U.S. Foreign Policy and Peru

SPECIAL PUBLICATION OF THE

Institute of Latin American Studies

THE UNIVERSITY OF TEXAS AT AUSTIN

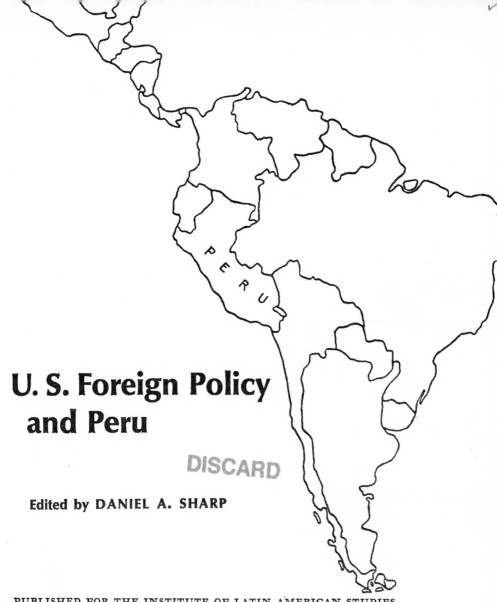

U. S. Foreign Policy and Peru

Edited by DANIEL A. SHARP

PUBLISHED FOR THE INSTITUTE OF LATIN AMERICAN STUDIES
BY THE UNIVERSITY OF TEXAS PRESS • AUSTIN AND LONDON

This book was produced by a citizens' constituency on U.S. foreign policy under the auspices of the Adlai Stevenson Institute of International Affairs, the Chicago Council on Foreign Relations, and the Johnson Foundation. The authors have agreed to contribute their profits from this book to the Peruvian Earthquake Relief Committee.

Library of Congress Cataloging in Publication Data
Main entry under title:

U. S. foreign policy and Peru.
  (Special publication of the Institute of Latin
American Studies, the University of Texas at Austin)
  Includes bibliographical references.
  1. U. S.—Foreign relations—Peru. 2. Peru
—Foreign relations—U. S. I. Sharp, Daniel A.,
1932–   ed. II. Series: Texas. University at
Austin. Institute of Latin American Studies. Special
publication.
E183.8.P4U5   327.73'085   73-39097
ISBN 0-292-78500-3

© 1972 by Daniel A. Sharp

Composition by G&S Typesetters, Austin
Printing by The University of Texas Printing Division, Austin
Binding by Universal Bookbindery, Inc., San Antonio

To the improvement of relations between
Peru and the United States

Sponsors of the Peru Policy Seminar

CONTENTS

PREFACE

All of the papers in this book resulted from a series of meetings in 1970 of an experimental constituency on foreign policy. To understand each chapter, it would be helpful to know the unique purposes and procedures that produced it.

Origins and Purposes

In the summer of 1969, while studying U.S. policy concerning Peru, I was reminded of Barbara Ward's explanation that bad foreign policy derives partially from the lack of a constituency. I was struck by the application of this general notion to Peru. Specific U.S. policies appeared to reflect the efforts of only a few people with a strong but narrow interest: some fishermen, a corporation, the Pentagon, a congressman from a sugar-growing district. I do not imply the *presence* of a military-industrial conspiracy, but rather the *absence* for foreign policy of the broad cross-section of citizens who constitute an effective, democratically representative constituency on many domestic policies.

This hypothesis moved me to take advantage of the neutral qualities of the Adlai Stevenson Institute, with which I was then associated, to create a model constituency of leading U.S. citizens from all sectors of society to interact both among themselves and with policy makers.

With the prompt backing of the Chicago Council on Foreign Relations and with much help from their senior staff and officers of their board, a carefully selected group of thirty were accepted for a study group, including leaders from business, university, church, labor, media, banking, law, government, and concerned citizens. A list of the members is included at the end of the book.

✓   The study group agreed upon two purposes: first, to activate a constituency of leading U.S. citizens on foreign policy, which would harness its experience and commitment to educate itself, form a framework of analysis and policy alternatives, and relate to foreign policy through a dialogue with policy makers and through discussion and publication of original papers. The second purpose was to create an environment conducive to improving relations between the United States and Latin America, taking Peru as the first case study.

We chose Peru because it was much in the news as a leading experiment in new structures that would likely be emulated by many other countries and that would therefore soon require consideration of new U.S. policies in response. Besides, it was my personal preference because happy years living in Peru increased my ability to locate and involve the most helpful relevant people.

Starting in September, 1969, the study group convened every few weeks with senior policy makers from the United States and Peru to consider early drafts of working papers. Among the government officials who came to the group were U.S. Assistant Secretary of State Charles A. Meyer, former U.S. Ambassador to Peru, J. Wesley Jones, Peruvian Ambassador to the United States Fernando Berckemeyer, and former Peruvian President Fernando Belaúnde Terry. Early in the project, I visited Peru at the Peruvian government's suggestion to meet with their foreign minister, General Edgardo Mercado Jarrin, who indicated his government's great interest in participating actively in our project.

We then sought outside experts to prepare those papers that were beyond the special competence of our group. Substantial contributions were secured from those foundations and corporations listed in the acknowledgments. Both the U.S. and Peruvian governments gave very strong encouragement, advice, and introductions, but only after expressing initial skepticism that a group of citizens would carry out such a project without complicating matters at a time of increasing tension.

SELECTION OF TOPICS AND AUTHORS

Each government also helped us to define the subjects of greatest interest and importance. During this period, a systematic effort was made to identify the leading authorities on each issue. Hundreds of names were compiled and cross-referenced on card files. Friends and colleagues gave many hours of their time in suggesting people, materials, and subjects; their names are listed at the end of the book. The topics finally chosen constitute the contents of this volume. Omitted for final publication were background papers, which are on file at the Adlai Stevenson Institute, 401 N. Michigan Avenue, Chicago, Illinois.

The final decision on topics to include was based on two practical criteria. The first, of course, was those topics suggested by either government. But the second criterion was the availability of a competent authority to prepare the kind of paper that we sought.

Preparation of the Working Papers

Each selected expert prepared a working draft, which we circulated to both the Peruvian and the U.S. governments and to experts representing varying points of view. Written critiques were secured that, together with the first draft, were submitted to a meeting of our study group attended by the author of the paper and specially invited experts. Following a full discussion of the paper, each author prepared a second draft for submission to the final conference, May 24–26, 1970. After further deliberations at the final conference, a final draft was prepared.

We realized that if our purpose was to affect policy, we would have to find ways to communicate effectively with policy makers. ✓ Without a power base, our impact would depend upon how useful our words were. While this may seem quite obvious, we made a conscious decision to prepare documents specifically calculated to be understood by the policy makers. I have noticed that most human communication, whether in person or on paper, is ineffective in accomplishing its purpose because of a failure to observe the difference between two categories of communication. Category one consists of true statements uttered in good faith for the satisfaction of the speaker or his own constituency. Category two consists of true statements uttered in good faith, but which are phrased and calculated to be heard by the intended listener, hopefully understood, perhaps also agreed to, and even favorably acted upon.

It is my observation that almost all communication is category one, whether between nations, spouses, parents and children, administrators and students, or between constitutents and policy makers. Our task was to calculate how to express the results of our citizens' interacting constituency so they would be useful in the category two sense. We concluded that because policy makers might resent a group of concerned but amateur citizens trying to help them, our usefulness would lie more in identifying alternatives rather than pressuring them with our opinion.

Our theme became the words spoken during his early visit to our study group by Assistant Secretary Meyer: "From Confrontation to Consultation."

For all of these reasons and more, each author was given the following instructions: "Your paper should be policy oriented, which means you should look forward rather than backward. Your primary responsibility is to identify the principal alternative policies for your subject. An analysis of past policies is of course necessary. Please answer the following four questions in this order as applied to your particular subject before expressing your own personal preferences:

1. What has been United States policy?
2. What have been the results of that policy?
3. What are the alternative policies available to the United States?
4. What are the probable consequences of each?"

THE FINAL CONFERENCE, MAY 24–26, 1970, AT WINGSPREAD

The culmination of many months of work was the three-day conference at the Johnson Foundation's hospitable Wingspread site in Racine, Wisconsin. More than seventy-five leading policy makers, senior business executives, scholars, labor leaders, clergy, reporters, and representatives of other sectors, were present from both countries. Twenty came from Peru, including an official delegation designated and sent by President Juan Velasco Alvarado, and a group from the Peruvian private sector, who came mostly at their own expense. The U.S. government sent senior policy makers directly concerned with Peru. Several international organizations were represented. A specific list of the participants in the final conference is set out at the end of the book.

The principal reason for holding this final conference was to bring to bear on the papers, which had previously been considered only by specialists on each topic with our study group, the interaction of the leading authorities on all related issues. It was our expectation, substantially realized, that the interaction of the final conference would strengthen the papers as well as provide increased perspective and understanding to the policy makers. Spokesmen for most of the alternative policy positions presented in the papers personally worked with each author who also heard the discussion of the various points of view, prior to publishing his paper in this book.

Thus, the conference had two primary purposes: one, to create an environment for broadening the understanding of the policy makers from both countries and two, to perfect the papers.

To accomplish these two purposes, certain unusual decisions were made:

1. No speeches.

2. No votes, resolutions, or seeking of a consensus. Because of the nature of this project and the people invited, to have sought agreement would in most cases have produced fuzzy, useless compromise language. We preferred to emphasize the differences rather than to obliterate them, and this step was necessary to ensure the participation of many of the people who wanted to preserve their independent point of view and not be associated with an opposing resolution.

3. Most conference time was spent in small workshops of twenty to twenty-five people, selected to balance points of view. The function of the workshop was to criticize and improve the papers and to permit a full exposure of points of view.

4. No interpreters. Ninety percent of the participants were bilingual, so that direct personal communications during and outside of the sessions took place continuously in both Spanish and English.

5. Free time. A fundamental ingredient of the meetings was the free interchange of ideas among the leading policy makers and experts.

6. Role of the discussion leader. The discussion leaders, selected from among the regular conference participants, and including substantial representation from both countries and all perspectives, ensured that the discussions moved logically and fairly through the four questions answered in each paper.

7. Discussions were off the record, except in a few cases where by unanimous agreement sessions were taped. Again, this was felt

necessary by many of the participants to ensure a frank and open discussion, but with the realization that the discussion would influence the final form of the chapters of this book.

RESULTS AND LESSONS

Among the many results was one that was not quite expected. There was an expression on the part of both business leaders and government officials from Peru about how much the conference improved their own internal communication. For example, a government representative during the final plenary session said: "One of the very important results of this conference has been to clarify the position of Peru and what is happening in Peru. But one important part of it is that it has also clarified the misunderstanding which has existed between the private sector of Peru and its government."

A prominent Peruvian industrialist later said:

As far as the American private sector is concerned, let me assure you that we have heard. We have understood your point of view. I think that most of your points are valid and I hope the Peruvian government takes that into consideration.

I think that you should also consider the points that we have tried to get across and I think you will find that as a result of this conference further progress will be very much easier and very much quicker because of the frank talk that has taken place, but which very often has not made it possible for us to comment directly on some of the things you have said.

Finally, and perhaps of greater satisfaction from the standpoint of the purposes of the project, was this statement by another prominent Peruvian corporation executive: "I am very happy to be here because we have been spending two and a half wonderful days meeting with very, very interesting and important people. I must say that I have been coming to the United States for, I don't know, nine years, a great deal of time, and this is a very honest and true statement: You have a better friend now after these two and a half days."

A major objective, only partially realized, was the identification of new alternative policies. In a few of the papers and meetings this was accomplished very well, but in others we fell victim, despite strenuous efforts, to traditional patterns in which information and argument are marshalled to support previously held personal views. The gap between policy makers and academics, derived from the latter's alleged inability to be "policy relevant," became understandable to project members in the only partially successful efforts to bridge it.

Nonetheless, the thorough interaction among many points of view during the rewriting produced much better work in most cases. In a few other cases, one can criticize the paper only in the sense of the observer who objects to the bad grammar of a talking dog. What is remarkable here is that a paper was produced at all by a concerned but previously unspecialized member of the new citizens' constituency.

It was clear that there was an unusually warm and open environment at the conference that produced generally effective communication.

Postconference Activities

Immediately following the three-day conference at Wingspread, the official Peruvian delegation along with several of the American participants spent a day or more in Chicago, Washington, D.C., and New York at the invitation of the Chicago Council on Foreign Relations, the Overseas Development Council, and the Council for Latin America. To these luncheons were invited other government policy makers, community leaders, leading businessmen, and specialists concerned with Peru. Discussions in many cases emanating from the three-day Wingspread meeting took place at a very high level of interest and openness. Press conferences followed. A few weeks thereafter, the project director and several conference participants participated in similar meetings sponsored by the same organizations in the same cities.[1]

---

[1] A further statement of a result of the conference was in a letter from a U.S. participant, living in Lima, who wrote to me in June as follows:

"The earthquake hasn't blotted out the effect of the Peru Conference. Rather, I think the papers, the discussions and the post-conference visits to New York and Washington actually helped prepare the ground, so that when the earthquake hit it took only a few days for the United States government to see that 12 million Peruvians, with a popular and reformist government, are of interest to the U.S. that overrides the dubious claims of an oil company and the confu-

An object of this experiment was to demonstrate the feasibility of a model of a citizens' constituency on foreign policy. Based upon its success, organizations in Chicago and other cities are engaged in developing projects on other foreign policy issues following the model. Discussions are underway, started by the Peruvian representatives at the final conference, to develop a similar project in Lima directed by Peruvians.

All of the Peruvians, both from government and the private sector, have met as a group several times in Lima during the first few weeks after their return to Lima. Newspaper and magazine stories have appeared in the United States and in Peru. A pamphlet illustrated with photographs of the conference and including extracts from each of the chapters of this book is in preparation under the sponsorship of two of the sponsoring foundations. Finally, of course, a major postconference activity is the publication of this book in English and Spanish.

It follows from the purposes of this project that this book is different from other compilations of conference papers.

First, as to the audience. This book is written for a relatively narrow group of important people: policy makers and potential participants in the new citizens' constituency including, of course, university students and faculty, as well as hopefully large numbers of newly involved citizens.

We include as policy makers all U.S. government officials concerned with policy for Peru in the Department of State, Congress, and the White House, as well as the other executive departments. Also included are senior executives of U.S. corporations presently doing business in Peru or considering it, as well as the senior executives of labor unions, church groups, foundations and universities, who are involved in or are considering projects related to Peru.

By a citizens' constituency, we mean the concerned specialist or amateur who wants his voice to be heard as part of a general perspective on U.S. long-term interests overseas, but who may have

---

sion of U.S. policy on maritime limits. We are giving aid generously, effectively and without conditions, and it's much appreciated. Now if we could just keep our priorities on people and not amendments!"

felt a great sense of frustration because of an inability to take an appropriate part in the formulation of foreign policy.

The object of this book is not to give advice to Peru, but rather to help in the formulation of policy by the United States. Of course, we hope Peruvians will read it in large numbers and that it will help them also to understand U.S. policy.

To assist readers concerned with policy alternatives, chapters are organized as briefing papers, which separate the past from the present, and description from analysis. Much effort is made to present all available policies rather than emphasize only the author's personal preference. Thus, the book is not advocacy, but hopefully scholarship designed more to aid than persuade.

My principal editorial task therefore has been to help each author stay within our unusual format of structure and objectivity rather than the more traditional one of marshalling his research to defend a conclusion, and each author's paper has really been "edited" during the series of project meetings.

Despite these efforts, some advance readers in the United States have complained that this book is essentially pro-Peru and not neutral. This may result from the fact, we hope, that in this book a description and analysis of the Peruvian point of view is included, in some cases perhaps for the first time in English. We have been assured by senior policy makers in both countries that most of our papers give a fair statement of their respective positions. If having done that equally well for both sides, it does appear pro-Peruvian in the United States, or pro-United States in Peru, that must be a risk we have assumed. We believe, on balance, that the book is neutral in that it includes a fair and representative series of articles describing a fairly complete range of opinions. Though we must indicate the preponderance of U.S. authors, there is a very full range of U.S. opinion included.

All intentions were not realized. Some papers do not fairly separate description of past policy from personal analysis, nor do they give enough thought to describing alternative U.S. policy response to those events. Of course, true objectivity is never possible, but we could have come closer. "The United States" is not a monolith, yet the term is sometimes used to mean the government and at other times an individual or a corporation, indicating a failure of thinking or writing.

These inadequacies, among others not mentioned, are acknowledged at the start to invite the reader's critical attention to each
chapter.

Because U.S. foreign policy is always in some measure a response to the policy of others, we are pleased that we have a paper
prepared officially by the Peruvian government to describe its view
of relations with the United States and its present national program. All the papers published have benefited from the discussions
of our study group with former President Fernando Belaúnde
Terry and from discussion with others closely associated with him
and also with other political parties. Because of the neutrality of
this book and project, communications were sought from all points
of view. The book includes the statement of the present government because that in fact is the government for whose policy the
United States must fashion appropriate decisions.

WHY SOME SUBJECTS WERE INCLUDED OR OMITTED

Increasingly, some people in both countries are saying that the
United States has no right to have a policy concerning what are essentially internal Peruvian affairs. Lengthy discussions were held
during several of the study group meetings concerning the proprie-
ty of our including them. Finally, we decided, more or less unanimously, that a failure to include these subjects would be a disserv-
ice not only to those who believed the United States should have a
policy but also to those who did not. Because in fact the United
States and U.S. organizations have had, or appeared to have had, a
policy in the past, it was a proper purpose of our project to examine objectively and thoroughly what that policy has been and what
its results were before deciding whether in fact we could avoid the
issue and not have a policy.

Still, some subjects, such as population control, were intention-
ally omitted, because we believed that for us to discuss it would
lead some Peruvians who might otherwise be sympathetic to the
project to reject participation. In retrospect, I think we made the
wrong decision, but it was made early on for what then seemed to
be good reasons. Similarly, we did not seek a discussion of the most
famous incident between our two countries: the IPC situation. Because the object of this project was to look forward and not backward, it was felt that to introduce a subject so controversial and so

loaded with history and commitment could lead to a long analysis of the past without the likelihood of a useful result for the future; it might further run the risk of interfering with our more creative hopes. Besides, it is not now a current policy issue at least from the Peruvian government point of view and perhaps not even from the United States.

We included discussions concerning the rural sector of Peru (Indians and agrarian reform) but do not have a chapter on the urban situation. This was not the result of conscious planning, but rather of our inability to obtain a paper from an appropriate expert.

Foreign investment is discussed in general, but little treatment is given to the new mining and industrial laws, because they emerged too late for adequate coverage at the final conference. The principal criterion for inclusion of a subject was its immediate priority for U.S. policy makers. The second criterion was the availability of a willing, competent author.

THE AUTHORS

The authors of the main chapters of this book are, in many cases, the leading authorities on their subjects. They include some members of the study group. In other cases, we were unable to secure the leading authority or felt none existed, and a paper was prepared by a nonspecialist in our study group. While each paper is an effort to provide objective answers to the fundamental questions, still it is a very personal work of the author concerned. For this reason, a biographical sketch of each author is included at the end of the volume.

The authors have asked me to express their usual disclaimer here for each of them. The facts and opinions reflect their best efforts to be accurate, fair, and objective with their own research and with their efforts to reflect the ideas expressed by advocates of alternative policies during study group and final conference sessions. A great many people have been extremely helpful with their time, materials, advice, and assistance. But, of course, each author individually, or government in the case of the official papers, is solely responsible for his own published work. Nothing in this volume should be construed in any other way.

As concerns the entire project including the book, all policy decisions were exclusively those of the study group, the authors, and myself. Neither government nor any sponsor attempted to influence any aspect of the project, beyond answering questions we put to them. And none of those questions concerned project policy. In my judgment, neutrality was successfully accomplished.

No discussion of a project aimed at improving relations between the United States and Peru can omit reference to the tragic earthquake that struck Peru on May 31, 1970, only days after the spirit of our Wingspread meeting had brought us so much closer together. Each of us involved with the project has been preoccupied with the fate of our friends and the citizens of their country. Almost every participant has in some way made an important contribution to the Peruvian Earthquake Relief Fund, which was organized by many project participants with assistance from Senators Edward Kennedy and Birch Bayh, among others. It has been difficult to complete this book without constantly being aware of this tragic human suffering. Perhaps that is why the authors of this book have unanimously and spontaneously agreed to offer their royalties to the Peru Earthquake Relief Fund.

DANIEL A. SHARP
Project Director
Chicago, June 1970

ACKNOWLEDGMENTS

Because of the unusual nature of this project, I think it is important to list by name and title all the people who participated in it. The project was designed to develop a constituency within the United States and within Peru of representative sectors within the society concerned about improving relations between our two countries. For this reason I felt it indispensable to the context of this undertaking to list all the people in both North and South America who contributed to what for us was a very successful project. Their names will be found in an annex at the end of the book.

The following are the people who at strategic points in the development of the project kept it going with accelerating impetus and enthusiasm, and who therefore deserve special acknowledgment here.

President Juan Velasco Alvarado of Peru, who by his personal attention to the selection and support of the Peruvian government delegation and his helpful communications provided the appropriate atmosphere of official support for the aims and objectives of this project.

Fernando Berckemeyer, Peruvian ambassador to the United States, who in our first conversation immediately communicated with his government, which resulted in their prompt support of the project and invitation for me to go to Peru to meet with their foreign minister.

The officers and board of the Chicago Council on Foreign Relations, who listened to the idea in its embrionic stage, gave encouragement and moral and financial support from the very beginning, pledging the first five thousand dollars. Particularly, their president, Alex Seith, their treasurer, Bruce Blomstrom, and their executive director participated fully in the project from its very beginning through to the final publication and encouraged the active involvement of other officers, board members and members of the council.

The Council for the Americas, previously known as the Council for Latin America, whose entire senior staff provided ideas and contacts in the private sector. Particular assistance was received from Harry Geyelin, executive director, Ralf Brent, special assistant to the president, and Enno Hobbing, staff director.

General Marco Fernández Baca, a friend and primary contact with the Peruvian government.

Among our sponsors, John Gallagher, vice-president international operations, Sears Roebuck & Co., gave the most time and the strongest support when requested for advice concerning the shape of the study-group session on the role of the private sector, which he ably chaired.

Robert C. Helander of IBEC, president of the American Chamber of Commerce in Lima, and Carlos Zuzunaga Florez, who together offered more time and friendly assistance than anyone could ever have thought to request.

Ambassador Douglas Henderson, friend and primary contact with the U.S. government.

General Edgardo Mercado Jarrín, foreign minister of Peru, who assisted in meeting and securing continuing collaboration from key Peruvian government officials at a time of increasingly strained relations between our two countries.

Dr. John L. Johnson, director of the Center for Latin American Studies, Stanford University, invited me as a Visiting Scholar to Bolívar House at the Stanford University campus in the summer of 1969, where I was able to work out the first outline of the project.

Ambassador J. Wesley Jones, who from the beginning volunteered time and thought and detailed assistance.

Assistant Secretary of State Charles A. Meyer, for his time and thoughtful analysis of the situation in Peru and for support of the U.S. government involvement in the project.

Leslie Paffrath, president of the Johnson Foundation, without whose assistance in providing the ideal environment for our final conference and an all-day study group meeting, the meetings would have been considerably less effective, and for his under-standing and restrained advice.

John Plank, for very thorough and understanding advice and as-sistance from the beginning of the project through to the end of the final conference.

Charles Robinson, president, and Richard Pettit, vice-president and treasurer of the Marcona Mining Co., for ideas, contacts, and support in carrying out the project.

Former President Fernando Belaúnde Terry, who sympatheti-cally and thoroughly collaborated with us from the beginning and spent a day with our study group, which was full of facts and insight.

My wife, Jacqueline Borda Sharp, who attended all the meetings of the study group and final conference, and who, with the whole family, understandingly permitted me the time away from them to complete this project.

U.S. Foreign Policy and Peru

Daniel A. Sharp

1. THE CONTEXT OF U.S. POLICY FOR PERU

Seven general themes emerge from the separate chapters of this book and especially from the Peru Policy Seminar meetings that produced them. As explained in the preface, no effort was made to determine the best policy, nor were the meetings used to seek a consensus, adopt resolutions, take votes, or even to permit speeches. Nor were conclusions requested in the conference working papers. Still, there was substantial agreement on the general context of Peruvian-American relations, which will now be described to offer the reader a perspective on the book. The reader is cautioned, however, not to overlook the essential disagreement on each specific policy issue, which was the stimulus for the project and is the essence of all succeeding chapters of this book.

Two themes were about Peru:

1. Peru has an increased sense of national competence.

2. Peru has a declining confidence in U.S.-led economic development.

Two themes were about the United States:

3. The United States has a waning sense of confidence in its ability to produce desired economic, social, and political development in other countries. There is a new consensus that U.S. policy is and should be of only marginal significance to Peru, that the United States has a primary responsibility first to protect and de-

velop its own society, and that it is therefore deemphasizing its international involvement and seeking—however impossible it is to accomplish—a policy of "neutrality."

4. The history of U.S. relations with Peru demonstrates significant lost opportunities where a different policy might have ameliorated the major areas of present conflict and misunderstanding.

The other three themes apply more or less equally both to Peru and the United States:

5. There is a mutually one-sided yearning for certainty. In the case of the United States it is a clearly stated desire that Peru indicate stable "rules of the game," especially concerning the role of U.S. private investment. Peru, for its part, is asking the United States government for a clear-cut indication of its Peruvian policy. Yet, dynamic changes within both societies seem to make uncertainty the only predictable certainty. This leads to the next general statement.

6. In both countries, there is an increased sense of urgency to deal with internal problems of social justice.

7. There is an increasing mutual understanding of the internal complexities in each other's country.

Each of these seven contextual conditions will now be discussed briefly.

1. *Peru has an increased sense of national competence.* There are many popular phrases that refer more or less to the same thing: nationalism, dependence, domination, intervention. These are the words one hears so often to express an emerging national consensus shared increasingly by all articulate segments of the Peruvian society. Peru wants to determine its own destiny without excessive dependence on the United States and without domination by the United States of its culture, politics, economy, development, and certainly without U.S. control of its industrialization and exploitation of natural resources.

Mindful of the importance of the United States and the necessity for outside capital for resource development, still Peru wants to have the decisive power in all decisions affecting her national development. Elaborated in the paper prepared by the Peruvian government and in all our discussions with the Peruvians, the following principal programs, therefore, have priority to accomplish this general purpose:

a. Peru will take a determining role in all important industrial activities, including those where foreign investors now are dominant. Two alternative models will be available. The preferred model will involve at least 51 percent Peruvian government or Peruvian private-sector control of all important industrial development. For the second model, where foreign interests hold generally 100 percent of a particular activity, a limited time schedule will be established for "fadeout" or divestment. In both cases, foreign investors will be guaranteed complete repatriation of their investments plus a "reasonable profit," as yet not specifically defined. This national policy is based on the judgment that the economic and social cost of permitting foreign-owned and controlled investments has been too great for Peru. Discussion of this policy area is found in many of the chapters, including those by Blomstrom and Cutter, and Goodsell.

b. Peru will control, at least for purposes of conservation, the rich resources of her seacoast, and will hold the right to freely dispose of all of its own natural resources. In the chapters on the two-hundred-mile issue by David Loring of the United States and Admiral Llosa of Peru, the reader will find perhaps one of the most comprehensive discussions available in the English language. The reader will also find, I believe, examples of lost opportunities when the United States could have, years ago, more thoroughly and sensitively identified itself at little political and economic cost, with Peru's purpose of conservation. Such a policy would have ameliorated one of the most intense areas of misunderstanding between our two countries and would have built a foundation of considerable good will. Concerning control of the natural resources, important discussions will be found in sections on the role of foreign investment by Blomstrom and Cutter, on diplomatic protection of foreign investment by Professor Goodsell, and in Dr. Strasma's work on agrarian reform.

c. The first major program of the current revolutionary government of the armed forces in Peru was agrarian reform. As Professor Strasma describes in thorough detail, the present program in large measure follows the lead of the United States and the Alliance for Progress. Yet Peru complained that the United States is attempting to prevent its successful completion by blocking specific credit requests in the international lending agencies,

as discussed in the chapter by Professor Powelson. Consistent
with its new national philosophy, Peru is saying to the United
States: We do not need your public statements of approval or
your direct support; rather, we need the withdrawal of your obstacles to our progress.

d. Education, a major priority of the new Peruvian government, as well as the last, not yet clearly visible to the outside
world in the form of a new program, is discussed in the chapters
by Professor Robert Myers and by the Peruvian government.

e. A corollary to increased national pride is the new sense of
the role of the military. Increasingly the senior officers are perceived in Peru as agents of social and political change rather
than as the handmaidens of the oligarchy. Dr. Luigi Einaudi
provides historical background of this development in his chapter on relations with the military. He describes how the present
senior officials of the Peruvian government come from a military
service that carries, under the Peruvian Constitution, the responsibility to "guarantee the Rights of the Republic [and] the fulfillment of the Constitution." Military officers are professionals
trained to the workings of rational bureaucracy who also, through
their own origins, life styles as junior officers, and career experiences, have had extensive contacts with the poor sectors of Peruvian society. To the extent that Peruvian officers in fact combine
social sensitivity with technical competence, they may be a
unique political resource which some observers have called the
New Military.

2. *Coinciding with the increased sense of national pride on the
part of the Peruvians is a declining confidence in U.S.-influenced
economic development.* In assessing the results of the Alliance for
Progress and other U.S.-influenced efforts to assist their country in
its development, many Peruvians are coming to the conclusion that
the United States does not know how to accomplish the change that
is needed in Peru. This view comes perhaps not coincidentally at a
time of declining U.S. world prestige resulting from our own internal crises and our Indochinese involvement. Looking at the role of
the United States in the Far East, the generals in Peru have been
struck by the remarkable failure of the most powerful nation in the
world to subdue rural guerrillas. As Professor Einaudi concludes in
his paper, this has produced not only a lack of confidence in U.S.

ability to assist Peru in its problems, but also the conclusion that Peruvians must resolve their own internal conflicts because nobody has the will or the ability to come to their assistance.

Peru is, at the same time, asking the United States for increased flexibility and forbearance. Being so large and strong, Peru suggests, the United States should have the grace to yield on matters which for itself are so small, but which for Peru are so crucial.

A seeming contradiction to her new independence, Peru regrets our diminishing attention to foreign assistance budgets in the new "low profile" approach, which has been characterized, in Moynihan's terms, as "benign neglect" and by Richard Goodwin as "malign neglect."

As a result of increased national pride and decreased faith in the United States, Peru has been seeking a new *in*dependence and *inter*dependence. Its new independence has been described above. Its new interdependence consists of its commitment to the Andean Group, an effort to align itself with several similar Latin American economies in a bloc capable of competing with the strongest Latin American economies, and a further step in the development of its independence from the United States.

3. *The United States has a waning sense of confidence in its ability to produce desired economic, social, and political development in other countries.* Coincident with Peru's diminishing confidence in us, we are losing some confidence in ourselves. We even doubt our ability to produce economic, social, and political development for ourselves.

a. Participants in our project generally agreed that it was enough for us in the past merely to be aware of the great *need* of help for us to find that we had a *moral duty* to meet that need. Recently, however, greater emphasis has been given to a third element, our *ability to meet that need*. Thus, even if there is a great need, and, granting just for the sake of argument that we might have a moral duty, we now doubt that we have the ability to accomplish very much. This has brought disillusionment and frustration to the idealistic, charismatic, morally committed but chauvinistic architects of the Alliance for Progress. They did not find evidence of substantial accomplishments commensurate with their ambitions and at the same time, found much evidence of hostility toward alleged U.S. "domination" or "cultural imperialism." Thus, a few liberals now conclude that the need does not exist, and even more now believe that it is not the obligation of the United States to take care of the world's poor and oppressed in any event.

There seems to be a ready acceptance of the new conventional wisdom that while there probably is a great *need* to help increasingly large numbers of poor, illiterate, sick, and oppressed people, the United States has no moral obligation to solve those problems on the world scale.

An interesting footnote arose during the final conference when several of the participants disagreed strongly that the Alliance for Progress was dead by stating that "the successor to the Alliance for Progress in Peru is the new government of Peru." In reading the papers that follow, one might conjecture about the extent to which the priority programs of the revolutionary government of the armed forces of Peru are inspired by the Alliance for Progress and by the United States, and the extent to which such programs, which at Punta del Este were to be accomplished by increasingly democratic systems, might be realized by this military government.

b. A direct corollary to the above discussion is the view that *U.S. policy not only is, but ought to be, of only marginal significance to Peru* in terms of the success or failure of the revolution.[1] In part, this feeling may derive from the lack of persuasive evidence of success from our prior aid programs. It also emerges from our faltering efforts as world policemen.

Peru appears to welcome this approach, as exemplified by her government's position on agrarian reform. Official representatives in our meetings expressed their desire that the United States not even have a policy concerning agrarian reform and that Peru does not need public declarations of support. The reader will note the expression of this desire that the policy alternatives considered be of marginal importance, for example, in chapters concerning the church (by D. McCurry), labor (by Father McIntire and W. Douglas), and Indians (by Dr. W. Mangin).

---

[1] That a policy of such "marginal significance" is almost impossible to achieve is also considered below in the discussion of neutrality.

It was even suggested by one official U.S. representative that our policy impact concerning the international lending agencies ought to be marginal, even though we are the major contributor of funds.

c. This new self-image of the United States involves a changing sense of its world responsibilities. In earlier times, the United States believed that it had a moral duty to harness its economic and social power to feed, cure, protect from oppression, and guarantee the freedom of the world, in its own image. Now, however, it is moving to the position that its first responsibility is to protect its own society and to use what power it has, both economic and military, in a restrained and humane manner. (In conference discussions, a few even suggested that the restraint include an effort to prevent certain types of development from taking place in the Third World because we had produced such terrible pollution and ecological dislocation.) There appeared to emerge a growing acceptance of the idea that each society must seek its own image appropriate to its own unique circumstances.

I would speculate that the pendulum will swing back again as we will take new note of the accelerating separation between the few rich powerful nations and the very many poorer, weaker ones. Once again, we will probably reestablish a national commitment based not only on humanity but also on self-preservation, which will take some new form hardly imaginable today.

d. The Cold War context of United States–Peruvian relations emerged in many of the discussions. For the United States, Peru is a relatively small element in the myriad of its global relationships. Yet even such issues as U.S. policy concerning the Indians, labor, and the two-hundred-mile issue seem to be caught up in a Cold War context. For example, Peru sees the two-hundred-mile fishing issue as essentially a question of Peru's economic and social development, whereas, for the United States, an important impediment to agreement with Peru lies in its view of the difficult military precedents involved. David Loring's chapter highlights these opposing approaches in a thorough and dramatic fashion.

As another example of the world-wide context, a final resolution of the IPC problem was apparently partially inhibited by concern with the possible impact of additional precedents being

established in Peru which would affect the U.S. position throughout the world, particularly in the Middle East. Again, for Peru,
however, it was a unique case of national honor.

e. The most elusive of the major emerging areas of agreement
was the almost unanimously supported notion that the U.S. policy toward Peru should be one of "neutrality." How can the
United States, with all of its power, its world economic and political involvement, and its past history of relationships ever be,
or at least be perceived to be, neutral? In a very real sense, any
policy of a world power is intervention and therefore not neutral.
This is implied in most of the papers that follow.

Consider education policy for example. Any assistance other
than support of an entire national budget changes internal priorities, and could be thereby considered intervention. To assist
education rather than housing, universities rather than rural
grade schools, science rather than the humanities—any specific
policy along the continuum of policy choices concerning where
to help, is also a policy to intervene in changing the percent of
resources allocated to alternative national priorities, and is therefore in a sense unneutral. Professor Myers's chapter considers the
education situation in detail.

Because of the long and predominantly friendly relationships
between Peru and the United States, and also because of Peru's
increasing economic and political dependence upon us during
certain periods, efforts to assume a neutral stance at this time are
perceived as hostile, if not actually interventionist. Threats to
withdraw AID commitments or the sugar quota as part of a new
approach are also viewed as threats to intervene in undermining
the Peruvian economy.

Concern for unneutral—even hidden—power of the U.S. presence also emerges from U.S. missionary and labor movement
presence, as discussed by two churchmen. Father McIntire and
Mr. McCurry find increasing activities on social issues in Peru
by U.S.-based institutions are but expressions of U.S. policy in
other ways. Mr. Douglas defends the U.S. labor policy, but not
really in terms of the new "neutrality."

Dr. Strasma's agrarian reform discussion also highlights this
dilemma at the beginning of his final section on policy alternatives. He discusses how U.S. influence helped to create the ex-

pectation of land reform. Therefore, "even silence speaks very loudly." Because the United States gave support to a different agrarian reform program under Belaúnde, a failure to do so now would be interpreted as opposition. Neutral programs tend to favor the status quo and since Peru's national policy is to restructure society, again neutrality could be viewed as favoring the established landowners.

Those considering the new "low profile" position toward Latin America might apply this analysis of neutrality to each of the specific policy papers in this book.

4. From the discussion principally of the two major areas of conflict between Peru and the United States—IPC and the two-hundred-mile fishing issues—it appears that there were acceptable opportunities to have avoided some present areas of misunderstanding.

If we were now in the year 2000, could we in retrospect isolate 1971 policy decisions that, if made differently, could have helped the U.S. policy better? The reader is encouraged to test this approach on each policy area. It might perhaps lead to a hypothesis that will help us to identify those cases in the present and near future where a projection of certain trends will lead us to a policy of more immediate identification with directions of history that we are unable to reverse. There were also three general themes applicable more or less equally to Peru and the United States.

5. *There is a mutually one-sided yearning for certainty.* Each side is seeking from the other a degree of certainty which it is resisting giving on its own part. The United States, in this case the private section, is saying to the Peruvian government: "If you will only tell us once and for all what the rules of the game are, we will probably continue to invest happily."[2] On the other hand, the Peruvians are telling the Americans: "If you will only tell us for certain what your policy is toward us, we can make our own clear plans concerning our economic development and also foreign investment." And each country is saying to the other: "We cannot

---

[2] EDITOR's NOTE: This was written prior to the Peruvian law creating an "Industrial Community" in which substantial ownership and resulting membership on the Board of Directors must pass to the community of workers over a period of years.

tell you our policy with such clarity because of the internal ferment within our society."

Dynamic changes evolving from powerful conflicting sources within both societies have, justifiably or not, made it quite difficult for clear policies to emerge and to be stated. While this all may appear somewhat contradictory, still, what each side is asking is in fact quite reasonable, because neither side is seeking absolute certainty. Each side is asking for indications of directions of policy in a situation where neither side has yet given a very firm indication. Neither side really is asking for the elimination of all uncertainty, but it certainly appeared that way at times during the discussions, and it also appeared that neither side was quite aware of how complete was the mutuality of their yearnings.

As a result of its view, U.S. business is searching to invest elsewhere in a competitive world market where risks and uncertainties are less and profits are more. Peru, for its part, is reaching out for alternative sources of financial, technical, and political support from people who it presumed were more willing to play by the not-yet-finalized rules of the game.

6. *Each country spoke with great feeling of its increased sense of urgency to deal with the internal problems of social injustice.* Similar goals were described with very different labels: nationalism, socialism, and revolution, when discussed by Peruvians; equality, integration and local participation, and radical restructuring of the society when spoken by North Americans.

For Peru, the transition was from a dependent, somewhat colonized, underdeveloped country moving toward a role of national unity and independence, combined with interdependence within Latin America.

For the United States it was a question of overcoming the results of 160 years of dealing essentially with its internal problems through the 1940s, and then finding after 30 international years that it must now turn inward to face and resolve three decades of relatively neglected social problems at home.

It was generally agreed that the increased emphasis on the home front has caused more or less the same three results in each country:

a. Unclear foreign policies, at least as perceived by the other country, because the conflicting internal forces are not yet resolved.

b. The dislocation of the traditional friendship between Peru and the United States.

c. The realization that the only certainty reasonably available is the continuation of uncertainty.

7. *There is developing an increasing mutual awareness of the complexities in the U.S. and Peru and in their relations with other countries.* As one example concerning Peru, there was a discussion about the fundamental tension between apparent economic requirements on the one hand and, on the other, political requirements to maintain the revolution. As an American scholar explained in the final meeting:

If the Peruvian government were to clearly define itself and follow the rules of the game, then it would lose a very great deal of its revolutionary momentum, and a very great deal of the support that it has managed to generate within Peru. In fact, if it were to define the rules of the game, it might even lose that element of uncertainty which is the only thing that has gained it the attention of the United States in a period when the United States has been busily ignoring the rest of Latin America.

An official Peruvian representative responded:

We are not playing with uncertainty. We are making good laws. That takes time. You are asking for a system of immediate laws. . . . Perhaps it would be too pretentious to say today we make the revolution and today we have all of the laws. It is impossible to have everything at the same time. And perhaps that is one of the secrets of our success, not the fact that we are trying to make everybody guess what is happening next, but rather that when the next thing is done, it is well done.

Near the end of the discussion, another senior Peruvian government official added:

You are asking that a revolutionary process be previously planned. This is impossible. It is more impossible even in a dependent economy where internal decisions are heavily influenced by external reaction. You should understand that the principal political leaders of the military government for almost 18 months have been almost exclusively preoccupied with whether or not the United States would apply the Hickenlooper Amendment. That is something of great importance in planning taxes and new industrial laws. And that was going to be decided outside of Peru.

A senior North American representative subsequently replied that this Peruvian rationale sounds very appealing, but no one—not even a Peruvian—invests his money in a revolutionary situation. And this is not an international conspiracy to inhibit Peru's revolution. The revolution is clearly Peru's affair, but the generals should not expect foreigners to invest their money in Peru while the revolution is going on.

Comparable conflicting discussions took place in an atmosphere of warmth and good will concerning the pressures affecting each U.S. policy regarding Peru. In the chapters of this book, the results of each of these thorough discussions are reflected.

In this chapter I have sought to create a helpful perspective by emphasizing some general themes on which most participants from both countries agreed. In doing this I have violated the prescribed format described in the introduction and followed in succeeding chapters, but, consistent with our format, I have felt it appropriate to resist the temptation to express my own view of the *validity* of major policy positions.

Luigi Einaudi

2. U.S. RELATIONS WITH
THE PERUVIAN MILITARY

Peruvian events have acquired increased prominence since the seizure of power in 1968 by the revolutionary military government headed by General Juan Velasco Alvarado. Although they reflect both the tensions and the general deterioration of U.S. relations with Peru, past U.S. military policies have been marginal in these developments. Future U.S. military policies toward Peru, in my opinion, should have as their major objective the maintenance of correct state relations.

The achievement of this apparently simple goal is hindered by mutual suspicions about the political roles of the military. Peru's military forces are often viewed in the United States through the lenses of what is called in this paper the "myth of primitivism," which suggests that they are politically reactionary, militarily irrelevant, and economically wasteful. Partly because of these considerations, the United States initially refused to recognize a mili-

NOTE: The views expressed in this paper are those of the author, a staff member of The RAND Corporation, and should not be interpreted as reflecting the views of The RAND Corporation or the official opinion or policy of any of its governmental or private research sponsors.

tary government in 1962, and in 1967 reduced economic assistance to an elected civilian government because it had purchased military jet aircraft in France (after being turned down in the United States). These and similar policies based on the distorted presuppositions of the myth of military "primitivism" have been either irrelevant or actually counterproductive to U.S. interests and have added to Peruvian suspicions of U.S. intentions.

Peru's armed forces cannot be ignored. The combined pressures of political frustration and economic development have broken down historical military conservatism and made them advocates of major changes in Peruvian society. Punitive antimilitary measures, although perhaps domestically popular in the United States, have helped to alienate the Peruvian military in their political as well as military roles. Future U.S. policies, therefore, though they need not necessarily foster close relations with the Peruvian military, should distinguish between the military as military forces and the military in their political roles and, since 1968, as government.

Discussion of policy alternatives centers on diplomatic recognition, combined with political distance on the governmental level, and the maintenance of decent working relations on a technical basis on a military level.

The analysis begins by considering matters that relate primarily to the military institutions themselves in Peru. After developing aspects of their structure and history, the paper examines the military in their domestic political relationships with the rest of Peruvian society, considering particularly the roles of the military government in Peruvian developments since 1968. Against this background, a review of military relations with the United States since World War II leads to a discussion of some of the policy alternatives open to both countries in the essentially political matter of their military relations.

THE PERUVIAN BACKGROUND

Structure and Composition of the Armed Forces

The armed forces of Peru consist of fiercely independent air, navy, and army establishments, which are loosely coordinated by a small joint command (Comando Conjunto). Each service operates under similar internal regulations within its own ministry, traditionally headed by the senior active duty officer of each service. Together, the budgets assigned the three service ministries have accounted for just under 20 percent of central government expenditures over the past decade.

Precisely how military appropriations are spent and on what is not clear. The ferocity with which the Peruvian military defends itself from prying outsiders shrouds most military operations, whether budgets, personnel, or plans, in a veil of mystery. This policy of secrecy, in effect since the Peruvian-Ecuadorian conflict of 1941, complicates any attempt to come to grips with Peruvian military matters and often heightens civilian suspicions about military activities and even motives.

Enough is known about Peruvian budgetary practice, however, to know that budgets of the military ministries include funds for military pensions, but exclude the police force, the Guardia Republicana and the Guardia Civil. A very substantial proportion of military expenditures, perhaps three-quarters, is for personnel costs. Though comparisons are difficult (Chile's military budgets seem significantly lower, but exclude pensions as well as police), it would appear that Peru's military expenditures are in a middle-to-high range in Latin America, which spends less on defense than any other area of the world. Within Peru itself, all three services combined spend less than the Ministry of Education.

With a total active military officer corps of approximately 5,000 (of which some 3,500 are army) and approximately 50,000 soldiers operating what is in many cases antiquated military equipment of World War II and Korean War vintage, and even then in limited quantities and of dubious quality, Peruvian military power looks insignificant compared to the military might available to the major world powers.

Peru's military forces also lack the modern armaments available to many other countries in the Third World (particularly in Asia and the Middle East), but which are available only to Cuba in Latin America. What military materiel Peru does have, however, it manages efficiently enough to be rated by most military observers at or near the top in Latin America.

The army is organized into six divisions, including armored and jungle divisions and elite mobile paratroop and commando units.

The air force inventory includes twelve French Mirage III's (Latin America's first supersonic fighters other than Cuba's MIG's) and sixteen British Canberra bombers as well as older U.S.-built F86s, F80s, and C47s. The navy's flagships are two cruisers bought from Great Britain in the late 1950s. Army engineer battalions, air force air transport services, and the Naval River Fleet all make significant contributions to development of remote areas, and are capable of major efforts during emergencies like the 1970 earthquakes.

MILITARY EDUCATION

What is often lacked in operational capacity and materiel, Peruvian officers traditionally have striven to make up in professionalism, particularly at the top ranks. This seriousness of purpose of the Peruvian armed forces is particularly evident in the training and quality of the officer corps. The Peruvian officer is a graduate of a military academy. Even in the army, the only service open to promotion from the ranks, a majority of officers have been academy graduates since 1930. Specialized training is provided routinely for all branches beginning shortly after academy graduation. A competitive entrance, two-year general staff course has functioned continuously since 1902, and has become a prerequisite for line promotion to general officer.

Since the turn of the century, advanced military training available in Peru has been supplemented by attendance at foreign military schools, until the Second World War largely in France and since then more frequently in the United States. In 1960 nearly half of the Peruvian general officers had attended specialized courses in nearly a dozen foreign countries.

Since World War II the training available to military officers has included increasing emphasis on the nonmilitary elements related to national defense, including public administration, economic planning and political studies. Since 1950 much of this has been concentrated at the Center for Higher Military Studies (CAEM). During the past decade, however, it has with increasing frequency also included attendance at civilian universities and international training institutes both in Peru and abroad. Peruvian officers have attended both MIT and the training courses offered in Chile by the United Nations Economic Commission for Latin America.

By relating this highly developed training system to the promotion process, the Peruvian military leadership made educational activity and achievement the cornerstone of a rationalized bureaucratic structure without parallel even in the major military powers (where combat performance has often contributed to lower correlations between formal education and promotion). It is impossible to predict, on a statistical basis, for example, the future of a West Point graduate from his class standing alone. In Peru, 80 percent of the division generals serving between 1940 and 1965 were in the top 25 percent of their academy graduating class.

The structure of skills represented by this military bureaucracy has gradually evolved in the direction of the more technical services. Although infantry officers and cavalry officers predominated during the nineteenth century, artillery became an important service after the turn of the century. Engineering and other traditional support services, including veterinary medicine, became accepted military subspecialties between the World Wars, and have been followed more recently by economics and public administration. By 1960 the Peruvian army had more engineers than cavalrymen as officers.

In sum, although he operates within a largely underdeveloped society, often with inferior and dangerous equipment, the Peruvian officer seeks the status of a modern professional. Indeed, one of his greatest frustrations is that modern warfare, at least in its technologically more sophisticated forms, is beyond the capacity or interests of his country, despite his best efforts to keep educationally prepared. As we shall see below, this phenomenon has important implications for the relations of Peruvian officers to their own society as well as to the United States. Unexpectedly, perhaps, the "irrelevance" of modern military skills in an underdeveloped country like Peru also emphasizes the importance of the officer corps as a reservoir of technical and organizational skills for national development. To most officers, the question is not *whether* their skills should be exploited to that end, but *how*.

Military History and Functions

The dominant myths commonly affecting American perceptions of the military institutions as such in Peru might well be labeled those of "primitivism" and of "irrelevance." The first centers on the view that the Peruvian armed forces are primitive by modern military standards; the second suggests that this military "primitivism" does not matter in any case because there is no legitimate function for military forces in Peru.

Peruvian realities are more complex. The Peruvian military, as we have seen, is relatively underdeveloped if measured in terms of armaments or size; but is rather more modern in the officer corps. In this, as in other characteristics, Peru's armed forces reflect the unevenness of Peruvian development, with modernity and feudalism coexisting virtually side by side.

Similar complexity is evident in considering whether there is a need for national defense forces. Most U.S. observers are not impressed by the seriousness of Chile or Ecuador as conventional external military threats to Peru's territorial integrity. Most Peruvians, though often differing on the details, agree on the need for the maintenance of military institutions for the defense of national sovereignty. The independence of Peru and of Latin America from Spain was won on the battlefields of Junin in the Peruvian Andes in 1824, and reaffirmed in the naval engagements of 1866. Peru was the loser in the nineteenth century's most important war in Latin America after the struggles for independence. Following a protracted campaign from 1879 to 1881, which saw Lima, Peru's capital and "city of kings," occupied by Chilean troops, Peru resigned itself by 1883, through internal war and exhaustion, to the loss of the nitrate-rich southern provinces of Tarapaca and Arica.

The pattern exemplified by Peruvian involvement in nine international skirmishes during the nineteenth century has continued during the twentieth, but on a reduced scale. Peru has participated in two of Latin America's last four major conflicts. Leaving aside the Chaco War of 1932–1935 between Bolivia and Paraguay and the Honduran–El Salvador conflict of 1969, Peruvian troops fought Colombia in 1932 and Ecuador in 1941. Both of these conflicts involved relatively undeveloped and unpopulated territories generally believed to have great future potential.

These past conflicts reinforce present arguments for the maintenance of military preparedness, even in the absence of clear and present foreign threats. Peru's defeat at the hands of Chile in the War of the Pacific, generally attributed to profligacy and the disregard of military preparedness in the 1870s, strengthens more than

might be the case in more successful or powerful countries the desire to maintain military forces in readiness for conflict with neighboring states. Peru's historic legal claims in its boundary dispute
with Ecuador were not accepted internationally until after Ecuador's defeat in the Zarumilla Campaign of 1941. The association of
might with right in the 1942 Rio Protocol implies that the inter-
American system is not an exclusive alternative to military preparedness.[1]

To believe that Latin America would have long since disarmed
had it not been for militarist selfishness abetted by the hemispheric
defense doctrines of the Cold War is thus to ignore Latin American
and certainly Peruvian history. Most of today's Peruvian senior
officers were youths during the Colombian conflict and lieutenants
at the time of the conflict with Ecuador. They find it difficult to
conceive of themselves as lacking an external defense function.

The viability of maintaining conventional forces is severely
tested nonetheless—by their costliness. Modern armaments are increasingly expensive. Military aircraft and naval vessels produced
in the industrial nations require massive capital outlays that tax
Peruvian resources even if bought only in token quantities and
with little or no electronic support systems. Rising armament costs
are particularly hard to bear in times of rising social consciousness
and popular demands. Yet not to make certain acquisitions may
seem, particularly for the air and sea services, tantamount to sur-
rendering even the option to develop modern capacities at a later
date. Foreign military assistance may in this sense reduce the economic drain and act as a link to future modernization, though at
the risk of political costs.

[1] An incident at the Rio Conference in 1942 serves as a poignant reminder of
the continuing importance of military power to an equitable international order.
When the Ecuadorian foreign minister complained (somewhat guilefully, as
Ecuador's army no longer existed as an operational force after Peru's decisive
military victory) that his country had depended on the principles of international law and Pan Americanism in its conflict with Peru, an unnamed Latin
American delegate replied that those principles "exist to solve problems. You
are not a problem for America. You, with your lack of military resistance, have
not made your problem an American problem." Cited by Bryce Wood, *The
United States and Latin American Wars, 1932–1942* (New York and London:
Columbia University Press, 1966, p. 315). The reference to "America" was to
the inter-American system as a whole, not to the United States.

But declining external defense functions and increasing costs are not alone in threatening military conventions. The guerrilla campaign of 1965–1966 posed a different kind of threat to the military institution. Ultimately, of course, the MIR guerrillas were crushed, but not without making military leaders acutely aware of the pressing need for the economic and political modernization of their country. In addition to their internal organizational concerns, the Peruvian military had long maintained an interest in public order and the control of remote areas, foreign policy, and boundary questions. Beginning with the great depression, these concerns began to extend to national development, including under that rubric education, industrialization, control of strategic materials (petroleum and telecommunications), and general national planning and support for central government authority and administration.

The rise of military leaders advocating basic structural reforms and an altering of international relationships is the culmination of an extremely complicated process involving a general crisis of Peru's economic, social, and political system. Military attitudes reflect growing uncertainty and changing life styles, as well as the evolution of new doctrines of social responsibility supported by Church and military intellectuals.

But it took the guerrilla campaign of 1965–1966 to force theory out of the schools and into the barracks, thereby making the political immobilism and economic decline of the late 1960s a matter of urgent military concern. Two fairly well-planned and organized guerrilla fronts opened in the summer of 1965 in the central and southern Andes with ambushes of police units. The outbreaks forced military intervention to replace the ineffective rural police and ultimately led to the discovery of other fronts that were in semi-formation in other parts of the country.

Despite forebodings in elite political circles about "revolution in the Andes," within a period of six months the military forces completely eliminated the guerrilla foci and almost entirely wiped out the MIR leadership. And the military did this without forcing a change in government, and without the prolonged suffering and mounting casualties characteristic of other cases of political violence, such as Guatemala and Colombia.

Containment of the guerrilla threat also confirmed military commitment to reform. The guerrillas had chosen for their headquarters a remote mountain top called Mesa Pelada near the Convención Valley in the province of Cuzco, where the famous Trotskyist labor organizer Hugo Blanco had successfully organized peasant unions in the early 1960s before his capture in 1963. But the Convención Valley had also been the scene of construction of a penetration road from Colca to Amparaes by military engineer battalions, and had been the site of a pilot agrarian reform program by the military junta of 1962–1963. The failure of the region's peasants to provide significant support to the insurgents appeared in military circles to confirm the wisdom of their earlier reform policies.

The sense of success was tempered, however, by the fear of recrudescence of violence. If a relative handful of radicalized urban intellectuals could occupy thousands of troops for months, what would happen if popular forces and the peasantry were enlisted in future disorders? The Ministry of War's published account of the guerrilla campaign concluded that Peru had entered a period of "latent insurgency."

Nor was this a matter to be readily resolved with foreign assistance. Guerrilla war had proved the undoing of France in Indochina and then in Algeria, where military operations had been observed by Peruvian officers with French ties through training and connections. Now Vietnam was proving the Achilles' heel of the United States, demonstrating the difficulties irregular warfare could create even for the world's foremost military power. The conclusion the fate of Peru's two historic foreign military mentors seemed to suggest was that internal subversion, if it could be controlled at all, would have to be controlled by Peruvians on their own.

The "latent insurgency" dilemma appears to have opened many officers to the idea that Peru needed agrarian reform combined with industrialization, or, in the more abstract language of the Ministry of War, a "General Policy of Economic and Social Development."[2] According to this view, largely parallel to the McNamara-Rostow thesis that violence springs from economic backwardness, conditions of injustice in the countryside needed to be removed so

[2] Peru, Ministerio de Guerra, *Las guerrillas en el Perú y su represión* (Lima, 1966), p. 80.

that no longer would the absentee landowner and his local hench-
men exploit and oppress the rural peasant masses whose marginal
living conditions were in effect making them future recruits for
potential subversion and movements against the military. These
views were strengthened by the fact that most military men had
few social ties to the elite, had served in rural areas during regular
tours as well as during the guerrilla campaign, and often found
emotional and ideological comfort in paternalist Catholic social
doctrines that also stressed that every man has a right to an existence offering material and spiritual dignity. For a combination of
reasons, therefore, many officers, particularly in the army, were
moving toward authoritarian preemption of traditional left-wing
positions, especially agrarian reform, under the aegis of a nationalist military dictatorship pledged to the modernization of Peru.

Before turning to the exploration of these explicitly political
matters, however, I will discuss the political and constitutional traditions that previously and repeatedly offset Peruvian military desires to maintain professional autonomy from politics, plunging
military men instead into very partisan political involvements.

Political Participation of the Military

The political participation of the Peruvian armed forces has
some legal sanction. Article 213, Title 12, of the Constitution of
1933 provides that "the purpose of the Armed Forces is to guarantee the rights of the Republic, the fulfillment of the Constitution
and the Law, and the conservation of public order." The explicit
provision of a political role of constitutional guardianship to the
military is uncommon in North American and European constitutional practice, but is found in a majority of Latin American constitutions and appears to have been viewed historically as enlisting
the military as a check on executive abuse.

Particularly at times of crises, such provisions traditionally tended to involve the military as an "arbiter" between continuing political factions. In Peru, with the increased capacity and self-confidence of the military (particularly the army, the only service from
whose ranks have come presidents), this legal sanction for political
activity seems to have been interpreted as the basis for an increasingly policy-oriented military role, culminating in the attempt to
lead Peruvian structural change initiated by the 1968 coup.

Before considering that revolutionary military experiment, how-ever, it is important to discuss the general evolution of military po-litical activity in Peru. Among foreign observers particularly, the myth of "primitivism" alluded to earlier in discussing perceptions of military roles provides a highly simplistic interpretation of the political role of the military. As seen from the United States, Peru, like much of Latin America, is an underdeveloped country with the primary characteristic of having few wealthy and many poor. In popular political mythology, the politics of Latin America are often dismissed as being merely an unfair competition between a rich "oligarchy" and "the people," normally resolved in favor of the oligarchy by the directed use of military force.

This perspective converts the military into an enemy of progress, preventing the full and just development of the nation it is theo-retically sworn to defend. With various embellishments (among some Peruvian nationalists and American radicals the military has been considered an arm of the U.S. Pentagon; among Americans generally it is seen as a devourer of economic resources that would otherwise be devoted to development) the military is thus often perceived as a veritable army of occupation in its own country.

This general perspective (which derives more from abstract val-ues than from empirical observation) is often indiscriminately ap-plied to all of Latin America, without regard to time periods or to distinctions among the very different situations and levels of devel-opment among and within countries. In Peru, where the condition of the Indian is a genuine (as well as politically convenient) sym-bol of the need for popular redemption, the generalized perspective finds its climax in the mythology of the confrontation between the military and the American Popular Revolutionary Alliance (APRA) founded in Mexico in 1924 by Victor Raúl Haya de la Torre, and the most famous of Latin American revolutionary na-tionalist parties.

APRA has long been presented in the United States as the cham-pion of nationalist revolutionary change in Peru. The military has opposed APRA. Logically, therefore, the military must be oppo-nents of nationalism and revolution. In fact, neither the military nor the Apristas have behaved as consistently as this simple scheme suggests. Both have changed dramatically since the days of their early, frequently armed confrontations of the 1930s.

In essence, APRA has evolved in the direction of moderation and even political conservatism, but without being effectively replaced by any single radical movement of equivalent stature. The aging of its leadership and the rise of younger men seeking to supplant the trade unionist accommodations of APRA by appealing to increased consciousness among newer social strata have been central factors in this evolution. So also has been APRA's desire to avoid conflict with the United States. Since 1956, when APRA threw its electoral support to Conservative Manuel Prado, the erosion of APRA's moral and political preeminence as a nationalist or revolutionary party has been increasingly apparent.

The army, meanwhile, largely as a result of the increasing professionalism and social consciousness of its officer corps, has moved in the direction of increasing independence and autonomy from traditional social and political elites. The officer corps, which always tended to be predominantly middle class and provincial in origin, became more so in life style and consciousness as well, reflecting the tensions and frustrations of development since the 1950s in a manner more typical of many civilians than previously. It could be said that having started, APRA on the left, and the army on the right, the two have moved toward and perhaps passed each other in opposite directions until today many military officers may be more favorable toward social innovation than the Aprista leadership, which lives increasingly in the past.

As we saw earlier in discussing the guerrilla campaign of 1965, the political evolution of the military drew upon developments within the military as well as in the Peruvian polity as a whole. The major change within the military relates to the increase in military self-confidence and capacity derived from improved nonmilitary education. No longer do civilians with degrees or pedigrees or foreigners with power and money automatically intimidate military officers. Since 1968, in fact, military confidence seems to have temporarily overcome some of the caution normally derived from the presence of internal political diversity within the military.

The increasing institutional autonomy and capacity of the military made them appear to be substitutes, acceptable to many, not only for the immobilism of the political parties, but for the presumed ineptitude of the civilian bureaucracy. So it certainly seemed to the increasing numbers of military men who felt threatened by the continued frustrations of Peruvian development and were, therefore, open to formulas promising action to break the impasse of backwardness.

The formula that reconciled direct political intervention with the greater bureaucratic development of the modern Peruvian military was the "institutional coup." In both 1962 and 1968, coup leaders acted only under the command of the chairman of the joint chiefs of the Peruvian service, thereby preserving institutional unity. Not since the 1948 coup by General Manuel A. Odría has an individual military commander been able to exploit his personal following to carry off a successful coup.

The military junta installed in 1962 behaved with the caution typical of traditional Peruvian military interventions conceived as a temporary "arbitral" stewardship of the state. Under the surface, however, a strong commitment to reform of the Peruvian state and society was contained only by the bad taste left behind by the corruption and excesses associated with the Odría dictatorship, and by the presence of a civilian alternative, Fernando Belaúnde, who seemed to promise effective reform. As it was, the junta's record in 1963, though mixed, included a tentative agrarian reform law as well as the founding of the National Planning Institute, which was to formulate many of the programs of the military government after 1968.

By 1968 these generally well-received reformist efforts of the 1962–1963 junta had replaced the memory of Odría as the standard against which to measure the wisdom of previous military attempts at government. By 1968, also, the political pressures of Peruvian development had led to the disintegration of the Belaúnde movement and to a sense of cynicism about the efficacy of external assistance.

Indeed, although Belaúnde began his presidency in 1963 with the strong support of military leaders, whatever opportunity existed for a coherent reform program instituted by democratic procedures was lost in the labyrinth of a political process marked by an opposition-controlled congress and presidential indecision. Simultaneously U.S. economic assistance was rendered ineffective by continuing unresolved disputes over the status of some U.S. investments, particularly the La Brea y Pariñas holdings of the International Petroleum Company (IPC), a wholly owned subsidiary of Standard Oil of New Jersey.

The military seizure of power of October 3, 1968, which deposed the civilian president whose election had been assured by the military five years earlier, was followed three days later by the seizure of the IPC's oil fields and refinery. This act, though probably critical to the coup itself, may have received more attention than it merits, largely because of the threat it poses to U.S.-Peruvian relations and therefore to Peru's economy.[3] But the IPC matter must be seen against the more general crisis of Peruvian society running through these pages. The political process set off by the 1968 coup has many of the earmarks of revolution: political upheaval, administrative reorganization, adoption of agrarian and water reforms, nationalization of a major foreign enterprise, diplomatic recognition of the Soviet Union, to mention only a few innovations.

These innovations may enable the military to manipulate the general myth of Latin American primitivism to its favor in its relations with the United States. Since the 1968 coup, the myth of the oligarchical military has been weakened in a number of important ways by the government's nationalism and reformism beginning with the nationalization of the Talara oil complex. By undertaking a series of reform measures, including agrarian reform, which clearly differentiate the current regime from previous military governments, the government of General Velasco Alvarado has made it difficult for the United States to invoke (or easier for the United States not to invoke, depending on perspective) the punitive provisions of the Hickenlooper Amendments without appearing to oppose progress.

A "progressive military dictatorship" provides some interesting problems for Americans, who tend to consider that a contradiction in terms. In Peru, also, the policies that accompanied the suspension of liberal democratic procedures have produced confusion, re-

---

[3] The Hickenlooper Amendments (1962) to the Foreign Assistance and Sugar Acts direct the president to cut off assistance and quotas to any country seizing property more than 50 percent owned by U.S. citizens, if the country does not take "appropriate steps" to pay "speedy compensation in convertible foreign exchange" within six months. The IPC matter has been remanded to Peruvian courts for litigation over back taxes, and there it rests, with no compensation paid.

minding some observers of another contradiction in terms: an attempt by the military to lead a bourgeois revolution against the will of the bourgeoisie.

What are the implications of this new political participation by the military for Peru and for U.S. military policy? The answers can be sought only after considering the military experiment in revolution before turning to a review of recent relations between the two countries on military matters.

The Experiment in Military Government since 1968

A number of commentators, including Fidel Castro as well as President Juan Velasco Alvarado, have taken to referring to the political process under way since the military coup that deposed Fernando Belaúnde in October of 1968 as a "revolution." Although it is not my intent to analyze its program in this chapter, I will briefly discuss some general considerations about the present military government.

There are many ways in which to look at what has happened since October 3, 1968, when the Peruvian military, acting institutionally, that is to say, with the commanding general of the Joint Command leading the coup but supported ultimately in disciplined hierarchical fashion by the three services, proclaimed the assumption of executive authority in behalf of a Revolutionary Government of the armed forces, dedicated to the eradication of an "unjust social and economic order." It is likely that some military leaders, and certainly most civilians, expected matters to evolve along fairly traditional lines. The military government, that is, would hold power, maintain order, bring about some necessary changes, and would then return power to elected civilians after a decent interval.

Once in power, however, even military conservatives have been faced with arguments that what was needed was not a coup, but a revolution. In other words, what Peru needed was basic change, starting with the elimination of the discredited parliamentary system, and continuing with all of the reforms Peru's "sham democracy" had "endlessly discussed, but never implemented." The urgency about the need for striking change also gained acceptance as a means of demonstrating that October 3 had been more than "just a coup." Finally, the difficulty of carrying out even moderate reforms became, given the initial commitment of institutional prestige, a source of pressure to produce significant results.

Although military isolation and secrecy had combined with civilian intellectual suspicions of military motives to divide them, military and civilian progressives actually had a good deal in common. Already, before 1968, military and civilian intellectuals had come together over the petroleum issue, which often seemed to make strange bedfellows, through a newspaper, *El Comercio*, which espoused conservative nationalism, and through two institutions, the National Planning Institute, founded originally by the military junta in 1962, and the Center for Higher Military Studies (CAEM), where civilians had for more than a decade occasionally served as guest lecturers. Catholic-inspired social and political activities formed still another point of contact between military and civilian elites.

With some of the barriers of mutual suspicion lowered, a number of attitudes common to both civilian and military progressives emerged. This process of mutual discovery accelerated in the months following the coup, often with surprising results. Among many Peruvians politically socialized since World War II, APRA seemed just another part of the Peruvian establishment. Dislike for APRA was no longer proof of conservatism. The search for a progressive nationalist solution to Peru's problem often seemed to be taking place in a political vacuum, occupied verbally by all the major parties, but implemented by none.

As the search developed after the 1968 coup, a startling amount of shared ground appeared between often somewhat disenchanted left-wing civilian intellectuals and professionals and military intellectuals and intelligence specialists. As my phrase suggests, these were and are very diverse groups. Many have been educated in the United States, others in France and are receptive to modern social science, particularly as represented by the economic views of the United Nations Economic Commission for Latin America (ECLA). Most are strongly anti-Communist, though there is some confusion over what that means in the 1970s in a country with insignificant Communist groups but a mounting social problem.

The political diversity of persons associated with the regime is most visible among the civilians, many of whom had engaged in prior political activity. Some, like the progressive priests who have helped to obtain public endorsement by Peru's Catholic church of the government's agrarian reform program, had acted outside of organized party channels.[4] Other civilians in this relatively small but technically competent group included former Apristas, Christian Democrats, and even a few who had belonged to the Social Progressive party (MSP) before it dissolved after the 1962 elections. Most, however, were political independents whose political philosophies ranged from Marxism to conservative Catholicism, and whose political views were often equally discordant.

Through this diversity, however, important common attitudes unite military and civilian technocrats. One such attitude is *elitism*, or acceptance of revolution from above. The military's views of discipline and paternalism are matched by the intellectual's fear of the masses which will neither vote for him nor support his guerrilla adventures. A second common attitude is dislike for politics, hatred for congress and for the traditional political party system. From the military side, there is the dislike for debate, disorganization, and corruption. From the radical intellectual side, the view asserts that politicians are "always selling out" to the Americans and to the upper classes, that they play petty politics instead of making a revoluion.

For many military and civilian intellectuals, therefore, there is an element of hatred for the historically dominant Peruvian elites on the grounds that they are antinational. The social and financial elites tend to be whiter in skin, they tend to have "foreign" attitudes—perhaps to the point of betraying national honor. The often conspiracy-minded nationalists made a reputedly missing "page eleven" in a proposed settlement of the IPC matter the basis of the political scandal that undid the Belaúnde government.[5]

Nationalists, of course, have no monopoly on conspiracy theories. Ever since it became clear that the Revolutionary Govern-

---

[4] See, in this connection, the discussion on pages 51ff. of our book *Latin American Development: The Changing Catholic Church* (RM-6136-DOS, The RAND Corporation: Santa Monica, California, October, 1969) by Luigi Einaudi, Richard Maullin, Alfred Stepan, and Michael Fleet.

[5] Richard Goodwin described the intricate background of this matter in his "Letter from Peru," *New Yorker*, May 17, 1969.

ment intended substantial changes, the accusation has been voiced that somehow the military were being "dominated by extremist civilian advisors," presumably Communists intent on moving Peru into the Soviet (or Chinese) orbit, or on emulating Cuba. These accusations reflect the fears and ignorance of their originators rather than any serious analysis of the internal workings of the Peruvian government. The suspicion that somehow all progressive intellectuals are "red" and that if they are they will automatically brainwash the military does more than ignore recent Peruvian history: it also reveals a characteristic Peruvian civilian upper-class refusal —often shared by liberal Americans—to believe that the military can ever be expected to do anything competently on their own.

In my view, in any case, the internal political diversity of the Peruvian armed forces as a whole will continue to block dominance by any narrowly partisan political group even if one exists. This military diversity, in fact, may perhaps even prevent the adoption of consistent development policies by the military institutions as such over any extended period of time.

The possibility that the military might adopt some form of "revolutionary" strategy has been fed in recent years by increased military concern over the need for modernization of society as a whole as a prerequisite to military survival as a modern institution. Likewise, the possibility that the military might adopt a strategy with "anti-imperialist" overtones has been fed in recent years by increased military suspicion of U.S. military and economic policies.

Such language, by its very breadth and vagueness, generates confusion and uncertainty. The military government may, as it did with the nationalization of the IPC petroleum complex at Talara, briefly take dramatic steps of considerable symbolic significance. This is particularly likely in those instances that are apparently amenable to executive action and the issuance of decrees, like that for agrarian reform. Similar acts may even be called for by radical elements of left and right who see the military as a means of outmaneuvering conservative and liberal democratic political opponents. Policies adopted under such circumstances may thus be the result of the development strategy of a specific political group but they are most decidedly not the strategies of the military as an institution.

INTERNAL CONSTRAINTS

Taken as a whole, it is unlikely that the military institutions as such will be able to resolve what they are likely to see as a contradiction between military discipline and the partisan political activity required for the organization of development. Internal political diversity constitutes an automatic internal self-regulating mechanism ensuring the development of internal counterweights to controversial policies that threaten military discipline, unity, and hence institutional survival. This dynamic makes it quite unlikely that the military can be bureaucratically controlled for long by any single partisan clique. Should the military officer corps produce individual leaders with a personal vision of the struggle for development, such men will in practice cease to be military officers, becoming instead what Peru's current leaders denounce almost daily, "politicians," while the military institutions withdraw to a less partisan posture.

This analysis implies that if the military is not the counter-revolutionary tool it is often painted to be, neither can it be regarded as a guarantee of progressive development. The thesis of "military as salvation"—for any partisan group—fails on the fact that the normal internal political diversity of the military is heightened by the assumption of responsible political power and the encounter with complexities of government. This transfer of politics into the military institution itself is often shrouded with secrecy because of the threat of fragmentation and hence of possible danger to the very survival of the military institution itself.[6] The result can be sudden swings and shifts in policy within apparent overall government stability, but repression and ultimate withdrawal from power are possible alternative outcomes of reliance on military power for the resolution of political problems.

EXTERNAL CONSTRAINTS

Additional sources for skepticism about the military's capacity for sustained revolutionary innovation derive from the nature of

[6] The illusion of the "apolitical" military and the tension between the military as institution and the military as government is discussed in the Brazilian case by my former RAND colleague Alfred Stepan, *Patterns of Civil-Military Relations: The Brazilian Political System* (RAND R-477-RC, forthcoming, Princeton University Press).

Peruvian society rather than from the nature of the military itself. I suspect that revolution from above by the military is likely to fail in Peru for reasons similar to those for the failure of guerrillas to lead revolution from below. One of the most important of these common reasons is the unmanageability of Peru, whether it be measured in social, political or administrative terms. Peru, one-third of whose people do not speak Spanish, has nearly twice the population of Cuba spread out over an area more than ten times as large, but with less than one-fifth as many television sets per capita. With neither a charismatic leader nor an overwhelming external enemy against whom to unite, can any Peruvian government hope to find and communicate the emotional cement necessary to hold a revolutionary effort together?

The problem is all the greater if there is uncertainty over the programs required to implement the general principles of change. To maintain momentum while the internal policy debates raged, the military turned immediately after assuming power to their traditional interest in "public morality." Few things are more de-moralizing than public displays of habitual ineptitude and corrup-tion. A major public scandal over smuggling implicating some offi-cers as well as highly placed civilian friends of President Belaúnde had contributed in the spring of 1968 to the atmosphere that later led to the military intervention. One of the first acts of the new revolutionary government, therefore, was to proclaim the need to eliminate graft and corruption. The moralization campaign that ensued included a series of measures to increase efficiency, includ-ing a reform of the basic structure of government, creating three additional ministries.

The attempt to improve public administrative services included the unheard-of introduction of time clocks for all public employees (to be punched by supervisors and employees alike) and the slogan *hora exacta, hora Peruana* to replace the traditional Peruvian habit of tardiness accompanied by the statement that the employee who was on time was operating on *hora inglesa.*

The incoming military ministers made a largely unprecedented (except for some members of the 1962 junta) public accounting of their wealth upon assuming office, and there can be no doubt that the government leadership as a whole has good intentions. Some ministers, in fact, appear to be incorruptible to the point of fanaticism. Harsh and immediate legal proceedings were instituted in the spring of 1969 against those officials of the Ministry of Finance and of the Central Bank, military as well as civilian, who could be charged with corruption or incompetence in the granting of an export license permitting the International Petroleum Company to withdraw funds from Peru.

The government's severity sent a shudder of fear throughout the civilian bureaucracy, and appears also to have frightened many private citizens with the technical competence needed if Peru is to enlist intelligence and knowledge to public service.

Excessive zeal in the eradication of corruption and ineptitude can heighten the deficiencies of public administration. This irony is perhaps most evident in an underdeveloped country with a large marginal population. In such a society, any educated man has means disproportionate to the environment as a whole. A sensitive member of the middle or upper classes, from which senior public officials must of necessity be drawn, finds it almost impossible to live in Peru without somehow feeling corrupt, if only because he lives well while others subsist in a near-animal state.

To offset the shortages in administrative personnel automatically imposed by the adoption of new government programs such as agrarian reform, the government has attempted to turn to retired officers and to Church personnel. Again, a quick consideration of the numbers involved reveals the poverty of Peru's resources compared to the magnitude of the task. There are fewer than 2,500 priests in all of Peru. Even assuming that most clerics are prepared (and free) to cooperate with the authoritarian military in the common cause of development, this is simply not a very large pool from which to draw. Finally, the limits on resources external to the military as a means of expansion of the bureaucracy are underscored by the fact that there are even fewer retired officers still young enough to be useful than priests.

As the time has passed, therefore, increasing numbers of officers have been assigned to the nonmilitary ministries, often occupying senior and even middle-level posts previously occupied by civilians. This proliferation of military officers in what would normally be considered civilian functions can be explained partially as attempts at reform and partially as a method of political control. The presence of many of Peru's best young generals in the ministerial portfolios should also be considered a sign of the depth and likely continuity of military governmental commitment.

The assignment of officers to previously civilian administrative functions may create tensions within the military itself, however. Officers holding administrative posts draw extra basic pay allotments denied those remaining on line duty in the barracks. This irritant may act as a catalyst for morale and other issues contrasting military "politicians" unfavorably with military "professionals."

Of greater immediate concern is the possibility for demoralization of the senior civilian element of the bureaucracy. Many civilian public servants have long practical experience in day-to-day management of affairs in areas only vaguely understood by the military men who now not only block their chances for promotion, but seem, with their insistent demands for revision and change, to imply that previous efforts were incompetent. Bureaucrats know too well the difficulties of innovation.

One of the political functions of the military in Peru has traditionally been to act as a means by which ambitious and talented civilian leaders could take office without having to undertake the messy business of organizing or currying the favor of political parties. As a means of bypassing the party system, which certainly has not always been a paradigm of statesmanship, the military has enabled the nation to draw in more or less "routine" fashion upon the intelligence of some of its more competent civilians.

Whatever the merits of such a pattern (and to one raised in the United States they appear dubious), the current military intervention, with its insistence upon military decision making and military control of key positions, suggests that the Peruvian military, under the leadership of the army, is attempting to erect itself as a super-bureaucracy dominating the state in the search for a modern nation. This attempt to run a government that is military to this degree is without precedent. It is a marked change even with regard to contemporary military regimes in other Latin American countries such as Brazil and Argentina, where civilians have continued to exercise key policy making functions.

For Peru, the ultimate problem may be that its strength may not lie in its bureaucrats and intellectuals, military or civilian (both of whom are generally looked down upon by social and economic elites), but in the private sector. The tragedy is that this private sector has until now acted in such a private manner as to discredit itself by appearing to deny the national goals to which the military, more than any other group in Peru, is dedicated. Military dictatorship and perhaps even ultimately stagnation may thus be the price of the selfishness of past Peruvian elites. The extent of that price will be determined by the political wisdom and flexibility of the military and their civilian associates as they seek to lead Peru to an improved accommodation with the pressures of modernity.[7]

What role can U.S. policy play in this process? What role should it play? For the United States, the extent and nature of military participation in the governing of Peru since 1968 complicates the already difficult question of the American role in events on foreign shores.

From an intellectual viewpoint also, the recent history of the Peruvian military should underscore the inadequacies of the often arbitrary and uncertain distinction between "military" and "civilian" governments.

Part II opens by considering recent U.S. relations on military matters rather narrowly and traditionally conceived. It then concludes by suggesting some implications of a distinction between the military understood "as military," and the military "as government."

PERU-U.S. MILITARY RELATIONS

Patterns of Past Relations

United States military relations with Peru were, with the exception of a naval mission, minimal until the Second World War. Wartime led to a vigorous U.S. military policy throughout Latin America seeking the ousting of Italian and German military missions, and, with the collapse of French missions, to their gradual replacement by United States Army and later Air Force missions in an attempt to establish U.S. regional military supremacy.

The doctrine covering the military relations with Latin America, which arose during World War II, was given institutional form in

[7] Brilliant descriptions of these pressures, and of the military response to them are to be found in articles by Jorge Bravo Bresani, "Naturaleza del poder peruano," and François Bourricaud, "Los militares: ¿por qué y para qué?" both appearing in Aportes (France), no. 16, April, 1970.

the Inter-American Defense Board, and led to the signing of the 1947 Rio Pact, aimed at hemispheric defense. Defense of the hemisphere against external attack, presumably from the Soviet Union and its allies, reached its height after the outbreak of the Korean War with the signing of mutual defense pacts with most Latin American countries. In Peru, this agreement was signed during the (elected by imposition) presidency of General Manuel A. Odría, who was later decorated by the Eisenhower administration.[8]

The Mutual Defense Assistance Agreement of February 22, 1952, between the United States and Peru (3UST2890-2900) committed both governments to make available to each other "equipment, materials, services, or other military assistance . . . designed to promote the defense of the Western Hemisphere . . . in accordance with defense plans under which both Governments will participate in missions important to the defense of the Western Hemisphere." Under the agreement, Peru undertook not to use such assistance for "purposes other than those for which it was furnished" and committed itself to "take all reasonable measures which may be needed to develop its defense capacities."

U.S. military grant assistance to Peru under this and subsequent agreements has been substantial. Cumulative grant material deliveries from fiscal years 1950 to 1965 inclusive were $59.3 million, equivalent to about 6 percent of Peru's military expenditures. This sum is but one-third of that provided to Brazil during the same years, but otherwise Peru is second only to Chile (and comparable to Colombia) in receipt of U.S. grant military assistance in dollar value. Public breakdowns of these deliveries by item rather than by value are not available. All three services have apparently benefitted, though it is likely that the navy has had the most success over the years in obtaining desired equipment. Deliveries under hemispheric defense concepts appear to have peaked with support for antisubmarine warfare operations, which led in 1959–1960 to loans to Peru of U.S. naval vessels, including a floating dry dock and a destroyer. In the mid-1950s, the U.S. Export-Import Bank had provided credit for the purchase of two submarines. This program, however, did not exclude continuing Peruvian purchases of impor-

---

[8] The classic (often highly critical) analysis of U.S. military policy in this period, written just before the Cuban Revolution, is Edwin Lienwen's *Arms and Politics in Latin America* (New York: Praeger, 1960).

tant equipment, including, for example, two naval cruisers obtained from Great Britain in 1958. A similar pattern held for the other services.

This development of the military assistance program brought about a subtle change in the U.S. military missions to Peru. Previously, U.S. missions, like those of other foreign powers, were contracted on a service-to-service basis. The Peruvian ministries of air, navy, or war (army) would separately contract with the appropriate foreign military department, often also at a service level, for individual officers and training services. American military missions had been operating in this fashion in Peru since the naval mission of 1922. By the mid-1950s, when a new army mission agreement was signed in 1956, the naval mission agreement dated from 1940, the military aviation mission agreement from 1946. Peru traditionally shared the cost of the missions with the United States, leading Peru to consider the missions as in their service. With the advent of MAP, however, military missions' functions and responsibilities were somewhat clouded by their assumption of the duties of supervision of use of American supplied equipment normally performed by military assistance advisory groups (MAAG) in countries where no missions had existed previously.

This political, if not legal, confusion was compounded in the early 1960s by new U.S. regulations designed to ensure effective coordinating of military policy with political and economic considerations. To this end the U.S. missions were to be brought under a single head, who would himself be a member of the U.S. country team under the ambassador. The missions were thus collectively redesignated a "Military Group" although the Peruvians never recognized the Military Group and continued to operate under the terms of the individual mission agreements.

Since 1966, when the Military Group (or three missions, depending on to whom one talked) had sixty-six members, including thirty-two officers, thirty-three enlisted men, and one civilian, the numbers of U.S. military personnel serving in advisory capacity in Peru has steadily declined. In part, this has been due to a general reduction of the U.S. military presence in Latin America.[9]

[9] See in this connection the statement and testimony, May 7, 1969, of William E. Lang, deputy assistant secretary of defense (international security affairs) for Africa and the Western Hemisphere in United States House of Representatives,

Increasing Peruvian military disappointment at the failure of the
U.S. missions to provide access to equipment suitable for external
defense functions, or other services desired by the Peruvians, also
contributed to the decline. By early 1969, the Military Group was
down to a level of nineteen officers and nineteen enlisted men, as
officers whose terms of duty had expired were not replaced. Finally, in May, 1969, after U.S. military sales to Peru were halted by
application of the Pelly Amendment because of Peruvian navy enforcement of two-hundred-mile claims at the expense of U.S. tuna
boats, the Peruvian government requested that the U.S. missions
be withdrawn by July 1.

The ambiguity of function was underscored when the United
States indicated that such a withdrawal, unless Peru accepted a
MAAG, would require the termination of all MAP deliveries. Un-
willing to lose all contact, the governments compromised on a
MAAG attached to the U.S. Embassy of three officers and four en-
listed men supervising delivery of items already in the pipeline.[10]

The reduction of U.S. military advisory activity paralleled in
many ways similar reductions in the overall military assistance
program. According to information supplied to the Senate Foreign
Relations Committee, the grant military aid program for Peru for
fiscal year 1969 contained no materiel grants and a total of $800,-
000 for training only.[11] Undelivered materiel from prior years,

Committee on Foreign Affairs, Subcommittee on Inter-American Affairs, "New
Directions for the 1970's: Toward a Strategy of Inter-American Development,"
Hearings March–May, 1969, 91st Congress, 1st session (Washington, D.C.: U.S.
Government Printing Office, 1969, pp. 497–539). The levels authorized at that
time for July 1, 1970, for all of Latin America totaled 505 U.S. military personnel, a reduction of one-third from previous levels. Additional reductions have
been announced since, and Governor Rockefeller has recommended the elimination of "permanent U.S. military missions in residence in other nations," advocating their partial replacement by temporary training missions provided on
request.

[10] These developments and their status in the spring of 1970 are discussed in
U.S. House of Representatives, Subcommittee on National Security Policy and
Scientific Developments, Committee on Foreign Affairs, "Reports of the Special
Study Mission to Latin America on Military Assistance Training and Develop-
mental Television," 91st Congress (Washington, D.C.: U.S. Government Print-
ing Office, 1970).

[11] United States Senate, Committee on Foreign Relations, Subcommittee on
Western Hemisphere Affairs, Hearings April, 1969, "United States Relations

plus amounts delivered to Peru after the coup of October 3, 1968, included vehicles ($138,000), maintenance equipment ($40,000), aircraft support equipment ($12,000), ship support equipment ($13,000), and other spares and support equipment. Grant assistance was thus down to less than 1 percent of the Peruvian military budget. The absolute amount is placed in some perspective when compared to the order in March 1970 by the Peruvian Air Force of sixteen De Havilland of Canada Buffalo STOL transports for development purposes at a cost of $60 million. In fiscal year 1970, U.S. grant military assistance, *for all of Latin America*, was $21.4 million, down from the fiscal year 1966 peak of $80.7 million.[12]

SHIFTING U.S. POLICIES AND DOCTRINES

Behind the changes in both amounts and types of assistance lies a story many of whose details are still unclear, although its lessons may have implications for U.S. policy that far exceed either Peru or the purely military sphere. Beginning under the Kennedy administration, after the Soviet Union's discovery of the potential autonomy of the "Third World" from the former colonial powers, and given added immediacy in Latin America by the rise of Cuban-inspired guerrilla activities, the United States adopted a military policy in support of what came to be known as "counter-insurgency and civic action," to provide the security for the Alliance for Progress. This virtual abandonment of the hemispheric defense doctrines in favor of new internal security doctrines was also partially based on the desire to give a new orientation to U.S. military policies, which had in the late 1950s come under increasing attack from American liberals critical of military dictatorships, particularly those of Generals Fulgencio Batista in Cuba and Mar-

---

with Peru," 91st Congress, 1st session (Washington, D.C.: U.S. Government Printing Office, 1969, p. 126).

[12] The decline is probably partly attributable to the U.S. belief, according to Assistant Secretary of State Charles A. Meyer, that "today insurgent forces are not a direct threat to the governments in any of the Latin American countries." United States Senate, Committee on Foreign Relations, Subcommittee on Western Hemisphere Affairs, "United States Military Policies and Programs in Latin America," Hearings June–July, 1969, 91st Congress, 1st session (Washington, D.C.: U.S. Government Printing Office, 1969, p. 59).

cos Pérez Jiménez in Venezuela, but including also that of General Manuel Odría in Peru.[13]

At a programmatic level, the doctrinal shift led to U.S. support for mobility, communications, and "nation-building" activities designed to win popular support for the military and thereby to deny it to potential insurgents.[14] In Peru, after 1961, the military assistance program helped equip four engineer battalions. AID and Export-Import Bank loan funds were also made available to purchase road-building equipment, which the Department of Highways turned over to the military to operate.[15]

The U.S. switch from hemispheric defense concepts to the newer internal security doctrines was also accompanied by a subtle reversal of the United States's implicit position on military expenditures. Under the mutual defense agreements, countries had accepted the responsibility of maintaining certain units for the common defense. This effectively associated the United States, by international agreement, with an obligation to maintain certain expenditures. The internal security emphasis now was accompanied by pressure to reduce military expenditures to free additional funds for development purposes. Suddenly, liberal U.S. congressmen in particular pictured the Latin American military as engaged in massively unnecessary military expenditures.

This new emphasis coincided in Peru (as in most other Latin American countries) with the increasing obsolescence (and hence danger and costliness) of much military materiel obtained after World War II and Korea. So long as the United States considered itself a military ally with an interest in hemispheric defense, there

[13] Or, as Ralph A. Dungan commented nearly a decade later at the hearings just cited, the "preoccupation with counterinsurgency as the major thrust of U.S. military and policy is nothing more than an incomplete evolution of an intention on the part of the Kennedy Administration to eventually disengage from significant military activity in Latin America." (Statement of June 24, 1969, U.S. Senate, ibid., p. 5.)

[14] A general account of the reorientation of MAP in the early 1960s is contained in Willard F. Barber and C. Neale Ronning, *Internal Security and Military Power: Counterinsurgency and Civic Action in Latin America* (Columbus: Ohio State University Press, 1966).

[15] A useful account in English is "East of the Andes: Internal Development Operations of the Peruvian Armed Forces," by John G. Waggener, Lieutenant Colonel (now Colonel), Corps of Engineers (U.S. Army War College, Carlisle Barracks, Pa., January 18, 1968).

was the possibility it would defray, through assistance programs, some of the expense associated with the increasingly sophisticated equipment the United States and other superpowers were building for their own use (but which tended to be the only equipment available, thereby forcing smaller states to either opt out or to escalate, even if merely replacing one aircraft with another). The shift in the Latin American military doctrine of the United States dashed hopes of cushioning the economic and political impact of military "modernization," and seemed even to deny validity to the hemispheric regional or other external defense functions of the Latin American military. Implicitly, "counterinsurgency" doctrine also tended to confirm the military as wardens in their own societies, an aspect of their traditions few officers relished, and which (at least in Peru) they were increasingly coming to question.

Under these circumstances, the changed emphasis seemed to suggest to many (including both military men and anti-American radicals of left and right) that the United States sought to deny the very institutional being of the Latin American military by making of them a special political police. These suspicions were heightened by U.S. delays and later refusals to allow acquisition of "sophisticated" military weapons. When the Peruvian air force sought to purchase Northrup Aviation's F-5 (a relatively cheap jet fighter, barely capable of breaking the sound barrier unloaded, but which would have amply replaced the FAP's disintegrating F-80s), the U.S. government procrastinated under congressional pressure until it was too late to prevent the angry purchase of the more expensive and sophisticated French Mirages, which were capable of twice the speed of sound.

After Peru's elected civilian government had made this purchase in 1967 with the unanimous support of Peru's Congress, the United States, which had resumed economic assistance in 1966 after freezing it in 1965 because of the ever-present uncertainty over the status of the International Petroleum Company, reduced economic assistance again because of legislation and pressures emanating from the U.S. Congress. First, Peru's elected civilian government was forced to spend more than it (or its air force) wanted to spend. Then, Peru's elected civilian government was weakened by a fine from the leaders of the Alliance for Progress.

Civilian and military leaders were united in baffled resentment at a U.S. policy that refused to sell them aircraft the U.S. was simultaneously providing to Ethiopia on a grant basis.

Before exploring the implications of these views, however, it seems necessary to consider other aspects of U.S. military relations with Peru. The F-5 case suggests that considerations characteristic of general Alliance for Progress policy were applied to arms sales, whether or not this was in the long-run interests of the United States. Did the same hold true for U.S. mission and training activity? One of the chief sources of Congressional concern over armaments was the fear that U.S. military policies were contributing to the militarization of Latin America in direct contradiction of the Alliance for Progress.

EFFECTS OF U.S. MISSIONS AND TRAINING PROGRAMS

Difficulties of definition, accounting, and secrecy make it hard to draw an accurate picture of the specific content of the military assistance program, whether in deliveries or training, and even less so in results. A review of the nature and impact of the foreign training of Peruvian military officers, for example, reveals both how little is actually known about the relevant details and how infinitely complex any assessment of the effects of training must be.

Generally speaking, it is clear that increased professional education, whether within Peru or abroad, has obviously not taken the military out of politics. On the contrary, by promoting self-confidence and international awareness, training may actually increase the military's desire and capacity for political participation. Incomplete quantitative data suggest that the more highly trained officers are, the more likely they are both to attain the top ranks and to participate in politics.

Of the army general officers serving in Peru in the period from 1960 to 1965, some 49 percent had received foreign training of some kind. This training had varied from brief orientation sessions in the Canal Zone to attendance at technical courses of some months' duration in the United States to *étages* of up to two years "on assignment" with a unit in the French army before World War II.

By comparison with previous periods, the 1960s saw the rise to numerical predominance of general officers whose training had taken place in the United States instead of France. Of those who had studied abroad, often in more than one country, 75 percent had done so in the United States, 30 percent in France, and 10 percent in other countries, principally Italy, Britain, and Belgium. Although the absolute numbers were larger on a relative basis, foreign-trained officers were fewer in the 1960–1965 period than previously. In 1940, for example, eight out of Peru's nine army general officers had received training in France, and even in 1950 three-fourths of army general officers had received foreign training compared to but one-half in the 1960s.

Actual numbers for individual students and types of training are difficult to obtain in global terms except from individual installations. The single largest block I know of is made up of 562 Peruvian air force enlisted specialists (not officers) trained from 1950 to 1969 in aircraft maintenance and related skills at the Inter-American Air Force Academy at Albrook Air Force Base, Canal Zone. The technical proficiency established as a result of these bilingual courses is a matter of pride to both the FAP and the USAF. It is difficult to assign major political importance to this training effort, however, other than the maintenance of cordial working relations between similar components of Peruvian and American society.

During approximately the same period, from 1947 to 1967, some 324 Peruvian officers, 80 percent of them lieutenants or captains, attended courses at the U.S. Army School for Latin America at Fort Gulick on the other side of the Isthmus of Panama. Initially, course offerings appear to have been standard World War II type weapons and logistics courses. From the early 1960s on, they centered increasingly on unconventional warfare operations and communications, subjects that were also taught to some 127 enlisted specialists from Peru in the 1964–1967 period. Not until the 1980s will significant numbers of the junior officers taking Canal Zone courses occupy senior command positions in the Peruvian army. By 1990, however, about one field-grade officer in three may have had at least a cadet orientation from the United States.

Seen against the background of substantial and improving Peruvian military educations, the assessment of the impact of this American training would suggest that it is relatively marginal on most matters of day-to-day behavior, and that its effects must be sought at the level of technical skills and general values rather than in support of specific U.S. policies or operations.

If any broad generalizations can be made on the basis of individual conversations, they would include the likelihood that, in addition to supplemental competence in the specific (generally technical) subject matter studied, the officers develop more realistic assessments (negative as well as positive) of the United States than if they had never been exposed. Indeed, U.S. training, while often producing admiration for many things American, is more likely to produce critics than supporters of specific U.S. policies toward Latin America.

Such mixed emotions have been more common than not among Peruvian officers since at least the early 1960s. In 1962, when the Peruvian military, acting under the chairman of its joint staff, installed a military junta, the United States refused to recognize the new government and suspended both military and economic assistance. This act shocked many military leaders who believed they had acted out of progressive and nationalist sentiments essentially in harmony with the social and economic reform goals of the Alliance for Progress. In fact, given their own constitutional mandate "to guarantee the fulfillment of the constitution and the laws" (Article 213, Constitution of 1933), most officers were probably no more ethnocentric in their belief that they acted democratically than were the Americans who criticized them for not living up to the precepts of the U.S. Constitution.

Peruvian military criticism of the United States tends, nonetheless, to be more realistic on most issues than that of many civilians. Most Peruvian officers know too much through their visits and training to harbor many illusions about the extent of American power. Officers may not, however, be as sophisticated about economic relations with the United States as success in the rather cosmopolitan world of international finance may require. Past U.S. policy reversals under pressure, particularly after the 1962 coup, may have convinced some Peruvian military leaders (possibly erroneously) that the United States will change its policies and even ignore U.S. legislation, such as the Hickenlooper Amendment, if challenged firmly enough.

Relations between the United States and Peru since the 1968

coup can be described on the whole as cool, but with varying degrees of hostility kept generally under control. The recognition of the Soviet Union was a clear demonstration of a desire to assert Peruvian independence of the United States. The expulsion in May, 1969, of the United States military missions from Peru was primarily an attempt to retaliate politically for suspension of U.S. military sales under the Pelly Amendment, but was also a sign of the prior deterioration of military relations between the two countries. This deterioration, it seems clear, was probably more the result of political considerations (IPC, 200-miles, etc.), than a reflection on the technical military record of U.S. advisors.

Relations between U.S. military personnel in the missions and their Peruvian counterparts had historically been cordial, though increasingly distant. Much of the American military personnel's activity was dedicated to the maintenance of complicated records in Lima on military assistance program support. Peruvian officers who valued their American contacts and training in the United States nonetheless pointed out that U.S. military personnel assigned to Peru never exceeded the rank of colonel and had not, to their knowledge, ever included officers who ultimately later attained general officer rank before retiring. Peruvians who attended regular U.S. officer training in the United States knew their best American classmates were not assigned to Latin America.

Professionally, Peruvian military officers often seem to feel a love-hate relationship for the United States. The United States often seems to ignore Peru and its problems, but it is nonetheless the world's leading military power. Peruvian officers, therefore, while often happy to turn toward France, England, or Japan for the acquisition of armaments and for certain types of training, nonetheless would like to continue to have access to the United States for equipment and advice when necessary, despite the United States' continuing relegation of Peru to second- or third-class status militarily.

Under these conditions, U.S. military policies are likely to be marginal, except for the rare occasion where they effectively preclude an action beyond appeal. The attempt to prevent Peruvian acquisition of supersonic military aircraft revealed that the United States could deny its own suppliers, and perhaps even delay the ultimate acquisition from France. But despite punitive legislation and previously good military relations the United States was unable to prevent the purchase in the long run.

Similarly, to argue that an officer has participated in a coup attempt merely because of his U.S. training is as arbitrary as to claim that this training has made him more democratic. Worse, such claims betray an arrogant refusal to take seriously the internal resilience and resourcefulness of Peruvians. When such attitudes become translated into policies, as with the F-5, the result is to provoke unnecessarily the hostility of a critical segment of Peru's political class. The F-5 case did not of itself change the direction of Peruvian government policies. But it went into the equation that did.

Each situation, of course, must be examined on its own merits, for the subtleties of politics are such that even a marginal impact may be decisive in a given instance. Our consideration of the place of future military policy in overall U.S.-Peruvian relations, however, will be significantly aided by the realization that we have as a nation and government frequently lacked the capacity for such subtle analyses in the past.

Alternatives for the Future

Peruvian conditions may determine the success or failure of U.S. policy in Peru itself, but they affect the formulation of U.S. policy toward Peru only to the extent that they are understood by the policy-relevant community in the United States. Discussion of policy, therefore, requires that descriptions and analyses of events be related to the perceptions the political actors affected by the policy have of each other.

This apparently trivial distinction is of critical importance, because U.S. policies toward Peru have often resulted from the application of U.S. political mythologies about Latin America as a whole. The individuality of countries and situations can best be reconciled with relatively abstract formulations that allow considerable latitudes in the choice of action or inaction. Activist policies as envisaged by the Alliance for Progress, on the other hand, place particularly taxing demands on discriminating knowledge of individual situations and the affects of attempts to influence them.

The discussion that follows therefore analyzes the military and political dimensions of U.S. policies with the implicit aim, not only of examining Peruvian conditions, but of deriving abstractions capable of more general Latin American application. In keeping also with our findings about the political importance of the military, the discussion of policy toward the military "as military" is followed by a discussion of policy toward the military "as government."

THE MILITARY AS MILITARY

That there is a clear and present interest of the United States that requires close cooperation between the military forces of the United States and Peru is not obvious. Neither hemispheric defense nor Peruvian internal security appear at this time to present military threats to the United States. There are no extra-hemispheric dangers on which it is possible to agree that requires U.S. bases in Peru.

Sensible military policy objectives for the United States in Peru would therefore appear to be limited to the maintenance of *decent working relations on a technical basis* with the Peruvian military and the avoidance of military programs that would jeopardize broader U.S. political interests in Peru.

There are essentially two reasons for insisting on decent technical working relations with the Peruvian military as a policy goal for the United States. The first is to have a basis for cooperation should a military threat develop in the future to require common action. The second, and more important, is to avoid unnecessarily alienating military forces whose leaders are clearly an integral part of the Peruvian political elite.[16]

---

[16] In P-4109, *Latin American Security Issues*, April, 1969, I argued with my colleagues Richard L. Maullin and Alfred C. Stepan that the outline of a U.S. security policy to conserve influence without exacerbating nationalisms might be as follows:

1. Maintain working relations with Latin America's military institutions to complement the multilateral alliance structure. These relationships should include some training, military sales, and advice, although the political costs of maintaining a mission monopoly should be evaluated.

2. Do not attempt to dictate missions or armaments for Latin American military forces. U.S. preferences and even opposition to given courses of action can be made clear, but without punitive restrictions if possible.

3. Strive to keep security policy politically neutral by avoiding entanglement in civil-military relations and in internal budgetary and operational matters.

Given these general requirements for a successful policy, however, a number of important policy alternatives still remain. Military relations may have a variety of components giving them greater or lesser prominence and volume as the situation requires. Though American policy objectives are for American policy makers to establish independent of Peruvian conditions, the details of their implementation will require adaptation to Peruvian needs.

I believe that a military policy least offensive to both countries, yet providing a basis for decent relations, could:

1. Allow military *sales* on an internationally competitive basis, without regard to the nature of the equipment (but with neither sales promotion nor the use of selective sales as a political weapon as had been done in recent years).

2. Give *credits* only under conditions comparable to other world military credit patterns (as opposed to credit arrangements that are in fact disguised grants or subsidies).

3. Eliminate *grants* except in such limited cases as might serve specific United States interests as determined by the executive branch in specific consultation with Congress.

4. Provide *training* in technical military matters whenever both the United States and Peru agree through appropriate political channels on the need and on the absence of partisan political involvement.

5. U.S. *missions* could also be provided, when requested, on a technical service-to-service basis to promote in-country training to supplement training provided in the continental United States. (The elimination of grants would render unnecessary the inflated missions often presently required by U.S. legislation to supervise the use of material.)

From an American viewpoint, of course, the fact that potential conflicts exist with Peru's neighbors must be taken into consideration. The United States presumably wants to avoid either contributing to conflicts or becoming identified with them, as might happen if the United States were to be an exclusive source of weapons or military advice to either side. As we have seen, however, standardization of equipment has not taken place in the past. It is even less likely today, particularly in the absence of military grant programs.

This discussion underscores, however, the political sensitivity of military programs. The mythology of domestic Latin American politics is full of partisan exploitation of military relations with the United States. To avoid providing ammunition to those who fear U.S. opposition and to prevent governments from claiming U.S. support on issues in which the United States does not have an interest, some might suggest the elimination of any military assistance program at all. This proposition may be considered in the specific case of military weapons. Should the United States grant or even sell military weapons to Peru?

The question of grants is most easily dismissed. U.S. policy since fiscal year 1969 has eliminated grant materiel support to the major Latin American countries, including Peru. Despite some skeptics who argue that the United States may thereby jeopardize military relations (on the theory that other relations, particularly training, follow equipment, and that the United States is not in a position to compete without grants), there seems to be no disposition to restore weapons grants.

The two extreme alternatives with regard to sales would seem to be either that the United States make *no sales* of military equipment or that it make *unrestricted sales*. Broadly speaking an argument for unrestricted sales must either attempt to divorce military sales from politics or to defend military establishments on political grounds. To make no sales at all requires the assumption that the United States desires to discourage the maintenance of military establishments and does not fear to incur their wrath.

Present policies seem to be a hodgepodge of *selective sales* imposed by a case-by-case consideration of requests in light of political and military situations and the legal requirements imposed by the Symington and Conte-Long amendments to the Foreign Assistance Act. Unless there were a total arms embargo, including small arms, communications equipment and military vehicles, a no-sales policy would implicitly involve the same, often arbitrary, judgments of the present selective sales system which has done considerable damage to U.S. influence and credibility.

The desire to prevent sales of major armaments is deeply rooted in the belief that whatever funds Latin America possesses should be devoted to productive economic expenditures. The paternalism in this argument is deeply resented by even many outside the military establishments; but its real weakness lies in the United States's inability to cut off alternative sources of supply. When Peru turned to France for the Mirage aircraft, it not only acquired supersonic military jets, but did so at a cost greater than if we had acceded earlier to its request for the F-5, a less-sophisticated (and much cheaper) craft specifically designed for the underdeveloped countries.

In practice, therefore, it would appear that the objective of decent working relations, *given present levels of demand*, can be best met by working toward unrestricted sales. Certainly it would be difficult to defend U.S. sales of military aircraft to the repressive military dictatorship of Brazil while refusing similar treatment to the progressive and generally not repressive military dictatorship of Peru.

Whether sales or a modest technically oriented policy should be termed an *assistance* program, with all the connotations that implies, including acceptance of the myth of primitivism, seems doubtful. What seems clear, however, is that the *absence* of decent military relations could simultaneously increase Peruvian military hostility to the United States and open commercial as well as military opportunities to U.S. competitors, including the Soviet Union. To some extent this has already been the result of past policies, which seem to have led to an almost purposeful alienation of a major political force: Instead of significantly weakening the Peruvian military, complete elimination of the MAP/mission program would only increase military anti-Americanism and would, given the centrality of military political roles, inevitably find additional expression in Peruvian government policies toward the United States.

THE MILITARY AS GOVERNMENT

Our discussion of relations between the United States and Peru suggests that a precondition for successful military policies affecting the two countries is recognition of the political traditions of both Peru and the United States. From this viewpoint, the most important of these traditions in Peru is the high rate of military participation in the affairs of government. The most important U.S. tradition, on the other hand, is that of civilian dominance and control of the military.

The result is that, when a military government is in power in

Peru, the two extremes of policy theoretically available to govern relations between the United States and Peru, *nonrecognition* and *full support*, are both equally untenable because of their contradiction of political realities.

Nonrecognition of a Peruvian military government, for example, although fully in harmony with domestic U.S. constitutional traditions, is unsound because of its contradiction of Peruvian constitutional traditions sanctioning military participation in government. Attempts by the United States in 1962 to deny and in 1968 to delay recognition of military governments have been to no avail. Ultimately unsuccessful also have been attempts to eliminate economic and even military assistance to Peru under military regimes. The costs to U.S. political relations with Peru have proven too great for such blanket denials of aid to last.

Full U.S. support and cooperation with a Peruvian military government, on the other hand, though perhaps desirable under certain Peruvian conditions, is equally unsound. Military participation in the government of Peru will inevitably be considered in some U.S. circles as an invitation to military dictatorship. Even the conferral of the Legion of Merit on General Manuel Odría during the 1950–1956 period of more or less constitutional rule ultimately provoked sharp negative reactions in the United States. American policy, despite the prominence of military factors and the exceptions generated by the Cold War, is more comfortable in the long run with liberal democratic ideals. Furthermore, extensive support for any Latin American government, of whatever coloration, is unlikely in the 1970s, given the decline in U.S. external activism and the inward diversion of U.S. energies and attentions.

The two basic requirements, then, for relations likely to be reasonably stable, because they deny neither country's vital interests, would seem to be *diplomatic recognition* and *political distance*. But does this rather abstract formula fit the situation that has developed since October, 1968?

In favor of strong relations of political support for the Peruvian military government would be the view that Peru's revolutionary experiment represents a major and appealing attempt at progressive political innovation at a time and on a continent where such progress is sorely lacking. Peru would, therefore, present the United States with an unusual opportunity to associate itself with positive social and economic reform in the style of the Alliance for Progress. This is a political, not a military argument. Even if it is valid, there is no necessary reason for U.S. support to be manifested in military policies, except in so far as these are required to avoid hostile relations and to maintain decent working relations on a technical basis with the politically important military forces.

There are, moreover, important political reasons for avoiding overly close identification with any regime merely because of its aspirations. Good intentions in themselves are unfortunately no guarantee of success. Even assuming, as we have, that there is no simple operational distinction between "military" and "civilian" governments, inter-American politics and public opinion often behave as if there were. The endorsement of a "military" government in Peru, for example, must be examined for its implications for "military" governments in Brazil and Argentina and for "civilian" governments in Chile and Colombia.

Under present circumstances, therefore, it is hard to escape the impression that the maintenance of correct diplomatic relations provides a sound and feasible middle ground for policy. But it may be that correct relations are also the "best" as the most morally defensible policy available to the United States. Correct relations are in accord with basic noninterventionist principles of mutual respect and with not imposing our values on others; they may also be most practical given our uncertainty over the ends, means, and effects of assistance.

Nonintervention in a strict sense is of course impossible in our increasingly interdependent world. The attempt of state relations, therefore, should be to avoid the fact or impression of partisan involvement. Government policy makers must be continually aware that either past policies or present relations at other than state levels (particularly private economic ones) may lead others to interpret "neutrality" or "nonintervention" in a partisan fashion. To ensure that neutrality is not misunderstood for hostility by those with the power to react in a fashion hostile to U.S. interests may thus require specific correctives.

In the face of the Peruvian government's takeover of the IPC, for instance, American government attempts at nonintervention, through nonapplication of the Hickenlooper Amendment, have been interpreted by some as a sign of tacit support for the Peruvian action against an American company, but by others as tacit support for alleged company claims against Peru. The fact that American law requires, and that defense of American citizens' interests in this and other cases would seem to encourage, prompt settlement of the IPC dispute has placed the U.S. government in the extremely difficult position of appearing to be tied to the outcome of this one dispute, no matter what other interests are at stake.

U.S. *assistance*, military or economic, could in this context be used to symbolize the desire of the U.S. government to avoid entanglement in the economic affairs of some of its citizens to the disregard of the economic interests of other citizens and of other political, ideological, and security interests of the United States. Under these circumstances, even assistance that might otherwise be considered marginal, might play a decisive role in preventing the further deterioration of relations by demonstrating the variety of U.S. interests.

In a similar vein, assume, for example, that the failure to provide grant materiel assistance or even the maintenance of restrictions on sales antagonizes Peruvian officers aware of U.S. wealth and programs elsewhere in the world. If the basic structure of state relations is intact, it becomes relevant to ask whether there are any compensatory strategies in related fields that can soften denials of military assistance. In the early 1960s, AID supported some military civic-action activities. The present military government is deeply committed, for example, to the agrarian reform program. Assistance in this area, whether for public administration, technical services, or credits, would certainly be deeply welcomed, even if not provided to or through military channels. This is true, of course, only if the military is serious in its reform intentions. If it is not, then presumably that would be another reason for not wanting close association and for choosing to provide assistance selectively in pursuit of correct state relations.

Paradoxically, as these examples demonstrate, even an avowedly "noninterventionist" policy must be militantly alert, constantly seeking to restore equilibrium to state relations threatened by private disputes. In such cases, if diplomatic recognition and related aspects of correct state relations are treated independently of formalistic distinctions between "military" and "civilian" government, the instruments of foreign assistance, economic and military, can also be used to demonstrate support or opposition to specific policies or programs as desired.

It should be clear, however, that the success or failure of the policies of the United States toward the Peruvian military will depend not on the primarily military but rather on the essentially political matters relating to the general welfare and interests of both countries. The likelihood is that the Peruvian government's current desire for development independent of outside influence or control can best be reconciled with the U.S. government's desire for nonintervention in Peru's political affairs by the maintenance of cordial, though not close, relations.

David C. Loring

3. THE FISHERIES DISPUTE

For nearly a quarter of a century, the United States and Peru have argued whether Peru may exercise jurisdiction over U.S. fishing vessels within two hundred miles of Peru's coast. As the dispute evolved, it generated bitterness and nationalistic considerations on both sides. Since 1948, Peru and the United States have been determined to defend their positions, and both the U.S. State Department and Peru's Foreign Ministry have failed to find any permanent solution. The controversy goes to the heart of the international order.

The United States, with vital global interests, is firmly committed to establishing general rules of international law. It approaches the question by asking, "What is the international rule?" It concludes that no state may unilaterally extend fishery jurisdiction beyond twelve miles. The United States believes, therefore, that Peru's claim is invalid and not binding on the United States or its nationals. The United States argues that if coastal states could claim whatever seaward limits they wanted, the result would be

EDITOR'S NOTE: While some of the early portions of this chapter are rather technical, it gives a fine perspective on relations between a big and a small nation, in addition to a very full analysis of alternative policies.

international conflict and chaos. In addition, the United States feels that "freedom of the seas" is fair to all and in the best interests of all nations. It views two-hundred-mile jurisdiction as an ancient and conservative position, which threatens to push world commerce back into the "closed sea" of the fifteenth century. The U.S. position is deeply rooted in Anglo-European culture and is based upon vital U.S. interests.

Peru, on the other hand, with interests essentially limited to its own territory, has an entirely different frame of reference. Peru starts from the premise that all states are "equal, sovereign, and independent." It follows, therefore, that every state is under a duty and obligation to recognize and respect the "sovereign acts" of other states—otherwise international controversies and chaos will result. Peru tends to ignore and resent the concept of "customary international law." In its opinion, Peru is bound by nothing it has not signed and ratified. And Peru argues that even if a general twelve-mile "rule" existed, it would not affect Peru's claim, for it is based on unique geographic and economic conditions entitled to special treatment. Peru regards the two-hundred-mile doctrine as modern, progressive, and the most practical and equitable means for promoting fishery conservation and development. Peru's position reflects a tradition of fierce individualism and independence inherent in the Latin American culture and a strong desire to protect Peru's own vital national interests.

The purpose of this paper is to provide an impartial analysis of the U.S.-Peruvian two-hundred-mile controversy. It examines present national positions and policies, the history of the dispute, national interests, and, finally, U.S. and Peruvian options that could lead to a mutually acceptable solution.

ORIGINS OF THE CONFLICT

Developments Leading to the Two Hundred Miles: 1493–1947

FREEDOM OF THE SEAS AND THE THREE-MILE LIMIT

For a century following discovery of the New World, European commercial development was hindered by a closed sea. The Papal Bulls of 1493 divided the oceans by a line one hundred leagues west of the Azores and Cape Verde Islands and granted exclusive rights to Spain to the west and Portugal to the east. Other countries were prevented from trading with the East Indies, and England was thereby prevented from exploiting its 1497 discovery of North America under the reign of Henry VII. Following England's defeat of Spain's Invincible Armada in 1588 and the consequent rise of British naval supremacy, a new order emerged; as the seas were freed from the Spanish-Portuguese monopoly, Europe began its modern growth. Within a few years, new trading companies, such as the East India Company, were chartered; colonies were founded in North America and other parts of the world; and the volume of world trade expanded substantially.

A new juridical regime was established at the beginning of the seventeenth century as a justification for the new economic order. Hugo Grotius, a Dutch lawyer retained to defend commercial interests, published *The Freedom of the Seas or the Right which Belongs to the Dutch to Take Part in the East Indian Trade* in 1609. Although his arguments were based on classic and ecclesiastic writings, he later concluded that the seas were open to all due to their inherently indivisible nature. The doctrine of freedom of the seas —that no state could subject them to its sovereignty—soon became a fundamental principle of the developing law of nations. Vattel expanded the rationale in 1758 with the argument that the sea could not be appropriated because its resources were inexhaustible. As absolute freedom of the seas developed, essentially as a reaction to the closed sea, it was perhaps inevitable that exceptions to the rule would arise. Gradually exceptions were made for piracy, control of the slave trade, hot pursuit, pollution, rescue, and others. The most significant exception was the doctrine of the "territorial sea," which began in the late eighteenth century and continues to the present time.

By the opening of the nineteenth century, it was widely accepted that the territorial sovereignty of coastal states extended over a narrow belt of adjacent sea, subject only to other states' right of "innocent passage." The first attempt to limit the width of coastal state jurisdiction was the so called "cannon-shot rule": a coastal state could exercise jurisdiction as far as its cannons would fire. Later the rule was formulated in terms of "three miles," although Secretary of State Thomas Jefferson and others regarded three miles as only a minimum limit. The "three-mile rule" has never been universally accepted as a maximum limit; nor has it ever been accepted by a general international convention, in spite of three world attempts to codify it. Since the eighteenth century, many states, including the United States, have from time to time asserted exceptions to the "three-mile rule" for special purposes.

The movement away from absolute freedom of the seas and the three-mile limit gained momentum during the presidency of Franklin D. Roosevelt, when the United States took a highly liberal view of the exceptions to the three-mile rule (see following section). Latin America's two-hundred-mile movement is an outgrowth of U.S. liberalism prior to 1947. Having opened what Morton A. Kaplan and Nicholas B. de Katzenbach characterized as a "Pandora's Box,"[1] the United States later retreated to the ancient doctrine of freedom of the seas and the three-mile limit, declaring such to be in the best interests of all nations and fair to all. The developing nations, however, became increasingly skeptical of this retrenched proposition. Peru, for example, regards its theoretical right to fish off California of no present value when it is technically unable to exploit resources off the U.S. coast, when excellent fishing grounds are located off Peru, and when California fishermen travel thousands of miles to fish there. As the established maritime powers attempt to maintain the traditional order against the demands of the developing world for a greater share in control of the ocean's wealth, the developing nations consider freedom of the seas as little more than a pretext for continued great power control and exploitation of the sea bed and fishery resources at their expense and perhaps contrary to the best interests of mankind. It is within the context of the current debate on freedom of the seas that the U.S.-Peruvian fisheries question arises.

UNITED STATES ACTIONS

U.S. frustration with the principles of freedom of the seas and the three-mile limit reached a high point during the administration of Franklin D. Roosevelt. An attitude—shared by President Roosevelt himself—developed that the historic regime was inadequate to protect U.S. economic and military interests. The attitude—re-

---

[1] M. A. Kaplan and N. B. de Katzenbach, *The Political Foundations of International Law* (1961).

flected in U.S. actions affecting customs enforcement, national defense, and fishing and oil interests beyond three miles—brought crisis to the law of the sea.

The Anti-Smuggling Act of 1935[2] granted the president authority "to proclaim an area extending one hundred nautical miles north and south from the point in which a suspected foreign ship is hovering and including all of the waters sixty-two miles from the coast within the area of two hundred miles thus designated."[3] The British government protested the law, saying that "the United States cannot be held in international law to have the right, by virtue of municipal legislation, to extend beyond the three-mile limit, as is done in the present bill, the area within which jurisdiction may be exercised over foreign vessels."[4]

Four days after Hitler attacked Poland, President Roosevelt ordered the organization of a "neutrality patrol" to operate as far as two hundred miles from U.S. and West Indies coasts to observe the belligerents' activities. When Roosevelt was asked whether this action meant the United States was extending its territorial sea, he gave the interesting, if perhaps ambiguous, reply that the territorial waters of the United States extend to the distance required by U.S. interests and not necessarily the two hundred miles patrolled.[5] The United States then called a meeting of hemisphere foreign ministers to support the action. The Declaration of Panama,[6] of October 3, 1939, establishing a three-hundred-mile defense zone around the hemisphere (except Canada), resulted. The American states declared their "inherent right" to have the zone "free from the commission of any hostile act by any non-American belligerent nation," and they agreed to "consult together to determine upon the measures which they may individually or collectively undertake in order to secure the observation of the provisions of this Declaration." Several governments objected. The British government

[2] 49 Stat. 517; U.S.C., paragraphs 1701–1711, Aug. 5, 1935.

[3] Lauterpacht, "Sovereignty Over Submarine Areas," *British Yearbook of International Law* 27 (1950):376, 405–406.

[4] M. M. Whiteman, *Digest of International Law* 4 (1965):490–492.

[5] International Law Commission. "Memorandum on the Regime of the High Seas," p. 34, U.N. Doc. A/CN.4/32 (1950).

[6] *Foreign Relations* 5 (1939):15–41; see also 62 Stat. 799; 18 U.S.C., paragraph 2152.

viewed it as a threat to "the well-established principle of international law relating to the freedom of the seas and the rights of both neutrals and belligerents to utilize the sea as a public highway open to all alike."[7]

Following the war, the zone was extended from pole to pole and made permanent by Article 4 of the 1947 Inter-American Treaty of Reciprocal Assistance.[8] Article 3 provides that armed "attack by any State against an American State" within the defined region" "shall be considered as an attack against all the American States." The International Law Commission later criticized the treaty, but it continues in force.[9]

President Roosevelt, in a 1943 letter to the secretary of state, proposed division of the Gulf of Mexico between Mexico and the United States:

> For many years, I have felt that the old three-mile limit or twenty-mile limit should be superseded by a rule of common sense. For instance, the Gulf of Mexico is bounded on the south by Mexico and on the north by the United States. In parts of the Gulf, shallow water extends very many miles off shore. It seems to me that the Mexican government should be entitled to drill for oil in the southern half of the Gulf and we in the northern half of the Gulf. That would be far more sensible than allowing some European nation, for example, to come in and drill.[10]

The proposal produced the 1945 Truman Proclamation on the Continental Shelf, which regarded the "natural resources of the subsoil and sea bed of the continental shelf beneath the high seas but contiguous to the coasts of the United States as appertaining to the United States, subject to its jurisdiction and control."[11] This unilateral action was without precedent. It rested only on the follow-

---

[7] Ibid., p. 29.

[8] 62 Stat. 1681; U.S. TIAS 1838; 21 UNTS 77.

[9] International Law Commission, "Memorandum on the Regime of the High Seas," p. 36.

[10] 4 Whiteman (1965) p. 947; MS Dept. State file 811. 0145/11–2844.

[11] Proclamation No. 2667, "Policy of the United States with Respect to the Natural Resources of the Subsoil and Sea Bed of the Continental Shelf," Sept. 28, 1945, 10 Fed. Reg. 12303, 3 C.F.R. 1943–1948 Comp., p. 67; 13 Dept. State Bull., No. 327, Sept. 30, 1945, p. 485

ing principles: "recognized jurisdiction over these resources is required in the interest of their conservation and prudent utilization . . . ; the exercise of jurisdiction . . . is reasonable and just . . . ; self-protection compels the coastal nation to keep close watch over activities off its shores."[12] Thus for the price of printer's ink and the bold assertion of a newly conceived right, the United States acquired effective sovereignty over submerged lands equal in area to the Louisiana Purchase. (The U.S. government emphasizes that no nation ever protested this proclamation.)

U.S. hostility toward the three-mile rule as applied to fishing peaked during the Roosevelt years. During the nineteenth century, the United States had attempted to justify its claim to exclusive jurisdiction over seals in the Bering Sea by drawing a distinction between territorial or "sovereign jurisdiction" and the mere assertion of "a right of self-protection and self-defense."[13] The United States was unable, however, to convince an arbitration tribunal and lost the case to Great Britain. One factor working against it was that U.S. relations did not restrict its nationals but merely excluded foreigners.[14] During the 1930s, coastal fisheries of the Pacific Northwest, particularly salmon, among the most important U.S. fisheries, were under growing pressure from foreign fleets (mainly Japanese). Americans sought some way around the three-mile rule to protect the salmon fishery. In 1938, Professor Joseph W. Bingham of the Stanford Law School published a *Report on the International Law of Pacific Coastal Fisheries*. The report (well known in Peru) is basically a lawyer's brief attacking the three-mile rule as "developed and persistently advocated by Britain in pursuance of British commercial, naval and fishing interests." It finds that "there is no established international law which categorically denies exclusive fishery rights beyond the three-mile limit" and urges "the direct and frank abandonment by [the U.S.] government of the rigid application of the three-mile rule to coastal fishery problems."

Congress considered several bills during the late 1930s which

12 Ibid.
13 Cited in Leonard, *International Regulation of Fisheries* (1944), p. 69.
14 D. M. Johnston, *The International Law of Fisheries* (New Haven, 1965), p. 210.

would have expanded U.S. fishery jurisdiction. One would have established U.S. jurisdiction over the waters above the continental shelf (the "epi-continental sea") in the Bering Sea.[15] And during the Roosevelt years, Texas and Louisiana extended state sovereignty to twenty-seven miles.

The most significant development, however, resulted from President Roosevelt's request to the State Department for development of a new fishery policy to get around the three-mile rule: "I suggest that you proceed immediately to the study of the possibility of adopting a new policy relating to off-shore fishing in Alaska. The policy would be based on the fact that every nation has the right to protect its own food supply in waters adjacent to its coast in which its fish, crabs, etc., leave at certain times of the year on their way to and from the actual shore-line or rivers."[16] This request resulted in the Truman Fisheries Proclamation,[17] issued the same day as the Continental Shelf Proclamation. It regarded as proper the establishment of "explicitly bounded" fishery "conservation zones in those areas of the high seas contiguous to the coasts of the United States wherein fishing activities have been or in the future may be developed and maintained on a substantial scale." Fishing by U.S. nationals alone would be subject to "the control and jurisdiction of the United States," while fishing involving other nationals, fishing *legitimately*,[18] would be regulated by mutual agreement. The Fisheries Proclamation, also without precedent, rested on the following principles: "fishery resources have a special importance to coastal communities, the inadequacy of present ar-

[15] See P. C. Jessup, "The Pacific Coast Fisheries," *American Journal of International Law* (1939):129.

[16] Memorandum from Franklin D. Roosevelt to R. Walton Moore, Counselor, Dept. of State, Nov. 21, 1937, MS Dept. State file 711.008 North Pacific /264; 4 Whiteman (1965), p. 945.

[17] Proclamation No. 2668, "Policy of the United States with Respect to Coastal Fisheries in Certain Areas of the High Seas," Sept. 28, 1945, 10 Fed. Reg. 12304; 3 C.F.R., 1943–1948 Comp., p. 68.

[18] The proclamation implied that if agreement could not be reached, the United States would act unilaterally. See E. W. Allen, "The Fishery Proclamation of 1945," *American Journal of International Law* 45 (1951):177. Careful and repeated use of the word "legitimate" in the proclamation, an accompanying press release, and a 1946 note to Mexico's government suggests the United States may have been considering a future attempt at excluding foreign fishermen it deemed "illegitimate."

rangements for the protection and perpetuation of the fishery resources, the possibility of improving the *jurisdictional* basis for conservation measures, an urgent need to protect coastal fishery resources, and the special rights and equities of the coastal State and of any other State which may have established a *legitimate* interest therein" (emphasis added). The proclamation recognized "the right of any State to establish conservation zones off its shores . . . provided that corresponding recognition is given to any fishing interests of the United States which may *exist* in such areas" (emphasis added).[19]

Mexico soon followed the U.S. lead. On October 29, 1945, the Mexican president signed a single proclamation that claimed jurisdiction over the continental shelf and fisheries.[20] Although the proclamation was ambiguous, it appeared to recognize only the *existing* present interests of other states and claimed, or "reclaimed" (the verb used was *revindicar*, which to most Latin American lawyers would suggest, I believe, a reassertion of title or sovereignty) all resources, including fisheries, for the benefit of Mexico. The U.S. government cautiously granted a qualified recognition on January 24, 1946, conditioned on "adequate recognition" for "United States fishing interests in the area affected by the establishment of such zones."[21] The U.S. note said, "The Government of the United States regards the recognition by the coastal state of such rights as a necessary prerequisite to recognition by other states of an extension of jurisdiction over high seas areas for purposes of fishery conservation," clearly indicating that U.S. policy in 1946 contemplated coastal state jurisdictional extensions for fishery conservation purposes and also implying that the United States was prepared to recognize them, providing its *existing* interests were respected.

ARGENTINE, CHILEAN, AND PERUVIAN CLAIMS

The Anglo-American concept of "sovereignty" has retained its absolute quality since Chief Justice John Marshall's 1812 definition

[19] "Exist" suggests coastal states need not respect *future* interests. (This is why Peru later made no mention of respecting U.S. interests in its 1947 two-hundred-mile decree: none then existed.)

[20] 4 Whiteman 1219.

[21] Ibid., pp. 1220–1223.

that it is "necessarily exclusive and absolute . . . susceptible of no limitation."[22] In Spanish there is a word *soberanía* which is almost invariably translated into English as "sovereignty." In 1812, *soberanía* and "sovereignty" had similar absolute meanings. By the early part of the twentieth century, however, Latin American lawyers regarded *soberanía* as nearly synonymous with "jurisdiction," for an assertion of jurisdiction is an exercise of sovereignty; thus *soberanía* should not always be translated as "sovereignty," but in many contexts means "the right to exercise jurisdiction." The Spanish equivalent of the English notion of "sovereignty" is *dominio*, a term very close in meaning to John Marshall's 1812 view of "sovereignty." *Soberanía*, therefore, may be limited or qualified.

On October 11, 1946, the Argentine president, citing the U.S. and Mexican proclamations as precedent for national *soberanía* over the continental shelf and "epi-continental sea" (meaning the waters above the shelf), decreed the Argentine continental shelf and superjacent sea subject to national *soberanía*.[23] The decree expressly recognized "freedom of navigation," probably the only foreign interest then existing within the affected area. The U.S. government made no immediate public objection.

Citing the U.S., Mexican, and Argentine actions as "categorically" proclaiming *soberanía* over the adjacent continental shelf and sea "within the limits necessary to preserve for the said States the natural riches belonging to them," the president of Chile, on June 23, 1947, issued the world's first two-hundred-mile declaration. Chile's declaration is important, for it became a model for Peru's decree and other early two-hundred-mile limits: Article 1 proclaimed *soberanía* over the continental shelf. Article 2 proclaimed *soberanía* over the sea "within those limits necessary in order to reserve, protect, preserve, and exploit the natural resources . . . placing within the control of the government especially all fisheries and whaling activities with the object of preventing . . . exploitation . . . to the detriment of the inhabitants of Chile."[24] Article 3 did

[22] Schooner Exchange v. McFadden, 7 Cranch 116, 136 (1812); 11 U.S. 287, 293.

[23] Argentina, Presidential Decree N. 14, 708 of Oct. 11, 1946, *Boletín Oficial*, Dec. 5, 1946, p. 2.

[24] *El Mercurio*, Santiago, June 29, 1947, p. 27.

not mention *soberanía*, but declared the right to establish explicitly bounded fishery "protection zones," and to change them at any time in the light of current scientific knowledge. Almost as an afterthought, a temporary and "explicitly bounded" zone of "protection and control" of two hundred miles was declared immediately. The "legitimate" rights of other states were recognized in Article 4, which also stated that "freedom of navigation" was not affected. According to former Chilean President Gabriel Gonzales Videla, who issued the declaration, it was inspired by information developed through studies by a U.S. fisheries mission to Chile.[25] Two hundred miles was considered the approximate distance covered by land-based whale catchers, which were very important to Chile in 1947. Although Peru was not a whaling nation in 1947, it followed Chile's example almost verbatim, including the two hundred miles, on August 1, 1947.

Precipitation of the Conflict: 1948–1955

UNITED STATES PROTESTS OF 1948

In 1947, no U.S. fishing interests existed within the areas affected by the Argentine, Chilean, and Peruvian claims. But the booming southern California tuna fleet expected to expand its operations off Peru and Chile in the near future. The United States evidentally miscalculated. The U.S. Fisheries Proclamation—recognizing the "right" of other coastal states to establish "explicitly bounded" high seas conservation zones, provided U.S. fishing interests "which may *exist* in such areas" were "adequately" recognized—failed to provide for *future* U.S. interests. To protect its future interests, the United States might have asked its ambassadors to discuss the situation with the respective governments. They could have praised the Latin American actions as progressive conservation measures, could have proposed joint conservation pograms, explained that the purpose of the U.S. proclamations was not exclusion of foreign fishermen but to provide a rational and joint basis for conservation, and could have expressed the hope that the claims would not harm future U.S. fishery development. The United States had other op-

[25] Interview with former President Gonzales Videla in Santiago, Chile, April 9, 1969.

tions. It could have waited to see whether the claims would have harmed U.S. interests in fact. (Given Latin American bureaucracy, a good chance existed that the claims would never be enforced on a regular basis, if at all.) Instead, the United States passed up its first and best opportunity to avoid conflict, departed from its Good Neighbor Policy, abandoned the Truman Fisheries Proclamation, and challenged the actions.

The U.S. government declared, in nearly identical protests of July 2, 1948, that the "principles underlying" the three actions "differ in large measure from those of the United States Proclamations and appear to be at variance with the generally accepted principles of international law."[26] Even though the Chilean and Peruvian documents made no claim of two-hundred-mile *soberanía* nor delimited the assertion of *soberanía*, the United States said they had claimed "sovereignty . . . outside the generally accepted limit of territorial waters." The United States not only failed to understand the distinction between *soberanía* and sovereignty, but misread the texts of the documents themselves. (Had the United States been more skilled in understanding Peruvian, Argentina, and Chilean internal law, it might have noticed that none of the three actions was law. Chile's action was merely a "declaration." The Peruvian and Argentine actions were "decrees" that neither president may have had authority to issue under the respective constitutions.) In addition, the United States said that the actions *failed* "to accord recognition to the rights and interests of the United States." The protest surprised and angered the South Americans, who considered the distinction between the "principles underlying" their actions and the Truman Proclamations intellectually dishonest, since the same U.S. "principles" were cited in the preambles of their respective decrees. The U.S. charge that they *failed* to take U.S. fishing interests into account was viewed as arrogant, for no U.S. fishing interests existed in the areas, and Chile's declaration expressly recognized the "legitimate" interests of other states. The United States appeared to say indirectly that it alone had authority to determine the course of international law—even as applied to waters off the South American coast—or that only the United States possessed the legal skill to accurately perceive the law. Peru-

[26] 4 Whiteman 796–797.

vians considered the protest a personal insult to their president, Dr. Bustamante y Rivero, who was a recognized authority on international law and later was elected and served as president of the International Court of Justice.

Peruvian and Chilean reaction to the U.S. protest was swift. Rather than putting the question to rest, the U.S. protest produced the opposite result and caused an aggressive Chilean-Peruvian foreign policy dedicated to establishment of two-hundred-mile limits throughout Latin America. Within the same month of the U.S. note, Costa Rica adopted an identical two-hundred-mile decree. This phase of Peru's foreign policy continued until shortly after the Anglo-Norwegian fisheries case, by which time, El Salvador, Honduras, and Ecuador had joined the two-hundred-mile club.

THE DECLARATION OF SANTIAGO

By August, 1952, Peru, Chile, and Ecuador felt threatened by U.S. and other great power policies they deemed hostile to their aspirations for economic development, particularly fishery development: Ecuador adopted a twelve-mile territorial sea in 1951. The United States, rather than congratulating Ecuador for not adopting a two-hundred-mile limit and seeking a mutually acceptable adjustment, passed a second opportunity for avoiding conflict, and protested.[27] Ecuador responded by seizing U.S. tuna boats. Peru's tuna industry, built during World War II at the request of the U.S. government for export to the U.S. market, was threatened by the U.S. tuna industry's 1950–1952 campaign to increase tariffs on imported tuna. And Chile, whose most important fishing interest was whaling, regarded regulations adopted by the International Whaling Commission as discriminatory.

Thus at Chile's invitation, Peru and Ecuador sent representatives to Santiago, Chile, in August, 1952, for the First Conference on the Exploitation and Conservation of the Marine Resources of the South Pacific. The main reason for the conference was to increase political support for a Draft Convention prepared by the OAS sanctioning the two-hundred-mile limit.[28] The Inter-American

---

[27] 4 Whiteman 800–801.

[28] See Hearings on H. R. 9584 before the Committee on Merchant Marine and Fisheries of the House, 83rd Cong., 2nd sess. (1954), p. 39.

Juridical Committee approved the Draft Convention on July 30, 1952, by only one vote. Colombia, which had voted with the United States against the draft, was also invited to Santiago and sent an observer. On August 18, 1952, the three countries signed the Declaration on the Maritime Zone (the Declaration of Santiago) and three other agreements. The declaration pledges the three countries to a joint "international maritime policy" dedicated to the principle that each of the three possesses "sole sovereignty [*soberanía*] and jurisdiction" over a maritime zone "extending not less than 200 nautical miles from the said coast." The new principle also included *soberanía* over the sea bed to two hundred miles. In the final article, the three agreed to sign conventions in the future that would bring these "principles" into being.

PERUVIAN SEIZURES OF U.S. TUNA BOATS

The U.S. protest notwithstanding, Peru might never have seized any U.S. vessels had it not been for three events in 1954. In March, 1954, the United States, "by combination of luck, diplomatic skill, and parliamentary maneuver which were not likely to be repeated at a second conference,"[29] defeated a two-hundred-mile resolution at the Tenth Inter-American Conference at Caracas. In August, 1954, due to fear that the OAS would adopt a two-hundred-mile limit within a year, the United States enacted the Fisherman's Protective Act of 1954, which transferred the burden of any fines from the fishermen to the U.S. Treasury. And Aristotle Onassis sent a whaling fleet from Germany on August 4, 1954, with the avowed purpose of challenging Peru's limit.

Confronted with an embarrassing public challenge by Onassis, Peru asked Panama, under whose flag the fleet was registered, to inform it of Peruvian regulations and to ask that it refrain from whaling without first obtaining Peruvian permits. Panama refused. The fleet left Panama for Peru on August 25, 1954. As the fleet neared Peru, Chile and Ecuador promptly "ratified" the Declaration of Santiago. Between August and October, 1954, Great Britain, the United States, Norway, Sweden, Denmark, and the Netherlands formally protested the Declaration of Santiago (incorrectly

[29] Hearings before the Subcommittee of the Committee on Interstate and Foreign Commerce, U.S. Senate, on S. 3594, 83rd Cong., 2nd sess. (1954), p. 8.

assuming it to represent a two-hundred-mile claim).[30] In October, 1954, the Permanent Commission (inactive since its establishment in 1952) held an emergency meeting. On November 13, an Onassis spokesman in Hamburg, Germany, announced that the fleet had carried out its objectives "within the two-hundred-mile zone claimed by Peru, in spite of announcements that it would be captured."[31] Two days later, Peru's navy captured two Onassis whale catchers, thereby avoiding international humiliation and possible political consequences. Three additional ships, including the factory ship, ironically named "Olympic Challenger," were seized a few days later. The expedition, insured against the risk of seizure beyond three miles by Lloyd's of London, was fined U.S. $3 million by the Port Captain of Paita, Peru. While the navy searched for the fleet, it began stopping U.S. tuna boats (which had operated peacefully near Peru's coast for several years) for the first time, and early in 1955 began seizing them.

Efforts to Resolve the Legal Questions: 1950–1960

INTER-AMERICAN ACTION

The first meeting of the Inter-American Council of Jurists, held in 1950, called on its Inter-American Juridical Committee to prepare a draft convention on territorial waters and related questions. Over strong U.S. objections, the committee presented its draft convention on July 30, 1952, sanctioning two hundred miles. At the Tenth Inter-American Conference in 1954, Ecuador introduced a resolution "reaffirming" coastal states' right to two-hundred-mile sovereignty.[32] Stripped of the two-hundred-mile provision, the resolution was approved together with a call for a Specialized Inter-American Conference on the subject. In 1956, the third meeting of the Inter-American Council of Jurists approved the "Principles of Mexico." Inter-American consideration of the two hundred miles ended on March 28, 1956, at Ciudad Trujillo, where the United States skillfully led the Inter-American Specialized Conference to

---

[30] See R. Ferrero, *Derecho Internacional*, vol. I, Lima, 1966, p. 151–171.

[31] E. García Sayán. *Notas sobre la Soberanía Marítima del Perú: Defensa de las 200 Millas de Mar Peruano ante la Recientes Transgresiones*. Lima, 1955, p. 51.

[32] Hearings on H. R. 9584, 83rd Cong., 2nd sess., p. 33.

the conclusion that unanimous agreement did not exist within the
OAS.

THE SANTIAGO NEGOTIATIONS OF 1955

Following Peruvian seizures in 1955 and a serious shooting incident with Ecuador, the United States called for a conference with
the signatories of the Declaration of Santiago to reach some understanding on fisheries that would not alter either side's legal position. The United States was led to believe by high officials of the
three South American governments that the reason for the two
hundred miles was strictly fishery conservation. Thus the United
States believed it could provide an affective conservation program
obviating the need for the two-hundred-mile claims. At the negotiations, it was immediately clear that Peru, Chile, and Ecuador
wanted more than a conservation agreement. At first, the three
tried to win U.S. two-hundred-mile recognition by arguing their
"bioma theory" (see p. 87). The U.S. delegation rejected this defense in a manner considered by Peruvians to be a sarcastic mis-
representation. The United States said, among other things, that the
theory "could have at most limited, if any, validity."[33] In the interest of reaching agreement, however, the three offered to compromise their legal position by limiting their exclusive jurisdiction to
twelve miles plus certain areas "traditionally fished"; over the
remainder of the two hundred miles, they would exercise shared
conservation authority with the United States.

The proposal was unacceptable to the U.S. delegation, because
the "areas traditionally fished" covered most of the best tuna
grounds, and the proposed conservation organization would have
given effective control to the three. Although the United States was
unwilling to concede more than three-mile exclusive jurisdiction it
offered to consider any proposal for exclusive jurisdiction around
small fishing villages "dependent directly upon the sea for their
sustenance." At that point the discussions reached an impasse.
Both the United States and the two-hundred-mile claimants lost
an opportunity to settle the question, for with new instructions or
more bargaining on the proposals, some middle ground might have

[33] U.S. Dept. State, "Santiago Negotiations on Fishery Conservation Problems," (1955) (USA Doc. No. 8), p. 36.

been found. Instead, both sides left on October 5, 1955, empty-handed.

THE AMERICAN TUNABOAT ASSOCIATION ACCORDS

Following the Santiago Negotiations, representatives of the American Tunaboat Association (ATA) met privately with Peruvian officials to approve a previously drafted and mutually acceptable set of regulations for foreign fishing. This agreement—based on the fact that the tuna clippers of the 1950s had to come within or near the three-mile limit for bait—was the most successful and brilliant way around the legal problem yet discovered.[34] It proved that private negotiations can be more effective in some cases than relations between governments. Although the ATA agreements and regulations resulting from them did not affect the legal controversy between the U.S. and Peruvian governments, they kept the peace until the 1960s.

LAW OF THE SEA CONFERENCES

One of the major lost U.S. opportunities was the U.N. Conferences on the Law of the Sea. After many years preliminary work by the International Law Commission, the United Nations called a world Conference on the Law of the Sea, which the United States hoped would resolve all legal questions concerning the two hundred miles. The two conferences, held in 1958 and 1960, failed to settle the matter. Peruvian and other Latin American delegates have said privately that they were snubbed by the U.S. delegation and made to feel that they were being "held on trial."[35] Whether this was the U.S. strategy is not as important as the fact that Latin Americans felt it was. Although Chile, Peru, and Ecuador de-emphasised the two-hundred-mile aspect of their claims, they voted against the United States. Perhaps had more been done to court their friendship and understanding the result might have been dif-

---

[34] The ATA claims its members never purchased licenses unless they entered the three-mile limit. Peru's experts claim that bait was available beyond three miles and that U.S. fishermen bought licenses regardless of whether they came within three miles.

[35] Off the record comments by Peruvian and other Latin American delegates to the 1953 and/or 1960 conferences, during interviews with the author in Latin America in 1969.

ferent—the United States lost by only one vote in 1960. The two failures probably left the two-hundred-mile claimants in a stronger position than before.

Renewed Vessel Seizures and Claims: 1961–1970

TUNA FLEET'S CONVERSION TO "PURSE SEINERS"

A technological revolution in the tuna fishery rendered obsolete the ATA's agreements with various Latin American governments. Until the early 1960s, most of the U.S. tuna fleet operated with "bait boats." The ATA accords were based on the fact that tuna clippers had to come close to shore to get bait. The clippers simply bought one license, valid throughout the two-hundred-mile zone. Tuna fishermen had long known they could improve efficiency if they could fish with nets, but an adequate net with a means for bringing it in had not been developed for large-scale operations. The breakthrough occurred in 1956 with the development of the all-nylon net and "power block" system. Net, or "purse seine," fishing did not require bait; thus vessels no longer needed to come near shore or purchase licenses. By the early 1960s, most of the larger vessels had converted to purse seiners. With the conversion, the apparent respect for Peruvian law ended together with the revenue it generated, and seizures began again.

THE MODUS VIVENDI WITH ECUADOR

One of the most costly U.S. errors in the two-hundred-mile controversy was a secret agreement made with Ecuador in 1963. U.S. interests in Latin America will suffer for many years to come because of this agreement. By 1963, the boat seizure problem had become critical. Within twelve months prior to May, 1963, Ecuador seized, fined, or harassed at least twelve U.S. tuna boats. On May 25, 1963, Ecuador seized two vessels within thirteen miles of the coast and fined them more than $26,000. Nineteen to twenty-one U.S. tuna boats in the area sailed into Salinas, Ecuador, in protest. Secretary Rusk called for their release and asked for negotiations. Ecuador rejected the plea. At the same time, Fishermen's Union Local 33, ILWU, representing California tuna fishermen, picketed an Ecuadorean vessel in southern California. International Longshoremen refused to cross the picket line, threatening losses to a large shipment of Ecuadorean bananas, a commodity representing more than 60 percent of Ecuador's export earnings. In the face of pressure from the U.S. government and a powerful U.S. labor union, Ecuador defiantly continued seizing U.S. tuna boats, one on June 13, another on June 29, 1963.

Although the domestic political situation had been relatively calm during the first half of 1963, the Ecuadorean government was overthrown on July 11, 1963, under the efficient direction of army, navy and air force officers. Radio Havana immediately charged that the U.S. government instigated the military coup d'etat. The Kennedy administration then reversed its nonrecognition policy for military governments (having withheld foreign aid and diplomatic recognition only one year earlier when Peru's military seized power), and recognized Eucador's military junta before the end of July 1963. Negotiations with the United States on the fisheries question were then held, but they terminated in September without any public announcement of agreement. The United States and the military junta, however, entered a secret agreement or modus vivendi in which the United States agreed to respect twelve-mile Ecuadorean jurisdiction to tax U.S. fishermen, plus exclusive fishing jurisdiction over certain areas. Ecuador agreed to grant licenses to U.S. fishermen and refrain from seizures beyond twelve miles— a de facto renunciation of the two hundred miles as applied to U.S. vessels. For more than two years, the modus vivendi prevented major conflicts with Ecuador. Discovery of the modus vivendi in June, 1965, was one of the major issues which later brought down the military junta and inspired Ecuador to claim a two-hundred-mile "territorial sea." The secret agreement caused an indignation across Latin America on which Peruvian diplomacy was quick to capitilize. (Some responsible, noncommunist Latin Americans believe that the CIA was responsible for the July 11, 1963, coup and secret agreement, and this view has harmed U.S. interests.)

THE U.S. TWELVE-MILE EXTENSION (1966)

Prior to 1966, the modus vivendi notwithstanding, the United States maintained publicly that international law did not permit assertions of fishery jurisdiction beyond three miles and that, in any event, a greater width could only be established by international agreement. In October, 1966, however, the U.S. Congress, under pressure from coastal fishing interests, unilaterally extended U.S. exclusive fishery jurisdiction to twelve miles.[36] Neither the Defense nor State Department objected; the lone dissenters were tuna and shrimp fishermen and some legal scholars. The law, arguably, was contrary to U.S. obligations under the 1958 Convention on the Territorial Sea and Contiguous Zone.[37] The convention did not authorize twelve-mile fishery jurisdiction. The U.S. action appeared hypocritical to Peru, weakened U.S. moral authority, and strengthened Peru's contention that it could unilaterally assert fishery jurisdiction to the distance served by self-interest.

Under the Bartlett Act of May 20, 1964, the United States claims exclusive fishery jurisdiction over sedentary fisheries on or within its continental shelf.[38] (The U.S. continental shelf extends to more than two hundred miles off New England and Alaska.) The act provides fines of up to $10,000 and/or imprisonment for the taking of any continental-shelf fishery resource by a non-U.S. flag vessel. It has been justified under the 1958 Convention on the Continental Shelf, although it was passed before the convention entered into force. Peruvians regard this claim as hypocritical, because the convention has been ratified by less than fifty countries, and because the International Court of Justice has suggested that it does not reflect customary principles of international law, but merely a contractual relationship among the parties ratifying it.[39]

THE TWO-HUNDRED-MILE "TERRITORIAL SEA"

The two-hundred-mile "territorial sea" is essentially a post–modus vivendi development. It may be one of the U.S. costs for the modus vivendi and the 1966 unilateral extension. Prior to discovery of the secret agreement, no Latin American state had deliberately intended to create a two-hundred-mile "territorial sea." From 1948 through 1965, the United States expressed fear of two-hundred-mile sovereignty, the two-hundred-mile territorial sea, the Declara-

---

[36] P.L. 89-658; 80 Stat. 908, approved Oct. 14, 1966.

[37] U.N. Doc. A/CONF. 13/38; U.S. TIAS 5630; 15 U.S.T. 1606.

[38] P.L. 88-308; 78 Stat. 194; see also S. Rept. 500, 88th Cong., 1st sess., and H. Rept. 1355, 88th Cong., 1st sess.

[39] *North Sea Continental Shelf Case*, I.C.J. Reports (1969).

tion of Santiago, and sovereignty over two-hundred-mile air space. After 1965, Peru led a psychological and political campaign against the United States for its intervention in imposing the modus vivendi on Ecuador in 1963. Peruvian diplomats actively supported the two-hundred-mile doctrine throughout Latin America, and in 1965, Peru claimed sovereignty over the air space above its two-hundred-mile zone.

In November, 1966, Ecuador established the world's first unequivocal two-hundred-mile "territorial sea." Under intense Peruvian and Ecuadorean lobbying, the Costa Rican Legislative Assembly purported to "ratify" its 1955 "adhesion" to the Declaration of Santiago, but under U.S. pressure, the president vetoed the legislation. Peru, which had enjoyed a special friendship with the Argentine military since San Martín's liberation of Peru, effected a diplomatic coup by encouraging Argentina's new military government to decree two-hundred-mile "sovereignty" in December, 1966. The Panamanian Assembly, refusing to consider ratification of the four laws of the sea conventions, hastily introduced in November, 1966, instead passed a perfect model of all that the United States feared: aluding to the Declaration of Santiago, Panama established a two-hundred-mile "territorial sea," expressly including "sovereignty" over the air space. Calling for "Latin American solidarity," Peruvian diplomats were able to get two-hundred-mile legislation introduced in Brazil and Uruguay and to increase support for Colombia's pending two-hundred-mile "territorial sea" bill. Despite strenuous U.S. efforts to block Uruguay's legislative approval of a moderate two-hundred-mile fishing limit, in December, 1969, the president of Uruguay decreed a two-hundred-mile "territorial sea," expressly claiming the air space. Brazil followed with a two-hundred-mile "territorial sea" decree in March, 1970. Others were expected to follow. The 1970 Declaration of Montevideo on the Law of the Sea,[40] signed by nine Latin American governments, may be the first step in Peru's drive to unite all two-hundred-mile claimants and other developing coastal states in a Third World alliance dedicated to the proposition that every coastal state has the right to exercise exclusive jurisdiction over the resources adjacent to its coast.

[40] For text, see *El Peruano: Diario Oficial*, May 13, 1970, p. 4.

THE EXISTING IMPASSE

U.S. Position and Policies

U.S. LEGAL CONTENTIONS

The Government of the United States, in conformity with the general practice of the World Community, maintains that the International Law of the sea does not sanction the assertion of jurisdiction by a coastal state over the activities of fishing vessels of other states beyond 12 nautical miles from its coasts. Because of this well-known legal position of the United States Government, the operators of United States flag fishing vessels, while pursuing their calling beyond twelve miles from the coast, cannot be subjected to the jurisdiction of any Government but their own, nor can they be obliged to pay a fee to other Governments in order to secure freedom from interference with their legitimate operations.[41]

The U.S. legal position is based on several arguments. The United States considers Peru's two-hundred-mile limit a violation of the historic principle of "freedom of the seas" and contrary to international law limiting national jurisdiction to twelve nautical miles. In addition, the United States maintains that international law imposes no duty to recognize unilateral claims in excess of twelve miles. The U.S. position is also based on practical considerations, for in the case of yellowfin and skipjack tuna in the eastern tropical Pacific Ocean (the two species in which the United States has an immediate interest), a two-hundred-mile limit for conservation purposes would be ineffective, because tuna migrate over vast areas. These arguments, advanced by the U.S. government and distinguished U.S. legal scholars, are examined in greater detail, but the author offers no judgment on their merits.

The first argument is that Peru's claim violates the doctrine of "freedom of the seas." The 1958 Convention on the High Seas[42] states, "The high seas being open to all nations, no State may validly purport to subject any part of them to its sovereignty." The convention defines "high seas" as "all parts of the sea that are not included in the territorial sea or in the internal waters of a State."

---

[41] Diplomatic Note No. 196, from the U.S. Embassy in Quito, Ecuador, to the Ecuadorean Foreign Ministry, October 25, 1968.

[42] Adopted by the United Nations Conference on the Law of the Sea, April 29, 1958 (U.N. Doc. A/CONF. 13/L.53); U.S. TIAS 5200; 13 U.S.T. 2312.

Peru's government makes no claim that its two-hundred-mile zone is either "territorial sea" or "internal waters." Peruvian law, however, establishes limited "sovereignty" up to two hundred miles. If the word "sovereignty" in the convention embraces the term "sovereignty" under Peruvian law, that law is contrary to the express language of the convention (although Peru has never ratified it) and is therefore—according to the United States—invalid and a violation of the principle of "freedom of the seas."

A second U.S. argument is that Peru's limit violates a customary rule of international law that coastal states may not extend jurisdiction beyond twelve miles. Although such a "rule" has never been drafted into a world convention, evidence of a customary twelve-mile rule is based on findings of the International Law Commission, records of the 1958 and 1960 United Nations Conferences on the Law of the Sea, and current international practice. In 1956, the Law Commission concluded that "international law does not permit an extension of the territorial sea beyond twelve miles."[43] At the 1958 and 1960 conferences, near unanimity existed that the proper limit of territorial and fishing jurisdiction was twelve miles or less, and at the 1960 conference a U.S.-Canadian resolution to establish a twelve-mile limit failed to win two-thirds approval by only one vote.[44] That close to 90 percent of the coastal states now limit their territorial and fishery claims to twelve miles or less is good evidence that customary international law prohibits extensions beyond twelve miles. Peru's two-hundred-mile extension, therefore, violates customary international law. And even if Peru's limit is binding on some states by their own voluntary actions, the United States believes that international law imposes no duty to recognize it. If such a duty existed, the result would be "chaos on the seas [endangering] the free use of the oceans for the production of food and transportation both on the seas and the airspace over the seas."[45]

As a practical matter, a two-hundred-mile limit would be ineffective for tuna conservation. Unlike most species of fish, tuna

---

[43] *Yearbook of the International Law Commission* 2 (1956):256.

[44] Second U.N. Conference on the Law of the Sea, A/CONF. 19/L. 12 Annex, April 26, 1960.

[45] Donald L. McKernan, "Background Paper for the Adlai Stevenson Institute," April 14, 1970, p. 2.

travel great distances. Even if Peru were to effectively prohibit all yellowfin and skipjack tuna fishing within its two-hundred-mile zone, according to the United States, these stocks of fish could be depleted by fishing effort entirely outside Peru's two-hundred-mile limit. Thus two hundred miles can never form the basis for a rational tuna conservation program, for unilateral action, or even action by several coastal states together would be insufficient to prevent overfishing. The only adequate conservation technique is international cooperation. In addition, Peruvian fishing regulations for foreign fishing are not conservation measures but purely for revenue.

On the other hand, the United States recognizes that its right for its nationals to fish off Peru is not absolute but subject to the "special interest" of coastal states in fishery conservation, as defined by the Convention on Fishing and Conservation of the Living Resources of the High Seas.[46] The United States also recognizes Peru's "sovereign rights for the purpose of exploring . . . and exploiting . . . natural resources" in Peru's continental shelf, as defined by the Convention on the Continental Shelf,[47] but it rejects Peru's claim to two-hundred-mile jurisdiction over the sea bed and subsoil.

U.S. OBJECTIVES AND POLICIES

From the U.S. legal position, certain specific objectives emerge: to establish internationally accepted rules limiting coastal state jurisdiction over the sea, to find a working arrangement with Peru to avoid conflict, to prevent future unilateral claims and/or enforcement of them, to provide effective mechanisms for fishery conservation, and to protect U.S. fishermen. To achieve these objectives, particular policies (meaning here plans or means of reaching objectives) are formulated. Due to diverse and conflicting interests in the United States, different policies and objectives have been followed. Congress, for example, developed its own policy dealing with U.S. vessel seizures, and the State Department created

---

[46] Adopted by the U.N. Conference on the Law of the Sea, April 29, 1958 (U.N. Doc. A/CONF. 13/L. 54).

[47] Adopted April 29, 1958 (U.N. Doc. A/CONF. 13/L. 55); U.S. TIAS 5578; U.S.T. 471. (Thirty-nine ratifications by 1969; Peru signed it.)

a strategy to cope with congressional attempts to legislate foreign policy. Nevertheless, some basic U.S. policies are clear.

The two most important aspects of present U.S. policy are essentially the same as those followed in the 1950s. Fifteen years ago, the United States decided to negotiate directly with Peru, Chile, and Ecuador (the three parties to the 1952 two-hundred-mile Declaration of Santiago) without discussing the source of the difficulty: the conflicting legal positions—while at the same time attempting to resolve the legal issues by international convention. In 1955, the United States met with Peru, Chile, and Ecuador to enter a "fishery conservation" agreement that would have supposedly left both sides' legal positions unaltered and would have prevented boat seizures. No agreement was reached however. Meanwhile, the United States worked to bring about a world conference to draft a convention definitively settling the legal issues. Although four conventions were signed at the 1958 Conference on the Law of the Sea, it failed to reach any agreement on the two most important questions: the widths of the territorial sea and exclusive fishery jurisdiction. A second conference in 1960 also failed to reach agreement. Peru never ratified any of the four conventions, and the two-hundred-mile controversy continued into the 1970s.

In the 1970s, the United States followed the same approach. Believing either that it could not afford to compromise its legal position, or that Peru, Chile, and Ecuador were unable to modify their positions, and also believing that some way around the legal controversy could be found, the United States again tried to negotiate a "practical solution." After several years of preliminary work, an informal conference was held at Santiago, Chile, in April, 1968, where the United States proposed the creation of a "regional fisheries institute" as a way around the impasse. In August, 1969, the four countries met formally at Buenos Aires, where the United States offered several modified formulas for avoiding the legal controversy and also considered requests for reductions in U.S. tariffs on fishery products and for financial and technical assistance for fishery conservation and development. The delegates agreed to meet again before the end of 1969, but as of June, 1970, no further meeting had been scheduled.

At the opening of the 1970s, the United States was working to bring about a new world conference to resolve the questions left unsettled in 1960. At the 1958 conference, the United States made a slight concession to coastal states in the Convention on Fishing by recognizing coastal states' "special interest" in fishery conservation beyond the territorial sea, but this concession was too slight to win Peruvian interest. The United States, in 1970, appeared willing to broaden that "special interest." It proposed that coastal states be entitled to a quota of the catch off its shores—beyond the territorial sea—based on the percentage of the catch they presently take. This proposal would preserve the status quo, but the U.S. position was not fixed, and it was willing to consider reasonable proposals from Peru or any other country.

U.S. policies to prevent two-hundred-mile claims and enforcement of them include formal diplomatic protests and representations. The U.S. government formally protests two-hundred-mile claims to protect the U.S. legal position by showing that the United States does not accept the validity of the coastal state's action, to deter continuation of that action, and to demonstrate to congressional and industrial leaders that the State Department has at least done something when they complain that the problem has not been solved. U.S. diplomatic representations usually begin with an explanation of the U.S. position to the foreign ministry. If it is unable to control the situation, a U.S. ambassador might talk with the local president, or individual legislators to dissuade them from going to two hundred miles or to encourage them to eliminate or moderate an existing two-hundred-mile limit. If necessary, pressure might be exerted on influential constituents. (In one case, the United States persuaded a president to veto two-hundred-mile legislation approved by a national legislature.)

One important U.S. policy is tuna conservation. The United States supports the Inter-American Tropical Tuna Commission, founded by the United States and Costa Rica in 1950.[48] The convention establishing the Tuna Commission is open to adherence by other governments whose nationals fish in the eastern tropical Pacific Ocean. Panama joined in 1953; Ecuador was a member from 1961 through 1968; Mexico joined in 1964, Canada in 1968, and Japan in 1970. The commission supports independent research

[48] Convention for the Establishment of an Inter-American Tropical Tuna Commission, May 31, 1949 (1950), 1 U.S.T. 230; TIAS 2044; 80 UNTS 3.

and makes conservation recommendations to member governments. The United States would like to see Peru and other states bordering on the eastern Pacific join the international program of the commission.

The U.S. Congress has adopted at least six pieces of legislation to protect the interests of U.S. high-seas fishermen. Although the U.S. government has discouraged, but not prohibited, the purchase of Peruvian fishing licenses for the two-hundred-mile zone, the Fishermen's Protective Act of 1954[49] established the unique precedent of compensating U.S. vessel owners for fines paid to foreign governments as a result of seizures the United States deemed unlawful. Although the act created incentive not to purchase licenses, Congress considered the policy necessary to protect U.S. rights on the high seas. Another important law is the Fish and Wildlife Act of 1956.[50] Congress, declaring "protection of [the] opportunity to fish on the high seas in accordance with international law" to be essential to the health of the U.S. fishing industry, consolidated the functions of all departments and agencies relating to "protection of commercial fisheries" in the Department of the Interior and gave the secretary of the interior authority to make policy to protect U.S. fishermen. Government restructuring assured a hard-line policy defending U.S. fishing interests.

During the 1960s, as congressional impatience with the State Department's handling of the two-hundred-mile controversy grew, Congress passed and the president signed four laws retaliating against countries seizing and fining U.S. vessels. While the new laws may have been partially intended to deter seizures and to encourage the Latin American countries to negotiate, they seem to have been more carefully calculated to light a fire under the State Department. In some instances, the legislation exacerbated the situation by arousing intense nationalism and anti-U.S. emotions in Latin America and limited the State Department's flexibility.

The Foreign Assistance Act of 1961, as amended,[51] contains former Senator Thomas Kuchel's so-called Freedom of the Seas Amendment, which provides that imposition of fines or other sanc-

---

[49] Act of August 27, 1954, 68 Stat. 883; 22 U.S.C., paragraphs 1971–1976.
[50] 70 Stat. 1119; 16 U.S.C., paragraphs 742a–742j, Aug. 8, 1956.
[51] P.L. 89-171; 79 Stat. 660, Section 620 (o), approved Sept. 7, 1965.

tions on U.S. fishing vessels for activities in international waters shall be a factor "in determining whether or not furnish assistance." (Neither Peru nor any other country has yet been excluded from the foreign assistance program under the amendment.)

Laws Relating to Loan or Sale of Vessels to Foreign Countries[52] requires the immediate termination of specific naval loan agreements upon a presidential finding that the country "has seized any United States fishing vessel on account of its fishing activities in international waters." (Although the law renewed the loan of one destroyer to Peru, in spite of continued Peruvian seizures, neither Presidents Johnson nor Nixon made any finding. As of June, 1970, the loan had not been terminated.)

The United States maintains, as one aspect of its legal position, that fines paid by its nationals for activities beyond twelve miles give rise to a U.S. government claim for reimbursement against the fining government. Section 5 of the Fishermen's Protective Act of 1967[53] provides that if the offending government fails "or refuses to make payment in full within 120 days after receiving notice of any such claim of the United States, the Secretary of State shall withhold, pending such payment, an amount equal to such unpaid claim from any funds programmed for the current fiscal year for assistance." (If the act were construed to carry out its obvious congressional intent, it should apply—at least in theory—to fines totaling more than $50,000 paid to Peru by four U.S. vessels in 1969 and one in 1970. It is believed that the amendment has not yet been applied.)

The toughest law to date, proposed by Representative Thomas Pelly, is Section 3(b) of the Foreign Military Sales Act of 1968.[54] It declares that no defense article or service shall be sold by the U.S. government to any country that "seizes or takes into custody or fines an American fishing vessel engaged in fishing more than 12 miles from the coast of that country." The act does permit a presidential waiver. When the law was applied to Ecuador in December 1968, the U.S. ambassador to Ecuador averted a crisis by pointing out that Ecuador was free to purchase arms and services directly from private U.S. companies. When the United States publicly announced

[52] P.L. 90-224; 81 Stat. 729, Section 3, Dec. 26, 1967.
[53] P.L. 90-482; 82 Stat. 729, approved Aug. 12, 1968.
[54] P.L. 90-629; 89 Stat. 1320, approved Oct. 22, 1968.

in May, 1969, that it had suspended arms sales to Peru in February, 1969, the Peruvian government apparently did not wait to hear that it could still buy U.S. arms privately. It immediately expelled the three U.S. military missions, canceled the scheduled visit of U.S. Presidential Emissary Nelson Rockefeller, and considered breaking diplomatic relations. U.S. arms sales were resumed in July, 1969, as part of an arrangement whereby Peru, Chile, and Ecuador agreed to negotiate with the United States.

Should the State Department fail to make meaningful progress in its discussions with Peru, Congress will probably amend the Fishermen's Protective Act by prohibiting the importation of any fish or fishery products from any country that seizes U.S. vessels or refuses to negotiate.

Peruvian Policies and Position

PERUVIAN LEGAL CONTENTIONS

The Peruvian government has strongly maintained that its two-hundred-mile limit is valid under international law and binding on the United States. The government, Peru's leading legal scholars, and some of the most able legal minds in Latin America have advanced numerous arguments in support of Peru's position. The following arguments will be briefly summarized: that the two-hundred-mile limit is consistent with current trends in an evolving law of the sea, that it is valid under the principles of the Anglo-Norwegian fisheries case, that it is valid as a compensatory right, that the claim is a justifiable exercise of the right of self-protection, that it is valid under "inter-American international law," and that the United States is "estopped" to deny its validity. No judgment will be made, however, on the merits of these contentions.

According to one Peruvian view, the law of the sea is in a process of evolution toward the two-hundred-mile limit. The failures of the 1930 Hague Codification Conference and the 1958 and 1960 United Nations Conferences on the Law of the Sea to define any rule limiting the breadth of the territorial sea or fishery jurisdiction are evidence that international law does not presently deny the right of each state to set its own limits in accord with national needs. Under this Peruvian theory, it is argued that no state claimed a two-hundred-mile limit in 1946, but by 1970, eleven Latin American countries had adopted such limits, and the concept of extended national jurisdiction for fishery conservation or other purposes had spread beyond Latin America. Peruvians argue that jurisdiction up to two hundred miles will be adopted by many other nations in the future for practical reasons. Most of the world's fishermen are coastal, and as they come under increasing pressure from modern foreign fishing fleets, they will demand protection in the form of exclusive jurisdiction (as U.S. coastal fishermen successfully extended U.S. exclusive fishery jurisdiction from three to twelve miles in 1966). In addition, Peruvian fisheries experts consider the two-hundred-mile limit superior for fishery conservation; they point out that nearly all of the world's fishing grounds are located within two hundred miles of land. Thus a two-hundred-mile limit would be effective, in their opinion, for most species, particularly in the case of a country with a long coast line, such as the United States. Where a particular stock of fish overlaps an adjacent two-hundred-mile zone, regulations could be adopted on a regional basis (as Peru, Chile, and Ecuador have attempted to do with their Permanent Commission of the South Pacific). For these reasons, Peruvians deny that two hundreds miles is an ancient, conservative, or illegal position; they firmly believe it to be the order of the future.

The Anglo-Norwegian fisheries case,[55] decided by the International Court of Justice in December, 1951, appeared to permit coastal states to make unilateral claims to exclusive fishery jurisdiction beyond limits generally accepted by international practice, provided certain "geographic realities" and economic factors are present: "One consideration not to be overlooked, the scope of which extends beyond purely geographic factors: that of certain economic interest peculiar to a region, the reality and importance of which are clearly evidenced. . . . Such rights, founded on the vital needs of the population and attested by very ancient and peaceful usage, may legitimately be taken into account in drawing a line which, moreover, appears to the Court to have been kept within the bounds of what is moderate and reasonable."[56]

Peruvians argue that the "reasonableness" of the two-hundred-mile figure is demonstrated by a 1947 study indicating that the

[55] United Kingdom v. Norway, Judgment of Dec. 18, 1951, I.C.J. Reports (1951), 116.

[56] Ibid., p. 142 (dicta).

biological limit of the Peruvian or Humboldt Current is approximately two hundred miles.[57] The lawyers point out that Peru's coastal belt is arid, receiving almost no rainfall because the unusually cold Humboldt Current prevents cloud formation over the coast. The high Andes' close proximity to the sea results in a high rate of erosion that fertilizes the adjacent sea with nutrients (nitrates and phosphates), thus making the Humboldt Current one of the world's richest areas of marine life. Consequently, Peru must rely more heavily on the sea than most other countries. In the nineteenth and early twentieth centuries, Peruvian agriculture and foreign trade depended on a large population of guano-producing sea birds. Today Peru's economy depends on the fish-meal industry, which earns more than 25 percent of Peru's foreign exchange. A twelve-mile exclusive fishing limit is inadequate to protect the fully utilized anchovy fishery from foreign exploitation. Peruvian lawyers conclude, therefore, that jurisdiction over the Humboldt Current is vital to Peru's economy and future growth and that Peru's claim meets all criteria established by the International Court of Justice. (This is the most popular defense and has been termed the "bioma" or "eco-systems" theory.)[58]

A related argument, advanced by the late Colombian jurist and member of the International Law Commission, Dr. Jesús María Yepes, is that Peru is entitled to extended jurisdiction as a "compensatory right."[59] Because Peru has almost no continental shelf and is faced with scarce agricultural products due primarily to the coldness of the Humboldt Current, Peru should be entitled to jurisdiction over the sea bed and fisheries beyond its narrow continental shelf up to a reasonable distance.

Dr. Enríque García Sayan, a former Peruvian foreign minister and professor of law at the University of San Marcos, has defended

---

[57] E. Schweigger, El Litoral Peruano, pp. 70–72 (Lima, 1947).

[58] For a concise statement of the "bioma" theory, see the explanation by Peruvian Ambassador Edwin Letts at the 486th meeting of the United Nations General Assembly's Sixth Committee, 11 U.N. CAOR, 6th Comm. 31, U.N. Doc. A/C. 6/Sr. 436 (1956). For a collection of Peruvian legal arguments, see *Revista Peruana de Derecho Internacional*, no. 54, July–December, 1958.

[59] J. M. Yepes, "El problema del mar territorial o jurisdiccional y de la plataforma submarina ante el nuevo derecho internacional," *Revista Universitas*, no. 8, pp. 45–69. Bogota, Colombia, 1955. "El mito de la pretendida 'regla' de las tres millas," *Separada de la Revista Universitas*, no. 12, 1957.

Peru's two-hundred-mile limit as an exercise of Peru's inherent right of self-defense, self-preservation, or self-protection.[60] While a state's right of self-defense or self-protection has not been seriously questioned, such rights have generally been asserted in time of war. The United States, however, has relied on the right as a justification for the Monroe Doctrine, as a defense of its claim to exclusive jurisdiction over seals in the Bering Sea,[61] and as a support of the U.S. claim to jurisdiction and control over the continental shelf.[62] Thus Dr. García Sayan contends that Peru's limit is a valid assertion of Peru's inherent right of self-defense or self-protection. (Philip C. Jessup, a former member of the International Court of Justice and a distinguished U.S. authority on the law of the sea, has said of the defense, "In essence . . . the claim is supported on the strongest possible ground, namely, the national interest in the conservation of the natural resources of the adjacent seas and sea bed, coupled with a general right of self-preservation.")[63]

Peruvians also argue that the two-hundred-mile limit is valid under so-called inter-American international law. Under this theory, the limit is rooted in precedents of hemispheric defense, principles adopted by the Inter-American Council of Jurists, and regional state practice. The U.S. obligation to recognize the limit follows from the OAS Charter, a 1936 Protocol on Non-Intervention, and from moral obligations.

One regional precedent that Latin Americans feel supports the two-hundred-mile limit is the 1939 Declaration of Panama. The declaration, instigated by the United States, created defense zones around the Americas extending, at some points, to three hundred miles. If the American states may jointly set three-hundred-mile limits for defense of vital national interests against foreign *military* harm, then the same states, or a portion of them, may certainly establish a two-hundred-mile limit to defend vital national interests from foreign *economic* harm. Like the defense zones, the two-hundred-mile zone is based on a multilateral agreement (the Declaration of Santiago) and not simply unilateral action.

[60] Sayan, *Notas sobre la Soberanía.*

[61] Leonard, *International Regulation of Fisheries.*

[62] See note 11.

[63] P. C. Jessup, book review, *American Journal of International Law* 49 (1955):593.

The 1956 Principles of Mexico, approved by the Inter-American Council of Jurists, with only the United States voting against,[64] declared the three-mile rule "insufficient" and not "a rule of general international law." The principles affirm: "Each State is competent to establish its territorial waters within reasonable limits, taking into account geographic, geological, and biological factors, as well as the economic needs of its population, and its security and defense. . . . Coastal States have, in addition, the right of exclusive exploitation of species closely related to the coastal population."[65] While the United States attempted to dilute the Principles of Mexico at a subsequent conference on technical and scientific matters, Peruvian lawyers note that the Council of Jurists' 1956 action represents the most authoritative OAS statement by inter-American legal experts. Another important precedent is the 1970 Declaration of Montevideo, in which nine Latin American countries reaffirmed and expanded the Principles of Mexico.

The third step in the inter-American law argument is that current hemispheric practice evidences a customary two-hundred-mile principle accepted as law. As of June, 1970, the following states had claimed two-hundred-mile limits (ranging from limited fishing jurisdiction to two-hundred-mile territorial seas): Chile (1947, 1952), Peru (1947, 1952), Costa Rica (1948, 1955), El Salvador (1950, 1962), Honduras (1951), Ecuador (1952, 1966), Nicaragua (1965), Argentina (1966), Panama (1967), Uruguay (1969), and Brazil (1970). Two-hundred-mile legislation introduced in Colombia in 1962 had passed the lower house of Congress and was expected to receive Senate approval in 1970. Venezuela was also considering adopting a two-hundred-mile limit, and Canada seemed determined to extend national jurisdiction to one hundred miles to regulate shipping in the Northwest Passage. The two-hundred-mile limit is now more commonly accepted within this hemisphere than is three miles, six, twelve or any other outer limit of national jurisdiction. The two-hundred-mile position is accepted among these states, say the Peruvians, and this practice is evidence of a customary regional rule of law that is at least binding among the two-hundred-mile claimants.

---

[64] 34 Dept. State Bull. 296, No. 869, Feb. 20, 1956.
[65] Ibid., p. 298.

The next argument is that this customary regional rule is binding on the United States. The United States is bound under the OAS Charter to observe Peru's "fundamental rights." One of Peru's Charter rights is "to defend its integrity and independence, to provide for its preservation and prosperity, and consequently to organize itself as it sees fit, to legislate concerning its interests, . . . and to determine the jurisdiction and competence of its courts."[66] Peruvians argue that the two-hundred-mile claim is an exercise of this sovereign right which the United States must respect. The minority of Peruvian lawyers who argue that Peru claims a two-hundred-mile "territorial sea" contend that U.S. nonrecognition violates U.S. Charter obligations to respect the "territory" of the American states.[67] In addition, the United States signed and ratified a Protocol Relative to Non-Intervention,[68] in which it pledged not to intervene, directly or indirectly, for any reason whatever in the internal or external affairs of certain American republics. Latin Americans tend to view even U.S. diplomatic protests on the two hundred miles as "acts of intervention." Thus Peruvians conclude that because the two-hundred-mile limit is a regional rule of law and because the United States has special legal obligations in this hemisphere, it is under a greater legal obligation to respect Peru's claim than are nonhemispheric states. Finally, there is a moral element: due to the historic U.S. role as protector and defender of the Americas and U.S. economic, political, historic, and military ties with Latin America, Peruvians feel that the United States is under a greater moral obligation to respect the two hundred miles than any other great maritime power.

Another Peruvian argument is that the United States is "estopped" to deny the validity of Peru's claim. The International Court of Justice, holding in the 1969 North Sea continental shelf case[69] that Article 6, section 2, of the Convention on the Continental Shelf does not embody a rule of customary international law, conceded that the Federal Republic of Germany might nevertheless have become bound by section 2 through estoppel, by its actions.

[66] Charter of the Organization of American States, April 30, 1948 (1951), Article 9; U.S. TIAS 2361; 2 U.S.T. 2394.

[67] Ibid., Art. 17.

[68] Signed Dec. 23, 1936 (1937), 51 Stat. 41; T.S. 923 (Peru was not a party.)

[69] *North Sea Continental Shelf Case*, I.C.J. Reports (1969).

Thus it has been argued that the United States is estopped to deny the validity of Peru's original two-hundred-mile limit, because, through its actions, the United States caused Peru to detrimentally change its position in reliance on the expectation that the United States would not object. Prior to Peru's two-hundred-mile decree, the United States asserted jurisdiction beyond three miles for many purposes. These unilateral assertions led Peru to believe that the United States would tolerate reasonable exceptions to the three-mile limit. In addition, the United States granted qualified recognition of a broad Mexican claim to fishery jurisdiction, subject only to the condition that Mexico give "adequate recognition" to U.S. fishing interests.

In reliance on U.S. assertions and actions, Peru changed its legal position. The change proved detrimental, for it caused conflicts. As a result of the formal U.S. protest in 1948, Peru was unable to reverse its position for domestic political reasons. The U.S. protest was therefore unexpected and unfair, and the United States should be estopped to deny the validity of Peru's claim.

THE SCOPE OF PERU'S TWO-HUNDRED-MILE JURISDICTION

Much confusion exists concerning the precise status of Peru's jurisdictional claims as a matter of Peruvian law and policy. While some Peruvian lawyers believe that Peru claims a two-hundred-mile "territorial sea," this is a minority position. The Foreign Ministry has never expressly stated that Peru has a two-hundred-mile territorial sea; in recent years, Peru has deliberately adopted an ambiguous position concerning the width, if any, of its territorial sea. Peruvian law does not presently deal with the subject. Four laws or decrees form the basis of Peru's two-hundred-mile jurisdiction:

The first is Presidential Decree No. 781 of August 1, 1947. It declared "sovereignty and jurisdiction" over the continental shelf adjacent to the coasts of "the national territory" and also over the adjacent sea to the extent necessary in order to protect, conserve, and utilize the resources found therein. The state reserved the right to establish explicitly bounded conservation zones and to modify them in the light of future needs and information. An immediate and temporary two-hundred-mile zone for fishery "protection and control" was then established. The decree expressly recognized the right of "freedom of navigation," suggesting a possible intent to leave unchanged the character of the waters as "high seas." Peruvian Petroleum Law No. 11780 of March 12, 1952, extended the concept of a two-hundred-mile fishery protection zone to oil deposits.

Legislation Resolution No. 12305 of May 6, 1955, "approved" the Declaration of Santiago of 1952 and nine other conventions, declarations, and regulations creating the "legal regime of the South Pacific." The Declaration of Santiago establishes the concept of the two-hundred-mile maritime zone. At first, the declaration was not considered a claim but merely a statement that Chile, Peru, and Ecuador would coordinate their international maritime policies to achieve international acceptance of a two-hundred-mile concept. Later, the maritime zone was interpreted as a claim of exclusive sovereignty and jurisdiction to a minimum distance of two hundred miles. In the mid-1950s, it was construed to be no more than an assertion of nondiscriminatory conservation jurisdiction. At present, it appears to mean no more than exclusive fishery jurisdiction.

The fourth Peruvian law concerning the two hundred miles is the Civil Aviation Law of 1965. Article 2 provides: "The Republic of Peru exercises exclusive sovereignty over the air space which covers its territory and jurisdictional waters within the 200 miles." For the Peruvian lawyers who had maintained Peru had a two-hundred-mile "territorial sea," the 1965 law proved what they had always said. For the majority, however, the law proved the opposite: by distinguishing between "territory" and "jurisdictional waters," the law showed that the two hundred miles was not "territory" but merely "jurisdictional waters."

PERUVIAN OBJECTIVES AND POLICIES

As in the case of the United States, Peru has many foreign policy objectives concerning the two hundred miles, and these are not generally a matter of public knowledge. Peru's primary objective appears to be universal acceptance of the principle that every coastal state has the right to exploit, conserve, and develop the natural resources of the sea and subsoil adjacent to its coasts and to exercise jurisdiction to the distance necessary to protect such resources, according to geographic, ecologic, and economic factors.

One specific objective is to secure U.S. recognition of Peru's two-hundred-mile limit. Since the United States appears adamant in its refusal to consider recognition, Peru seems to be trying to force U.S. acceptance.

In Peru, there is a saying that iron cannot be shaped unless it is hot. If Peru merely sat on its claim and did not enforce it and did not encourage others to follow, it could not interest the United States in negotiating anything. Consequently, it appears to this author that the seizures may be a tactic to force U.S. concessions. Peru has never publicly advocated a universal two-hundred-mile limit, and indeed, from 1952 until 1965 it discouraged other countries from claiming two-hundred-mile limits. Nevertheless, since 1965 it seems that Peru has decided that its position is strengthened when other states claim two-hundred-mile "territorial seas." At some future time, Peru may point to the modesty of its two-hundred-mile maritime zone to win U.S. and world recognition as a means of halting spread of the two-hundred-mile "territorial sea." Thus Peruvian policy may be designed to keep the heat on so that the United States will ultimately bend.

Peru is reluctant to enter any agreement with the U.S. government, at least in part because any arrangement securing U.S. rights within the two hundred miles would undermine Peru's legal position. On the other hand, Peru is willing and anxious to negotiate directly with the U.S. tuna industry, for any agreement with the industry would not affect its legal position, and Peru is relatively stronger. Peru also has important conservation objectives. It is willing to cooperate with the United States on conservation matters, but its interests are slightly different. While the United States is concerned mainly with conservation of yellowfin and skipjack tuna, Peru seeks an effective regional conservation system for all the living resources in the Humboldt Current, not just tuna.

Peru's government has made an effort to accommodate the U.S. tuna fleet. It has given tuna fishermen preferential treatment not accorded other fishing fleets. Supreme Decree of January 5, 1956, which was acceptable to the American Tunaboat Association (representing U.S. boat owners) provided regulations for granting fishing permits to foreign vessels in jurisdictional waters of the country. Under the regulations, the government is required to grant fishing licenses to foreigners for yellowfin and skipjack tuna, whales, and tuna bait-fish. Foreign fishing within Peru's "jurisdictional waters" for all other species is prohibited. The only permissible restriction on the number of permits granted are those recommended by the Permanent Commission of the South Pacific for Conservation, and it has never restricted foreign tuna fishing. The 1956 regulations provided that if restricted licensing were adopted, preference would be given to foreign fishermen who had previously held permits.

ANALYSIS OF U.S. AND PERUVIAN INTERESTS

U.S. Interests

MILITARY

Considerable confusion exists in both the United States and Peru concerning U.S. interests in the two-hundred-mile controversy. Peruvians and other critics of U.S. policy tend to believe it is controlled by a small group of southern California tuna fishermen, and this view is reinforced by the fact that nearly all U.S. congressional action in this area has been designed to protect U.S. fishermen. That the hot spot in the conflict involves U.S. tuna fishermen off Peru and Ecuador obscures the fact that the U.S. government strongly believes that its most vital national interests at stake are *military*. The Defense Department determines U.S. two-hundred-mile policy, and it was this department that discouraged tuna fishermen from reaching an accord with Peru in 1969.

Peruvians and some U.S. Latin American experts have difficulty understanding why Peruvian two-hundred-mile resource jurisdiction would threaten any U.S. military interests. As a matter of first impression, it would appear that U.S. military interests are harmed more by opposition to the two hundred miles: the United States has obvious military interests in maintaining good U.S.-Peruvian relations; U.S. opposition to the two hundred miles has created an anti-U.S. issue on which communists and other subversives are able to capitalize; U.S. opposition has been an important factor in Peru's move toward the Soviet bloc in search of new markets; and U.S. sanctions against Peru for seizures was the immediate cause of Peru's expulsion of U.S. military personnel in 1969. (The U.S. Naval Mission to Peru was the oldest U.S. military mission in Latin America.)

The Defense Department is well aware of these facts. It would like to improve U.S.-Peruvian relations as much as the State Department or U.S. business interests in Peru. Defense experts realize that the benefit to U.S.-Peruvian relations of U.S. recognition would far outweigh the value of the small amount of tuna taken off Peru's coast. If the world consisted only of the Western Hemisphere, the Defense Department would probably not oppose Peru's claim. But this relatively peaceful and friendly hemisphere is only one part of a hostile world. Because the U.S.-Peruvian controversy has been one of the outstanding disputes on the law of the sea for nearly a quarter of a century, whatever the United States does in relation to Peru's claim is likely to have repercussions throughout the world. The United States, unlike Peru, has vital strategic and commercial interests throughout the world, and those interests could be seriously injured by the precedent of a U.S.-Peruvian settlement. Succinctly stated, U.S. military experts believe that Peru's claim—when considered in relation to U.S. global interests— threatens "immobilization of an eighty-billion dollar a year department of the U.S. Government," the Department of Defense.

This conclusion is based on a complex chain of reasoning that is not without merit and certainly deserves careful analysis. The threat to U.S. military interests can best be understood with a partial consideration of U.S. alternatives. The first proposition is that any settlement with Peru in which the United States compromises its position would encourage other coastal states to make outrageous claims in order to secure U.S. concessions. U.S. recognition of any form of Peruvian two-hundred-mile jurisdiction would be the most important precedent supporting Peru's thesis that coastal states may assert jurisdiction to the limits they alone believe are reasonable and would give every coastal state incentive to make similar or greater claims. While Peru argues that it has never advocated a universal two-hundred-mile limit and believes that universal application would be impractical, this argument is irrelevant to the United States. Nothing would discourage some small country from claiming a thousand-mile corridor across the Atlantic Ocean and demanding tribute from all vessels and aircraft passing through. The precise claims that might result from the precedent of U.S. recognition may be unforeseeable, but there is good reason to believe they would be made. On the other hand, if the United States gives Peru nothing—or imposes economic sanctions—other countries will gain little advantage by asserting bold new claims.

This leads to the conclusion that the United States could only adjust the conflicting legal positions by an international convention, for this would eliminate the danger of chaotic unilateral actions. The United States believes that it must grant two hundred miles to all nations or to none. Before the United States could accept a two-hundred-mile regime on a world-wide basis, it would have to be shown that such an arrangement was in fact in the best interests of the world community. Assuming for the moment that such a universal two-hundred-mile regime (perhaps dividing overlapping claims by a median line) could be constructed that would serve the best economic interests of the world, the United States would still have great difficulty accepting it, because of its deep belief in what might be termed the "doctrine of creeping jurisdiction."

The "doctrine," simply stated, is that any jurisdictional limit, however narrowly defined, tends to grow into a "territorial sea"— if not in name, then in substance. A good illustration of "creeping jurisdiction" is Peru. In 1947, Peru established a two-hundred-mile fishery conservation zone. In March, 1952, drafters of Peru's new petroleum law decided that two hundred miles was a convenient distance for regulating oil concessions. In August, 1952, Peru proclaimed, as a principle of its international maritime policy, its right to assert *exclusive* sovereignty and jurisdiction to a *minimum* distance of two hundred miles. In 1965, Peru established two-hundred-mile sovereignty over the air space for its new civil aviation law. In 1969, Peru's new Code of Waters established *dominio* (roughly equivalent to absolute ownership) over the waters extending to two hundred miles. While Peru has never claimed a two-hundred-mile "territorial sea," as a practical matter its jurisdiction has "crept" from a modest fishery claim towards absolute sovereignty. Hundreds—perhaps thousands—of similar examples of "creeping jurisdiction" could be cited (including U.S. cases). Assuming the validity of the "doctrine," it follows that any two-hundred-mile limit, even if defined narrowly by international agreement, would inevitably lead—perhaps not in all cases, but at least in many—to two-hundred-mile "territorial seas."

The final question concerns the effect of world-wide two-hundred-mile territorial seas on the Defense Department. Under universally recognized principles of international law, a coastal state exercises absolute territorial sovereignty over the air space above its territorial sea; no foreign aircraft may enter the air space without the coastal state's consent. Commercial vessels have a right to pass through the territorial sea without coastal state permission (the right of "innocent passage"), but this right is much more limited than "freedom of navigation," which all vessels enjoy on the "high seas." No universal agreement exists, however, that military vessels have a right of "innocent passage."

International acceptance of the two-hundred-mile territorial sea would place a vast area—about the size of the entire Atlantic Ocean—under national control; many of these areas would be in strategic military locations. All of the world's straits would be closed to free navigation and aviation. The Caribbean Sea, for example, would be under the control of several states, and Cuba would have a large segment of it. This could make U.S. defense operations in the region extremely difficult or impossible. Two-hundred-mile territorial seas would close the Mediterranean Sea and could exclude the U.S. Sixth Fleet. In the Middle East, they could make it very difficult for the United States to defend Israel. The United States could no longer conduct reconnaissance flights within two hundred miles of North Korea, China, North Vietnam or other strategic areas. In short, the United States is the world's leading air and sea power. If critical areas of the sea were under national control, the power and influence of the United States would be reduced and in some cases eliminated altogether. The United States cannot afford a settlement with Peru, according to U.S. military experts, because the risks are far too grave.

There is little reason to doubt the Defense Department's conclusion that it would be immobilized if the two-hundred-mile territorial sea were adopted throughout the world. The Defense Department has no interest in fishing or other resources off Peru and has every reason for seeking peaceful and cooperative relations between the two countries. It is because Peru's claim—not in itself, but in its world-wide implications—threatens what the United States firmly believes are its *vital* national interests that the United States must oppose (perhaps reluctantly) Peru's claim. U.S. policy

is not designed primarily to protect such a narrow parochial interest as California fishermen; they are merely beneficiaries of a policy designed primarily to protect U.S. military interests.

NONMILITARY INTERESTS IN THE SEA

Vital U.S. economic interests are similarly threatened by Peru's
position. (All of the analysis concerning the harmful precedent of a
bilateral settlement and "creeping jurisdiction" is incorporated
here by reference.) The United States has a wide range of nonmilitary interests in maintaining maximum "freedom of the seas,"
or minimum coastal state control. These interests might be broadly
grouped under the headings "trade and commerce," "science and
technology," and "resource development." Trade and commerce
includes U.S. interests in transporting people, raw materials, products, and information on, under, and over the seas with minimum
interference by coastal states. While Peru argues that it has no intention of interfering with foreign shipping or other aspects of
trade and commerce, according to the United States, the argument
is irrelevant. Peru stands for what the United States deems a radical proposition: that each coastal state may exercise jurisdiction to
the limits it alone considers reasonable. That proposition, if endorsed by the United States, could be used by other coastal states
(Canada's proposed hundred-mile limit for foreign oil tankers is a
good example) to restrain international trade and commerce. The
United States believes that coastal states should not regulate scientific research off their coasts beyond the territorial sea, for it is in
the best interests of the world that human knowledge about the sea
be maximized. While Peru apparently disclaims any desire to regulate scientific research within its two hundred miles, the disclaimer
is immaterial in the U.S. view. The principle on which Peru's
action rests has been used by Brazil and Ecuador to regulate, restrict, and even prohibit scientific research far from their coasts.

Resource development includes exploitation, conservation, and
development of all of the sea's resources (including fishing, which
is treated separately). The United States believes that national
jurisdiction over these resources should be limited by international
agreement to assure their maximum and most efficient development for the benefit of mankind. Peru's claim of resource jurisdic-

tion is in direct conflict with U.S. interests—not that the United States is concerned with having its own nationals exploit resources off Peru's coast, but that it is concerned with the international order. U.S. experts willingly admit that Peru's claim is in Peru's self-interest. But the United States would challenge the claim even if no U.S. interests ever contemplated exploitation off Peru. The United States wants a rational world order that will produce the greatest benefit for mankind; this is because the United States has vast global interests. It wants to promote world economic development and stability, because what is good for the world is good for the United States. The United States doubts that Peru's approach would provide the most efficient allocation of the world's resources. Thus Peru's position threatens a series of vital U.S. nonmilitary interests in the uses of the sea.

SPECIAL RELATIONSHIP WITH PERU AND LATIN AMERICA

Aside from its vital national interests in the sea, the United States has important national interests in maintaining good relations with Peru and other Latin American countries. Like the sea, Latin America is vital to U.S. military and economic interests. Any conflict dividing the United States from Peru and other Latin American countries is harmful to U.S. interests in their good will. Immediately after World War II, and for many decades before, the United States enjoyed a high degree of control over political and economic matters in this hemisphere. Since the mid-1950s, however, U.S. influence in Latin America has been undermined by the Soviet Union's "good neighbor offensive" and by subversive forces who are quick to exploit every possible issue against the United States, including the two-hundred-mile issue. U.S. interests are best served by elimination of such divisive issues whenever possible. Although the costs of such conflicts are difficult to calculate, they affect U.S. military and commercial interests in this hemisphere.

As a military matter, Latin America may be the U.S. "soft underbelly." Had Franklin D. Roosevelt not initiated the so-called Good Neighbor Policy during the early days of his administration, the United States could have easily confronted a neutral, divided, or even pro-Axis Latin America during World War II. Thus the

United States has vital strategic interests in keeping Peru in the "Western camp." The Rockefeller Report on the Americas warned: "Forces of anarchy, terror, and subversion are loose in the Americas. Moreover, this fact has too long gone unheeded in the United States."[70] Mr. Rockefeller found, "At the moment, there is only one Castro among the twenty-six nations of the hemisphere; there can well be more in the future. And a Castro on the mainland, supported militarily and economically by the communist world, would present the gravest kind of threat to the security of the Western Hemisphere and pose an extremely difficult problem for the United States."[71]

The two-hundred-mile issue is a popular anti-U.S. question that is exploited by the Soviet Union (in spite of its official twelve-mile position), Castroists, Maoists, and others from Central America to Chile. It would be impossible to determine precisely how much power this issue has given them, but it definitely provides one additional tool for attacking the United States. The issue has sufficient political glamor in some countries (Peru, for example) that it could conceivably bring a strongly anti-U.S. government to power.

The U.S.-Peruvian conflict has been an important factor in Peru's move away from dependence on the United States. Because the United States threatened to cut off imports of Peruvian fish meal in the event of seizures, Peru has established trade relations with the Soviet bloc. As a direct result of application of the Military Sales Act to Peru for its seizures, Peru ordered nearly all U.S. military personnel out of the country. U.S. legislation providing termination of ship loans and military sales to countries seizing U.S. vessels caused Peru to question the value of U.S. military aid. Thus the controversy appears to be undermining vital U.S. military interests.

As an economic matter, U.S. interests in Peru and Latin America are substantial. The United States annually imports more than $4 billion worth of foodstuffs, fuels, raw materials, and other products from Latin America. The region is also a vital market for U.S. goods; more than 10 percent of all 1968 U.S. exports went to Latin America—machinery, chemicals, and other manufactured goods—

70 *New York Times* edition (1969), p. 60.
71 Ibid., p. 38.

valued at nearly $5 billion. In addition, the United States has more than $10 billion worth of direct private investment in Latin America (more than 17 percent of all U.S. foreign investment).

It would be naive to suggest that the fishing controversy was a significant factor in Peru's expropriation of the International Petroleum Company. On the other hand, it would be unwise to ignore the fact that many years of unfavorable publicity resulting from U.S. vessel seizures helped create a climate in which the Peruvian government could take assets of the IPC without serious domestic opposition. The U.S. position on the two hundred miles is used by anti-U.S. forces in Peru and elsewhere to discredit U.S. business generally and to support the charge that U.S. policy protects narrow private interests and is economically imperialistic.

On February 14, 1969, the U.S. tuna boat *San Juan* was allegedly fired upon by a Peruvian naval vessel. The ATA believes the Peruvian captain was drunk and acting contrary to orders. Peruvians deny that the *San Juan* was hit by any Peruvian shots. Cynics observe that Peru signed its first trade agreement with the Soviet Union three days later, on February 17, 1969, while the incident (reported in the Peruvian press as another example of U.S. "piracy") was still fresh in the minds of the Peruvian public. Regardless of the facts of the incident, its timeliness (or untimeliness for the United States) may have blunted possible pro-U.S. domestic criticism of the Soviet-Peruvian trade agreement.

In addition, the United States has a vital interest in Peruvian economic growth and development. To the extent that two-hundred-mile resource jurisdiction would help build a strong Peruvian economy such jurisdiction is consistent with this U.S. interest.

Thus U.S. policy on the two hundred miles has undermined vital U.S. interests in Peruvian good will. To the extent that present U.S. policy has subverted these interests, the benefits of that policy must be balanced against its costs to U.S.-Peruvian and Latin American relations; similarly, the costs of alternative policies must be balanced against the possible benefits to U.S. interests in Latin America. Such analysis is not easy, but it must be made.

FISHING

U.S. fishing interests affected by the two hundred miles include high seas, coastal, and sports fishing; fishing investments in Peru and other Latin American countries; and fishery conservation and development.

From an economic standpoint, sports fishing is the most important U.S. fishing interest. U.S. salt-water sports fishermen numbered more than thirteen million in 1965, and they spent more than $3 billion on their fishing activities. By the year 2000, the United States will have an estimated thirty million salt-water anglers. Extended fishery jurisdiction is generally in their interest, from whatever country they fish, for it can be used to exclude foreign commercial fishermen. In one case, U.S. sports fishermen even instigated a Panamanian seizure and fine of a U.S. tuna boat, beyond limits recognized by the U.S. government.

U.S. commercial fishing contributed about $500 million annually to the U.S. economy during the 1960s and employed approximately 225,000 fishermen in 1968. The industry is predominately coastal. Between 1964 and 1966, for example, about 89 percent of the value of the U.S. catch came off U.S. coasts, while only 11 percent was taken off foreign coasts. Between 1964 and 1966, about 22 percent of the value of the U.S. catch was taken between twelve and two hundred miles off the U.S. coast, or twice the value taken off foreign coasts. U.S. coastal fishermen would like very much for the United States to claim two-hundred-mile exclusive fishing jurisdiction. But it is not even clear that the balance—if limited only to fishing interests—would favor coastal fishermen, in spite of the fact that they take twice as much between twelve and two hundred miles off the U.S. coast as the high seas fleets take off foreign coasts. The United States could go to two hundred miles with only marginal benefits for coastal fishermen at the expense of destroying the U.S. tuna fleet.

The U.S. tuna fleet, more than all other U.S. fishing interests combined, needs access to waters between twelve and two hundred miles off foreign coasts. The U.S. fleet cannot afford to pay taxes to coastal states for the right to fish, because it is not in a monopoly position, but operates in an extremely competitive world market with Japanese and other tuna fleets, which, for economic and technical reasons, can fish profitably for tuna beyond two hundred miles (which the U.S. fleet cannot yet do). Thus the Japanese fleet would not be subject to coastal state taxation if a two-hundred-mile limit existed.

While most U.S. commercial fishing is in a period of economic decline, the tuna fleet presents a sharp contrast. One of the most modern and rapidly growing U.S. fleets, it is the world's most efficient tuna harvester. It is one of the few U.S. fishing industries able to compete on world markets. Since its founding in the early 1900's, it has survived and prospered without any tariff protection. This has benefited Peru and Japan, which have both been able to export tuna to the United States duty free. The U.S. fleet is not owned by great corporations but by individual entrepreneurs; while some have become wealthy, the risks of the industry are great and unpredictable, and future profitability is clouded by unrestricted new-vessel entry. In reliance on U.S. policy, boat owners have invested more than $100 million in more than a hundred boats. If the two-hundred-mile doctrine could be confined to Peru, or if the two-hundred-mile doctrine did not include taxation power, or if it were economically possible to fish beyond two hundred miles, the U.S. fleet could live with the two hundred miles. But unrestricted coastal state authority to tax or to exclude foreign fishermen could bring collapse of the tuna fleet. It is understandable, therefore, that tuna-boat owners, led by the well-organized and well financed American Tunaboat Association have fought the two-hundred-mile doctrine vigorously.

The U.S. tuna industry has other important elements. While U.S. fishermen land on the order of $50 million worth of tuna annually, a half-dozen canneries (Star-Kist, Van Camp, Westgate-California, Bumble Bee, Del Monte, C.H.B., and I.B.E.C.) convert the U.S. catch, plus imports, to canned tuna valued at approximately $250 million retail. Canners are primarily interested in obtaining as much raw tuna as possible at the lowest possible cost; they would also like to control their sources of supply. Through long-term financial arrangements, canners indirectly control about half the U.S. tuna fleet. Because the two hundred miles threatens the U.S. source of supply, canners tend to support the fishermen.

Probably the most vigorous champion of the boat owner's cause is organized labor. In southern California, tuna fishermen are organized by two unions: Fishermen's Union, Local 33, ILWU (Independent) and the Cannery Workers and Fishermen's Union of the Pacific, SIU, AFL-CIO. The unions, particularly Local 33, have taken strong stands on the two hundred miles, because the controversy not only threatens members' jobs, but also their lives. Following Peruvian and Ecuadorean seizures in 1970, the executive secretary-treasurer of Local 33 wrote President Nixon threatening to take private retaliatory action unless the conflict was settled.

New U.S. retaliation against Peru is likely to bring Peruvian retaliation against U.S. fishing investments in Peru. Van Camp, Del Monte, and Star-Kist have investments in Peru and Ecuador. Star-Kist controls Peru's fourth largest fish-meal enterprise. U.S.-controlled companies produce roughly one-fourth of Peru's fish meal; the annual value of their production is about $70 million—nearly twice the total value of U.S. tuna landings.

The United States also has important conservation interests affected by the two hundred miles. A two-hundred-mile conservation limit, internationally recognized, could greatly simplify conservation problems, by eliminating the need to negotiate conservation agreements in many cases. Another U.S. conservation interest is the Inter-American Tropical Tuna Commission. The United States would like Peru to become a member. U.S. opposition to the two hundred miles is probably the major reason why Peru is not a member. Thus U.S. policy may undermine U.S. conservation objectives.

Peruvian Interests

ECONOMIC

Peru has vital economic interests in the two-hundred-mile doctrine. Its largest present economic interest, the fish-meal industry, developed many years after the claim. Beginning in the 1950s Peru began exploiting its vast anchovy fishery, and by the early 1960s Peru was the world's number one fishing nation (by volume). (Peruvian lawyers claim this could not have happened without the two-hundred-mile limit.) In 1967, for example, Peru landed more than twenty-two billion pounds of fish—16.7 percent of the world's total. The anchovy is converted to fish meal (used as an additive in poultry feed) and to fish oil, for export to European markets, although about one-fourth goes to the United States. In 1967, fish-meal and fish-oil exports earned more than $200 million for Peru—close to 27 percent of exports.

Because the anchovy fishery is being utilized at its maximum sustainable yield, for economic and biological reasons no additional fishing effort should be applied. Although most anchovy fishing occurs within twelve miles of the coast (about 50 to 60 percent), the fishery extends up to forty miles from shore, but some years currents shift and it might move farther out. Twelve-mile fishery jurisdiction is inadequate to protect Peru's "ownership interest" in the anchovy fishery from foreign exploitation. The Declaration of Santiago is particularly beneficial to the fish-meal industry, because it precludes Chilean anchovy fishing off Peru. (Chile also has a large fish-meal industry, and some incidents have occurred along the Peru-Chile sea border.) Peru's fish-meal industry would probably be pleased with the new U.S. proposal to expand the "special interest" of the coastal state to include the right to a fixed percentage of the catch. Since Peru's industry now takes nearly all the anchovy, its interest would be protected against the threat of foreign fishing.

But Peru also has important *future* interests in fisheries off its coasts. Present Peruvian fish catch is valued at about $300 million annually. It has been estimated that this could be increased to $800 million or more if hake, tuna, and other resources within the two hundred miles were fully developed. Because fishery development requires relatively little capital, skilled labor, or infrastructure, it offers one of the most promising areas for future growth in Peru's economy.

Another vital aspect of Peru's claim is its future interests in mineral deposits in the sea bed out to two hundred miles. Although the resources located in this zone are not fully known, some Peruvian experts believe that Peru's interest in these minerals may well exceed the value of all living resources in the sea above. In any event, Peru feels that its exclusive jurisdiction over these mineral resources is essential to its future economic growth and development.

Peru has other economic interests affected by the two hundred miles. It is genuinely interested in development of an effective conservation program for all Humboldt Current resources. Consequently, with Chile and Ecuador, it supports the Permanent Commission of the South Pacific in its efforts to formulate regional regulations covering fisheries overlapping its maritime frontiers

with Chile and Ecuador. Peru also has a slight revenue interest in
the two-hundred-mile regime, for under its foreign fishing regulations, it earns a few hundred thousand dollars annually, but would
earn substantially more if the limit were generally recognized.

Some Peruvian economic interests are adversely affected by the
two-hundred-mile doctrine and the controversy. For example, one
of the Star-Kist–owned Peruvian companies fishes tuna off Peru,
Ecuador, and other countries. Consequently, its vessels must purchase licenses to fish within two hundred miles of some of these
countries; such license fees add production costs and reduce profits.
Perhaps the most serious economic harm is indirect. The conflict
affects the climate for foreign investment, although it would be
impossible to estimate the volume of investment it has deterred.
The conflict also affects U.S. congressional attitudes toward Peru,
but it would be difficult to calculate how much has been slashed
from foreign assistance requests due to the conflict.

POLITICAL

The two-hundred-mile question is probably one of the most effective political issues in Peruvian politics. Defense of national
"sovereignty" has emotional appeal. In a country where bravery
and courage are more important than friendship with the United
States or economic and scientific arguments, the picture of tiny
Peru standing up against the "great economic colossus of the north"
wins votes. The fact that no Peruvian interest group is greatly
harmed by the claim could allow politicians to take extreme positions in its defense. While the two-hundred-mile issue has not been
exploited in Peruvian political campaigns as it has been in other
countries, no political figure, including members of a military government, could advocate a change in Peru's position without risk-
ing political suicide. The political force of the two hundred miles is
heightened by Peruvian mass media, which has publicized the
claim and seizures of U.S. "pirate" boats for so many years that the
average man on the street in Lima is aware of the two-hundred-
mile "Peruvian Sea" and the U.S. challenge.

It is the kind of political issue that serves anti-U.S. subversive
forces. It is also the type of political issue that inevitably leads to
international conflicts. David F. Belnap of the *Los Angeles Times*,

an astute observer of the two-hundred-mile controversy, has noted, "So sacred has the issue become that a government functionary who even appears not to accept it in all of its blind, nationalistic aspects seriously risks being accused of treasonous behavior."[72] No Peruvian government could abandon the claim, or enter any agreement that seemed to be a retreat, and remain in power very long.

PSYCHOLOGICAL FACTORS

Powerful psychological forces have been generated in Peru by U.S. policy and action. From Peruvians' point of view, the United States challenged Peru's sovereignty and independence, questioned its judgment, repudiated its well-reasoned legal arguments, offended its president, and snubbed its diplomats. The United States unintentionally offended Peru's national pride and honor, and in Peru and all of Latin America defense of honor is extremely important. The desire to uphold national honor—to prove that Peru has not violated the law of nations—has combined with deep resentment of apparent U.S. inconsistencies and "economic imperialism" to form a deep psychological interest in Peru's legal position.

The desire to protect Peru's position produced two trends in Peruvian legal thinking. First was that Peru's claim was valid under existing international law. For more than two decades, Peruvian lawyers labored to prove the point. The second position—far more threatening to U.S. interests—was that if Peru had violated the law, then the law was wrong and ought to be changed. This attitude resulted in an aggressive foreign policy from 1948 through the early 1950s and again after 1965 and into the 1970s. It is a foreign policy aimed at hemispheric and Third World establishment of the two-hundred-mile thesis and the principles of the 1970 Declaration of Montevideo (which did not mention the two hundred miles). Peruvians obviously derive a certain satisfaction from being the world leader of this movement.

On a psychological level, the conflict may be a test of U.S. friendship, for if the United States is a true and understanding friend, then it will recognize the two hundred miles. Thus, Peruvians seek U.S. recognition not only for economic reasons, but also

[72] *Los Angeles Times,* Dec. 19, 1969, p. 32, col. 1.

for psychological reasons, and Peru's many written defenses of its position over the years reflect a strong motivation to rationalize and explain its past actions.

ANALYSIS OF U.S. AND PERUVIAN OPTIONS

U.S. Options

A vast range of U.S. options exist, including the possibilities of using an Antarctic Treaty as a basis for compromise, using private efforts to reach a settlement, modifying U.S. legislation to prevent vessel seizures, reducing or increasing U.S. tariffs, and using various military devices. Only four U.S. alternatives are considered here because these are the options most relevant to current U.S. policy: (1) a bilateral nonlegal settlement with Peru; (2) an international conference; (3) a bilateral legal compromise; and (4) acceptance of Peru's two-hundred-mile limit by international agreement.

Both the policy of a negotiated settlement with Peru avoiding the legal issues and the policy of an international conference to resolve the legal questions are to a large extent counterproductive. If the assumption that any U.S.-Peruvian compromise on the legal issues would produce new harmful claims in other parts of the world is correct, then it is difficult to see why a compromise on any other basis would produce a different result. A nonlegal compromise could have even more serious consequences. If Peru were to agree to stop seizing U.S. fishing vessels in exchange for U.S. tariff reductions, technical or financial assistance, or any other concessions, such an agreement would establish a precedent. Other countries would be inspired to make extravagant claims in order to secure whatever U.S. concessions they could. Thus a nonlegal settlement with Peru could be as harmful to U.S. interests as a bilateral legal compromise.

Similarly, an international conference could prove harmful to U.S. interests. The mere suggestion encourages coastal states to quickly make new claims. Also the United States seems willing to accept whatever two-thirds of the delegates adopt, although the final decision rests, of course, with the president and Senate. But the U.S. position, if carried to its logical conclusion, would be acceptance of the two-hundred-mile "territorial sea," if that is what the world decides. This stance gives Peru incentive it would not otherwise have to sign up new members in the "two-hundred-mile club" throughout Africa, Asia, and Latin America with the utmost speed. Thus instead of discouraging the two-hundred-mile movement, a conference may cause it to spread more rapidly.

In addition, both policies may fail. An agreement avoiding the legal issues that would stop boat seizures seems to me an impossibility. Under Peruvian law, foreigners may not fish within two hundred miles without Peru's consent. If Peru agrees not to enforce its regulations against U.S. fishermen, it has compromised its position. The United States has offered a number of "nonlegal" formulas since 1955; Peru has accepted none. As a political matter, it is unlikely that a Peruvian government could allow U.S. fishermen within two hundred miles in exchange for concessions—however favorable to Peru financially—for the agreement would be open to the political charge that Peru had sold "national sovereignty to the rich Yankees." Thus the prospects for such a settlement are dim. Talks, nevertheless, should continue, for they help improve relations even if no agreement is ever reached.

An international conference is based on at least two assumptions: that two-thirds of the delegations could reach agreement (i.e., that the law is ripe for codification), and that Peru would accept the outcome. Three world attempts in this century—in 1930, 1958, and 1960—have failed. National interests in the sea are greater now than in 1960, and world practice is more diverse. The odds that an agreement could be found are probably less than before the earlier conferences. Assuming an agreement is reached, it is doubtful whether Peru would feel any obligation to accept it. While Peru might be willing to negotiate its position on a bilateral basis, it is far less willing to reduce its claims for all countries. Peru's national interests are limited and do not require substantial concessions to world opinion. In addition, Peruvians feel that a conference is a U.S.-Soviet conspiracy to defeat the two-hundred-mile movement. Finally, the United States failed to gain Peru's trust and confidence before beginning work toward a new conference. While this omission might be remedied, it has already negatively influenced Peruvian attitudes. Thus it is possible that both aspects of U.S. policy toward Peru's claim will fail.

In view of this possibility, it is appropriate to reexamine the arguments against bilateral legal compromise. The United States has discarded this option, at least in part because it believes any recognition would risk disastrous repercussions throughout the world. This belief—based largely on fear of the unknown and deductive logic—may well be valid. It is beyond the scope of this paper to prove or disprove the assumption. That harmful consequences may follow from U.S. recognition is reasonable. The assumption, however, is also injuring vital U.S. interests in Peru and Latin America. The United States cannot afford to make important foreign policy decisions on reasonable assumptions alone. Common sense dictates that a more careful and thorough analysis be made.

Theoretically, an infinite range of possibilities for U.S. recognition exist. Some "recognition possibilities" might produce more harmful results than others. U.S. recognition of Peru's "right" to claim whatever it wants, for example, is more likely to provoke new claims than a more carefully qualified recognition.[73] Assume that several possible compromises would be acceptable to Peru and the United States (setting aside, for the moment, any external impact of the precedent). The next step would be to forecast probable external consequences within an acceptable margin of error. This determination must be empirical. It should be possible, for example, to contract an independent research organization to evaluate probable world reaction, on a country-by-country basis, to each "recognition possibility." A model might be constructed, based upon such studies and other relevant data about each country, for computer analysis of these questions so that answers would be based on scientific evidence rather than assumptions based more on fear than careful analysis. Such an approach might minimize the risks to the point where the benefits of a U.S.-Peruvian settlement would outweigh the foreseeable costs.

Another obstacle to a bilateral legal compromise is the U.S. as-

---

[73] As a qualified recognition, for example, the United States might, as a first move, consider recognition of Peruvian conservation over certain species, or exclusive exploitation jurisdiction over particular species, or areas for a limited period of time (such as until Peru recovers from its earthquake disaster) and upon other terms and conditions. The United States might explain its proposal in advance to all other countries: that the agreement would be a unique assistance program, that it would be part of U.S. inter-American policy and no change in international law, and that the United States would appreciate restraint and understanding.

sumption of "creeping jurisdiction." This assumption is also unproven. In some cases jurisdiction may creep, in others it may re-
cede. One possibility is that U.S. opposition to the two hundred
miles is a force moving some countries toward the two-hundred-
mile "territorial sea," since such a claim is more an anti-U.S. statement than an expression of real national interests. Ample evidence
supports the argument that U.S. opposition was a major factor in
the decisions of Ecuador, Panama, Uruguay, Argentina, Brazil,
and El Salvador to claim a two-hundred-mile territorial sea.
Whether "creeping jurisdiction" or U.S. policy is the greater threat
to stability in the law of the sea is a question of fact that should be
demonstrable by careful analysis. Information on this subject can
be quantified. Proposed and actual claims of each coastal state are
known. U.S. protests, diplomatic representations, official statements, and other actions are known, and it should be possible to
determine the correlation, if any, between U.S. policy and certain
claims. Until a working model is constructed, it will be difficult to
test the validity of either argument.

The fourth U.S. option concerns international acceptance of
Peru's claim. The United States, at some point, may have to deal
with the possibility that no agreement will be acceptable to Peru
that does not preserve the two-hundred-mile figure. In some countries, particularly Peru, the two-hundred-mile figure has powerful
political implications that overshadow the economic questions.
Even if Peru were to receive, by international convention, all the
economic benefits it now claims, the convention might be unacceptable for purely political and psychological reasons. Thus the
United States may have to deal with the political mystique of the
two-hundred miles. This might be approached in at least two ways:

First, the United States contends it cannot recognize Peru's
"right" to two hundred miles without conceding this right to every
other coastal state. This, too, is an unproven assumption. It is possible that if the case were properly handled, Peru could be given
two hundred miles for certain purposes, while other states would be
willing to accept less than two hundred miles, but for other purposes. In short, it might be possible to construct a stable world
regime that would take into account the specific geographic, ecological, and economic factors peculiar to each country. An international administrative body might be established to adjust claims

from time to time. A diverse but stable regime is one possibility meriting careful U.S. consideration.

Second, the United States refuses to accept two-hundred-mile jurisdiction for all countries because it believes that *no* two-hundred-mile regime would be in the best interests of the world community. The United States supports this contention with the Argentine case. After Argentina went to two hundred miles and substantially increased fees for foreign fishing, total fish catch off Argentina declined because it was uneconomic for foreigners to fish. This development was contrary to the best interests of a hungry world. Coastal state authority to tax foreign fishing without restriction—even within three or twelve miles—is contrary to the best interests of mankind. Unrestricted taxation deters fishing, increases production costs, reduces profits and competition; less fish is produced and at higher costs, while the coastal state enjoys revenue in exchange for which it produces nothing. But these considerations fail to prove the argument that no two-hundred-mile regime could serve world economic interests.

If such revenue could be used only for fishery research or if coastal states had authority limited to establishment of exclusive fishing zones within two hundred miles for particular species, based on the coastal state's actual exploitation capacity, such schemes might well produce more fish at lower costs and provide a beneficial reallocation of resources between developed and developing nations. It is not contended that this example would in fact provide a rational two-hundred-mile regime. The answer involves complex economic analysis of the comparative costs of fishery development and exploitation on a country-by-country basis, which is beyond the scope of this paper. Nor is it argued that a rational two-hundred-mile regime exists in theory, but it could. The Latin American countries may not understand the issues well enough to propose a two-hundred-mile regime that would serve world interests. It might therefore be appropriate and in the best interests of the United States for it to make such a determination. If a rational two-hundred-mile regime could be devised, it might form the basis for international negotiation. Nothing would be lost by such a study; if no rational regime could be conceived, the traditional U.S. position would be strengthened. On the other hand, if it were shown that the two-hundred-mile regime most favorable to world interests was less efficient than some other scheme, in the interests of securing agreement, it might be the best compromise. The benefits from stability and uniformity might far outweigh the costs of a slightly inefficient system.

Thus the United States must first identify all assumptions governing present U.S. policy. These assumptions must then be examined empirically to determine whether they are in fact valid or whether some alternative possibility is more likely to be true. The validity of none of the critical assumptions underlying present U.S. policy have been demonstrated beyond a reasonable doubt. A much higher degree of certainty is possible and essential to protect adequately the vital national interests of the United States.

Peruvian Options

Peru is the leader of the two-hundred-mile movement in Latin America and feels that vital national interests dictate that its claim be recognized by the United States. If the United States is unwilling to accept Peru's position on a bilateral basis or is dedicated to undermining Peru's position, then Peru is prepared to strengthen its position by making its claim, and other two-hundred-mile claims, invulnerable to foreign pressure. Peruvian options for making its position absolutely uncompromisable within Peru and nonnegotiable, through alliance with others in Latin America, Africa, and Asia are numerous, and the United States must be aware of these Peruvian alternatives. Some Peruvians feel that conflict with the United States serves Peruvian interests. (I pass no judgment on what Peru's best interests are.) Because of this view, even if the United States were to recognize two-hundred-mile Peruvian resource jurisdiction, the conflict might continue and affect U.S. aviation and shipping. If a Peruvian government wants conflict with the United States, no settlement is possible. Other Peruvians believe that Peru's highest national interests are best served by friendship and cooperation with the United States. Assuming the latter proposition to be true, Peru can do several things to improve relations in this area:

First, if boat seizures continue, the United States Congress will retaliate, and such retaliation will only intensify the conflict and make rational settlement more difficult to the detriment of U.S.-Peruvian relations. If U.S. congressional retaliation is not desired, then Peru could eliminate this risk by refraining from seizing U.S. vessels.

Second, Peru could address itself to the questions the United States has raised concerning world interests. Peru has asked that changes be made in the international legal order to permit it to exercise two-hundred-mile jurisdiction. Peru has justified this request by showing that the United States has been inconsistent and hypocritical in its position. This appears to be true. Peru has also justified its action with a rational argument based upon geographic, ecological, and economic factors unique to Peru. If the international order should be changed (even if the change is limited to Peru), this should only be done if it serves the best interests of the world community. It should not matter that the United States has acted on self-interest in the recent past; nor should it matter that Peru's coast is arid and that its people are poor. If resources were to be allocated on the basis of equity, then all of Peru's vast fishery wealth should go to the people of India, China, or to others more needy than Peruvians. No argument yet advanced by Peru shows that the change Peru advocates would serve the best economic interests of the entire world community. Peru's claim may well be in the best interests of the world, but the burden of making this showing is Peru's.

To meet its burden of proof, Peru and other two-hundred-mile claimants could commission a comprehensive economic study, not by Peruvians, but by disinterested professional economists. It should not be based on speculation or reasonable assumptions but should be rooted in world economic realities. Such a study could be costly, for it would require the most advanced tools of econometrics, comparative economics and considerable computer time. The hypothesis Peru must test is whether exclusive coastal state resource jurisdiction to conserve, develop, and exploit living and mineral resources to the distance the coastal state believes is reasonable would produce a net benefit for the world. If Peru's thesis could be persuasively demonstrated—and it would require a country-by-country analysis—the United States and others would have few alternatives other than supporting Peru.

Third, Peru might consider the alternatives for achieving the objectives of the two-hundred-mile doctrine without using the figure "two hundred miles." It may be that the two-hundred-mile figure is the best way of protecting vital Peruvian interests; on the other hand, this is also an unproven assumption. If protection of Peru's vital economic interests is more important than vindication of the two hundred miles, then alternative means may be more effective. The two-hundred-mile figure was intended as only a *means* and not an *end* in itself. Because of U.S. reluctance to accept the two-hundred-mile figure, it has obvious limited utility. At the present time, the United States appears willing to make substantial concessions in the interest of securing international uniformity. Through constructive cooperation with the United States, Peru may be able to protect all or most of its economic interests in marine resources without reference to two hundred miles. It is not only for protection of U.S. tuna fishermen that the United States opposes the two-hundred–miles, but primarily for military reasons. If Peru can offer creative alternatives to the United States, it may be possible to find a mutually acceptable solution protecting Peruvian economic interests and U.S. military interests. At any rate, both the United States and Peru have options that could lead to a rational solution.

Supplementary Materials on the Fisheries Dispute

The Proclamation signed by President Truman on September 28, 1945, on the "Policy of the United States with Respect to the Natural Resources of the Subsoil and Sea Bed of the Continental Shelf" read:

By the President of the United States of America

A PROCLAMATION

Whereas the Government of the United States of America, aware of the long range world-wide need for new sources of *petroleum and other minerals*, holds the view that efforts to discover and make available new supplies of these resources should be encouraged; and

Whereas its competent experts are of the opinion that such resources underlie many parts of the continental shelf off the coasts of the United States of America, and that with modern technological progress their utilization is already practicable or will become so at an early date; and

Whereas recognized jurisdiction over these resources is required in the interest of their conservation and prudent utilization when and as development is undertaken; and

Whereas it is the view of the Government of the United States that the exercise of jurisdiction over the *natural resources of the subsoil and sea bed* of the continental shelf by the contiguous nation is reasonable and just, since the effectiveness of measures to utilize or conserve these resources would be contingent upon cooperation and protection from the shore, since the continental shelf may be regarded as an extension of the land-mass of the coastal nation and thus naturally appurtenant to it, since these resources frequently form a seaward extension of a pool or deposit lying within the territory, and since self-protection compels the coastal nation to keep close watch over activities off its shores which are of the nature necessary for utilization of these resources;

Now, therefore, I, Harry S. Truman, President of the United States of America, do hereby proclaim the following policy of the United States of America with respect to the *natural resources of the subsoil and sea bed* of the continental shelf.

Having concern for the urgency of conserving and prudently utilizing its natural resources, the Government of the United States regards the *natural resources of the subsoil and sea bed* of the continental shelf beneath the high seas but contiguous to the coasts of the United States as appertaining to the United States, subject to its jurisdiction and control. In cases where the continental shelf extends to the shores of another State, or is shared with an adjacent State, the boundary shall be determined by the United States and the State concerned in accordance with equitable principles. *The character as high seas of the waters above the continental shelf and the right to their free and unimpeded navigation are in no way thus affected.*

In witness whereof, I have hereunto set my hand and caused the seal of the United States of America to be affixed.

Done at the City of Washington this twenty-eighth day of September, in the year of our Lord nineteen hundred and forty-five, and of the Independence of the United States of America the one hundred and seventieth.

Harry S. Truman

President Truman's Proclamation, signed September 28, 1945, known as the "Fisheries Proclamation," read in full:

Policy of the United States with Respect to Coastal Fisheries
in Certain Areas of the High Seas
By the President of the United States of America

A PROCLAMATION

Whereas for some years the Government of the United States of America has viewed with concern the inadequacy of present arrangements for the protection and perpetuation of the fishery resources contiguous to its coasts, and in view of the potentially disturbing effect of this situation, has carefully studied the possibility of improving the jurisdictional basis for conservation measures and international cooperation in this field; and

Whereas such fishery resources have a special importance to coastal communities as a source of livelihood and to the nation as a food and industrial resource; and

Whereas the progressive development of new methods and techniques contributes to intensified fishing over wide sea areas and in certain cases seriously threatens fisheries with depletion; and

Whereas there is an urgent need to protect coastal fishery resources from destructive exploitation, having due regard to conditions peculiar to each region and situation and to the special rights and equities of the coastal State and of any other State which may have established a legitimate interest therein;

Now, Therefore, I, Harry S. Truman, President of the United States of America, do hereby proclaim the following policy of the United States of America with respect to coastal fisheries in certain areas of the high seas:

In view of the pressing need for conservation and protection of fishery resources, the Government of the United States regards it as proper to establish conservation zones in those areas of the high seas contiguous to the coasts of the United States wherein fishing activities have been or in the future may be developed and maintained on a substantial scale. Where such activities have been or shall hereafter be developed and maintained by its nationals alone, the United States regards it as proper to establish explicitly bounded conservation zones in which fishing activities shall be subject to the regulation and control of the United States. Where such activities have been or shall hereafter be legitimately developed and maintained jointly by nationals of the United States and nationals of other States, explicitly bounded conservation zones may be established *under agreements between the United States and such other States*; and all fishing activities in such zones shall be subject to regulation and control *as provided in such agreements*. The right of any State to establish conservation zones off its shores in accordance with the above principles is conceded, *provided that corresponding recognition is given to any fishing interests of nationals of the United States which may exist in such areas*. The character as high seas of the areas in which such conservation zones are established and the right to their free and unimpeded navigation are in no way thus affected.

In witness whereof, I have hereunto set my hand and caused the seal of the United States of America to be affixed.

Done at the City of Washington this twenty-eighth day of September, in the year of our Lord nineteen hundred and forty-five, and of the Independence of the United States of America the one hundred and seventieth.

                                                     Harry S. Truman

CRITIQUE OF "THE FISHERIES DISPUTE" BY DAVID C. LORING*

Vice-Admiral Luis Edgardo Llosa, Peruvian Navy (retired)

Importance of Mr. Loring's Paper

"The Fisheries Dispute" by Mr. David C. Loring, written for the Peru Policy Project of the Adlai Stevenson Institute of International Affairs is, in my judgment, serious, objective, and, above all, courageous because, by studying in depth the causes of the conflict that have harmed relations between Peru and the United States, the paper reveals, as with a surgeon's scalpel, the errors of U.S. foreign policy and exposes them to the light of reality, showing the "solutions" over the past quarter of a century that have led to a very difficult situation.

* Translated from the original Spanish by the editor and Miss Molly Older and approved by Admiral Llosa.

Over such a long period of time, almost enough to form a new generation, I have read about this topic in more than one hundred pieces in newspapers, magazines, and books by reporters, writers, and other professionals in the field, and I must confess that I have never encountered the clarity, objectivity, and sincerity in recognizing one country's errors (those of the U.S. State Department) as in the work by Mr. Loring.

I may disagree with some aspects of his study, but I cannot deny that it is inspired by the sincere and rational proposition of finding solutions that will be acceptable to the governments and to the highly sensitive public opinions of both countries.

What the Paper Proves

1. The intransigent attitude of the United States in opposing the Peruvian declaration proclaiming exclusive Peruvian jurisdiction and sovereignty over the two-hundred-mile zone, does not respond, as the government says it does, to a traditional juridical position, since there exists an impressive record of transgressions of customary norms of International Maritime Laws, which occurred each time U.S. economic interests or military security were involved.

2. The need to change the limit of the territorial sea for the protection of the fishery areas, or the need to establish a special jurisdiction of a coastal state over such a fishery area, has not simply been a Peruvian invention but rather has existed in fact and in law, and in the minds and in the actions of many statesmen, congressmen, and intellectuals in the United States, particularly in the mind of President Franklin Delano Roosevelt.

3. As Peru has always said, it was precisely the unilateral action of the United States, effected through the two declarations by President Truman in 1945, that generated the chain reaction in other countries in favor of changing the norms and concepts of the law of the sea, which no longer is responsive to the advances of science and technology, nor, fundamentally, to the needs of a nation on the road to development.

4. The twelve-mile fishing-maritime jurisdiction of the United States, by unilateral declaration in October of 1966, invoking reasons that do not substantially differ from those used now by nations of the South Pacific, places the United States in the same legal position as those nations.

5. The attitude of the United States, upon becoming the opposition leader against the new principles and norms of the law of the sea is, for the above reasons, unacceptable to Peru and to the other Latin

American countries that have denied the moral and legal validity of
the North American position, because of contradictions with previous
declarations and actions of the United States. (In effect the United
States is therefore "estopped.")

6. Since the individual Peruvian and Chilean declarations of 1947
and the Declaration of Santiago of 1952, which created the two-hundred-mile maritime zone and the South Pacific System, the majority of
the Western Hemisphere nations with a seacoast have adopted similar
legislation that reinforces the position taken by Peru, Chile, Ecuador,
and the Regional Maritime Zone, which these three nations created.

7. Therefore, it is wrong to attempt to restrict the solution of the
problem to any unilateral action Peru might take, inasmuch as the
matter has taken on continental dimensions. Each day the issue ac-
quires more momentum, which will soon bring it to the attention of
the other nations of the Third World that are now beginning to realize the importance of the new rights of coastal states.

8. The greater extensions of their territorial sea that some nations
have proclaimed, including the so-called two-hundred-mile zone, respond without a doubt to socioeconomic rather than to political or
military purposes. Therefore, if recognition is given to the right of the
coastal state to exclusive jurisdiction over the fisheries and other natural resources of its contiguous sea, the width of this territorial sea
need not be modified; and the "high seas" would still maintain all
their present area; freedom of navigation and free use of air space,
which so preoccupy the United States and other naval powers, need not
be modified either.

Results of U.S. Policy

In evaluating the results of U.S. policy toward Peru (the policy of
absolute opposition to the two-hundred-mile theory and to recognition
of the preferential rights of coastal states) on the attitude in Latin
America and the rest of the world, I must conclude that the effect is
negative.

The right of coastal states to establish limits of their territorial waters in accordance with their geographical and ecological peculiarities
and with the necessities and responsibilities resulting from their various levels of development is a right that the United States has sought
to have indirectly rejected by the international community of nations. The United States supported the two conferences in Geneva in
1958 and 1960 for this purpose and to obtain approval of the three-
mile territorial seas. These efforts failed.

The problem continued to exist, with the additional irritation that the conferences served to make evident that the law of the three-mile limit, if it ever had existed as an international norm, was definitively buried in the Palace of the Nations in Geneva, leaving the road open for a larger number of states to effect unilateral proclamations extending their maritime jurisdiction.

The measures taken directly against Peru had even more negative results and have only served to cool relations between the two countries that in the past were characterized by a close friendship within a mutual respect.

The elaborate legislation adopted by the U.S. government to discourage Peru, Ecuador, and Chile from declaring a two-hundred-mile limit, such as the Foreign Assistance Act of 1965, the Naval Vessel Loan Bill of 1967, the Fishermen's Protective Act of 1967, the Foreign Military Sales Act of 1968, the famous Hickenlooper Amendment, and many other proposed laws still pending legislative approval, have not only been useless, but also counterproductive.

The threat of application of the Hickenlooper Amendment, following the IPC expropriation in Peru and the capture and fining of a North American fishing boat, brought the two countries to the point of breaking diplomatic relations and brought about Peru's turning to the East in search of markets that would replace the North American market.

The May 1969 application of the Foreign Military Sales Act in Peru over the capture of a North American clipper, brought as a consequence the immediate departure of the U.S. military missions that had been in Peru since 1923, when the first North American naval mission arrived in Peru. (This was also the first U.S. naval mission in Latin America.)

Later, when the United States tried to put up an economic embargo around Peru in order to keep her from receiving any outside help, the reaction was to look for continental solidarity which took concrete form in the "Consensus of Viña del Mar," which was approved in the meeting of CECLA on the ministerial level in May of 1969 and which adopted almost without modifications the Peruvian Doctrine on International Cooperation, formulated by the Peruvian Foreign Ministry.

This Consensus constitutes the most open rejection of the above-named legislative amendments by approving the principle that says, "Foreign aid must be given without any conditions whatever which would pervert its real purpose and which, moreover, would be harmful to the dignity and sovereignty of nations, would have prejudicial consequences for the economic and social development of the people."

Finally, as stated above, new nations were added to the list of the "two-hundred-mile club" practically closing the chain that protects the maritime interests of South American countries.

This has been in summary the result of a U.S. policy toward Peru that I am sorry to have to label as mistaken.

Analysis of Options Open to Peru and the United States

UNITED STATES DIPLOMATIC OPTIONS

1. It is almost impossible to imagine an agreement between the two countries in which fishing rights are traded for economic concessions granted by the United States.

2. It would also be useless to seek approval of the "abstention principle" at a new world conference, since such a principle, in the unlikely case it were approved, would cover only fishing for anchoveta, but would leave other fishing interests of equal importance to Peru without protection.

3. The measures to maintain the status quo, which prevent the aggravation of the conflict, particularly because of the sensitivity on both sides, seem reasonable and convenient.

4. The same can be said of the private action of the North American tuna industry, which can, by means of direct negotiation, try to better the present situation, thus avoiding the political and juridical aspects of the controversy.

5. Economic measures of a repressive nature should be forgotten because of the natural reactions they can generate in the economic and political fields of the country to which they are applied. For example, there is the experience of what happened in Peru when application of the Hickenlooper Amendment and the Foreign Military Sales Act was threatened.

6. On the other hand, positive economic incentives could help in an indirect way—if not in the definitive solution of the conflict, at least in the alleviation of the causes of tension.

7. Any military sanction considered against Peru should be discarded because of the grave repercussion it would have.

PERUVIAN OPTIONS

1. Peru might exercise her influence over the other countries that have proclaimed the two-hundred-mile limit, in order to bring the new maritime rules into being. She might cease her political activity in Latin America in order to obtain favorable legislation on the two-hundred-mile limit and to encourage the rejection of the two-hundred-mile limit by other countries. But it would be quite naive to think that such measures could be adopted by our country.

Peru needs to fortify her position, and it is logical that she would look for support not only from South American nations but also from all the nations of the Third World that find themselves in similar situations. It is necessary to recognize that the policy which up until now has had the most complete success is that of the "two-hundred-mile club," which gains more adherents each day, and that the proclaimed doctrine of the three countries of the Pacific Coast appears in process of conversion into a truly Latin American Doctrine on Law of the Sea.

2. To cease capturing U.S. tuna boats while negotiations are taking place can be favorable, but only under the condition that the proposal come from the tuna-boat owners themselves. Peru as a nation cannot negotiate its sovereignty, but it can listen to reasonable requests that tend to eliminate the causes of the conflict.

3. Reduction of domestic publicity could be an immediate consequence of measures taken by the press, the economic sectors, and the political sectors of the United States.

4. Abandonment of the two-hundred-mile territorial sea theory in exchange for obtaining exclusive jurisdiction over the two hundred miles is a proposition that seems reasonable but one that requires the previous assurance that the right of that coastal state will be recognized in any world conference. It is up to the United States to initiate a movement along these lines, and the sooner the better.

5. Scientific cooperation between the United States and Peru for the conservation and development of the fisheries of the southeastern Pacific is necessary and convenient. Peru has not opposed this, nor will she ever oppose it. At present there is an exchange of information and consultation among the scientific organizations of both countries. This cooperation should be increased.

6. The possibility that a new world conference will be convened at the request of the United States and the Soviet Union to attempt to adapt in definitive form the twelve-mile territorial sea seriously preoccupies Peru and all other American governments. In the terms in which the conference has been proposed by both powers, a clear purpose emerges of ending the aspirations of the developing countries which, like Peru, base their hopes on the full utilization of the resources of the sea along their coasts. As long as the danger exists of such a meeting being convened, one cannot hope for an attitude favorable for the solution of the present conflict by means of conciliation. The advisable thing would be for the United States to influence its sometimes friend, the Soviet Union, to desist from trying to convene such a meeting. This would be, to our minds, the most positive and urgent step that the United States could take to avoid a deeper division within the nations that make up the international community.

Recommended Courses of Action

In summary, I believe that in the present circumstances the measures which would have the most influence in solving the existing conflict between Peru and the United States, or at least in preventing its deterioration, would be the following:

1. Elimination of all legislative amendments that threaten the economic and political independence of the country, as well as any other repressive measure of economic character.

2. Lifting the customs duties that impede the entry of Peruvian fisheries products into the North American market.

3. Elimination or modification of the Fishermen's Protective Act, which encourages violations of the Peruvian fishing regulations by fishing boats from other countries.

4. Reaching a direct understanding between the organization representing the North American tuna fishermen and the Peruvian authorities.

5. Desisting from the projected convening of a world conference on the Law of the Sea, which would attempt to obtain a uniform territorial sea limit of twelve miles.

6. Formulation of a policy that would encourage world-wide recognition of the right of coastal states to extend their maritime jurisdiction for the protection, conservation, and utilization of marine resources, maintaining reasonable limits on the territorial sea.

7. Keeping open the dialogue between the United States and the countries of the South Pacific so that, within a more favorable climate, they can seek compromise solutions while in the process of reaching a definitive agreement to the entire controversy.

I believe that prompt adoption of measures such as those suggested would bring an immediate alleviation of the tension existing not only in Peru but in all of Latin America and in nations on other continents, would help to improve relations between the United States and all of these nations, and would contribute toward the assurance of peace and well-being among the less-favored nations that are struggling to escape from underdevelopment.

Note of Clarification

Finally, I ought to state for the record that the opinions expressed in this document are my own and do not necessarily reflect the opinion of the Peruvian government or of the Peruvian Foreign Ministry, although I assume that there exists considerable coincidence between their views and mine.

John P. Powelson

4. INTERNATIONAL LENDING AGENCIES

Have the disputes over Peruvian fisheries and the nationalization of the International Petroleum Corporation influenced the behavior of the United States in the international lending agencies? Has the United States respected the independence and integrity of these agencies in carrying out their basic functions? Has the United States tried to put pressure on Peru through these agencies, and if so, is such pressure legitimate? These questions are the subject of this paper. The lending agencies examined are the Inter-American Development Bank, the International Monetary Fund, the World Bank Group, and the United Nations Development Program. Although the bilateral aid program is not examined here, nevertheless certain comparisons are made to operations through the Export-Import Bank and the Agency for International Development.

THE GRAND DESIGN

Whatever it may be, the behavior of the United States in international lending institutions must fit in "more or less" with some grand design, though the degree to which it is articulated or even fully agreed on by the players is debatable. Let us now propose three alternative sets of guidelines that might form this design. The United States does not adhere consistently to any one of these sets.

Given the pressures in a democracy such as ours, it inevitably bends, sometimes satisfying one criterion and sometimes another. Nonetheless, the extent to which the Administration leads in foreign policy, as opposed to shaping itself to dominant pressures, will be seen in how consistently it applies criteria.

The first of these three options is the "ideal," probably not achievable without the surrender of some sovereignty to international agencies. Practical choices therefore lie between the second and the third.

Option 1. The constituency of each international agency is the world community, and its purpose is to maximize world welfare in the area of its competence. By and large, such welfare coincides with the welfare of all member governments, though from time to time an agency may properly act in a way contrary to the direct interest of one. It is the duty of the United States to behave in such a way as best to achieve the goals of the agency, regardless of possible adverse implications of one incident on the welfare of the United States.

Option 2. International agencies are a means to bring about or to maintain certain world conditions that the United States deems to be in its own national interests and that are probably (and hopefully) in the interests of other member governments as well. "National" here covers interests of *all* citizens, such as their stake in international peace or in orderly world trade, and *not* the interests of particular groups.

Option 3. International agencies are a means by which each member government, the United States included, ought to promote the interests of specific groups of its own nationals, assisting them in winning competitions with nationals of other countries.

This study will show that the Department of State would handle the present Peruvian situation largely in terms of the second option. Congress, which by its nature does not represent a single opinion, is nevertheless strongly oriented toward the third option, although the so-called liberal legislators would gravitate toward the second. Though it might appear that the administration has also opted for the second ("liberal") option, for example in its unwillingness to implement the Hickenlooper Amendment, nevertheless there is evidence that it has had difficulty not only in formulating a policy but also in determining the criteria on which that policy should be based.

The second option requires further subdivision. What are the "certain world conditions" that the United States deems to be in its own national interests? With respect to both the fisheries and the International Petroleum Corporation dispute, it would seem that these conditions are the following:

1. The sanctity of contract, especially where government is a party.

2. The legitimacy of governmental continuity. Each government assumes the obligations of its predecessors.

3. The acceptance of international law in a country's definition of its rights and obligations vis-à-vis foreigners.

No one in the United States, it would seem—Congress, White House, State Department, or the business community—would deny these are goals. But the Peruvians deny them. The government of Peru also appears to be seeking "certain world conditions" deemed to be in Peruvian national interests. These would include agreement on the following:

1. The capacity to revise retroactively contracts entered into between a weak and a strong party, especially where there is no framework of national or international legislation or policy capable of adequately defending the weak. Revision would be done unilaterally by the weak party.

2. The sovereignty of governments over all matters of business activity carried on within their borders.

3. The reversal of previous breaches of sovereignty, for example decisions of international arbitration tribunals in areas that should have been subject solely to the sovereign government.

From each vantage point, both the IPC and the fisheries dispute may turn out to be only incidents in U.S. and Peruvian strategies aimed at a grand design. This is indeed why it is often so difficult for a contemporary observer to judge whether certain elements in the United States are more motivated by the second option or by the third. Yet if the U.S. strategy were entirely and consistently in favor of seeking the "world conditions" outlined above, and not at all for protecting particular interests, then it might occur to farsighted U.S. policy makers that the Peruvian and U.S. sets of conditions are not, in the long run, so contradictory as they appear in the static present. Indeed, the Mexican Revolution is a case in which sanctity of contract, legitimacy of governmental continuity, and acceptance of international law became part of the national culture (along with price stability and orthodox economic policy) when and only when the other conditions concerning abrogation of weak-strong contracts and security of national sovereignty had been properly won.

The basic facts of the IPC and fisheries disputes are covered in other papers in this volume; consequently, I will discuss the policy of the United States in international lending agencies. The National Advisory Council, consisting of certain cabinet members and the chairman of the Federal Reserve Board, is the executive vehicle for the formulation of this policy. The voices of the secretaries of state and treasury probably carry the greatest weight.

THE UNITED STATES IN INTERNATIONAL LENDING AGENCIES

Authorizations of loans for Peru by international lending agencies have appreciably slowed in 1968, 1969, and to date in 1970, and there is evidence that the United States has been instrumental in promoting the slowdown. The loans authorized to Peru by the international lending agencies from 1960 through 1969 are summarized in Table 1.

The World Bank Group authorized no loans to Peru in 1968 and 1969, and two that were in the mill at the time of the military takeover have been delayed. The signing of one Inter-American Bank loan (approved in 1968) was delayed for several months in 1969, and only one was approved (the United States abstaining) in 1969. Peru's standby with the International Monetary Fund expired in November, 1969, but was renewed in April, 1970. While this paper is not intended to cover the U.S. foreign-aid program, nevertheless it should be noted that no new AID loan authorizations for Peru were made in 1969 or to date in 1970, though technical assistance and disbursements of old loans has continued. The Export-Import Bank has approved no loans to the public sector in Peru since the IPC takeover, though some, but not all, negotiations with private business continue.

While some argue that the Hickenlooper Amendments have been informallly (though only partially) implemented by administrative decision, others explain the slowdown by the deteriorating

TABLE 1: LOAN AUTHORIZATIONS TO PERU (MILLIONS OF DOLLARS)
January 1, 1959–May 31, 1970

| | Inter-American Development Bank | | | World Bank | Export-Import Bank | Agency for International Development |
	Ordinary Capital	Fund for Special Operations	Social Progress Trust Fund			
1959	0	0	0	0	0	0
1960	0	0	0	95.8	166.8	34.9
1961	5.4	0	23.8	10.0	9.6	19.3
1962	2.5	0	2.5	0	15.3	6.0
1963	7.2	0	0	28.3	14.2	11.6
1964	1.7	0.5	9.7	3.1	38.5	24.8
1965	14.1	0	9.3	59.0	2.2	8.0
1966	*	40.7	0.5	19.1	7.7	11.1
1967	*	19.5	0	17.5	0	3.4
1968	6.5	15.1	0.9	0	28.2	14.6
1969	9.0	0	0	0	0	0
1970 to May 31	0	0	0	0	0	0

* Less than $500,000.
SOURCE: Organization of American States (unpublished data).

economic conditions in Peru from 1968 to 1970, as well as uncertainties in the economic and political structure brought about by statements of the government of Peru. It is therefore well at this time to review economic developments from 1968 to the present.

RECENT ECONOMIC DEVELOPMENTS IN PERU

From 1960 to 1964, Peruvian real gross national product increased vigorously, at an average annual rate of 6.1 percent (Table 2). In addition, the balance of payments position was strong (Table 3), with international reserves increasing from $76.1 million in 1960 to $175.7 million at the end of 1965.[1]

These healthy conditions, which were spurred by steady increases in export prices and volume, were accompanied until 1963 by only moderate increments in the money supply and consumer prices (Table 4) and only moderate government deficits, with a surplus in 1960 (Table 5).

With the advent of the Belaúnde government in 1963, however, a less orthodox economic philosophy emerged. Belaúnde's desire for "full speed ahead" investment in economic growth ran counter to an opposition Congress's reluctance to provide the necessary financing. Dominated by the unlikely bedfellows of Apristas and Odriístas, Congress seemed bent on stymying the president at every turn, whether it was in proposed fiscal legislation or in agrarian reform (although a mild law was passed in 1964) or in censure for his conduct in handling guerrillas on the sierra.

Belaúnde's response was to bypass Congress and initiate the development projects anyway. Heavy expenditures on infrastructure (such as the jungle-edge and other highways, public housing, expansion of the Chimbote steel mill, and public power plants) but inadequate taxing capacity to finance them led to increasing government deficits from 1963 on (Table 5). At first these were financed largely by foreign loans, but by 1965 they had outgrown the capacity of these sources and increasing reliance was made on the banking system. Whereas the net increase in bank claims on government from 1960 to 1963 was only 0.12 billion soles, from 1963 to 1966 it was 3.86 billion (Table 4).

The government deficits and expanding money supply led to

[1] International Financial Statistics.

TABLE 2: PERUVIAN GROSS NATIONAL PRODUCT IN REAL TERMS (BILLIONS OF SOLES) 1960–1968 (1963=100)

	1960	1961	1962	1963	1964	1965	1966	1967	1968
Personal consumption	46.84	48.82	52.70	57.12	60.41	64.00	68.60	71.68	71.79
Government consumption	5.83	6.75	7.20	7.71	9.28	9.72	10.50	11.40	10.61
Domestic investments	14.99	16.16	17.79	16.39	16.46	16.57	19.50	21.08	14.83
Exports less imports	.06	−0.94	−1.41	−2.51	0.20	−2.69	−3.54	−4.93	—
Gross national product	67.72	70.79	76.28	78.71	86.35	87.60	95.06	99.23	—

Source: International Financial Statistics, deflated by cost of living index.

TABLE 3: PERUVIAN BALANCE OF PAYMENTS

	1960	1961	1962	1963	1964	1965	1966	1967
Goods and services:								
Exports	430.0	494.2	537.9	539.8	665.6	666.2	763.0	774.2
Imports (—)	−372.8	−468.1	−541.3	−573.6	−584.1	−744.7	−817.0	−833.4
Other	− 55.5	− 42.5	− 41.2	− 58.0	− 74.4	− 87.9	−136.3	—
Transfer payments	6.2	8.1	8.5	11.1	9.0	16.1	28.5	—
Private capital	28.0	30.3	70.4	55.5	44.0	135.6	47.0	—
Government capital	− 9.3	− 11.7	8.0	3.7	19.3	64.8	182.3	—
Commercial banks	4.0	− 0.6	− 6.5	− 16.1	− 22.8	− 7.4	− 38.1	—
Monetary authorities (reserves)	32.7	− 34.3	− 5.0	− 17.9	− 23.9	− 14.3	22.0	—
Errors and omissions	2.1	24.6	− 30.8	55.5	− 32.7	− 28.4	− 51.6	—

Note: Minus sign indicates debit. Thus minus sign under "monetary authorities" means *increase* in reserves (no sign, *decrease*).
Source: International Financial Statistics.

TABLE 4: MONEY SUPPLY (BILLIONS OF SOLES) AND CONSUMER PRICES (1963=100) 1960–1969

	1960	1961	1962	1963	1964	1965	1966	1967	1968
International reserves	2.67	3.58	3.98	4.75	5.71	6.28	6.50	7.41	—
Claims on government	2.91	2.70	2.30	3.03	4.05	4.28	6.89	7.70	—
Claims on private	7.62	9.07	10.80	11.87	13.34	16.19	17.01	18.38	—
Other items	−6.64	−7.57	−9.01	−10.65	−12.60	−14.66	−16.10	−16.96	—
Total (money supply)	6.56	7.78	8.07	9.00	10.50	12.09	14.30	16.53	—
Consumer prices	82	88	94	100	110	129	141	155	185

Source: International Financial Statistics.

TABLE 5: GOVERNMENT FINANCE (BILLIONS OF SOLES) FOR YEAR ENDING DECEMBER 31

	1960	1961	1962	1963	1964	1965	1966	1967
Revenues	8.6	10.3	11.5	13.9	17.0	15.5	18.1	19.3
Expenditures	8.1	10.1	12.3	14.8	19.0	19.4	23.8	25.8
Surplus (deficit −)	0.5	0.2	− 0.8	− 0.9	− 2.0	− 3.9	− 5.7	− 6.5
Financing:								
Domestic banks	− 0.1	1.0	− 0.3	0.2	0.4	2.7	3.0	4.1
Foreign loans	− 0.3	− 0.3	0.8	1.1	1.6	0.5	2.7	2.9
Use of cash	−0.1	− 0.6	0.3	− 0.4	—	0.7	—	—

Source: International Financial Statistics.

increases in the consumer price level. Furthermore, until 1967 the exchange rate was held steady at 26.82 soles to the dollar, and rising prices coupled with no exchange depreciation led to increasing balance of payments deficits (Table 3). Though exports continued to increase because of the strong world market for Peruvian products, nevertheless imports rose faster. International liquidity, after its peak of $174.4 million at the end of 1965, dropped to $105.1 million at the end of the third quarter in 1968, just before Belaúnde fell.

The composition of foreign public debt became a serious concern. Not only did the demand for loans increase, but also the government found traditional sources unwilling to lend in the quantities needed. It therefore turned to commercial credits and other short-term debt, principally from Europe, Japan, the United States, and Canada. The foreign public debt, which had been $196.0 million at the end of 1963, rose to $754.6 million by the end of 1968.[2] The gross amount of such debt, which is less than Peru's annual exports, would be no cause for alarm, since it is not overly great in comparison to the norms of other nations. What was alarming, however, was the heavy amortization and interest foreseen over the next few years, owing to the short maturities of commercial credits. The foreign-debt service ratio (ratio of amortization and interest costs to exports) rose from 6.9 percent in 1963 to 15.6 percent in 1968.

By mid-1968, economic conditions had deteriorated so much that, to avoid complete collapse, the major political parties were obliged to reach some sort of *rapprochement* to allow the president extraordinary powers, by which he passed a new set of fiscal, monetary, and foreign exchange proposals worked out with the help of the International Monetary Fund. These included a new capital tax and revision of rates for taxes on gasoline and urban and rural property. At the same time, the government successfully negotiated a short-term rescheduling of some of its external debts, to spread them over a two- to three-year period. The prospects for sound economic policy were brighter than ever during the Belaúnde presidency before the armed forces ousted the president and assumed control of the government on October 3, 1968.

The military takeover did, however, provide the political condi-

[2] Agency for International Development (unpublished data).

tions under which the stabilization policy of 1968 could stick. The tax reform was vigorously implemented, not only through the new taxes but also through greater persistence in collection. Coupled with decreased government spending, these policies greatly reduced the fiscal deficit in 1968 and may have virtually eliminated it in 1969 and so far in 1970.[3]

Monetary policy was tightened in some ways and relaxed in others in 1969. Whereas the authorities had previously relied mainly on legal reserve requirements to control the supply of money (in 1970 the discount rate was still 9.5 percent, unchanged since 1959), in 1969 they introduced several measures of selective credit control. Since tighter fiscal operations and other government policies were already leading to economic stagnation, they decided against an all-out tight monetary policy, and marginal reserve requirements were revised in a series of steps occurring in April and May of 1969. The money supply increased in 1968 at an annual rate of about 17 percent; the increases slowed down to about 15 percent in 1969, and the slowdown was considerably greater in 1970 despite easier reserve requirements.

The sol had already been devalued from 26.82 to the dollar in 1967, and multiple rates were introduced. These quickly reached the neighborhood of 40 soles to the dollar and have held steady throughout 1968, 1969, and so far in 1970. There was a marked improvement in the trade account, so much so that—despite a decline in the inflow of foreign capital—the balance of payments at last moved into surplus in 1968.

The orthodox nature of monetary and fiscal policy is clearly consistent with what the United States government has preached to Latin America for two decades. In the cases of other countries previously adopting similar policies—such as Bolivia, Argentina, and Brazil—the United States has been quick to offer assistance against possible adverse repercussions. U.S. officials interviewed in connection with this study, however, cited the stagnation of the Peruvian economy as a reason why international agencies were *not*

[3] This statement represents the informed opinion of officials who have preliminary data they were unable to release. Tables 4 and 5 contain only officially released data.

in a position to assist, rather than as circumstances that ought to have compelled the participation of foreign capital.

This stagnation is depicted in Table 2. The increase in real personal consumption virtually stopped in 1968, while domestic investment declined from 21.80 billions of 1963 soles in 1967 to only 14.83 billions in 1968. Although data for 1969 are not yet published, nevertheless persons close to the scene report that, on the basis of preliminary figures, the gross national product increased by about 2 percent that year. However, there has been a distinct decline in both the inflow of foreign capital and the amount of domestic investment.

Opinions differ as to whether the stagnation is the outgrowth of restrictive fiscal policies or whether it results from uncertainties introduced by the government. The shake-up in the officers of the Central Reserve Bank of Peru, as well as statements by the government that private investment laws will be revised, enterprises must be reformed in as-yet unspecified ways, government control of exports such as fish meal may be imminent, and the threat of expropriation may have led both foreign and domestic investors to hold off.

At the same time, poor weather conditions caused declines in agricultural output, while over-fishing of anchovies adversely affected fish-meal production and exports in the latter half of 1969.[4]

THE INTERNATIONAL MONETARY FUND

The International Monetary Fund has recently been involved with Peru in two ways. First, it has advised in connection with Peruvian monetary and financial policies almost continuously since 1954, when the first stand-by arrangement was concluded. Second, it took part in the conference in Brussels in November, 1969, in which the rescheduling of part of Peru's foreign debt was considered.

[4] *Wall Street Journal*, Sept. 3, 1969. Also, International Financial Statistics reports the index of fish-meal exports (1963=100) to be 200 for 1968, but only 128 for the third quarter of 1969 and 56 for the month of October. The fishing itself is seasonal, dropping off sharply in the last months of the year, but the production of fish meal is less so; for example, in 1967 and 1968 the fourth quarter indices were 168 and 207 respectively.

As part of the above-mentioned series of agreements, on November 8, 1968, the International Monetary Fund concluded a one-year stand-by arrangement with Peru for $75 million. The agreement was not immediately renewed on its expiration, but a new stand-by for $35 million (the amount requested) was granted on April 17, 1970.

Until May, 1970, the only way in which Peru's behavior had not been exemplary according to IMF standards was the reestablishment of a dual exchange system in October, 1967 (under Belaúnde), followed by a 15 percent exchange surtax on imports in March, 1968, which was reduced to 10 percent in November (under the Junta). Its conversion into an import surcharge collected by customs in May, 1969, would remove it from being a technical violation of the Articles of Agreement. Arrears in remittance of profits and dividends, which might also be construed as a violation of the IMF agreement, developed in the first quarter of 1969 but were eliminated by August of the same year. From January through August, Peru drew nothing from the Fund, a fact leading one to speculate that the Fund may have informally considered it ineligible while the profit-remittance question was being settled. In September, Peru drew $9.6 million.

In May, 1970, Peru introduced controls on current purchases of foreign exchange, in violation of the Articles of Agreement of the Fund. The principal objective of these new regulations appears to have been the repatriation of capital held by Peruvians abroad. Stiff fines and jail sentences were stipulated. Since most Peruvians believe their mail has been censored in such a way that the government would have read their financial statements, there is widespread belief that the new edict will find compliance.[5]

Why, however, was the stand-by not renewed when it expired in November, 1969? Why the delay until April, 1970? Some Peruvians have charged that the Fund's reluctance somehow stemmed from the IPC controversy and the influence of the United States. Fund officials, however, argue that the delays were technical, approval awaiting only the working out of the Peruvian financial

[5] It could be argued that these regulations will only hit the small offender and the foreign resident and not be effective on the biggest offenders, because it is thought by some that principal exporters of money from Peru have for many years arranged for statements not to be mailed to them in Peru.

program, including the rescheduling of foreign debt. Officials of the U.S. State Department who were interviewed thought it inconceivable that the Fund should be used as a policy tool in the IPC dispute.

THE RESCHEDULING OF LOANS

The Fund's interest in the November, 1969, debt renegotiations stems from its concern for the balance of payments of Peru, a country currently using the Fund's resources. It participates in such conferences as an "honest broker," serving the interests of both debtor and creditor countries.

It has been mentioned earlier that the 1968 negotiations had led to a rescheduling of Peru's short-term debt over the ensuing two to four years. For European creditors, this rescheduling involved government guarantees. Once again, at the end of 1969, Peru's foreign public debt was not alarmingly great with reference to projected export earnings, but the shortness of maturities and the fact that the debt was owed by the public sector would have greatly strained Peru's finances in the next few years if full amortization were required.

In preliminary meetings in Lima during October, 1969, the Peruvians had proposed rescheduling amortizations of the greater part of the public debt over ten years. These terms were unacceptable to the creditors, who insisted on a shorter period of consolidation; that is, they would only reschedule maturities falling due in the next year or two.

Those who argue that the U.S. government initiated the slowdown in lending to Peru might have raised the same question with respect to debt rescheduling. Debt rescheduling is similar to untied foreign lending, for it releases foreign exchange reserves with no restrictions on their use. Furthermore, it constitutes budgetary assistance, which may be even more important to the Peruvians than balance of payments relief. A greater portion of the government budget might thus be devoted to development purposes. If the United States is, in fact, slowing down its foreign lending through AID and the Eximbank, and if it is also opposing operations by the international development lending agencies (World Bank Group and IDB), it would have been consistent for it to oppose the debt rescheduling as well.

To do so, however, would have involved a conflict with the interests of other U.S. nationals, the commercial banks. Throughout the negotiations, these banks were concerned not only for the repayment of their debts but also for the preservation of their financial relationships with Peru. Controversies come and go, but (the bankers say) everyday business must go on. They would object to their negotiations becoming a tool of foreign policy for a dispute that concerned them only marginally. There is evidence that the U.S. government maintained a careful watch but a strict hands-off policy in the proceedings.

The negotiations did not end in a binding agreement, but they did set a formula for individual bilateral agreements between Peru and each creditor group, which must now be transacted. By this formula, one-half of the maturities owed to U.S. and Canadian banks in 1970 and 1971 would be spread over the four years, 1972 to 1975 inclusive.

THE WORLD BANK GROUP

No member of the World Bank Group (World Bank, International Development Association, and International Finance Corporation) approved any loans to Peru during 1968, 1969, or so far in 1970. Spokesmen for the Bank who were interviewed explained this hiatus entirely in terms of Peru's economic situation, especially her budgetary problems that make difficult the contribution of local counterpart, and her international creditworthiness. They pointed out that the Bank had participated in the consultative group in 1966, which outlined the framework for long-term lending to Peru, but that the deterioration in the economic situation, especially with respect to the external public debt, had caused a lapse in lending that began several months before the Belaúnde government fell.

Two loan applications were under consideration at the time of the military takeover: one for educational improvement and the other for agricultural credit to be extended by the Banco Agropecuario. Though many Peruvians believe that the takeover and the IPC dispute largely explain the failure of these loans to be awarded, Bank officials deny that this is the case. The agricultural loan, they say, failed because the Bank and Peruvian government could not agree on relending terms by the Banco Agropecuario to the individual farmers, the Bank insisting on a maintenance-of-value clause in the face of currency devaluation, and the Peruvians objecting. The terms of the education loan also encountered some disagreement.

In assessing the World Bank's behavior, it is perhaps relevant to consider the current controversy over a loan to Bolivia, where the seizure of the Bolivian Gulf Oil Company presents certain parallels to the Peruvian case. The purpose of this loan was to finance a 334-mile natural gas pipeline to carry 150 million cubic feet daily from Yacuiba to the Argentine border. The project was to have been undertaken jointly by the Bolivian National Oil Company (Yacimientos Petrolíferos Fiscales Bolivianos, [YPFB]) and Bolivian Gulf. It would be financed partially by a loan from the World Bank, for which Bolivian Gulf originally offered its guarantee. Before the loan became effective, however, Bolivian Gulf was expropriated in October, 1969, its assets turned over to YPFB, and the guarantee withdrawn.

Since Bolivian Gulf would no longer be guarantor of the loan or partial operator of the gas lines once completed, the World Bank decided that a material change had been made in the terms of the loan, and it held up disbursements. In the meantime, the Argentine government, which considers itself an interested party (as potential purchaser of the gas) offered its guarantee in place of that of Bolivian Gulf. Currently, the Bolivians have negotiated sale of the oil to the government of Spain and spokesmen for the World Bank confidently predict that the loan will be implemented as soon as the negotiations are concluded.

Two explanations for the delay entered the rumor circuit. One is that the U.S. director pressed the Bank not to disburse, hoping that this pressure would be transmitted to the Bolivian government in its negotiations to settle the Gulf dispute. The other—which would seem the more likely explanation—is that the Bank is waiting until it is assured that all administrative and marketing arrangements have been made for the borrower to sell his product successfully.

The same rumor circuit is rife with respect to the World Bank and Peru. Why is it that, despite continuous consultations between the Bank and the Peruvian government, no loans have materialized in recent years? Possibly the answer is simply that negotiations take a long time, particularly under uncertain conditions of government policy. Implementation of the Bolivian oil loan, if it occurs soon, would lay to rest speculation that the World Bank is unduly influenced by pressure from the United States. What applies to Bolivia should apply equally well to Peru.

THE INTER-AMERICAN DEVELOPMENT BANK

Since the IPC seizure, the United States has faced two major decisions concerning IDB loans to Peru. The first was on a housing loan approved by the Executive Board during the Belaúnde presidency but not yet signed by the time of the seizure. Under Bank regulations, an approval expires if a loan is not signed within six months, unless the Executive Board votes an extension. No extension had been voted by the time of expiration, though in the spring of 1969 the extension was retroactively approved, and the loan was signed on April 25. Since the Executive Board conducts its meetings *in camera*, one can only speculate on the reasons for the delay. But the sequence is so out of keeping with ordinary practice that it must be related to some unusual circumstance.

In the second instance, a $9 million loan was proposed before the Executive Board in November, 1969, for the Corporación Peruana del Santa, a public corporation charged with promoting the economic and social development of northwestern Peru's Santa River area, to improve and expand the electric power system of the provinces of Ancash and La Libertad. The project was approved, though it is understood that this approval occurred with the abstention of the U.S. director. If this is so, then an even more curious question arises: why was a vote taken at all? It is the Bank's custom to approve loans by consensus. If an objection occurs during a Board meeting, the loan is usually recommitted for further negotiation until it can be resolved; otherwise, applications that have passed all tests prior to the Board meeting are generally passed without vote. If indeed a vote was taken in this case and the U.S. director abstained, there are two probable alternative explanations: either that the United States wanted to make a specific warning concerning Peru, or that the Peruvians were eager for a confrontation to clarify their position in the Bank. Without specific knowledge of what occurred at the Board meeting, further speculation is not productive.

At this point, it is useful to review the financial structure of the

Bank and the constraints on the behavior of the U.S. director. The Bank's capital is divided into three funds. Ordinary capital (slightly over $1 billion) is contributed by member government subscriptions (a little over $400 million, of which $150 million by the United States) and by borrowing from nonmember governments and in private financial markets (a bit more than $600 million). The Social Progress Trust Fund (originally $525 million, now slightly augmented by accumulated earnings) is legally owned by the United States and administered by the Bank for soft loans in specified areas defined as "social"—housing, sanitation, land settlement, and education. This fund was fully committed by 1967, and this type of operation was then passed to the Fund for Special Operations. This third fund, to which $150 million had been committed in 1959, was successively increased to over $2 billion by the end of 1969, with the United States contributing approximately 80 percent. Because the Social Progress Trust Fund belongs to the United States and because the United States has contributed most of the Fund for Special Operations, Congress required that the U.S. director be empowered to veto any loan proposed for financing by these funds. He does not have a veto over ordinary capital loans, however, since the votes of any government here are proportionate to the capital contributions of the country. If the Hickenlooper Amendment were to be applied to Peru, the U.S. director would be required to veto any loan to Peru proposed for the Fund for Special Operations, but he would not be required even to vote negatively on proposals for ordinary capital.

Evidence that the United States has probably been foot-dragging lies in the fact that no loans to Peru have come up for approval from the Fund for Special Operations since the IPC seizure, even though two such applications—one for a road and another for irrigation—have been under consideration by loan committees for over two years. At the time of this writing (May, 1970), it is expected that the irrigation loan ($23 million) will be presented to the Board shortly, and Bank officials see no obstacle to its being passed. If so, this would indicate that the United States is at last lowering its profile. Until now, there is reason to believe that the Bank's management may have wished to avoid confrontation in cases where a U.S. veto is permitted.

On the other hand, the Bank staff has been carrying on negotiations with Peru on a business-as-usual basis, and a new mining loan proposal is under consideration. Furthermore, in January, 1970, a Bank mission went to Peru to discuss the possibility of a loan for agricultural credit. Since the proceeds of this loan would probably be reloaned to participants in the agrarian reform promulgated by the military government, the prognosis is for delicate negotiations this year.

As in the case of the World Bank, it is necessary to consider whether the Inter-American Bank has delayed loans to Peru because of budgetary conditions in that country. While this is possible, the probability is less in the IDB than the World Bank for three reasons. First, the IDB is more flexible in its assignment of loans as between ordinary capital and the Fund for Special Operations than is the World Bank Group in allocations between the Bank and IDA. Hence, there is greater likelihood that a loan would be shifted from hard to soft, rather than denied. Indeed, virtually all IDB new loans to Peru in 1966 and 1967 were from the Fund for Special Operations. The IDB will admit soft loans for projects that do not meet the requirements of hard loans, whereas the World Bank Group distinguishes only on the basis of a country's per capita income. Thus, the IDB frequently makes ordinary capital and special operations loans to the same country in the same year, whereas the World Bank Group would have to consider that the income status of a country is changed in order to shift from Bank to IDB loans or vice-versa. Second, while the IDB does take account of a nation's creditworthiness, it has rarely refused to make *any* loan at all to a country on this ground. For example, while the World Bank might declare a country noncreditworthy and refuse to lend to it, the IDB would be more apt to distinguish between loans expected to have an adverse balance of payments impact and those not so expected, making the latter and declining the former. Finally, in recent years the World Bank has been paying more attention to the borrowing country's macro-economic policies (e.g., overall fiscal, monetary, balance of payment, and development financing), while the IDB has based its decisions more often on project criteria alone. It is far less likely for the IDB to turn down a loan because a government does not follow acceptable macro policies than for the World Bank to deny such loans.

Nevertheless, a possible contradiction of the second and third hypotheses is found in the case of Costa Rica. Although it is unusual for the Bank not to make *any* loans in a member country (other than the United States) during a given year, no loans were approved for Costa Rica in 1968. At the annual meeting of the Board of Governors (Guatemala, April, 1969), the Costa Rican governor complained that the withholding of loans had been caused by Costa Rica's failure to ratify the Protocol of San José.

Costa Rica, as a free and independent nation, can accept comments and suggestions from its sister countries of Central America on any problems related to the Common Market and to the other principles of integration that guide us. But it cannot and must not accept, as has already happened, that the granting of loans by international agencies outside the area be made conditional on approval by the country of the Protocol of San José, since that would entail an impairment of our sovereignty and an intervention in our internal affairs, the problems of which it is the exclusive province of the Costa Ricans to solve.[6]

The Protocol of San José, ironically enough, was initially sponsored by Costa Rican delegates at a meeting of the Central American Common Market in 1965. Its objective was to resolve the fiscal crisis facing Central American countries from the withdrawal of duties they had previously collected on imports from each other. Under the Protocol, all member countries would agree on a surcharge of 30 percent on imports from outside the area and they might optionally establish internal excise and consumption taxes of 10 and 20 percent. The Costa Rican Congress, however, refused to ratify the Protocol, despite urging by the government, preferring to rely on the sale of government bonds (at 10 percent interest) to cover its fiscal deficit. Between 1965 and 1968, banking system claims on government more than doubled, from 132.8 million colones to 284.1 million.[7] In their 1968 budget, however, the Costa Ricans added a new sales tax and a 10 percent surcharge on the personal income tax which, however, expired at the end of 1968.

---

[6] Address by Mr. Oscar Barahona Streber, alternate governor of Costa Rica and minister of finance, at the Fourth Plenary Session, Inter-American Development Bank Proceedings, Tenth Meeting of the Board of Governors, Guatemala, April, 1969, p. 127.

[7] *International Financial Statistics.*

Did the slowdown in loans to Peru and Costa Rica *in each case* represent concern on the part of the Inter-American Bank for fiscal problems within the country, including the incapacity to provide local counterpart to Bank loans? Or were they *both* the response to pressure—in the case of Peru, from the United States on account of the IPC dispute, and in the case of Costa Rica, from other Central American Republics on account of the Protocol of San José? It would take the wisdom of Solomon for an outsider to answer this query with confidence. Furthermore, there is no other case known to me where *either* the Bank has refused to make any loans in a given year on account of a country's fiscal policy *or* where it may have exerted political pressure of the natures indicated. The absence of precedents is indeed confounding. But either explanation is bound to contain profound portents for Bank policies now in the making.

OAS AND CIAP

The Organization of American States (OAS) and the Inter-American Committee for the Alliance for Progress (CIAP)[8] are not themselves international financial agencies. But their relationship to these agencies, both formal and informal, is close enough that they should be considered here. Although the Inter-American Bank is autonomous, it has a special relationship with the OAS. The CIAP, whose headquarters are located in the OAS and which utilizes OAS staff, is the coordinating agency for entities participating in development financing in Latin America (World Bank, IDB, AID, Eximbank, United Nations Development Program, national development planning bodies, and the like). Each nation receiving finance under the Alliance presents an annual country review, consisting of a resumé of economic and financial policies along with development plans. Other agencies concerned, such as the IMF, the Economic Commission for Latin America, and the Food and Agriculture Organization, join with the national delegates and those representing the agencies providing development finance, to form the country subcommittee of CIAP for review of the program. The reviews usually take place in Washington, where delegates comment on the plans and use them as guidelines for each agency's

[8] Comité Interamericano para la Alianza para el Progreso.

participation and for ways in which they can cooperate with each other in joint efforts.

The thorny questions relating to the role of the OAS in the current U.S.-Peru dispute may be stated as follows:

1. Why has not the OAS been used as a consultative or peace-making body?

2. Would the invocation of the Hickenlooper Amendment violate the charter of the OAS, which provides that no member state shall intervene in a way harmful to another, "measures of an economic or political character" being included?

Seasoned diplomats would shrug the first question off. In the first place, Peru considers the IPC matter, though perhaps not the fisheries, to be of internal concern only. The IPC and the Peruvian government are both residents of Peru, and any dispute between them should be the sole province of the Peruvian judiciary. In the second place, it is only natural that governments should try to solve problems bilaterally before referring them to an international agency.

The second question, however, raises some ticklish points. It would be hard to argue that the United States does not have the legal right to suspend foreign aid for any reason whatsoever, even whim. But the Hickenlooper Amendment to the sugar act is another question. Should the United States decide to cut off all imports of sugar from Peru in order to coerce settlement of the IPC dispute, it is likely that Peru would have a reasonable case charging the United States with wilful economic damage in violation of the OAS charter.

Just as the OAS has not been employed as a peace-making institution, neither has CIAP. Meetings of the subcommittee on Peru might have been an organ by which the United States and Peru could openly plead their cases before the participating agencies. There is even a question of whether the invocation of Hickenlooper would not be a direct violation of U.S. commitments to CIAP. *Unilateral* action on the part of the United States is not consistent with the concept of CIAP as a *multilateral* agency.

THE UNITED NATIONS DEVELOPMENT PROGRAM.

The United Nations Development Program (UNDP) is triply insulated from U.S. political pressure. In the first place, its headquarters is in New York, not Washington. In the second place, the amounts involved are relatively small compared to those of the major development lending agencies. And finally, the UNDP is an organ of the United Nations, which contains ample communist representation. Indeed, Cuba became a member of the Governing Council in January, 1970, and the UNDP is financing several projects in Cuba.

Two projects have been approved for Peru since the IPC takeover; one a fish-marketing and utilization project ($2.5 million) approved in January, 1969, and the other for the management of small enterprises ($.1 million) in June, 1969. One other is actively under consideration, a pilot project for the planning of human resources, and it is possible that the UNDP will cooperate, with technical assistance in an agricultural-credit program currently being considered by the Inter-American Bank.

U. S. GOVERNMENT LENDING PROGRAMS

The Agency for International Development has gone into low gear with respect to Peru. It has reduced its staff (though staff is being reduced in other countries as well, because of budgetary constraints), and it has authorized no development loans since 1967. Technical assistance continues, but at a level of $3.5 million in fiscal year 1970 compared with $4.5 million in fiscal 1969. Disbursements on prior loans continue on schedule, and there have been some grants and loans under the Food for Peace program.

The Export-Import Bank is conducting "business as usual" with the private sector in Peru (except, as noted below, with respect to Southern Peru Copper Company) but is not conducting any negotiations for loans to government or government agencies. During the fiscal year ended June 30, 1969, three loans were approved for private enterprises operating in Peru: Marcona Mining Company ($11 million), Sociedad Paramonga, Ltda. ($3.2 million), and Compañía Papelera Trujillo, S.A. ($8.8 million).[9]

ATTITUDES OF THE PRIVATE SECTOR

In assessing the pressures on U.S. government policy makers, it is well to have some appreciation of the attitudes taken by the

[9] Export-Import Bank, Annual Report, 1969.

private sector. Do the managements of U.S. companies investing in Peru propose the Hickenlooper Amendment and other diplomatic leverage to settle the dispute in the favor of IPC? There is evidence that the business sector is ambivalent; from their point of view, official pressure involves disadvantages as well as advantages.

While some U.S. government spokesmen and congressmen have reported letters urging a "get-tough" attitude, most of these seem to reflect the views of those in the private sector who, for nationalistic or patriotic reasons, do not want to see the lion's tail twisted. Businessmen and bankers interviewed in New York, who have direct relationships in Peru, were much less clear. Bankers in particular were concerned with the disruption of "business as usual" that might be caused by strained financial relationships. Other businessmen outside IPC were concerned that application of the Hickenlooper Amendment might imperil U.S. investments in other companies, principally mining. For example, the Peruvian government might take Hickenlooper as an excuse to initiate mass expropriations. Others, both within IPC and without, characterized Hickenlooper as "not well thought out," because it would force the United States to lay its cards on the table, stipulating a confrontation deadline that might not be consistent with optimum possibilities for negotiation. When Hickenlooper was not applied because negotiations were deemed in progress, then they were concerned that the United States would be characterized as a "paper tiger." The Council for Latin America, an organization of U.S. corporations operating through subsidiaries or other affiliates in Latin America, has taken no public stand, and even IPC has not insisted on the application of Hickenlooper. By contrast, spokesmen for Bolivian Gulf publicly urged that Hickenlooper be applied in the case of their own expropriation.[10]

---

[10] *New York Times*, October 31, 1969. There are substantial differences between the Peruvian and Bolivian cases. First, there are many more U.S. companies operating in Peru than in Bolivia. Second, Bolivian Gulf is almost totally dependent on exports, whereas virtually all IPC products are consumed within Peru; consequently Gulf, by refusing to transport Bolivian oil and by threatening to claim legal ownership of oil exported, is in a stronger position to put the squeeze on the government of Bolivia than Standard Oil of New Jersey is on the government of Peru. Third, Bolivia has been more dependent than Peru on U.S. aid, particularly budget support; aid suspension might be expected to imperil

The case of the Southern Peru Copper Company is very delicate. This company, 51.5 percent of which is owned by American Smelting and Refining Company and the remainder by Cerro, Newmont Mining, and Phelps Dodge, was affected by a decree law of September 2, 1969, providing that holders of major mining concessions granted before June 18, 1965, and not yet put into production would be required either to present a five-year timetable of operations acceptable to the Ministry of Mines, in which the company would abdicate any special privileges accorded by Article 56 of the mining code or to reach agreement with the government under Article 56 to exploit the concessions concerned. Article 56, which was last modified by the Belaúnde government early in 1968, details the foreign-exchange surrender requirements and the extent to which mining companies may repatriate capital, as well as regulations on tax treatment, import duty exemptions, reinvestment of earnings, and other financial matters affecting foreign mining companies. Southern Peru elected an agreement under Article 56, which would involve investments of $355 million for developing the huge Cuajone copper deposits. The agreement was apparently reached after tremendous pressure by the Peruvian government, and, some say, under the threat of expropriation as an alternative. On December 3, President Velasco announced that an appeal by Southern Peru to modify the agreement had been rejected, that the government's position had been solidified at a cabinet meeting on November 21, and that it was unchangeable.[11]

On April 8, 1970, however, the government of Peru announced its intention to construct a government-operated copper refinery.[12] It has not been clarified whether or to what extent that refinery would supplant the investment planned by Southern Peru. Without settlement of this question, Southern Peru has found itself in difficulties with the sources of capital it had counted on for meeting its commitment to the government of Peru.

Businessmen who were interviewed in New York reported that

Bolivian political stability far more than Peruvian. Mr. Lumkin, head of Gulf, has indicated he was misquoted in the newspapers, and in fact did not request that the Hickenlooper Amendment be applied concerning Gulf's problems in Bolivia.

[11] *New York Times*, December 4, 1969, p. 84.
[12] *Wall Street Journal*, April 9, 1970.

at the time of its agreement, Southern Peru was negotiating with the Export-Import Bank for a possible loan, but that the Bank had decided that under the circumstances it would be well to postpone discussions. If this is so, it constitutes an exception to the previously reported policy of "business as usual" with the private sector.

THE SLOWDOWN AS AN INSTRUMENT OF PRESSURE

From the above we conclude that there has been a significant slowdown in the authorizations of loans to Peru, as felt in the bilateral lending programs of the United States (AID and Eximbank) and in the World Bank and the Inter-American Development Bank. The five-month time lag in renewing the stand-by (November, 1969–April, 1970) might raise the question of whether the slowdown affected the Monetary Fund as well, but the explanation of this (that Peru's financial program was being negotiated) and the ultimate renewal would seem to exempt the Fund.

We now question the reason for the slowdown. Were there direct pressures from the United States connected with the IPC and fisheries disputes? Or did it stem from the uncertainties of Peru's financial conditions: her creditworthiness, her capacity to raise counterpart funds, or her inability to prepare lendable projects?

But this dichotomy is not clear-cut. Rather, it would seem that three forces are at work. First, U.S. officials have made polite but threatening statements, both in and out of directors' meetings in the international agencies. They hinted that careful thought would be required in loan proposals for countries that would not pay their debts. Second, the managements of the international agencies responded differently to these gestures. When interviewed, staff members of the Inter-American Bank believed that their management was reluctant to submit to the Board loan proposals involving the Fund for Special Operations, because they did not want to test whether the United States would apply the veto or not. Staff members of the World Bank denied that their institution would be so affected and insisted that the slowdown resulted from the Board's normal mode of operations. Third—and perhaps most subtle—international agencies may be so structured that any disturbance such as the IPC dispute will *automatically* lead to a reduction in lending. In this case, the only U.S. "pressure" would lie in the fact that the United States, like other purveyors of capital, was instrumental in structuring the institutions so that they would function in this manner.

This third force requires further explanation. First, whenever there is a sudden change in government, as by coup d'état, the international agencies tend to hold off lending until the confusion settles. The new government may not know whether it wants to endorse the loan applications of the old. The agencies for their part want assurance that the government is legal and capable of making agreements. But second—and this applies especially to the World Bank—international agencies tend to a certain conservatism inherited from the tradition of Euro-American financial circles. They think carefully about the financial responsibility of a government whose "rash" statements lead to stagnation in investment by its own private sector and to uncertainty over its expropriation and debt-repayment plans. Staff members argue that the World Bank must see to its own security; if it does not act "responsibly," its sources of funds in the New York and other money markets will dry up.

Suppose the United States were to apply direct pressure. What would it expect to accomplish? How would it decide which institutions to pressure?

What would be accomplished? It is difficult to believe that the U.S. pressures were implemented with the expectation of doing economic damage to Peru, since such damage would be slight and would be postponed for many years.

Disbursements to Peru from the IDB, World Bank, AID, and Eximbank together amounted to $62.4 million in 1966, $47.9 million in 1967, and $50.3 million in 1968,[13] compared to exports of $763.0 million, $774.2 million, and $865.0 million respectively in the same years.[14] Gross national product is currently running about $4 billion. Loan disbursements have therefore been approximately 6 percent of exports and 1 percent of gross national product. Furthermore, no agency can slow down its *disbursements* without abrogating its loan contracts. If the *authorizations* (or loan approvals) are slowed down, the effect on disbursements is spread over the entire period of the would-be loan. We must conclude

---

[13] Data collected by the Organization of American States.
[14] International Financial Statistics.

first, that the disbursements are but a small amount relative to Peru's economic indicators, and second, that a slowdown in loan authorizations would have a very slight immediate effect on disbursements. It is hard to see how enough economic damage might be inflicted to influence the government of Peru.

Rather, it would seem that the Nixon administration is motivated by another consideration, that of preserving the international agencies before Congress. Congress provided a blunt instrument, the Hickenlooper Amendment. While the administration has decided that Hickenlooper would impose more sanctions than are desirable, nevertheless it has apparently decided that some sanctions are necessary. There is no inconsistency in *not* applying Hickenlooper while instituting a slowdown instead. The administration decided not to slug with the ax but to do some fine tuning.

There is, however, some anomaly in the conclusion that one agency of the government must institute a policy that can be demonstrated to be ineffective vis-à-vis the foreigner because it *believes* another arm of our national government might insist upon it. How inflexible would Congress be? In large part, it would seem that the answer here lies in the pressures put upon Congress by the business community. Though I have taken no poll (and neither has the administration, to my knowledge), nevertheless it is clear from my interviews with the business community in New York that some officials of corporations with interests in Peru are ambivalent toward the use of Hickenlooper. These are intelligent men, capable of understanding the incidence of economic action, and—it seems to me—it would not be difficult to persuade them, in case they need to be persuaded, that a slowdown would be ineffective. All evidence leads to the probability that *they* did not initiate the idea of the slowdown, and neither did Congress. Rather, it would seem that the administration has assumed the role of the bogeyman, thus abdicating a leadership position that it might have taken before Congress, if indeed the administration has opted for Option 2 of the grand design (see p. 126).

Which institutions to pressure? Pressure is difficult to pinpoint. It can neither be measured nor substantiated; it is a matter of opinion. After intensive interviewing of U.S. government officials and the staff of international agencies, I am convinced that at no time between the military takeover in Peru and the present (June

1970) did a responsible U.S. official specifically threaten to veto any loan or potential loan to Peru. Strong but inconclusive statements are alleged to have been made in the board meetings of the Inter-American Bank and the International Monetary Fund. But even these can be deceptive. The platform that a spokesman selects may not indicate the agency through which action is contemplated.

Of the agencies under review (excluding the UNDP), only the International Monetary Fund has recently concluded an arrangement with Peru. Most likely, the IMF is the most immune to pressure, for three reasons. First, it is the only one that is fully independent of the U.S. Congress for funds (except when general increases in quotas are contemplated). While the World Bank is itself independent, nevertheless the International Development Association (part of the World Bank Group) is not, and IDA may reap the congressional consequences of actions by the Bank. Second, the IMF is directed by a European, strongly committed to institutional independence. But third—and most important of all—the IMF has a mission that the U.S. government endorses: the orderly management of the international monetary system and the encouragement of sound monetary, fiscal, and balance-of-payments policies by member governments. If the IMF were to be an instrument for the resolution of *ad hoc* political problems of the United States, it would lose prestige in carrying out its higher missions.

This prestige has not come easily. Over the years the IMF has been accused of imperialism and intervention in member governments' affairs. But almost a quarter century has done much to persuade borrowers that it is professionally managed, and its decisions are based on technical and not political grounds. It has a consistent ideology concerning the "right" way to develop: without inflation and with specific criteria for monetary management. It is to the interest of the United States that the legitimacy of this kind of pressure by the Fund upon its members shall be preserved in accordance with Option 2 of the grand design. This legitimacy would be diluted if the Fund were asked to employ other pressures that its members would deem illegitimate.

Most of what applies to the IMF also applies to the World Bank. It too imposes standards of behavior upon its borrowers with respect to both macro-economic policies (where it endorses the Fund's development ideology) and in analytical studies of loans under question. In addition, borrowers are expected to manage their investment funds well. The Bank's pressures upon them to improve their administrative capacities are highly approved in the United States. In all these respects, the Bank is similar to the Fund.

It differs, however, in two ways. First, it depends on the private money markets, as has already been mentioned. Second, the Bank has taken a formal position against expropriation without adequate negotiation for compensation. To date, it has not invoked this position against Peru. Possibly it considers that adequate negotiation is occurring. But staff members argue that the question has not arisen, since all loan proposals in the mill in October, 1968, have been tabled for other reasons, and no serious new ones have been made. Many observers believe, however, that this slowdown is related to the Bank's general philosophy opposing expropriation as well as its basically conservative nature.

While the IMF and the World Bank perform vital missions, the U.S. government does not believe the same of the Inter-American Development Bank. First, the IDB does not have the same reputation as the IMF and World Bank for pressuring clients into forms of behavior of which the United States approves. The IDB has never fully endorsed the requirement that an adequate macroeconomic policy, including inflation control, should be a requisite for borrowing. Second, the IDB does not have the same reputation as the World Bank for insisting on sound administrative practices on the part of all borrowers. To be sure, it does so in principle. Through the Fund for Supervision and Vigilance it performs engineering audits on projects in construction. Some staff members insist upon stipulations for improvement of management, the institution of sound marketing practices, and other reforms. But others argue that such stipulations constitute undue intervention in the affairs of clients. There is thus no internal unity in the IDB on this question. Furthermore, the IDB does not have the same leverage as the World Bank for imposing reform conditions on its borrowers. The management of the IDB is elected by its borrowers (the United States has only a minority vote), and borrowers are not pleased when that same management imposes difficult conditions upon them. The World Bank, by contrast, is managed by the lenders (the U.S. minority vote being bolstered by those of European governments), and it is not so likely to cater to the complaints

of borrowing governments. Because the IDB does not, in the eyes
of the U.S. government, have a mission as valuable as that of the
IMF or the World Bank, it is more likely to be "fair game" for the
exertion of political pressures in circumstances such as the present
problems with Peru. Here, then, is the logic for applying Option 3
of the grand design.

POLICY OPTIONS

In summary, the United States faces the following policy options with respect to international lending agencies. Following Option 2 of the grand design, it may view them all as designed to
bring about, in the borrowing countries, forms of behavior conducive to the efficient use of funds. (Nothing is implied concerning
the purposes or benefits of the lending, which are normally thought
of as the principal functions of the agencies.) Or, following Option
3, it may view them as designed to strengthen U.S. political relationships with governments in the borrowing countries. Finally, it
may view some institutions in one way and others in another. But
it should be recognized—by both the institutions and the U.S.
government—that the two views are not consistent. To the extent
that the former is accepted, the international agency will act with
independent, international criteria. It is to the interest of the U.S.
government that it do so. To the extent of the latter case, however,
the agency will always be vulnerable to U.S. pressures for whatever bilateral problem may occur.

U.S. policy choices with respect to Peru present an additional
dilemma: whether the government is concerned more with re-
solving each specific question (IPC and fisheries) to the best advantage of the U.S. parties, or whether its concern lies with promoting the general kind of behavior outlined at the beginning of
this paper (sanctity of contract, legitimacy of governmental continuity, and acceptance of international law). The first suggests a
short-run perspective and the second a long-run. Furthermore, they
are probably not consistent; that is, option of one may mean rejection of the other. As was suggested earlier, the government of
Peru may ultimately be willing, even eager, to behave according
to the international standards provided that old wrongs as they see
them are first righted. The question is one of whether or not Peru

will be another Mexico, whose revolutionary institutions have become stabilized over the years.

In one sense, the current case of Peru has no recent precedent in Latin America. U.S. policy makers are accustomed to a Latin America where left-wing revolutionary movements are associated with loose monetary, fiscal, and balance of payments policies that lead, through inflation, to a weakening of the economic fiber. Such was the case of Perón's Argentina, Paz Estenssorro's Bolivia, and Goulart's Brazil. Weakness is deemed a vacuum, and it is feared that if the United States does not intervene, some other power will.

But Peru has not followed this model. It has complied with all its obligations before the CIAP and the IMF, except for occasional lapses into exchange controls. It has instituted a vigorous tax reform, and its monetary policy is not extravagant. Instead of defaulting on its foreign obligations, as did Cuba, it has entered into serious negotiations with creditors. It has not made the same kind of break that Cuba (or even Mexico) did with prerevolution political and economic institutions. The army that controls the government is the same that put down guerrillas in the land seizures in Arequipa and Cuzco during the Belaúnde regime. The Peruvian government was one of the last in Latin America to recognize the Bolivian military seizure. Its establishment of relationships with the Soviet Union is clearly a gesture of independence rather than approval of communism. This same government has included in the administration such unrevolutionary characters as Jorge Grieve, President of Volkswagen in Peru and noted private-enterprise reformer (now adviser to the Ministry of Mines), and Edgardo Seoane, vice-president of Peru under Belaúnde (now president of the Agricultural Bank). Despite the expropriation of IPC, there is hardly evidence that the government is bent on destroying western institutions. Rather, it shows signs of wanting to settle down, like Mexico, into a stable relationship with the United States.

John Strasma

5. THE UNITED STATES AND
AGRARIAN REFORM IN PERU

After a decade of debate, legislation, and faltering first steps, Peru in 1969 suddenly moved into an agrarian reform worthy of that name.[1] The reform includes both land and water. It is massive, drastic and rapid. If it continues at its present pace, almost everyone in rural Peru (that is some six million people) will be affected in some degree by 1975.

Peru is a "classical" case,[2] starting from precisely the kind of unjust and stifling rural economy and society that the Alliance for Progress swore to overthrow throughout the Americas. Agrarian reform is at the heart of what development is all about in Latin

[1] "Agrarian reform" in this essay means redistribution of landownership in favor of cultivators and greater social control over the use of agricultural land and water resources. Reform tends to bring more radical increases in rural incomes, social mobility, equality before the law, and human dignity than do programs of colonization, rent control, or labor legislation that leave landownership intact in traditional agricultural areas. Redistribution is more effective if accompanied by improved credit and extension and marketing services.

[2] That is, modern plantations coexist with inefficient latifundia, minifundia, traditional communities, and laborers bound to the land in traditional ways that discourage productivity and tend to produce human relations reminiscent of the age of serfdom in Europe. See Carroll (1961).

America. The revolutionary military government is carrying out a reasonably effective reform without bloodshed.[3]

Social and economic reform is basically the domestic political concern of a sovereign government. Nonetheless, the agrarian reform being carried out in Peru in 1970 clearly reflects the influence and actions, over the last decade, of the U.S. government, business firms, and individual U.S. citizens. The future attitudes and actions of these same three groups, whether helpful or hostile, informed or ignorant, will also to some extent influence the outcome of the reform now under way.

This paper traces the history of land reform in Peru, summarizes the laws of 1964 and 1969, and describes actual accomplishments under each law. A final section analyzes the alternative paths that U.S.-Peruvian relations might take regarding agrarian reform. It also considers whether there is any way in which U.S. citizens and the U.S. government could be helpful without unacceptable intrusion in Peru's domestic political affairs.

THE UNITED STATES AND AGRARIAN REFORM IN THE AMERICAS

The United States has a long tradition of sturdy frontiersmen and a highly productive agriculture that developed on the basis of the family farm using little permanent hired help. Americans should logically be sympathetic to the elimination of the latifundia system, so reminiscent of their own slavery-based traditional Southern plantations a century ago.[4] Nonetheless, choosing and implementing a consistent U.S. policy stance on land reform everywhere in Latin America has been complicated by several sticky facts:

1. Some of the largest farming operations in Latin America are owned by U.S. corporations or individuals. They, and wealthy Latin landowners as well, know how to lobby in Washington in defense of their interests.[5]

[3] None of my interviewees in Lima could recall any public mention of land reform, and the U.S. ambassador managed to ignore the subject completely in a speech to the American Society (April 1970) on recent trends in U.S. aid programs.

[4] See Barraclough (1965).

[5] My knowledge of such lobbying is limited to owners of land in Central America, the Caribbean, and Chile. One interviewee in Lima denied that Peru-

2. Some of these large operations are highly productive, per worker and per acre, in comparison with most local farming units.

3. Some of these large operations have pioneered in developing new varieties and in processing agricultural products.

4. Many uncritical journalists, tourists, and even foreign service staff shown these outstanding farms by gracious hosts speaking fluent English, erroneously suppose these operations to be "typical" of all large estates in Latin America. They therefore respond sympathetically when any landowner asserts that the United States should oppose land reform because it would reduce production and lower efficiency.

5. Most Americans believe that land reform leads to lower agricultural output, at least in the short run. In Bolivia and Mexico, recent and more careful studies have shown that this was not the case.[6] The U.A.R., Japan, Korea, and Taiwan are other cases where land reform increased output.

6. Communist parties and Marxist ideologues also advocate land reform, and solely for that reason some Americans suppose they should be against it. A few perhaps remember how Joseph McCarthy abused those who once described Mao Tse-tung as "an agrarian reformer, probably no worse than the Kuomintang" for the Chinese people.

7. Some land reformers advocate large state-owned farms rather than family farms or producer cooperatives as the best post-reform organization for agriculture. Many Americans were taught as children that state or "collective" farms are the epitome of evil. If not assured that family farms will result from agrarian reform, these Americans would rather leave the latifundia system in place. Our agricultural attachés seem particularly prone to this view.

In view of these facts, it is no wonder that the views of the U.S. government on land reform have varied considerably over time and according to who was writing or speaking. The same could be said of many managers and employees of U.S.-owned business firms in Latin America.

---

vian landowners had lobbied in Washington for anything other than the sugar quota.

[6] See Eckstein (1968) and Clark (1968).

U.S. Attitudes toward Land Reform in the 1950s

After the Chinese Communists drove Chiang Kai-shek from the mainland in 1949, his government carried out a massive land reform on Taiwan. This reflected, at least in part, lessons learned in the land reforms carried out in Japan and in Korea over the preceding five years under orders of General MacArthur, commander of the American occupying troops.[7]

In Latin America, land reform was a major factor in the Bolivian Revolution of 1953 and in the events leading to the Guatemalan Counterrevolution of 1954. The issue was then dormant until the Cuban Revolution triumphed at the end of 1958. In Venezuela, land reform was a key part in the effort to restore functioning constitutional democracy after the overthrow of Pérez Jiménez. It was not a major factor in efforts to restore democracy after the fall of Rojas in Colombia and Trujillo in the Dominican Republic; this may have something to do with the greater success of democracy in Venezuela.

1. *Bolivia.* In the Bolivian Revolution of 1953, land reform took place spontaneously in the valleys around Cochabamba, and the MNR reform law in effect legalized it after the fact. When the law was enacted landlords abandoned their estates on the altiplano and a de facto land reform took place in virtually the entire country. Few U.S. investments were affected. After a survey visit by Dr. Milton Eisenhower, President Dwight Eisenhower committed the United States to support the Bolivian Revolution, including the land reform. For over a decade, very substantial grants and loans were made to cover fiscal deficits and carry out development programs in Bolivia, though few had any relation to land reform.

By 1964, however, the AID mission and the U.S. ambassador were concerned about consolidating the reform. Ten years after land reform, most beneficiaries still had no legal titles to their plots, nor could they get credit. Some landowners or their representatives visited their former estates, demanding and getting money in exchange for a title deed. Though legally worthless according to the Bolivian land reform law, this "sale" at least assured

[7] See Mitchell (1951).

the beneficiaries that the old landlord would not return after some future change in government.

In 1969, the AID program helped finance a program of land registration and titling, designed by Bolivians and University of Wisconsin Land Tenure Center staff members financed under an AID contract. Essentially, the program bypasses the maze of pitfalls and delays in La Paz. Mobile teams (a judge, surveyors, and notary public), go to the field, resolve all pending land disputes, and arrange for issuance of the titles and hence the security of tenure that has so long eluded the reform beneficiaries.

2. *Guatemala.* The land reform program began under President Arévalo, who served from 1945 to 1950 after the overthrow of Ubico. The reform gained momentum, and under President Arbenz (elected in 1950) some 100,000 landless families reportedly obtained land to till by 1954.[8] As in Bolivia, they often took the land without awaiting legal formalities, and no individual titles were issued. In contrast with Bolivia, U.S. investors held substantial land holdings, much of which they were not currently cultivating. It was decided that the CIA should overthrow the Arbenz government. This was done rapidly and with little bloodshed, mainly because President Arbenz regarded resistance as hopeless. He surrendered to the U.S. ambassador and fled the country.

It is not clear whether the U.S. intervention was motivated principally by the defense of property rights of U.S. citizens and corporations. Official statements stressed the possibility of communist bases being established in Guatemala, threatening the Panama Canal. However, the United Fruit Company did stand to lose 160,000 hectares of uncultivated land, as well as its accustomed ability to influence events affecting its interests in Guatemala. The company also protested the indemnity that the Guatemalan law set at that value which each landowner had declared for land tax purposes.[9]

The invasion itself was reported fully and candidly in *Time*, but the aftermath is described succinctly in a statement by the AID Mission in Guatemala, submitted in 1967 to the Reuss subcommit-

[8] The figure may be exaggerated; see Carroll (1961) and the CIDA report for Guatemala.

[9] Carroll (1961), p. 179.

tee: "With the fall of the Communists in 1954, the expropriated lands were returned to their owners. The campesinos were summarily removed from the land they had been occupying illegally."[10] While Colonel Castillo Armas, who led the CIA operation, attempted to start a land program in hope of rallying peasant support, in fact Guatemalan efforts since 1954 have been limited to colonization and resettlement. The 1965 Constitution even prohibits the issuing of bonds for paying for expropriated land, and no reform is in sight.[11]

3. *Cuba.* After Guatemala, little more was heard of land reform until Fidel Castro overthrew Batista in 1958. Cuba's land reform is recent, but reliable and quantitative information is scarce. However, we must note that Cuba was able to justify each confiscation of an American-owned sugar mill or plantation as a reprisal for some hostile act of the U.S. government. In turn, the United States regarded its acts as regrettable but necessary reprisals for some earlier act by Castro. The United States eliminated Cuba's sugar quota and banned the shipment of spare parts, fuel, and other supplies, which naturally affected agricultural operations.

At the end of the decade, several other events heralded the massive upturn in interest in land reform which was to characterize the 1960s. President Kubitschek of Brazil proposed "Operation Pan America" in August, 1958, and the Act of Bogotá was signed in 1960. Both stressed the need for social as well as economic progress if democracy itself were to survive. And in Venezuela, where democracy had just been restored, President Betancourt initiated a relatively large land reform. Appreciative and well-organized peasants helped him complete his full term of office, staving off attacks from Fidelista guerillas on the one hand, and military Golpistas on the other.

U.S. interests were not harmed in Venezuela, in part because Betancourt paid generously for their land as well as that owned by Venezuelans. This in turn was facilitated by oil, but also by the

---

[10] Reuss (1967), p. 118. In fact, of course, the campesinos had occupied the lands legally under Decree 900 of 1952. Their position became illegal only after the new government repealed that law. See Carroll (1961), p. 179.

[11] Reuss (1967), p. 118.

fact that a large fraction of the land required could be confiscated from the deposed Pérez Jiménez and his followers, who were accused of illegal enrichment during his government.[12]

U.S. Attitudes toward Land Reform in the 1960s

For many Latin Americans, the U.S. posture on land reform is directly linked to the personality of the U.S. president. Whether or not this has been the cause, overall U.S. "leaning" toward or against land reform does seem to have passed through phases that more or less coincide with presidential administrations.

1. *The Kennedy period: 1960–1963.* President Kennedy followed hard on the Latin American proposals (Operación Panamericana and the Act of Bogotá), with a dramatic speech in March, 1961. Kennedy mentioned the common revolutionary heritage of the Americas, and urged that all countries work together to prove to cynics that economic and social progress are attainable and most successful under democracy. He insisted that all levels of society must share in growth, and asked for an inter-American meeting to launch the proposed Alliance for Progress.

This meeting was held at Punta del Este, Uruguay, in August, 1961. It produced a "Charter" and a "Declaration to the Peoples of America," which together amounted to a declaration of intentions between the United States and the Latin nations (except Cuba). Agrarian reform was one of the measures to be undertaken, under the general category of self-help. In turn, the United States promised financial and technical assistance to those countries that came up with development programs, self-help measures, and policies and programs consistent with the Charter.

Even before President Kennedy's speech, the International Cooperation Administration (AID's more aptly-named predecessor agency) had organized a seminar in Chile on agrarian reform. Between February 21 and 24, 1961, staff members of country missions in Latin America debated the nature of reform and discussed the situation in their respective host countries. Invited speakers urged skeptical ICA staff to understand what land reform was all about, and to provide positive help to nations enlightened enough

---

[12] See the United Nations Secretary General's *Fourth Report on Progress in Land Reform*, 1966, chapter 2.

to carry one out before a violent revolution did the job. Solon Barraclough, an American formerly with ICA but by 1961 working with FAO, argued that U.S. domestic land policies and history should place it firmly against continuation of the status quo. He reminded the faint-hearted that "one of the most devasting criticisms to be found anywhere of the system of large semi-feudal estates is to be found not in Marx, but in Adam Smith's *Wealth of Nations*."[13]

The rapporteur at the ICA Seminar summed up what he thought agrarian reform meant, and why the United States should favor it for all peoples, as follows:

Agrarian reform should consist in peaceful evolutionary processes directed toward the development of rural societies comprised primarily of owner-operators of family size farms and of tenants who have the opportunity to become farm owners.

Such an organization of agriculture holds most promise of providing the economic efficiency and capital formation necessary to agricultural improvement and general economic development.

Satisfying as it does the deep aspirations of rural people for economic independence, personal security, equality of opportunity, and human dignity, it provides also the requisites for political and social stability.[14]

Pushing further the analogy between U.S. history and Latin American needs, the seminar brought out the difference in the impact of independence on land tenure. In North and South America alike, the colonial power had deeded most of the land in huge blocs, as political favors or to pay royal debts. After the Revolution in the United States, unsettled land was declared to have reverted to public ownership; earlier land grants by the British Crown were simply declared null and void. In Latin America, on the other hand, independence left the land ownership pattern intact. The residuum of structure developed in the colonial period still plagues many Latin American countries, including Peru.[15]

Under President Kennedy, then, the heady language of the Alliance promised a new day for the Latin American peasant. An

13 Barraclough (1961), p. 49.

14 International Cooperation Administration (1961), p. 1.

15 Of course, as Dr. Enrique Peñalosa has observed, the United States still has land tenure problems of its own, especially in the South.

enormous publicity operation was mounted at once; it may have heightened subsequent disillusionment, but it did convey the message that the United States was now officially in favor of social reforms, including land reform. President Kennedy was personally much interested in land reform. Yet with the exception of Venezuela, where land reform was already under way, nothing happened.[16]

2. *The Johnson years, 1963–1968*. The only major land reform during this period took place in Chile, where U.S. Ambassador Ralph Dungan gave active, visible support to President Frei's reform. However, this was clearly an exception, justified in part by the very clear electoral mandate for land reform given by Chilean voters in 1964 and 1965.

Even before Kennedy's assassination, people were beginning to ask why the Alliance had "failed." President Johnson's personality came over very differently among Latins; the landing of marines in Santo Domingo confirmed their suspicions. The appointment of Thomas Mann, regarded as a rather traditional "hard liner," was correctly interpreted by the traditional elites as a sign that the Alliance was now in cold storage. Actually, some of its difficulties were inherent in its original design. Perhaps all that should be laid to President Johnson is a lack of energy to overcome the difficulties in a program which, had it been more successful, would have been credited to his predecessor.

With hindsight, it is easy enough to see that the original model of the Alliance was doomed from the start, so far as land reform was concerned. While all governments (except Cuba) signed, few Congresses had the slightest interest in redistributing their own overwhelming political and economic privileges. The presidents were forced to sign both by Kennedy's charisma and by the threat that U.S. aid would go only to those who signed. They nonetheless did so with fingers crossed, and some relied on legalistic escape clauses.

For instance, the Charter does not actually commit *any* government to undertake agrarian reform. Thanks to weasel words an Argentine delegate reportedly added to an early draft, his government was subsequently able to argue that Argentina has no need and therefore has no commitment to do anything whatever in this

---

[16] See, for instance, Lowenthal (1970) and Alba (1970).

direction. The revelant goals as stated in the Charter are (emphasis added): "To encourage, in accordance with the characteristics of each country, programs of comprehensive agrarian reform leading to the effective transformation, *where required*, of unjust structures and systems of land tenure and use, with a view to replacing latifundia and dwarf holdings by an equitable system of land tenure so that, with the help of timely and adequate credit, technical assistance and facilities for the marketing and distribution of products, the land will become for the man who works it the basis of his economic stability, the foundation of his increasing welfare, and the guarantee of his freedom and dignity."

The Alliance was also done in by perfectionism. As the old Spanish saying has it, "The best is the enemy of the good." The Charter pledged the signatories to design reform programs on the basis of integral national economic planning. It took several years to recruit and train planners and gather the needed statistics. Meanwhile, reform was put off and the initial dynamism of the Alliance ran down. Congress asked in Washington why so little reform had been achieved, but by the time Latin American economic plans were forthcoming the Congress had itself begun a drastic series of annual reductions in aid funds. This provided a further excuse for Latin elites: now the United States was not keeping its side of the bargain.

At the outset, the Alliance raised expectations in both Latin America and Washington. Under President Johnson, the heady idealism in Washington disappeared. Occasional words still mentioned the need for social reforms. The deputy U.S. coordinator for the Alliance (James R. Fowler) tried hard to keep the program alive. Fowler welcomed redistribution, though he insisted that agrarian reform means more to the United States than simply expropriating land and redistributing it. Land is of little use without complementary facilities such as credit, know-how, and marketing. "It is these vital factors that turn mere land redistribution into true agrarian reform."[17]

The more typical U.S. official posture in these years was ex-

[17] James R. Fowler, "The Role of Agrarian Reform in Latin American Progress," a speech by Mr. Fowler to St. Joseph's College, Philadelphia, April 25, 1968; reprinted by the Office of Public Affairs, Bureau of Inter-American Affairs, U.S. Department of State, July, 1968.

pressed by Fowler's boss, Covey T. Oliver, who urged vastly expanded programs in rural education and health, the creation of more jobs, improved wages and working conditions, and "in some cases, redistribution of land to the landless, or colonization opportunities."[18] Land redistribution was tolerable, but not to be pushed, while the United States *would* push government programs that did not change existing structure at their tenure roots.

As the executive branch retreated, the Congress assumed the role of prodder. Title IX of the Foreign Aid Act, and some of the congressional committee visits to Latin America, were probably the most effective factors in holding alive the idea that the United States is officially committed to support social reform throughout Latin America, including land reform.

Had Latin American agrarian reform in fact depended on the U.S. government, perhaps it would have come to a halt by 1970. However, the revolutionary rhetoric of the Alliance, carried by transistor radio, had raised expectations and made it harder for landlords to call land reform a communist plot. The Alliance did succeed in creating or reinforcing indigenous pressures for reform, and in cases such as Chile and Peru these pressures eventually produced significant action despite the cooling of official U.S. attitudes.

3. *The Nixon Administration, 1969–*. Thus far, President Nixon has said little about land reform in Latin America, although he has come out in favor of social reforms in general. His appointments have not altered the "harder" U.S. image set in the Johnson years, though I do not believe they have worsened it. The Rockefeller mission was regarded in Latin America as both a lightning rod for complaints and an excuse for delay in making policy decisions. The Rockefeller Report mentions reform just once, in passing, in recommending program and project loans and technical assistance for rural development programs "including agrarian reform appropriate to the needs of the country." This was to raise production,

---

[18] Covey T. Oliver, assistant secretary of state for inter-American affairs and U.S. coordinator for the Alliance for Progress. The place where the quoted statement was originally made is not specified, but the quotation was placed on the back inside cover of the booklet with Mr. Fowler's speech—the boss having the last word—to tell the reader that Mr. Fowler's obvious enthusiasm for reform does not speak for the higher ranks.

improve the quality of rural life, and slow the exodus of the jobless to the cities.

There is a new factor, however, that may in time bring a significant change in the official posture. The staff of USAID itself, in Washington and at least some country missions, is increasingly perceiving that land reform is potentially productive and politically inevitable, and, therefore, must be taken seriously. The 1970 Spring Review in that agency will center on agrarian reform at the express request of Administrator Hannah—probably more attention than land reform has had in the agency since that 1961 seminar. There are still some AID employees and agricultural attachés who think it is morally wrong to expropriate privately owned land. But compared to just three years ago far more staff members now seem interested in the welfare of all rural families, and not only of the landowners with whom Americans abroad used to identify. Many of these newer staff members are veterans of the Peace Corps, other volunteer services, or campus concern over social problems—and this may have something to do with the changed attitude.

Should the U.S. posture under President Nixon shift significantly, U.S. personnel could treat credit, extension, and marketing programs as necessary complements to land redistribution in many countries, and not as programs to be pushed *instead* of land redistribution. Thus, the benefits of such programs will accrue to many; to new farm operators instead of the traditional landowning elite. The young and concerned know there is little point in trying to teach a peasant to grow two bushels of corn where one grew before, unless you first redistribute the land so the peasant *gets* the second bushel.

THE AGRARIAN PROBLEM IN PERU

In Peru as in much of Latin America, the hacienda was until recently the very keystone of rural society. It was regarded as a major barrier to economic and social change, and was the symbol most consistently assailed by reformers and revoltionaries. Agrarian reform was a basic plank in the program of the APRA from its very founding about 1930. In this section I will describe some of the man-land problems of Peruvian agriculture.

Nature of the Agrarian Problem

The overwhelming population pressure in relation to cultivated land in Peru has appalled economists for decades, though the use of cultivated land as the denominator somewhat exaggerates the problem. The following figures were taken from the 1961 National Census.[19]

Region	1961 Rural Population	Cultivated Area	Persons per Hectare
Coast	1,000,000	670,000 ha.	1.5
Sierra	4,200,000	1,700,000 ha.	2.5
Jungle	800,000	380,000 ha.	2.1
Total	6,000,000	2,750,000 ha.	2.2

However, the area actually cultivated in 1961 was far short of the area that—by declarations of the owners in the Census—could have been cultivated that year. Arable land not in cultivation was another 1,336,169 hectares. While some of this land was doubtless idle because rotations include fallow periods, it is far from clear that much of it is necessary or profitable for modern agriculture in Peru. It is a traditional method, cheaper than fertilizing, but hardly appropriate for the labor-abundant Peruvian circumstances.

Naturally, land-reform enthusiasts would like to get the cultivable land into cultivation—it fits perfectly the old slogan of "putting the landless man onto the manless land." However, there is another reason to question alarmists who insist that the country has only about one acre of cultivated land per person. That is that Peruvian agriculture, particularly in the sierra, is based on a substantial amount of grazing.

The grazing land is left out of most comparisons, though there is honest doubt about the figures. The 1961 Census reports 9,150,000 hectares of natural pasture in the country, with 8,000,000 of them in the sierra. Yet the Agricultural Statistical Yearbook of 1964 insists that the correct total is three times as great —27,600,000 hectares, of which 24,600,000 are in the sierra, 2,200,000 on the coast, and 800,000 in the jungle.[20]

Compared to either figure, there is very little cultivated pasture

---

[19] As reported in Mann (1970). One hectare=2.471 acres.
[20] Ibid.

—229,290 hectares in 1961. Yet according to FAO experts who have worked with Peruvian scientists in experiments in the sierra, improved pasture is the key to raising poverty-level incomes there, and indeed, of ending periodic famines caused by the frost that kills all the native grass every three years or so. There are varieties of grass that, once established, form a mat so thick that frost never kills it down to the roots, hence it comes back very quickly.[21]

Yields under present farming practices are far from satisfactory by comparison with world averages, nor are yields improving very fast. Potatoes, for instance, native to Peru, yielded in 1967 an average of 6,700 kilos per hectare, (about 6,000 pounds per acre), while the world average was 12,700 kilos.[22]

One practical problem that has arisen in efforts to introduce new techniques and farming practices is linguistic and racial. The majority of the population in the sierra is Indian, and only a minority speak Spanish. The rest speak Quechua or Aymará. This, plus historically justified misgivings about the good faith, intentions, and competence of white, Spanish-speaking people complicates the efforts of the typical University graduate in agriculture to communicate directly with the Indians.

A large fraction, perhaps the majority, of the sierra Indians live by preference or, for lack of alternatives, in communities that hold land collectively and assign plots to members on a long-term hereditary usufruct basis, much as in Inca and pre-Inca times. At least in theory, this should facilitate modernization, since large tracts are under one land use decision-making body. It may well be necessary to recruit and train technicians nominated from and by these communities in order to overcome gaps of language and trust.

Labor Relations

There are marked differences in the agriculture and in the degree of population pressure of Peru's three main areas: coast, sierra, and selva, yet there are some similarities among the traditional

---

[21] Dr. Clyde Mitchell estimates the carrying capacity of this kind of grass to be at least three times as many sheep per hectare as the natural pasture now typical of the sierra.

[22] The ICAP review for 1970 includes tables of Peruvian, tropical, and world average yields for various crops, as well as estimates of the trend for eight crops. See also the appendix to this chapter.

haciendas in all three. Until roads reached them, the traditional haciendas were self-contained. No one but the owner received much cash income, but resident laborers were given food rations, the use of a shack, and a small garden plot, and a paternalistic welfare system centered on the owner or his administrator. In medical or other emergencies they could count on a small loan, but they were also subject to instant dismissal and eviction, for insolence or any other signs of independence. Whipping and other violent disciplinary measures were once routine; they are still reported occasionally.[23]

In the traditional areas, the labor supply was thus kept docile and cheap. Workers could not leave voluntarily until they repaid loans and advances, and the landowner kept the books. This labor supply was regarded as an asset until recently; I have seen a copy of a 1951 title deed in which the seller transferred to the buyer a stated number of hectares in the sierra "and 600 Indians."

Along the coast, however, in irrigated valleys that relieve the desert from time to time, there are areas where sugar, cotton, and rice are produced on medium and large farming units. Some of the plantations are efficient by any measure, famed for the quality of their fibers and the ingenuity of their technicians. (For instance, W. R. Grace pioneered in making paper out of bagasse, the residue left after sugar and molasses are extracted from cane.)

In the earliest days of the plantations, the field work was done by Negro slaves. After the abolition of slavery, their place was taken by Chinese field hands. When the latter proved entirely too helpful to the invading Chileans in the War of the Pacific at the end of the last century, the plantations switched to their present labor force: Indians recruited in the sierra, at first for seasonal work and then persuaded to settle. The permanent labor force was largely trained on the job, and had to be given fairly attractive wages and other inducements to overcome their reluctance to live at sea level.[24] Together with modern, commercial cropping and processing, these plantations have developed strong industrial unions, which in turn were and to some extent still are part of the APRA core in Peru. W. R. Grace had a particularly nasty strike in

---

[23] See, for instance, Whyte (1970).
[24] See the National Planning Association on Casa Grace.

1960, with three dead in a battle between workers and police. One of the issues was the installation of time clocks. Shaken, the company began a modern labor relations program. Since 1960, there has been little violence, but wages and fringe benefits have risen far above the levels at other plantations.[25]

Nonetheless, it must be stated clearly that the coast is not made up solely of large sugar and cotton plantations, that not all of the coast irrigated land is intensively cultivated, nor are all workers there organized. To the surprise of many, a sample survey taken about 1965 but tabulated and available only in 1969 showed that it would be possible to provide a minimum family farm unit to a very large portion of the landless rural workers on the Coast, just by expropriation of idle or underfarmed land available under the terms of the 1964 reform law.[26] This was much more land than would be available if the modern sugar plantation and refinery were really typical of the coast.

Production, Productivity, and Investment

In Peru as in much of Latin America, traditional agriculture failed to keep pace with population growth and rising per capita incomes. Imports of food that could be produced in the country consume some $150 million in foreign exchange yearly, at the expense of capital goods for manufacturing or other sectors.[27] At the same time, cash incomes of farm workers (except in the sugar plantations) are too low to constitute much of a market for domestic manufactures. In the Sierra, the vast subsistence sector suffers from nutritional problems as well.

Yet it must be stressed that seven sugar plantations, occupying about half of the irrigated land in two northern provinces, did pay relatively good wages, had effective labor unions, and generated

[25] In 1970, Paramonga and Cartavio average labor costs were reportedly 100 soles a day (U.S. $2.40), twice the level at Tumán or other family-owned haciendas farther north. Including fringe benefits and costs of the company town, Grace's total labor cost at Paramonga in early 1970 was $5.74, which Grace estimates to be some $2.00 per day more than the formerly family-owned plantations.

[26] Carrasco (1969).

[27] This is 23 percent of all imports (1969). *Peruvian Times*, February 13, 1970.

substantial foreign exchange and tax revenues for Peru. These included cotton and sugar plantations owned by U.S. and German interests (W. R. Grace and Gildemeister), and others owned by wealthy Peruvian families. Actually, the Grace and Gildemeister personnel had been in Peru so long they were often regarded as part of the local establishment.[28]

In the sierra, well-run haciendas were decidedly the exception and not the rule. Two outstanding exceptions were the Algolan and the Cerro de Pasco livestock operations, yet even these fell far short of full utilization of all of their lands. The main reason was the insistence by the owners that the expansion of flocks be financed entirely by growth from existing animals, rather than by the investment of further capital.

Another reason—and for that matter, a reason for reluctance to bring in further capital—was the rising self-confidence and aggressiveness of the neighboring Indian communities. After centuries during which the Indians complained uselessly in the courts that the haciendas stole their lands,[29] the political situation had reversed. The boundary markers got moved again, but this time it was the hacienda owners who complained to the police and the courts.

Sometimes the police drove the Indians off, but other times they did not. Particularly in the central departments, to the interior of Lima, the Indians were allowed to keep what they took—in the South, around Cuzco, they were sometimes driven off with considerable bloodshed.[30] Even with police support, the haciendas were never able to end cattle rustling and the mixing of Indian strays with their purebred animals, and understandably they were reluctant to invest much new money in improved pastures and larger

[28] An interesting problem for chauvinists is posed here. Are Peruvian-born grandsons of German immigrants less Peruvian than the descendants of Spanish conquistadores? What of persons of traditional Peruvian surname who live in Germany and collect rents from properties in Peru? Similar problems arise with capital. The Ministry of Agriculture gave great publicity to the fact that a large fraction of the shares of sugar haciendas thought to be Peruvian-owned were in fact held by foreign interests. Apparently those who tabulated this data did not realize that the shareholding banks in Panama and the Bahamas are probably representing Peruvian owners seeking to evade taxes and exchange controls.

[29] Six communities in Puno averaged 9 percent of their budgets on legal costs. (CIDA, 1966).

[30] See, for instance, Neira (1961) and Whyte (1970).

herds. This meant that part of their land remained idle, making it all the more attractive to the neighboring Indians with their emaciated sheep on overgrazed hills.[31]

As we shall see in the next chapter, the Algolan property was bought for cash in order to start reform in the sierra during the Belaúnde government. The Cerro de Pasco farming operations were expropriated in early 1969 by the present government. So far as I have been able to determine, this is the only American-owned land in the sierra that has been affected, as the Grace plantations were the only coastal properties held by American companies and affected by land reform. Land reform in Peru was and is essentially a domestic matter, and because they have other investments in Peru, both companies are actively interested in its success.

Returning to the theme of productivity, then, we must note that much of the land in the sierra was owned by absentee landlords— and frequently by the very kind of owner least equipped to manage a modern farm: the board of trustees of a church, school, or other nonprofit institution in a city. Such institutions, as well as landowning widows and other elderly people in far-off cities, had not invested in the land for the purpose of farming it well. They had received the land by bequest or legacy, or had invested savings in land in order (they thought) to protect themselves against inflation and to produce a dependable annual income without managerial effort.

Such owners appointed farm managers or more often rented the entire hacienda for a few years at a time. The tenant then exploited the place (land and workers alike) as ruthlessly as possible, so as to make all he could before the lease or his contract ran out. Such managers and tenants had no incentive whatever to invest in soil fertility, build up pedigreed flocks, or improve pastures, orchards, and vineyards.

The logical solution of renting the land to the workers who lived on it seldom occurred because the owner lived at a great distance and hence wanted to rent it in one single transaction, and perhaps because it simply never occurred to the parties that the racial gulf

---

[31] This includes many very small holdings as well. For instance, my maid in Lima owns about three hectares near Cuzco and fears that her tenant (her brother) will "steal" it from her through the land-to-the-tiller policy. This is of course exactly what development requires.

could be bridged. When Cornell University Professor Allan Holmberg and his Peruvian colleagues suggested that an Indian community at Vicos itself, collectively, rent the hacienda and run it for its own long-run benefit, the trustees of the charitable institution that owned the land flatly refused the idea. Only persistent political pressure exerted by various interested parties in Lima succeeded in persuading the Beneficiencia to give in; even so, the government had to buy the land itself and sell it on long terms to the community.[32]

Later, after the Vicos precedent, a number of nearby land conflicts were settled by sale of the land directly by the owner to the community.[33]

Agricultural Credit

The distribution of agricultural credit was another sore spot in the prereform Peruvian agriculture. As in many Latin countries, many landowners were willing to invest in their farms—but only if they could borrow the funds at subsidized interest rates from a development bank. According to some critics, things were even worse than that: landowners borrowed for farm investment projects and then allegedly used the money for foreign travel or sumptuous consumption in Lima.[34]

Whatever the frequency of such behavior, there is no doubt that until recently most bank credit for agriculture, both at commercial banks and at the state-owned agricultural development bank (BFA), went to the relatively large landowners. It is also clear that they had a remarkably bad repayment record, at least in the period 1966–1967. Although the formalities were observed, with renewal notes and the like, an internal staff report of 1967 complains that large landowner borrowers had obtained the amazing total of eighteen separate laws and decrees in the preceding two years, ordering the bank to renew outstanding and overdue agricultural loans, usually at reduced interest and with repayment spread out over as much as twenty years. The reason given was the drought of 1966,

[32] Edward Kennedy personally took an interest in the project and persuaded President Prado to act: without this "Yanqui intervention," as well as Cornell's, the project might not have come off.

[33] Whyte (1970) describes several cases in detail.

[34] One such case is described in Whyte (1970).

but the fact remains that such subsidies were given only to borrowers and not to other drought victims who had not been able to borrow at the bank. The BFA now has a large program of credit for small holders and reform beneficiaries, but at that time it was still mainly serving the larger units.

A long-foreseen devaluation also took place in 1967. Some skeptics suspected that landowners had used borrowed money to buy dollars, and sought loan extensions in order to be able to repay with cheaper Peruvian currency once the long-delayed devaluation finally took place.

U.S. agencies and international organizations provided much of the agricultural credit resources in Peru over the last fifteen years, with very mixed results. Carey cites the Ellender Report of 1958, which tells of the largest single loan project to that time—and how it wound up helping those who needed help least.[35] This was the Quiroz irrigation scheme (San Lorenzo), for which the World Bank loaned $18 million, and ICA another $8 million, between 1955 and 1958. The project was supposed to benefit the small landholders, but by 1961 Richard Patch reported that the irrigated land had in fact passed almost entirely into the hands of a few very wealthy men who already owned other enormous haciendas in Piura.[36] Credit programs in the late 1960s were more oriented toward small and medium farmers, as we shall see in the next section.

Other large projects in which U.S. investors participated as businessmen are few; the most spectacular was the enormous LeTourneau scheme in the jungle. This project involved about a million acres and the investment of some $5 million, mostly the great machinery maker's own money. The jungle proved harder to tame than LeTourneau had expected, and in the end the discovery of oil in the area did more to develop it. Though the project began in 1954 during the Odría dictatorship, it was far from completed when Carey wrote (1963). A *Peruvian Times* article in late 1969 contained yet another optimistic statement by the management that they thought their problems were finally about licked.

[35] Carey (1964), p. 137, citing Ellender (1959).

[36] Patch (1961). Ing. Agustin Merea, a participant in the Peru conference that produced this book, has kindly pointed out that this is exaggerated; the San Lorenzo beneficiaries were relatives and friends of the wealthy and not the *hacendados* themselves.

Other U.S. Government Programs in the 1950s

Besides the loan for the San Lorenzo project, U.S. aid programs in the 1950s included ambitious agricultural production and planning programs for southern Peru, financing for a tannery in Arequipa, a fishing cooperative at Chimbote, and assorted dams and small irrigation projects. This effort was tarnished, unfortunately, by the fiasco associated with U.S. efforts to bring relief to the drought-stricken south in 1956.[37]

U.S. aid programs in the 1960s were much better managed, but some problems remained. These will be discussed together with President Belaúnde's reform program in the next section.

A Brief History of Agrarian Reform Efforts in Peru, 1956–1968

Agrarian reform was a basic plank in the APRA platform from the party's very founding. Although the party was banned and driven underground from the 1930s until after the elections of 1956, it grew and could not be ignored by ambitious politicians. The party was not allowed to present candidates itself in 1956, but all presidential candidates wanted APRA votes and therefore all of them came out for land reform. By this time, too, news of the Bolivian Revolution and the 1953 land reform had been carried by travelers and radio into even remote settlements.

As early as 1949 the Odría government promulgated a decree asserting the right of the state to expropriate idle lands. This decree was never implemented, nor were provisions in the Constitution calling for expropriation and redistribution of land to "promote the diffusion of small and medium-sized rural property," and to aid Indian communities. The Odría government did promote colonization schemes, vocational agriculture schools, and extension services. U.S. aid programs played a substantial role in some of these, in the San Lorenzo irrigation project, public works and extension. In the same period, U.S. and Peruvian scholars, led by the late Professor Allan R. Holmberg of Cornell University, started the Vicos project, which

---

[37] There was no doubt that the drought was serious. The United States donated some 30,000 tons of surplus grain under Title III of Public Law 480, and substantial amounts were shipped under other titles. According to a subsequent investigation, about 25 percent of the grain was still undistributed three years later—after the drought was over—while some 60 percent of the proceeds from what was sold were used improperly.

(with an assist from Edward Kennedy) was to create an irreversible awareness in the sierra of the possibility of change in centuries-old land tenure arrangements.

President Prado and the Beltrán Commission

The 1956 elections were won by Manuel Prado, who appointed a commission to study the agrarian problem (as well as housing). Most of the members came from conservative, upper-class families or from large enterprises—Pedro Beltrán was the first chairman of the commission, and the legal advisers of W. R. Grace and Cerro de Pasco also participated. Even so, the mere idea of making such a study was anathema to the Congress, which rejected the $22,000 budgeted for the commission. Beltrán turned to the Rockefeller Foundation, and, with a grant from that organization, the commission began its work. For technical advice, the commission called on Dr. Thomas F. Carroll, an American economist and expert on land reform who was then FAO's regional officer and specialist in land tenure and rural institutions.

The commission moved deliberately, taking four years to complete its report and a detailed land reform bill, which it submitted to the Congress in 1960. The attitude of some other members of the Prado administration was hostile; for example, Dr. Carroll was once refused a visa to return to Peru after a routine trip to another country on FAO business.[38]

While the commission was compiling and reflecting on the views of political leaders and agricultural experts, Indian uprisings had begun. Large estates around Cuzco were among the first invaded, though there is no unanimity on the reasons. Perhaps the abuses were the worst in this area, perhaps Indian pride and energy were highest near the former seat of the Inca Empire, or perhaps the Indians were driven to desperate measures by the massive drought that began precisely in that area in 1956.

Named premier, Pedro Beltrán promptly decreed the creation of the Instituto de Reforma Agraria y Colonización (IRAC), with

[38] With commission knowledge and permission, Carroll discussed land reform with many leaders. But when an opposition politician (Belaúnde) quoted him in political press releases, Carroll was declared *persona non grata* for two years. To prevent the commission from defending him effectively, Carroll was not actually barred until he had left the country on a routine FAO trip.

broad powers including the expropriation and redistribution of private property. However, funds were never provided for more than
a few modest colonization and road-building projects, plus a few
purchases of land (for cash) for redistribution where the pressure
was most intense. The most common government response to land
invasions during the Prado administration was to send in police to
drive out the invaders.

Though never acted on, the commission's bill was a comprehensive proposal that has been influential in framing the reform laws
of 1963 and 1969. Though it stressed measures to raise productivity
and bring more land into cultivation, the commission bill included
land redistribution and improvement of unsatisfactory forms of
tenancy. The scope of any reform would have been limited by the
requirement that all expropriated land be paid for at a just price, in
cash. Though maximum size limits were suggested for individual
landholdings, they would not apply to coastal estates, nor to any
land acquired before passage of the bill.

The Junta Militar, 1962–1963

In the 1962 elections, all candidates again promised agrarian reform. The election, very close, was clouded by accusations of whole-
sale fraud and bargaining among the candidates for support in the
congressional decision that is called for when no one candidate ob-
tains a decisive majority. The armed forces stepped in, and a military junta governed Peru for nearly a year. However, this clearly
did not imply antipathy to land reform: the junta favored reform,
and even in its brief period took several steps, however cautious, in
that direction.

In August, 1962, the junta decreed that all unirrigated and un-
exploited land claims reverted without compensation to state ownership. In January 1963 it renewed the life of the IRAC and shortly thereafter issued a decree-law setting forth "bases" or norms for
future action and legislation on land reform. Similar to the Beltrán
Commission bill but with more stress on social justice, this decree
called for expropriation of inefficiently farmed land. It also enunci-
ated clearly the doctrine that "the land belongs to the tiller." In
addition, the decree innovated by proposing significant rights and
benefits for rural laborers, who would not all receive land.

The junta began to implement this policy by expropriating and redistributing some land, especially in La Convención, near Cuzco. Some observers reported that this was mostly an ex post facto legitimization of land seizures, though during the same period the junta also used police to repel land invaders in other cases. Roads were built and some technical assistance was provided to land recipients, who rewarded the junta by abandoning their Trotskyite leader, Hugo Blanco (who was still in jail in 1970).

President Belaúnde and Law 15.037 (1964)

New elections in 1963 produced a clear mandate for Belaúnde, who was inaugurated in July. On August 12 he introduced his agrarian reform bill, which was joined by bills presented by APRA, the Christian Democrats, the FLN (Fidelista) and even UNO (a party that had supported ex-dictator Odría in the presidential elections). The Beltrán Commission bill was still before the Congress, along with at least two more that had appeared along the way. A compromise bill was hammered out in the lower house by December, 1963. It provided for compensation to landowners largely in bonds, but on APRA's insistence it excluded sugar plantations, efficient ranches and other agro-industrial operations from expropriation. By May, 1964, both houses had passed this bill and President Belaúnde signed it into law.

U.S. companies were apparently not affected, because sugar lands were excluded and because Article 25 said that land held by corporations would be subject to acreage limits only if the total holding divided by the number of shareholders exceeded the land that an individual owner was allowed to retain.[39]

Compared with experience in some countries, major reform legislation in less than one year sounds rapid, but the experience was a painful process for Belaúnde. His supporters were in the minority in both houses. APRA and UNO, the majority, agreed on very little except that they did not want Belaúnde to head a strong and effective government, and in this many observers would say they suc-

---

[39] Nonetheless, both W. R. Grace and Cerro de Pasco sensed the pressure for change, and worked on plans to sell off land to their workers on credit and with technical assistance. The U.S. Embassy in Lima was sympathetic, but both plans required legislation (on water rights, for instance), which neither the Junta nor the Belaúnde government cared to assign high priority to, so the projects were abandoned.

ceeded. UNO opposed any serious land reform. APRA could hardly summon its masses to march *against* reform, but it certainly did not want Belaúnde to get credit for what was, after all, APRA's oldest program.

1. *Massive land invasions.* As soon as Belaúnde was inaugurated, a new wave of land occupations far larger than those during the Prado regime swept over Pasco, Junin, Cuzco, and the sierra portions of Lima and Cajamarca. Some 350 to 450 communities and 300,000 persons were involved[40]—a number far larger than better-publicized uprisings in, say, Cuba. These land recoveries were accompanied by peasant union movements at the local level, and in Puno, Cuzco, Ayacucho, Pasco, and Junin there were federations of unions as well.

These movements did not materialize overnight, nor were they the work of fantastically effective outside agitators. Most of the villages involved had been trying for years to regain their lands through the courts and the Ministry of Labor and Peasant Affairs. They had spent money on lawyers and travel that could better have been used in community projects; even so, they seldom won their suits. With the election of Belaúnde and the introduction of a land reform bill, they felt that it was now all right to just take back their lands.

In the name of "law and order," the opposition majority forced Belaúnde to order the police to dislodge at least some of the occupiers. He persuaded others to withdraw temporarily, and wait for expropriation. Police repression in Cuzco and Ayacucho, and the arrest of the main leaders in Pasco, also weakened the labor movements in those areas. In Junin, on the other hand, the movement was ended without repression, by giving the communities much of the land they claimed. When would-be revolutionary leaders went from Lima to the hills in 1965, their potential followers either already had land or feared the police, and the guerrillas were easily crushed.

2. *Valuation and financing.* The Belaúnde law contained most of the provisions appropriate for a massive land reform—but other articles provided such extensive checks and safeguards that deter-

[40] Estimates by the Interamerican Committee for Agricultural Development (CIDA).

mined landowners could and did stall off expropriation for years. Various steps required approval at the highest levels in Lima. Valuations were to be set as an average of three values: tax value (generally grossly underdeclared), market price,[41] and potential income under good management, capitalized at 9 percent. (Since badly exploited land was to be expropriated first, actual income would have been a more logical index of what the owner actually lost by expropriation; the figure could be taken from his sworn income tax declarations.)

The law of 1964 included a novel provision that the value determined was then to be divided, 70 percent paid to the owner and 30 percent credit to the account of resident workers, on the grounds that their underpaid labor was the source of about that much of the land value.

3. *Resources.* The 1964 law specified that ONRA[42] was to have a budget not less than 3 percent of the total central government budget. At first, ONRA concentrated on building and training staff. By the time ONRA was ready to move, a fiscal crisis began, and ONRA never obtained anything like the 3 percent share specified in the reform law. The average for 1964–1967 was more like 0.6 percent, a third of which went into colonization programs instead of reform.[43]

I have no reason to question Belaúnde's own support of land reform, though his writings suggest that he preferred building penetration roads into new land as a way to improve the man-land ratio without making anyone unhappy.[44] During his government, however, little cash was ever budgeted for the down payment, and actual expropriations ran far behind the amount of eligible land all studied and ready for legal action. Worse, once ONRA established that an hacienda was eligible, neither the owner nor the workers farmed very well during the long wait for the transfer to take place.

---

[41] Determined by professional appraisers who tended until recently to think in terms of a hypothetical market of yesteryear, in which land reform and land invasions did not exist and land was a safe, inflation-proof, and status-conferring investment.

[42] Officina Nacional de Reforma Agraria, successor to IRAC.

[43] Carrasco (1968).

[44] Belaúnde (1965).

4. *Actual accomplishments.*[45] Between May, 1964, and September, 1968, 61 properties with 651,419 hectares were expropriated. Some 313,972 hectares were redistributed to 9,224 families, and the rest was supposedly in preparatory stages for redistribution.

Another 324 properties with 47,132 hectares were affected in Title XV actions. Under this title, resident laborers and small share-croppers could get title to the land they tilled on long payment terms, with fewer formalities than those required for expropriations. Some 128,000 applied by the end of 1966, and 54,800 had received provisional occupancy rights certificates by that time.[46]

5. *U.S. contributions.* The role of the U.S. government and of U.S. companies during this period was not great. AID provided funds for a credit program aimed largely at beneficiaries, administered by the Agricultural Development Bank. AID and U.S. foundations supported continuing work by agricultural economists and other university scholars to build strength in economic planning and agricultural sciences, in the government, and at the Agrarian University in La Molina.

U.S. banks also participated. While Congress stalled on his bill, President Belaúnde borrowed $5 million from U.S. commercial banks (Chemical and Bank of America), to buy the Algolan Ranch for cash and thus show some action on the land front to encourage his supporters.[47]

USAID contracted meanwhile with the Agricultural Development Bank (BFA) to administer a revolving fund for supervised credit to land reform beneficiaries, for animals, fertiziler, and similar production credit. Before the due date of the Chase Manhattan Bank loan, ONRA had set up much of the 309,000 hectare Algolan property for transfer to fourteen Indian communities and to twelve groups of former Algolan laborers. ONRA arranged for beneficiar-

[45] Dirección de Promoción y Difusión de la Reforma Agraria (1969).

[46] This was the basis for enthusiastic reports alleging that Peru had by 1967 carried out a massive land reform in terms of numbers of beneficiaries. Unfortunately, this massive creation of minifundia was not accompanied by any provisions for transferring additional land to reach a minimum family unit: this measure is contemplated in the 1969 reform.

[47] Hoping that the United States would make a big, soft loan or otherwise help buy out landowners (see next section), the Peruvian Congress had cut the budget for cash down payments—but authorized the president to borrow abroad to buy land for redistribution.

ies to borrow from the BFA in order to buy the Algolan sheep from ONRA. Some 3,160 families thus benefited, with U.S. assistance, even before Belaúnde's reform law was enacted.[48]

Later on, that credit program had problems. According to ONRA's 1967 evaluation exercise, many field offices reported that when beneficiaries repaid production loans, the Agricultural Bank sent the money to Lima, and it did not return. The revolving fund revolved only once, and then—as the reform agency staff saw it at the time—went to the bank's home office to make up for the decapitalization caused by the much worse repayment record of the large borrowers. There were also problems in persuading the government to put up counterpart funds, despite fiscal deficits.

Cerro de Pasco Corporation was another unwilling participant during this period. Despite their high quality, its 160,000 sheep were far fewer than justified by the carrying capacity of their 800,000 acres. Furthermore, neighboring Indian communities were still incensed over the manner in which Cerro had obtained the land.

Cerro had acquired the lands around 1920, under pressure from the government to buy it from the owners after fumes from Cerro's smelter had ruined the pastures. Some years after buying the land, Cerro installed a filter in the smokestack and went into the meat production business in a big way. While it did not buy Indian lands, Cerro did have to pay an indemnity for damages to them, and this obligation continues.

Regardless of apparent exemption, Cerro was unable to defeat pressures to divide its land and livestock among Cerro's workers and the over-crowded neighboring Indian communities. Expropriation was completed in early 1969, under the present Revolutionary Government, with payment negotiated under the terms of Belaúnde's law.[49]

The Peace Corps, together with hundreds of Peruvian university

[48] Some AID staff tried very hard to prevent this on grounds that it was practically the same as financing an expropriation. By forbidding a repetition of such financing, they managed to delay the expropriation of Cerro de Pasco's ranches.

[49] As of May, 1970, Cerro was still appealing the valuation in the courts. Cerro has already received cash for the livestock; it will receive bonds for the land once a definitive value is set.

students, made a valuable and generally appreciated contribution in this period by teaching principles of cooperatives and simple animal husbandry. The International Development Foundation encouraged and trained indigenous leadership in the Sierra, particularly in Puno and the Mantaro Valley.[50]

Bond Guarantees

By 1963 leaders of the landowners' association (SNA) were aware that some kind of reform was inevitable. They used resources skillfully, seeking the weakest possible reform law that would nonetheless assure generous payment when owners lost their land. Supposedly disinterested study groups sprang up overnight and published pamphlets arguing in favor of some kind of reform, but against payment in bonds rather than for cash. It is possible that the SNA hoped to slow reform with a cash payment requirement. However, I think it more likely that these owners expected to lose their land in any case—by expropriation or by invasion— and simply sought to have someone, somehow, buy them out on terms that would soften the blow.

Landowners had good reasons to be unhappy about payment in bonds. For lack of a capital market, they would be unable to sell their bonds at anything like nominal value should they want to leave the country completely. The bonds, like most government bonds anywhere, paid interest rates lower than customary profit rates from other kinds of investments.[51]

Finally, payment in bonds made it possible for a future government to review the procedure and to decide that the price set on expropriated land had been too high. Partial repudiation of the bonds would be a simple way of adjusting the price downward, a risk that would not apply when indemnization was paid in cash. (Of course, this would be less probable if the bonds had been sold and were

[50] Some of IDF's financial support during this period was provided indirectly by the CIA, although the reason is not obvious, and I am satisfied that many IDF staff members had no idea that support came from that source.

[51] Like other financial investments in Peru at the time, the bonds had no escalator clause for devaluation or inflation, and by 1964 it was obvious to all that both were not far off. (To be fair, inflation and devaluation were worsened by the behavior of the landowners' congressional friends who voted spending but denied tax reform to finance it.)

held by innocent third parties—but the lack of a capital market made sale difficult.)

President Belaúnde tried hard to obtain some kind of "solid" bond that would soothe the landowner bloc. The Peruvian delegation to the U.N. Economic and Social Council and General Assembly meetings asked for some kind of international guarantees, saying that this would accelerate land reform by making the bonds more acceptable to landowners. James Patton, president of the U.S. National Farmers' Union, liked and promoted the idea for a time. Nonetheless, it died quickly in the United Nations, where other members insisted that reform is a domestic matter, requiring only domestic currency for indemnization, whether in cash or in bonds. Other bilateral and multilateral institutions were equally unwilling to buy out the landowners, though some officials said that whenever a country did decide to carry out a reform, they would consider credit for the beneficiaries.

Essentially the same idea also appeared recently in the form of an insurance scheme. The risks are still those of money depreciation and of repudiation following a reappraisal of land prices for which bonds were issued. No one has yet found a way to design actuarial tables for these risks, which depend on future decisions by sovereign governments.[52] Worse, guarantees payable in foreign exchange (which is what the landowners asked) would give a government some incentive to repudiate. Also, any agency underwriting guarantees would have to participate in the valuation process to protect itself, and thus would be intervening in the very heart of the redistributive question.

Channeling the Capital from Land into Industry

One of the more common goals of economists planning land reforms is that of somehow converting capital "tied up" in landownership into working productive capital in a more dynamic sector—usually manufacturing. Thus it was natural for various persons to suggest that the Peruvian landowner be guided from landownership into industrial entrepreneurship. A U.S. contribution to the

[52] AID insures foreign investments against political risks, but only for specific projects. Agrarian reform involves larger amounts, and insurance would be for a "high risk" group. The problem is like insuring New York City against nuclear attack, not like fire or tornado insurance for one house.

notion was published by Professors Mann and Blase, of the Iowa Universities contract group, together with Peruvian colleagues. Essentially, they suggested that land reform bonds be exchangeable for shares in a mutual fund that would underwrite new manufacturing industries.[53]

In order that the proposed mutual fund could show some quick results, before it got any real capital through the payment of principal and interest on the land bonds, Mann and Blase proposed that AID make a rather large loan to the Industrial Development Bank, with which the fund could get started. In effect landowners would be bought off on better terms, to be made possible with U.S. soft loans.

The idea of channeling funds from land into industry is old, of course. It was accomplished successfully in Taiwan. What is often overlooked, however, is that in Taiwan the landowners received shares in four decrepit, state-owned enterprises taken over from the defeated Japanese government. The assets given landowners were no beauties, but they at least already existed. Schemes to create new industries in order to pay off landowners require that new resources be put into the system from somewhere.[54]

At any rate, the agriculture-to-industry idea thrived in Peru, and appears in the new reform law as well. In its present form, it serves to show good will (or at least an absence of bad will) toward the ex-landowner, and yet it appears that with proper management it will not lead to either waste of resources or a new kind of "latifundia" in manufacturing. Specifically, the quantity of bonds likely to be issued and presented in 1970 and 1971, at least, will not come close to exhausting the Industrial Bank's loanable funds. Also, the bank will presumably advance funds on the basis of the present value of the bonds; for 5 percent, twenty-five-year bonds, that is not much when discounted at the bank's normal interest rate of 14 percent. Conversion at face value is unthinkable for various

[53] Mann, Blase, and Paz (1964). Since inflation was a more immediate threat than ordinary business risks, the authors expected widows, nonprofit institutions and other unlikely potential industrialists to welcome expropriation of their land, provided they could turn in their government bonds for mutual fund shares.

[54] In any case, the real problem is usually a shortage of commercially feasible projects, rather than a serious shortage of loanable funds for sound projects.

reasons, one of which is that it would reward most those who deserve the least: those receiving thirty-year, 4 percent bonds.

Agrarian Reform under the Revolutionary Military Government

Between October 3, 1968, and the proclamation of Decree-Law 17,716 on June 24, 1969, it appeared that little was happening on the agrarian front. The IPC affair and subsequent sputtering, plus the capture of tuna boats fishing without Peruvian licenses, monopolized public interest in the United States and even in Lima. In fact, however, the bureaucratic machinery continued to operate and to grind out Title XV and other modest actions under the 1964 law, with more budget resources than it ever had under Belaúnde. The Cerro Corporation gave up its farm lands in January of 1969, and was lucky because it thus will get compensation under the 1964 law.[55]

With this major expropriation accomplished, and time for popular reaction to be sensed, the Revolutionary Military Government apparently decided that it was time to accelerate land reform. Its general planning strategy calls for expropriation of all large haciendas by 1975 in order to raise real incomes and hence create effective demand for domestic manufactures among the very large fraction of the rural population that has simply not been a part of the market economy. In June, 1969, President Velasco demanded and got the resignation of General José Benavides.[56] With the appointment of a "radical" and energetic minister, General Jorge Barandiarán Pagador, the stage was set for promulgation of the decree-law that was drafted during several months and then reviewed in depth by the president's advisers.

[55] Compensation included $1,800,000 in cash for 90,000 head of livestock, mostly sheep. The company has appealed the valuation of its 300,000 hectares of land and improvements, so delivery of cash for the installations and twenty year 5 percent bonds for the land requires a final court ruling on valuation. The amount will in any case be small in relation to the company's mining activities.

[56] Interviewees disagree sharply on the reason for Benavides' dismissal. He was known to be on cordial terms with conspicuous landowner association (SNA) leaders. He had expressed doubts about the wisdom of expropriating large and efficient plantations, and he fought for higher food prices (against colleagues trying to slow inflation). Still other reasons I have heard are implausible or impossible to substantiate.

Comparison of Law 17,716 and the 1964 Agrarian Reform Law

There is little need here to review in detail the contents of the new law; that has been done very competently in a recent publication of the Iowa Universities Mission (working in Peru under a contract with AID).[57] The 1969 law goes further in practically every dimension, maintaining the general structure but clearly reflecting the frustration experienced by ONRA in trying to carry out the 1964 law. Renters can get the land they till (up to the nonaffectable size), whereas before only sharecroppers and *feudatarios* (resident laborers with use rights to small parcels in exchange for labor) were eligible.

More importantly, whereas the 1964 law "froze" minifundia by granting *feudatarios* their plots, no matter how small, the new law provides that other lands of the same owner must be affected in order to give each such beneficiary at least a family farm unit. Not only that, the law obliges owners to transfer such land themselves, without waiting for reform officials, not later than June, 1970, on pain of a fine of half its value for noncompliance or tardiness.

Corporations, which in the previous law could own land provided the amount per stockholder did not exceed the permissible holding for individuals, were given just six months to get rid of their land or convert themselves into unlimited liability partnerships. The penalty for noncompliance, which has already been applied to some properties in 1970, is expropriation of the land and a fine of 50 percent of its value. The 1969 law also closes a loophole by adding together the land of spouses regardless of legal formalities concerning separate and community property of the spouses. Affectable land is increased (unaffectable land decreased) whenever labor laws are not complied with, or if the land has been occupied in adverse possession for five years.

In any case, the unaffectable land limit for land worked directly by its owner was reduced from the 1964 law to 150 hectares of irrigated land on the coast or its equivalent in other qualities of land and other regions. Owners must supply maps and titles upon demand. If maps or plans are not submitted, the reform agency will have them drawn up and deduct their cost from the compensation.

All formalities were accelerated, and valuation for most cases

[57] Mann, Morrissey, Huerta (1970).

where the owner operated the land will be based on the owner's 1968 real estate tax declaration. If no declaration was made, the price recorded when he bought the land will be the basis.[58] Appraisers only come in when the farm has increased or decreased in value since 1968. Appeals are generally limited to the indemnization amount and cannot be used to block or delay the actual transfer of possession of the land. If the owner fails to deliver the title deed in fifteen days, the Agrarian court issues it for him and grants possession in three days with police assistance if required.

The new land reform is complemented with a complete water reform, even more drastic. Present water allocations, often dating from the colonial period, are wiped out without indemnization, and a new, rational, and just pattern is to be ordained. Specifically, anyone with ten hectares or less will get water before larger owners get more. When implemented, this will be a drastic change in power as well as a real income redistribution.

Another provision of social and political significance was the moving of indigenous affairs from the Ministry of Labor (where strikes and protest movements were logical means of expression) to the new Dirección General de Reforma Agraria and Asentamiento Rural (ex-ONRA). The new emphasis is to be on production and technology, with organization in cooperatives. Land use rights are no longer inherited; death or absence causes reversion to the group. Indians are henceforth to be called peasants (*campesinos*); this is considered more dignified. The communities in effect are recognized as local governments.

On the legal side, one major innovation was the organization of separate Agrarian Tribunals, to hear all appeals on matters concerning agrarian reform, waters, unclaimed lands, and jungle lands. These courts, whose activities sometimes occupy as much space in the official gazette as those of all other kinds of courts tak-

---

[58] If he understated it to evade the transfer tax, so much the worse for him. Interviewees said most owners declared the "typical" values per hectare suggested for each province by the Cuerpo Technico de Tasaciones, an association of appraisers. No one recalled a single case in which an owner, anticipating land reform based on tax values, declared too high. This demonstrates that no one read the kind of advice economists were giving, or else owners were confident that the government was not heeding it. See Strasma (1964), United Nations (1966), Kozub (1967), or Carrasco (1968).

en together, started out with very low backlogs and have some expertise; their decisions emerge rather promptly. Decisions of the
land judges in each Agrarian Reform Zone are appealable to the
Agrarian Tribunal in Lima, and that is all.[59]

On payment for the land taken, the new law provides that cash
down payments will not exceed 100,000 soles ($2,400) for land,
and 1,000,000 soles for improvements. The bonds have slightly
longer maturities than before (twenty instead of eighteen years,
thirty instead of twenty-two years, etc., with down payment, interest rate, and maturity varying with the reason for expropriation).

The new bonds are non-negotiable. The only place bondholders
can convert them into other assets is the Industrial Development
Bank. Bonds will be exchangeable for shares of industrial enterprises which the Industrial Development Bank may decide to spin
off; such shares are themselves non-negotiable for ten years. The
bondholder may also apply to the Bank for the value of the bonds
as part of his capital for a new enterprise he himself proposes to
launch; in this case, he must put up the other 50 percent himself
in cash.

The maturities of the bonds, nominally twenty to thirty years,
may be even longer for some bondholders: annual cash disbursement for amortization and interest is limited to 150 "monthly minimum white collar wages."[60] The rest must be taken in shares in
enterprises spun off by the Bank.

Finally, the law contains drastic penalties for sabotage, with jail
plus fines equal to the value of expropriated land for owners who
dispossess feudataries, simulate parcelations, delay harvests, and
burn crops. Trial is before military courts, and no bail is allowed.
These provisions were extended to non-owners in March, 1970,
with another decree-law providing jail for unfounded criticism,
false statements about the reform, or trouble-making in general.

[59] The owners of the Tumán Hacienda tried an appeal to the Supreme Court,
based in part on alegations that the land reform law was unconstitutional and
that the sugar mill was a factory and hence should not be expropriated. Most
observers thought they were wasting their time, since any constitutional problems could be remedied at the next Cabinet meeting. At any rate, the Supreme
Court rejected the appeal.

[60] Since this is about $43 (U.S.) the maximum cash amortization payment is
about $6,500 annually.

This measure was used at once to jail several APRA leaders who tried to organize a work stoppage when a reform administrator forbade Haya to conduct a rally at a sugar plantation.[61]

Early Steps in Implementing the New Law

While Peruvians were still trying to digest the news of the new law, the government gave it a dramatic start by flying intervenors to start taking control of nine major sugar plantations and refineries of the coast, to the north of Lima. In a couple of days, the point was made: no one, however distinguished the surname, was exempt from measures of social reform. At the same time, the government carried land reform to the very heartland of APRA, the party that had so long advocated reform, but whose union leaders in the sugar mills and cane fields had insisted that it not affect their livelihood.

W. R. Grace, the only U.S. company affected,[62] went through some lively days of indecision and contradictory statements as to whether the reform would or would not include this part and that of the complex and integrated Grace installations. The government had no desire to include the paper mill and chemical installations, for instance, yet there are practical problems when distinct operations are carried out in one physical area and some of them must be expropriated.

Grace, in fact, was not even the biggest of the plantations, nor was it at all high on the "hate list" of the most revolutionary-minded. That distinction may go to the Gildemeisters, whose German and other highest-level technicians lived behind a rather high

---

[61] The measure appears harsh. It could conceivably even be applied to me, if something in this paper were to embarrass or offend the reform agency. Yet bitter experience in Chile and elsewhere has convinced some observers, including me, that it is necessary for redistribution to be done speedily. Landowners and their press can generate attacks, rumors, and even well-founded criticisms of misconduct and arbitrary action by reform officials—faster than the reform staff can refute the accusations. The tactic ties the staff up in internal investigations of steps already taken and effectively halts reform. This, in my opinion, is worse than any probable injustice or harshness in execution of the expropriation procedure. Delay raises political pressure, detains investment, and postpones the increase of output and peasant purchasing power.

[62] There appear to have been cotton investments and shares in some other holdings, including 49.67 percent of Laredo, though these appear to have been Peruvian owners with U.S. bank accounts and addresses.

wall that has a meaning to the Peruvian workers not too different from some of the meanings attached to the Berlin Wall.[63] The Gildemeisters had 11,714 hectares of cane; Grace was second with 9,504 hectares between Cartavio and Paramonga.

Since proclamation of the new law, then, most public attention has gone into speculation over how successful the government may be in training the workers to take over the plantations and refineries and run them as workers' cooperatives. One technician prepared a critical path program for the reform process for a sugar hacienda, finding 138 distinct steps up to the moment when the transfer of land ownership was to take place. Given perfect logistics, he thought it could be done in 318 days. Five to ten years, argued others. Yet by late February, a leftist magazine (OIGA) accused the responsible functionaries of having gotten to liking the life of plantation managers too much, and of behaving like Gildemeisters themselves.

Perhaps in response, perhaps to keep the staff concentrating on the heart of the process and not just on the formalities, the government has announced that the first three haciendas[64] will be turned over to the worker cooperatives on the anniversary of the reform decree law, June 24, 1970. Furthermore, says Minister Barandiarán, the other plantations[65] will be so turned over on October 3, the second anniversary of the Revolution. The motto is clearly, "Ready or not, here we come!"

Production Impact

Sugar output under the reform is up. For 1970, the harvest is expected to reach 7 million tons of cane, yielding 725,000 tons of sugar, about 20 percent over 1969. Critics will attribute the increase solely to greater rainfall, but the fact remains that output is not falling as a direct, immediate result of land reform. Had rainfall and crops declined—as in Chile from 1966 to 1968—critics would undoubtedly have blamed land reform for a large part of the resulting reduction in output. In fact, however, it will require several years to establish any causal relationship at all between output

---

[63] The wall was knocked down by the beneficiaries one month after the expropriation.

[64] Laredo, Tumán, and Cayaltf.

[65] Pomalca, Pucalá, Cartavio, Paramonga, and Casa Grande.

and reform. The problem is even harder to study in the sierra, where increased output is likely to be overlooked because of deficiencies in the agricultural statistics data gathering, as happened in Bolivia.[66]

Land Reform in the Sierra

Critics from the left were unhappy with some of the retired colonels named as intervenors at the sugar plantations; they were equally unhappy with the loud silence from the sierra. Indeed, between June, 1969, and February, 1970, it did seem as though the sugar plantations had absorbed all the available staff, funds, and interests.[67] In fact, however, a major policy shift seems to have taken place about the end of February with a decision to encourage some political mobilization of the *campesinos*. Before, as in the junta of 1962–1963, political organization has been officially discouraged at all levels.

Suddenly, letters and declarations began to appear in the press from federations and sindicatos from the sierra, asking the government to accelerate the reform and, of course, congratulating it on the good job with the plantations.[68] In March, 1970, the first new decrees appeared, proclaiming additional zones of agrarian reform in much of the sierra. This means that private land transfer is more or less frozen, the amount of land owners can retain is reduced, and the expropriation process becomes even more agile. Several haciendas have been expropriated in the sierra, and various coastal plan-

---

[66] See Clark (1969).

[67] Except in Puno, at the opposite end of Peru, where twenty fundos, 169,358 hectares, were expropriated in November, 1969.

[68] The agrarian reform agency's publicity bureau also encouraged the formation of "Committees to Defend the Revolution." The name, identical to early Cuban "denounce your neighbors" organizations, alarmed the Lima press and even the *New York Times* imagined the worst. In fact, the army quickly made it clear that such groups were welcome but were to register with and be controlled by the government. The *Times* erred in its alarm; it should have stressed the fact that there is actually much less violence under the present government than in previous years, and that not even the most ardent revolutionists propose circus-style peoples' trials followed by firing squads. The role of the committees appears to be that of giving their members a sense of greater participation in the government's program. In time, this might even become genuine participation in the design of future programs—participation notably lacking now.

tations that were expropriated included associated farming units in the sierra. The flow of declarations and letters to the official gazette is unabated, and Limeños no longer speak of the reform as limited to sugar or to the coast north of Lima.

In sierra and coast alike, unions soon complained that some owners were dividing eligible farms by private sale, permitted in Title IX of the new law, but this left less land available for enlarging feudataries' plots. Decree-Law 18,003, at year end, gave preferences for such workers and regulated private divisions. Unions also complained that owners were going into the local courts on any pretext to evict or fire workers, so as to lose less land. The same Decree-Law therefore shifted all such cases to the agrarian tribunals, where the rights of the worker to land are relevant and known to the court.

Problems for Early Resolution

This paper does not pretend to analyze all of the dilemmas of social engineering posed by Peru's agrarian reform. Nor does it attempt to evaluate that reform in either social or economic terms; that will only be possible after there are several years' experience in operating Peruvian agriculture on the new basis.

It is worth noting some of the principal current problems, however, as a prelude to considering whether United States citizens, companies, and government agencies can and should have a position on Peru's reform.

Financially, the administration of the reform is not burdensome for the present year—perhaps because salaries are not high and the total staff of the Ministry of Agriculture has not been increased dramatically, as might be expected of a reform which intends to reach 500,000 families in five years. If 5,000 extension agents are to be added to present personnel, however, there may be a budget problem.[69] This would be the technician for every hundred beneficiaries, which agricultural development experts all regard as a minimum if the reform is to realize its economic potential. These technicians would have to be resident, Quechua-speaking, and competent. That means that a well-led, massive training program is re-

[69] Obviously, this depends partly on salary levels. These are now so low that many "field" staff now hold a second job in the evening in their base town, and hence are completely unwilling to stay in that field overnight.

quired, and that most of the trainees will have to be recruited among the beneficiaries or their sons.

Such a training program has been discussed by the Peruvian government and an advisory mission from FAO and the United Nations Special Fund. The requisite institution was created on paper in November, 1969, but as of April, 1970, it still had no director. Its budget for 1970 is a token 5 million soles (U.S. $120,000), and it cannot be seriously considered for international assistance until a director is in place and a reasonable budget provided for staff, vehicles, teaching and research materials, and quarters in the reform areas.

A second critical financial need is credit, particuarly for the sierra. Productive investments in fencing and livestock and improved pasture could use about U.S. $2,000 per family, to be repaid over five to eight years from higher output and earnings. If there is a capital shortage, reform will proceed but incomes and hence peasant purchasing power will not rise nearly as fast as reformers expect.[70]

The biggest current problem in the sugar plantations along the coast is that of organization for the future. A specialized cooperative training organization under military leadership (ONDECOOP) is holding seminars and classes in the field, but it too has a staff too small for the massive task assigned—that of preparing nine sugar haciendas for reorganization as producer cooperatives in just one year, while continuing its regular programs elsewhere.

For that matter, Peru is conducting an experiment so novel that there is no consensus as to how the cooperatives ought to be organized. If all nine haciendas were merged into one monster cooperative, the financially strong (e.g., Tumán) would tend to support the weak (e.g., Paramonga).[71] If each hacienda is a separate cooperative, but everyone from mill manager to seasonal cane field hands is to be a member on a perfectly equal basis, a different kind of problem is bound to appear. Only one country, Israel, has made

[70] Readers should remember that in the sierra a primary aim of land reform is the incorporation of the indigenous population into the market economy as potential customers for domestic manufactured goods. On the coast the aims were more political, as incomes of workers were already at that level.

[71] This would be highly unjust, especially since weakness often reflects higher cash wages than those paid at the more profitable plantation.

such inclusive cooperatives work, and the members there tended to be better educated and more highly motivated than appears to be the case in Peru.

The basic problem, according to many observers, is that the field hand cannot really grasp the complexity of the specialized work of the refinery technicians, but he can grasp and does covet the better housing, swimming pools, and social clubs of the technicians. Yet even if the entire profits that used to go to the owners were redistributed, there would not be enough to level wages upward to the level of the refinery technicians—who will leave if asked to take much of a cut.

Some observers suggest that the haciendas be divided into specialized cooperatives, each more or less homogeneous in race, language, living habits, and expectations, and each with specific tasks to perform in the hacienda. The state supervisors would intervene to set prices between the growers, refiners, and technical services groups. And if the higher-paid technicians were moved to nearby towns, their relatively more expensive living standard would no longer be flaunted daily in the face of the lower-paid field workers.

Particularly if the "one big happy family" model is imposed, it will also be necessary to create training facilities for upgrading workers to fill the technical vacancies. Peruvians with the critical refinery skills are already being recruited by sugar companies in Brazil and Colombia, and one of the "attractions" is the lack of any need to adjust to more egalitarian human relations in their work.[72]

A third major area in which reform creates problems is that of marketing. Supplies and services must now be delivered to hundreds of thousands of new farm operators, who do not have purchasing agents in Lima or other cities, and present marketing channels are likely to be swamped by increased output of fruit and vegetables, crops that reform beneficiaries on the coast are likely to plant on their three or four hectare irrigated plots.

Ordinary production credit (as opposed to medium-term invest-

[72] It is at least possible that foreign technicians will find it easier to adjust to the new social conditions and stay on the job than Peruvians brought up in the previous stratified society and accustomed to elite status. This was not as serious for the Grace organization, which was more professionally-oriented, and from which retired staff have been recruited for various reform tasks.

ment credit mentioned before) will also be needed, but the Agricultural Development Bank has already made significant progress in that direction. It has finally begun to embargo and auction the land of big borrowers who have overdue loans, and new loans are increasingly directed to small farmers and cooperatives. Even so, there has been a notable lack of planning and control of the entire credit supply to agriculture, public and private. If credit is not available to farm operators at a reasonable cost when needed, potential production will be lost. The United States has a great deal of know-how in farm credit, and could perhaps be helpful in the reorganization necessary if Peru is to absorb, lend, and collect the productive loans that land reform beneficiaries need.

ALTERNATIVES FOR A UNITED STATES POLICY POSITION

The "sticky facts" of American attitudes toward land reform, and unrelated conflicts that threaten the arbitrary halting of any joint program, make it extraordinarily difficult to propose concrete policies. It is not obvious that an activist stance in support of the Peruvian reform would be helpful at all. The U.S. government and one U.S. oil company were the "bad guys" in the IPC and fishing license matters as seen by Peruvians, so any program loudly endorsed by the United States would instantly become suspect.

The starting point in framing any position, however, is clearly a decision as to whether land reform of this type is "a good thing" for Peru and for the United States. In my own opinion, the reform in the sierra is "good" in both social and economic dimensions. It is a precondition—necessary but not in itself sufficient—for human dignity and economic growth. On the coast, the issues are political, except that there will be an economic impact resulting from possible changes in production, in the sugar quota, and lower foreign exchange requirements from the elimination of profits remittances abroad.[73]

For U.S. citizens and for their government, if a Peru with rising incomes and greater social equality is a better neighbor in the world community, then I believe the Peruvian reform is also a good thing for them. As for U.S. companies, particularly those with other busi-

[73] For more extensive discussion of the "why" of land reform in Peru, see CIDA (1966), Barraclough (1970), and Carroll (1961).

ness activities in Peru that may share in the increased domestic market, the agrarian reform could also be a good thing. In any case, since failure would presumably lead to more social unrest and perhaps to more drastic reforms in other areas, business in general—Peruvian and foreign-owned alike—surely has no desire to see land reform fail.

Some comments on an early draft of this paper urged strenuously that the United States should be "neutral" on land reform in Peru. It is not at all clear what this means, nor how it might be implemented.

Through the Alliance for Progress, as well as the other influences described above, the United States helped create the expectation of land reform in Peru. The United States influence in Peru has been so substantial that even silence speaks very, very loudly. During the Belaúnde period, the United States gave some credit and other help to the reform program; failure to do so now is interpreted as opposition.

"Neutrality" is also a sticky matter when a program deliberately seeks to change relative power and to redistribute income from the rich to the poor. In the 1950s, we were "neutral" in our help to extension and irrigation programs, and because we made no effort to see that the benefits were spread around evenly, they went mainly to the rich. "Neutral" programs tend to favor whoever is now on top and getting the most out of the existing social and economic structures. Therefore, unless we are willing to consider distributional questions and adjust our programs so that they do not merely reinforce existing non-neutral income and power structures, it would be "more neutral" to cancel our aid programs completely. That at least would not reinforce existing differences.

The same critics suggest that the United States should do whatever it does inconspicuously, seeking "a low profile." This is much more attractive, particularly because outspoken endorsement would —at this stage in relations over other issues—practically amount to sabotage of the reform. This might mean that anything done by the U.S. government to help the Peruvian land reform program should be done through multilateral agencies or by low-key programs in supporting areas rather than directly in land reform. The most obvious current example of the latter is the $5 million loan to strengthen marketing facilities; this loan is apparently frozen for reasons completely unrelated to its merits, and disbursement would clearly help in an area that will help land reform achieve its goals.

Within the multilateral agencies, such as the Inter-American Development Bank, World Bank, and United Nations Special Fund, it is again almost impossible for the United States to be genuinely "neutral." In the IADB, the U.S. representative has enough votes to amount to a veto. Even abstention amounts to opposition, so long as the United States normally supports similar loans to other nations. Here, the most "neutral" position can only be attained by a positive statement that the U.S. vote will henceforth be cast strictly on the merits, just as for other projects for other countries.

The amount of capital that could be absorbed productively in Peru's reform might be on the order of $150 million per year for five years, in order to finance production-increasing investments by some 500,000 farm families. Most of this would be channeled through cooperatives, but even so, a substantial reorganization of Peruvian credit mechanisms would be needed to process the needed amount efficiently. Still, it seems clear that the $30 million loan application that has been pending in the IADB for almost a year is well under the amount that could be used productively.[74]

Various other opportunities exist for U.S. citizens, companies, or agencies that might wish to help. Agricultural research centered on those crops and products that are now imported unnecessarily, and which are apt for farming in the reform structure, could be strengthened.[75] Agricultural schools at all levels could be reinforced, required to adjust their programs to train staff for the new structures, and helped to make their training more relevant and their trainees more competent than the present graduates. Rural electrification, health, and literacy programs are relevant and could be helped without diverting resources from, and thus weakening, the reform program.

Finally, U.S. citizens in general could seek to inform themselves

[74] The delay is only partly due to U.S. hesitancy, if at all; but if problems of project design and program administration had been resolved sooner in Peru, I believe U.S. footdragging would have become an effective barrier.

[75] Programs in wheat, corn, and potatoes are just beginning, with assistance from the Ford and Rockefeller Foundation–financed research center in Mexico.

better about the aims and relevance of agrarian reform to social and economic development in countries like Peru. Once we understand the issues and their meaning for Latin America's future then we can begin to ask whether there is any way we can relate to the Latin America we should like to have for a neighbor.

SOURCES AND ACKNOWLEDGMENTS

This paper is based on an extensive literature, cited below, and on personal research on the economics of Latin American land reform from 1962 to date. My first involvement in the Peruvian reform was in April, 1964, when I taught in the ONRA staff training course at Huampaní, organized by ONRA and the FAO. Since 1967 I have participated in a joint FAO-IADB study of the financing of agrarian reform in Latin America; Peru was one of the case studies. The findings, which refer to President Belaúnde's law, appear in Carrasco (1969). This text also reflects what I have learned from students and colleagues at the University of Wisconsin, based on their own work in Peru—particularly, Hugo Vega, José Chirinos, Howard Handelman, Elsa Chaney, and David Chaplin.

I want to express special thanks to friends and colleagues who read and commented on early drafts. In Peru these were Victor Alayza, Percy Barclay, Arthur Domike, James Freeborn, Abraham Lowenthal, Agustín Merea, Clyde Mitchell, Fred Mann, Luís Paz, and Pablo Salmón.

Equally valuable comments were made by members of the Peru Study Group of the Adlai Stevenson Institute: George Blankstein, Tom Carroll, Ed Crane, Paul Doughty, Georgie Anne Geyer, William Mangin, Kenneth Manaster, Russell Marks, Enrique Peñalosa, Dan Sharp, and William Whyte.

Marilu Bacigaludo, Elisa Flores, and especially Sylvia Cabegas (of the Land Tenure Center; Santiago, Chile) provided timely and much-appreciated translation and typing for the Spanish and English versions.

Naturally, none of these persons is responsible for any errors in the present version, and some of them disagree sharply with my interpretations or conclusions. The usual disclaimer also extends to my associates in my present assignment as an adviser to the Office of Tax Research and Development, in the Ministry of Economy and Finance, Lima.

EPILOGUE

The earthquake of May 31, 1970, damaged some sugar mills, but it is not expected to reduce agricultural output significantly. The government has asserted that the reform will proceed on schedule, with three haciendas being turned over to monolithic cooperatives in June, 1970. Many kilometers of irrigation canals were damaged; it may be necessary to accelerate expropriation in such cases because present landowners are naturally not interested in rebuilding for fields they will lose anyhow in a year or two. Meanwhile, the landowners' society (SNA) proposed that the government finance a massive program to rebuild worker housing on existing farm units. The priorities set in allocating resources will soon indicate whether structural reform continues on top in government priorities.

APPENDIX: SUGAR QUOTAS[1]

Peru's sugar exports in 1970 are expected to bring in about U.S. $55,417,000, up 40 percent over the 1969 level of $38,736,000. The 1969 exports were 61 percent below those of 1968, as a result of drought in part of the producing area. (Output was down 195,000 metric tons, of which 155,800 are expected to be restored this year.)

Total sugar output for 1970 is forecast at 750,000 metric tons. The U.S. quota assigned Peru for 1970 is 333,974 metric tons, plus possible waivers; all told, Peru hopes to export 383,500 metric tons. The U.S. price is also expected to be up very slightly over 1969, reaching $6.65/ quintal FOB, up 10 cents from the $6.55 received in 1969. The world market price for any exported sugar that cannot be placed in the United States is expected to be about $3.00 per quintal, FOB Peru. Peru's domestic price is one of the lowest in Latin America, about $5/quintal. This is about equal to the cost of production at the two or three efficient plantations, said to be $5.00/quintal.[2]

If the sugar quota were to be cut or ended, and if Peru were to maintain present expected output and to attempt to export all of the sugar to the world market, and if in fact the $3.00 price were to hold, there would be a loss of $3.65 per quintal, or 55 percent. The foreign exchange earnings loss would thus be approximately $30.4 million. That is, exports would bring $25 million instead of $55.4 million.

Total Peruvian exports for 1969 brought in about $867 million, and the annual economic plan for 1970 indicates that they should rise this year to at least $966 million. Imports are also expected to rise, as part of a general economic recovery from a recession that began with devaluation in 1967 and has continued through 1969. Imports and exports are also expected to rise as a result of economic integration in the Andean Zone. (For 1970 this may be wishful thinking.)

At any rate, if the sugar quotas were to be cut off, the foreign exchange earnings lost would be about $30 million, or about 3 percent of total earnings. Retaliatory measures that might reasonably be predict-

[1] Figures from the 1970 *Annual Economic Plan* except as otherwise noted.
[2] *Peruvian Times*, March 7, 1969.

ed against U.S. manufactured goods of low priority, particularly consumer goods, could easily reduce total imports by a similar amount,
shifting part of the burden back onto U.S. export firms and companies
producing for export.

The loss of half of expected earnings on about half of the total output would, of course, have the same devastating effect on sugar plantation earnings as would any other 25 percent cut in gross revenues. It
would postpone the hoped for improvement of worker earnings; it
would make it difficult for the plantations and refineries to keep up
current maintenance and continued improvement of their plants. The
impact would probably be more in the medium to long-run than immediate, if in fact the slack were taken up by putting off improvements and maintenance.

On the other hand, ending the quota would enrage 45,000 sugar
workers[3] and Peruvians in general. In a way, it would "help" Peru by
providing a recognized need to pull in belts and suppress differences
while facing a common enemy.

In the longer run, Peruvian planters recognize that the sugar quota
will not go on forever. The land is very good for growing cane, but it
will also grow other crops, and the reform agency has expressed interest in seeing whether some of the land cannot be put to substitution of
foodstuffs Peru now imports. The same question is raised regarding
cotton, which is expected to bring in $78,900,000 in 1970 but which
faces ever-tougher competition from synthetic fibers.

For purposes of comparison with future reports on production of the
expropriated plantations, we note here that output in thousands of
metric tons of sugar cane in recent years is as follows (sugar content
varies slightly):

1967	*1968*	*1969* (*preliminary*)	*1970* (*Forecast 2/70*) *Annual plan*
8,431	8,231	8,162	8,700

[3] Ibid.

REFERENCES

Barraclough, Solon. "Why Agrarian Reform?" *Ceres*, special issue, 1970.

——. *Atlantic Monthly*, September 1965.

——. In *Report of United Nations Operations Mission Seminar on Agrarian Reform, ICA*. Santiago, Chile, 1961.

Belaúnde Terry, Fernando. *La Conquista del Perú por los Peruanos*. Lima, 1965.

Carey, James. *Peru and the United States, 1900–1962*. Notre Dame: University of Notre Dame Press, 1964.

Carrasco, Gamaliel, et al. *Mobilización de Recursos Financieros y Económicos para la Reforma Agraria Peruana*. Washington, D.C.: CIDA, 1969.

Carroll, Thomas F. "Agrarian Reform." In *Latin American Issues*, edited by Albert Hirschman. New York: Twentieth Century Fund, 1961.

——. *Land Reform in Peru*. Agency for International Development Spring Review. June, 1970.

CIDA (Guatemala and Peru). *Financia de la Tierra y Desarrollo Socioeconomico del Sector Agrícola*. Washington, D.C.: Comité Interamericano de Desarrollo Agrícola, 1966.

Clark, Ronald J. "Problems and Conflicts over Land Ownership in Bolivia." *Inter-American Economic Affairs*. 1969.

Dirección de Promoción y Difusión de la Reforma Agraria. *Ciento Veinte Días de la Reforma Agraria*. Lima, 1969.

Eckstein, Salomon, and Edmundo Flores. *Informe sobre la Reforma Agraria en el Perú*. Lima, 1969.

Ellender, *A Review of U.S. Government Operations in Latin America, 1958*. Washington, D.C., 1959.

Fowler, James R. *The Role of Agrarian Reform in Latin American Progress*. Washington, D.C.: Office of Public Affairs, U.S. Department of State, 1968.

Larson and Bergmen. *Social Stratification in Peru*. Berkeley: Institute of International Studies, University of California, 1969.

Lowenthal, Abraham F. "Alliance Rhetoric versus Latin American Reality." *Foreign Affairs* 48, no. 3 (April 1970).

McCoy, Terry. "The Politics of American Reform in Peru." Unpublished. Madison: Land Tenure Center, University of Wisconsin, 1965.

Mann, Fred L.; Melvin Blase; and Luis Paz. *Financing Agrarian Reform and Industrial Development in Peru.* December 1963.

————, et al. *Preliminary Analysis of the Agrarian Reform Law.* Report T-4, January 1970.

Ministerio de Agricultura. *Informe ante el Sector Privado.* Lima, 1970.

Mitchell, Clyde. *Land Reform in Japan and Korea.* National Planning Association, 1951.

Neira, Hugo. *Cuzco: Tierra o Muerte.* Lima, 1961.

Patch, Richard W. "Peru Looks toward the Elections of 1962." *American Field Service Report.* Lima and New York, May, 1961.

Reuss, Henry S. *Food for Progress in Latin America: A Report on Agricultural Development in Latin America.* Washington, D.C.: House of Representatives, Subcommittee on International Finance, February 8, 1970.

Rockefeller Commission. *Report.* Chicago: Quadrangle Paperbacks.

United Nations Secretary General. *Fourth Report on Progress in Land Reform.* 1966.

Van der Wetering, Hylke. *Agrarian Reform: An Approach towards Measuring Its Impact on the Provincial Economy.*

Whyte, William. "El Mito del Campesino Pasivo: La Dinamica del Cambio en el Perú Rural." *Estudios Andinos* 1 (La Paz, 1970).

William P. Mangin

6. THE INDIANS

The subject of this paper is so clearly an internal matter for Peruvians to define and deal with that I hesitate to suggest that the U.S. government *should* have a policy toward Indians and what happens to them. On the other hand, for better or for worse, the United States has been involved in and with Peru for over a century and has had, not always consciously, a policy toward Indians. Business and development loans, cooperative decisions on roads, schools, food programs, Peace Corps and AID technicians, and religious missionaries have all involved a policy toward Indians.

During the Wingspread Meeting, Julio Cotler, as others have before and during our project meetings, noted that the concern of the United States to have a policy toward so many Peruvian matters, such as "the Indians," was testimony to the extent of U.S. intervention in Peruvian affairs. For better or for worse, the fact of the policy is there. That the policy toward Indians has not been consistent should not be surprising. That it has generally followed the policy of the Peruvian government (which has been to integrate Indians in the national culture) is evident in most cases. In some cases, however, both governments have seen the Indians as a potentially rebellious or revolutionary force and the policy has been defensive, for example in the joint AID-Peruvian counterinsurgency programs (including some of the penetration highways to the jungle).

The task of detailing the complete history of the U.S. policy toward Indians I will leave to someone else. For the purposes of this paper it is enough to mention the following: Knowingly or unknowingly, practically all decisions in Peru of U.S. public and private agencies and companies involve a policy toward Indians since they are so numerous in the population.

Cerro de Pasco's hiring and promotion policies involve differential treatment of Indians. The Maryknoll School in Puno (not to mention the radio network schools) and the Adventist School and Hospital in the same area involve differential treatment of Indians. The U.S.-Peruvian cooperative *servicios* (SCIPA, SECPANE, SCISP) in health, education and agriculture played an important role in setting future policies in those fields, particularly in the mountain area, and they have influenced the lives of thousands of Indians.

A partial list of the programs of the last twenty years that have involved a U.S. policy toward Indians would include, in addition to the counterinsurgency, the road building, the Maryknoll Schools, SCIPA, SCISP, and SECPANE, the following: the AID small-loans project, the AID crafts program, the Peace Corps, the Cornell-Peru project in Vicos, the Cornell–San Marcos Quechua teaching experiment in Quinua, extensive Catholic missionary activity, Protestant missions, Point Four Plan del Sur survey of southern Peru from 1957–1960, U.S. army civic-action programs with the Peruvian army, AFL-CIO involvement in FENCAP and other unions through AIFLD, AID, and Ford assistance to agricultural programs in La Molina, BID loans to National Council for Community Development, assistance to Cooperation Popular and to PNIPA of the Instituto Indigenista, plus the influence of Cerro, Toquepala, Anderson Clayton, Grace, and other private companies.

The following remarks, I hope, are not to be taken as advice to anyone or criticism of Peruvian or U.S. policy positions. My major purpose is to call to the attention of U.S. business and governmental policy makers an important social situation too often misunderstood in the formulation of policy.

Peru, in the international stereotype world of Uncle Sam, John Bull, and the Russian Bear, is generally depicted as an Andean

Indian. There is something tragically ironic about an abused, exploited, low status group (with a "glorious" past) being chosen as a national symbol. In the case of Peru, however, there is also something fitting and correct, possibly even prophetic, about the choice.

Over the past four centuries millions of people of Indian "blood," "race," or "ancestry" in the Andes have passed from living as Indians to living as Spanish-speaking Peruvians. They have moved as families both spatially and socially. They have also moved singly and intermarried with whites, mestizos, blacks, and orientals, giving rise to the vigorous, creative urban, coastal, and small-town populations of Peru today. This long-term change has been noted by many observers and has dominated the Peruvian social scene.

During the same four centuries, however, there has been a concomitant social phenomenon that has not been so well documented. In hundreds of mountain valleys, sometimes far from roads and sometimes on major highways, many Indians have maintained a distinctive Quechua- (or Aymara) speaking culture. They have contributed many individuals to the outside society, but they have also maintained themselves as culturally separate. They have not remained unchanged, but they have changed as Indians. They have learned to defend themselves and survive in the present state of Peru, to become part of that state while retaining their own culture. The migrant to the coast or to the city who so often denied a knowledge of Quechua belongs to a past generation. There is so much less self-deprecation today and, even, a growing pride in being bilingual.

The contribution of those who do not migrate is considerable. They form part of the national economic and social system. They do agricultural work on large haciendas owned by whites, on smaller farms owned by mestizos, and they work on their own fields and for one another. They are active in marketing. They are involved in extensive fiesta networks that include whites and mestizos, and that have wide social and economic implications. They serve in the army. They make some use of the school system. They take part in political, syndical, and rebellious movements. In some ways they can be equated with a general Peruvian nonwhite lower class that is poor, rural, hardworking, and nationalistic.

In 1951, many Indians in Vicos, in Ancash, did not recognize the name of the then dictator Odría and many did not know what the word "Peru" referred to. My own impression is that today it would be rare to encounter the kind of isolation that was common then. Indians have found out about the nation and about themselves. Vicosinos, for example, have now traveled around Peru selling potatoes, been in the army, and seen much of their country in other ways, and some of them have been to the United States on a program sponsored by the Farmer's Union and AID. They have learned Spanish and have found that they can communicate with Indians from other regions more easily in Spanish than in the different dialects of Quechua or Aymara.

At the same time, it is my contention that they do constitute a separate cultural group, even when they participate in the national economy and social system of Peru. They lose members to what I shall awkwardly call the national culture, and they gain no converts from that culture, but they maintain their population through natural reproduction and are, in fact, increasing in number.

INDIANS AND OTHERS

The characteristic sociological feature of all highland Latin America is the presence, in most areas, of large numbers of Indians. Their relative status is partly indicated by the fact that even though most of us know full well that Columbus didn't arrive in the Indies, we still haven't found a better name for the "Indians." The major areas of concentration are in Mexico, Guatemala, Ecuador, Peru, and Bolivia. Indians are also present in every other country with territory in the highland area in western Latin America, although the numbers are small in Costa Rica and Argentina. This paper will stress Peru over the others because of the focus of this book, but there are many similarities.

No one would dispute the statement that there are large numbers of Indians in highland Latin America, but there are many disputes over how to tell an Indian. (There are even more disputes over *what* to tell him, but I will bring that up later in the discussion of Indianism and political change.) After examining the literature and after many discussions with anthropologists, Indians, mestizos, cholos, politicians, and others, it seems evident that clusters of traits are used to identify Indians and that the traits differ from area to area. The two most commonly used, and there are exceptions, are speaking a native American language as a primary language and wearing clothing defined in the local area as "Indian." The first, language, is the best. To my knowledge, no writer has touched on related matters such as body movements, postures, gestures, and ways of sitting and walking. These, along with language, are distinct and change slowly. Clothing, on the other hand, can be changed in a few minutes, but, nonetheless, it is a useful criteria and is mentioned by all writers.

The biological aspects of race have been discounted by most writers as an important basis for differentiation in Latin America in general, particularly in Brazil. This may be true as compared to the prejudice and discrimination encountered in the United States, Great Britain, Germany, or France, but one has only to look at pictures of the almost exclusively white generals, colonels, senators, governors, presidents, businessmen, and other upper-class Brazilians to see that color plays a most important role in that culture. In highland Latin America color, height, and body hair play even more important parts in racial differentiation. It is the case, as many authors have pointed out, that it is possible to pass from lower-class Indian to lower-class mestizo within one's lifetime by leaving the home area, changing clothes, learning Spanish, and modifying certain other cultural practices. It is then possible for the children of one who so passes to rise in the mestizo and even the general national culture. But in all Latin American countries, whiteness, tallness, and body hair contribute to social mobility. Darkness (whether Indian or Negro), shortness, and straight, black hair or lack of body hair hinder social mobility. There is, however, variation in the importance attached to race in the various countries. At one extreme there is Mexico, with, at least on a sentimental level, an extolling of the virtues of Indians and some real possibility of mobility for Indians as Indians. At the other extreme is Chile, with a long history of anti-Indian attitudes and certainly the most voluminous anti-Indian literature.

In Peru there are many social class and castelike differentiations in the population, and each region has a slightly (or more than slightly) different composition. There has been no official legal distinction among Peruvians (except for some anti-oriental laws). The much discussed Comunidades Indigenas were created as legal entities with corporate identity but, as many observers have pointed out, they were not necessarily *comunidades* or *indigena*. Recently IEP students have studied a Comunidad Indigena in Chancay made up principally of Negroes.[1] Until last year there was a Bureau of Indian Affairs in the Ministry of Labor and Indian Affairs, but it made no attempt to define who was Indian. The division has now been abolished and the office most comparable is called Dirección de Asuntos de Comunidades and is located in the Ministry of Agriculture. The new agrarian reform law does not mention Indians, and the official pronouncements have eliminated the term in favor of the more general term *campesino*.

The mountain area, the sierra, is not one cultural unit, and there is variation from north to south and from east to west. The peoples of the coastal range are more Spanish-Peruvian than those of the central valleys. The central valleys are more so than the Amazon slopes. The northern valleys are less Indian than the southern altiplano. The following scheme is based mostly on my own experience of twenty years living in, visiting, and studying the Peruvian sierra, and is undoubtedly overinfluenced by my greater familiarity with the sierra of Ancash. It is also more applicable to the 1955–1965 decade than any other. I have numbered the groups for convenience in cross references. They might better be called categories, and I do not mean to imply that they are absolute. I present them to show that Indians live in conjunction with many other people and to indicate some of the complexity of highland social structure.

SOCIAL GROUPS IN THE PERUVIAN SIERRA

Group 1. A small upper-class group that resides in the major cities of the valleys or on their large estates part of the time and in the national capital or abroad part of the time. They are mostly white, and most of them are rich. They are "of good family." They generally do not work, but some of them occupy positions as justices of the court, provincial governors or state governor, or, in fewer cases, provincial military leaders. They interact with each other and with upper-class people in Lima, and they also occasionally admit resident foreigners to their social circle in the provinces.

---

[1] Instituto de Estudios Peruanos, Lima

Group 2. A small group of relatively rich people who form a regional upper class and have some contact with Group 1 in the provinces but very little in Lima. They are owners of small estates, mines, and businesses. This group also includes locally born or longtime resident employees of the national government, the military, the church, and private businesses such as banks, schools, and the Jockey Club. Group 2 people are whites and mestizos. It is a considerably larger group than Group 1 and contains more variation politically, socially, economically, and racially. They are generally in operational control of local affairs subject to control of the national government and powerful pressures from Group 1. They interact and intermarry with each other and with groups occupying similar positions in other cities and towns of the region as well as with Group 3. They often reside part of the time in the regional city where they have their businesses, part of the time on their estates and most of them manage to spend some of their time in Lima or on the coast. Their children frequently attend high school and college in Lima or in some other region or some other country.

Group 3. This group overlaps Group 2 in some cases but can be distinguished for many purposes. The members are mostly technicians representing the dozens of Peruvian governmental agencies maintaining regional personnel, such as tax collectors, road builders, agronomists, surveyors, prosecuting attorneys, army and police officers, detectives, architects, medical doctors, operators of government monopoly stores for salt, tobacco and coca, and others. This group of *doctores* and *ingenieros* is mostly a young group, which interacts and intermarries with Group 2 and, in some cases, with Group 1.

Resident North Americans and Europeans interact socially with Groups 1, 2, and 3. Priests, ministers, miners, landowners, and technicians seem to find easy superficial acceptance as long as they do not criticize local economic and social class institutions. Permanently residing Jewish, Arab, Japanese, and Chinese merchants operate on the fringes of the first three groups.

Group 4. As with the first three, Group 4 is both rural and urban but primarily urban. It is a group noticed by many observers but not singled out. The group is made up of working people participating along with the first three groups in the "national culture" of Peru, and includes all those working for more or less regular paychecks in the white-collar category, that is, bank clerks, governmental clerical employees, taxi drivers, primary school teachers, police, and army career noncommissioned officers. Two categories within Group 4 can be distinguished in Peru by the terms *empleado*, ("employee"), referring to white-collar workers, and *obrero*, ("worker"), referring to blue-collar workers. Unionization is strong in both groups.

Political party organization is also strong, and probably between a fourth to a third of the *voters* in Peru are in this group. They are largely literate and are in touch with national and international events. There is some antagonism between *empleados* and *obreros* and some feeling among *empleados* that manual labor is demeaning but organized factory and mine workers are not generally thought of as being *peones*, that is, serfs, or as Indians. There is overlap in pay between the highest-paid *obreros* and the lowest-paid *empleados*.

Since none of the groups in this outline represent discrete categories and are arbitrarily separated by me, it could just as easily consist of two groups, employees and workers, characterized by the heads of families having more or less steady work. Women contribute much more to income earned outside of the home in Group 4 than in any other group.

Group 5. I will call this the mestizo group. The word "mestizo" is not widely used in Peru except by writers and social scientists. I use it here to refer to people living on farms and in small towns who are historically descendants of early Spanish settlers, many of whom married with Indians. Racially they are mixed, and it would be impossible in most cases to distinguish them from Indians on biological grounds. There are more tall, light-skinned people among them, but the overlap in physical characteristics between Groups 5, 6, and 7 is almost total.

They constitute also an economically varied population of artisans such as potters, tailors, carpenters, hat-makers, barbers, blacksmiths, and tinsmiths, as well as small landowners, minor officials of the government, small store owners, and some teachers. Some would rank in wealth with members of Group 2, some would fall below the wealthiest members of Group 6, and, in a few cases, of Group 7. At the bottom of Group 5 socially are subsistence farmers and day laborers who are Spanish speakers and can trace their connections with a "good family" in the area and who are recognized locally as non-Indian. They are fairly numerous and constitute a mestizo peasantry.

The economically deprived of Group 5 are in some ways analogous to "poor whites" of the United States in that they are in direct competition and daily contact with cholos and Indians and often harbor the bitterest resentment.

Group 6. This group is widely recognized in Peru by the term "cholo." The word has many meanings, some derogatory, some friendly, and some descriptive. In this case I refer to a group similar in many ways to Groups 4, 5, and 7. They are people in transition from Indian to modern national Peruvian. Racially they are varied but with few whites. They are mostly Spanish speakers, but many speak Quechua as their primary language. More men than women speak Spanish. With regard to clothing they are generally bicultural, wearing on different occasions factory-made "western" clothes similar to those worn by mestizos and members of the other mentioned groups and on other occasions "Indian" clothes, or combinations of the two. Again, women are usually more Indian than men. Cholos are often born in Indian communities or are children of parents born in Indian communities. Their children, generally, along with many of the children of Group 5, pass into Group 4. Some few pass to Group 3. Some remain in the group, but in the main it is a transitional group. In Group 5 (the mestizos) there are few men between the ages eighteen and thirty in the mountains. They migrate to the large cities and plantation towns of the coast.

They are farmers, both hired and small owners, truck drivers and owners, market sellers (mostly women), organized and unorganized laborers, agricultural middlemen, policemen, soldiers, prostitutes, janitors, and are found in many small business operations. They have the great advantage of not only not being encumbered by the Spanish tradition of according low prestige to manual labor, but of still having the Indian tradition of respect for hard physical labor. In addition they exhibit a high degree of ambition for social mobility for their children. They save and reinvest in small enter-

prise. Many have joined cooperatives and many have also joined
Protestant groups, North American Catholic congregations or various sects of the Communist party, at least in part to break out of
the traditional mestizo and Indian pattern of spending any accumulated wealth on sponsoring religious fiestas.

There are other motivations, obviously, and many cholos do not
join these groups. They do, however, tend to be a highly political
group, participating in election campaigns and pressure activities.
They tend to be strongly nationalistic Peruvians while also being
strongly against or cool toward many traditional Peruvian institutions such as upper-class privilege, church power, landlord domination of local courts and governments, and certain criollo social and
recreational customs associated with non- and usually anti-Indian
Peru, particularly with people from the coast.

The cholos are the hard-core *serranos* (mountain people).
Groups 1 through 5 are also mountain people but they pass more
easily outside, and the cholos make much less of an effort to hide
their mountain origins. In recent years, judging from hundreds of
personal experiences as well as newspaper accounts, popular books
and songs, national advertising, political appeals, and other indications, there is an increasing pride in sierra origin and even in being
Indian. At a typical cholo celebration, even in Lima, criollo music
and food are rarely encountered. The music is mountain Indian,
Caribbean (such as pachangas and chachas) and North American
rock and roll. The food is mountain Indian and "modern" Peruvian
(such as hot dogs, hamburgers, Coca-Cola, and pizza). A popular
criollo recording artist, Luis Abanto Morales, perhaps misreading
some of the clues, recorded a waltz called "Grito del Pueblo" in
which he condemns the Americanization of popular taste as un-
Peruvian. He says that were Atahualpa to rise from the dead he
would not approve. I am not so certain.[2]

---

[2] In the song (Sono Radio, 10004A-X-45) Abanto Morales says that Atahualpa
and Cervantes would be upset by the anglicization of Spanish, and the Quechua
is thrown in secondarily. Most Peruvian Indians would have no idea that Atahualpa was a leader in the Inca empire.

Songs that appeal to the new Indian nationalism are quite popular and at
times are very topical; for example, "I Would Like to be a Congressman" (Sono
Radio 12036-A-45), where the singer, El Embajador de Quiquijana, says he
would bring electricity, drinkable water, and dignity to his community.

This group may acquire some intergenerational stability as it gains political power, particularly if it associates itself with a growing Quechua nationalism.

Groups 4, 5, and 6 form the majority of the population of the mountain valleys, perhaps some 65 percent, and comprise what we might call the lower-middle-class and working-class populations. They can be thought of as equivalent to Lloyd Warner's "middle majority" in the United States. They are primarily Spanish speakers, although many are bilingual in Quechua. They are racially mixed, although sociologically non-Indian. They are economically productive and consciously members of the Peruvian nation.

Group 7. The Indians form this group, as defined by themselves and by others. There were many different kinds of Indians, and local differences in dress, language, and custom (and even physical type) can still be distinguished. The spread of the Inca empire did much to standardize some aspects of language and social structure and to accustom people to changes at the top of the leadership pyramid. In some areas large-scale mining enterprises developed. In some others mammoth haciendas were created. In the Mantaro Valley and some valleys of the north smaller farms predominated. Land tenure is varied, and the numbers of landless Indians is greater in the south. Indians live in comunidades, haciendas, manors, small farms, towns, and high plains.

Indian forms of the family are different from national Peruvian forms, and, in many areas, descent and inheritance patterns are within patrilineal lines and obligations to certain groups of relatives are strong. Religion is nominally Catholic, but in many communities the mixture of Catholic and pre-Spanish religion is so great that a European or North American Catholic would not recognize the resulting product. The mythology, cosmology, and general view of man to nature and man to man are quite different from the European counterparts, and Indians do not start from the same "universal truths" as do Spanish-speaking Peruvians.

Indians in legal *comunidades*, because of the necessity to acculturate strategically and to protect their land from encroachment by hacienda owners, have had to learn enough law and politics to protect themselves. Indians on haciendas have often been cushioned against the national culture and against land encroachment by the hacienda owner who sees cultural isolation as a way to keep his cheap labor force. Indians far from roads and in communities of free landholders are often even more culturally isolated than hacienda Indians. There is variation, as I have said, but they are properly placed in the same category because of their common language and what this implies in terms of non-European culture and philosophy.

Anthropologists refer to a "trinity" of land, animals, and family as basic to Indian life. They certainly are, but this same trinity is also basic to upper-class and mestizo life. Indians are and have been involved in two economies. They have a local economy based on kinship, mutual obligation, and the fiesta system. They are also intimately related to the national economy. They are inveterate merchants. Most Indian women have an awareness of fluctuations in the national price of eggs and small animals, and most men trade in cattle and agricultural produce raised on their own fields. A good percentage of Indian families operate small stores in their houses and some have fairly large enterprises. Saving money is common, particularly hard money in the form of coins, and, as the credit cooperative movement has discovered, considerable capital has been out of circulation in Indian strongboxes.

A very appropriate characterization of Indian social organization in Peru is that of Ralph Beals (1953), who says that they participate in an "internal prestige system." The communities resemble what Wolf (1957) refers to as "closed corporate communities." Local politico-religious office connected with the fiesta system is highly prized and sought after but has little impact outside of a local community. Indians are at the bottom of the social scale in the valley and suffer from discrimination at all levels. They are effectively barred from justice in courts, equal treatment in the draft, educational opportunities, and general national participation. They are virtual slaves in the area, and Indians can be and occasionally are killed by whites and mestizos with impunity. A frequent comment to North Americans in the area is, "We should have killed them all the way you did." The term "brute Indian" (*indiobruto*) is used as frequently as the term "Indian."

Indians frequently have reciprocal feelings of hostility, but they manifest themselves in action much more rarely. There is an increasing awareness on the part of Indians that they are Indians.

Previously, most thought of themselves as natives of a small region and made little connection between themselves and Indians of other parts of the valley, to say nothing of the rest of the country. Improvements in transportation, communication (transistor radios and Quechua-language broadcasts), increased knowledge of Spanish, more men in military service, more two-way migration to coastal areas for short-term work contracts on sugar and cotton plantations, plus deliberate propagandizing by the government and by political parties have made Indians in Peru conscious of the existence of other Indians. If the Quechua nationalism now emerging around Cuzco in the south (Neira, 1964) should spread and combine with the general *serrano* (mountain Indian) nativism (Group 6), it would make Indians a much more important political force in the country than they have been in the past.

The purpose of this discussion of seven vaguely defined, overlapping social groups is to point out the complexity of the social situation. It can be further complicated by pointing out that just over the mountains to the west there are many more groups, many different kinds of land tenure, social class relationships, and power struggles. To the east in the upper valleys of the Amazon are still different patterns. In the Huancayo valley in the central Andes there are very few small estates, and an Indian group has a long, stable history of successful competition with whites and mestizos. The Cuzco region is again different, with stronger caste lines, strong communist and Trotskyist groups, guerrilla fighters, and Quechua nativism. In the far south the Aymara patterns are quite distinct and in many areas Aymaras, Quechuas, and mestizos live in proximity to each other. To the north in La Libertad and Cajamarca are large numbers of people who are "Indian" in every respect except the most important in other regions, speaking an Indian language. There is very little Quechua in Cajamarca. In the far north, in the mountains of Piura, there is practically no Quechua and no Indian culture. The north coast is different from the south coast. There are fishing communities, communities made up largely of Negroes, cities built around fish-meal plants, cities and camps built around mines, plantation communities, company railroad towns, oil company towns, and isolated Indian communities such as Cuyo-cuyo and Ayapata that use pre-Incaic agricultural calendars. There are various migration patterns of communities or individuals practicing different kinds of herding and agriculture or fishing. There are villages along the coast that have two locales, one on the sea and one inland.

In Q'ero most families have plots of land at four thousand feet in tropical jungle, plots in the temperate area partway up the mountains, and plots and pastures on the high plain from twelve to sixteen thousand feet. Many villages have regular migratory trips to jungle or coastal plantations to harvest crops. There are communities that move to the desert of Chancay each year to pasture sheep and goats on the vegetation that appears toward the end of the drizzly season, who then sell much of the livestock and return home.

Tarapoto, a few years ago a small, quiet jungle town, now has one of the continent's busiest airports. Pozuzo, in the jungle near Oxapampa, still has many traits brought by German colonists in the mid-1800's. Foreign influence is strong in many areas of the jungle because of missionaries and prospectors. One town is practically owned and controlled by a fundamentalist American Protestant road builder. There are third-generation German communist hacienda owners near Cuzco and Italian fascist hacienda owners near Tingo María. It would be impossible to understand the Puno area without understanding the pervasive influence of U.S. Maryknoll Catholics. North American and Western European technicians abound, as do Spanish, Irish, and North American priests. Foreign salesmen are everywhere. Some areas are controlled by U.S. or European mining or business firms.

The above variations exist outside Lima. Within this city of about three million residents, at least half of whom are migrants from the provinces, the variation is also enormous. In many ways Lima, although on the coast, can be thought of as a highland community for many of its residents. There are some attempts at re-creating highland communities in Lima, and many thousands of highlanders are making new lives for themselves in the city.[3]

---

[3] Unfortunately, little discussion took place at this project's meetings concerning U.S. policy toward urbanization in Peru as explained in the introductory portions of this book. AID and other agencies have been very active in housing, water systems, social services, and urban planning. Through technical assistance and direct and international loans, as well as through private U.S. companies

Were we to examine life histories of highland Peruvians, both those who have stayed at home and those who have migrated, we would find that many of them complicate the situation even more by belonging during their lifetimes (or even at the same time) to several of the groups I have described. We would also find a number who wouldn't quite fit any of the groups.

The Indian areas of Peru have also gone through a violent acculturation period with relocations, depopulations, and a few years of tranquility. Many of the problems of Indian-white relationships can be traced back to colonial times. It has become standard now to blame problems on communism, U.S. imperialism, or both, depending on one's political position.

But colonial institutions persist in present-day Latin America. Mariátegui's *Seven Interpretative Essays on Peruvian Reality* (1928) traces the development of problems of land tenure, concentration of wealth in few hands, relationships of Indians with other groups, public education, religious institutions, regionalism, and centralization. The book, with few changes, could have been written in 1966 (Mariátegui, 1957). Similar examples are available for other countries. The common problems presented by urbanization, industrialization, and overpopulation, plus the effects of improved communications and transportation on aspirational levels, outside and inside agitation for political and social change, and involvement in the cold war, continue to give a similar cast to the highlands.

INDIANS AND CHANGE

George Foster, an American anthropologist with broad experience in applied work in Latin America, has devised a scheme he calls "the image of limited good." He claims explanatory and predictive value for the model of "limited good." I have been impressed with how the scheme fits my own experience in Peru in

---

(IBEC, Hogares Peruanos) and church-related agencies (Credit Co-ops), the U.S. has had a direct, if somewhat ambivalent, effect on urbanization in Peru. In the massive area of squatter settlements there seems to be a trend during the last few years for the U.S. and Peruvian governments to emphasize rehabilitation rather than eradication and replacement with expensive public housing. It seems a much more realistic policy.

both mestizo and Indian communities and with migrants from the mountains to Lima. It also fits numerous other situations described in the highland literature, particularly in the fields of community development and introduction of technological change. Foster (1965, p. 296) says:

I mean that broad areas of peasant behavior are patterned in such fashion as to suggest that peasants view their social, economic and natural universes—their total environment—as one in which all of the desired things in life such as land, wealth, health, friendship and love, manliness and honor, respect and status, power and influence, security and safety, exist in finite quantity and are always in short supply, as far as the peasant is concerned. Not only do these and all other "good things" exist in finite and limited quantities, but in addition there is no way directly in peasant power to increase the available quantities.

He also says that the system is closed and that "an individual or a family can improve a position only at the expense of others" (p. 297). He points out that, particularly in the economic sphere, it is true that there is only a finite amount of wealth and progress and that one is usually at the expense of another. He says that extreme individualism is chosen over cooperation in preserving peasants' security because cooperation assumes leadership and peasants who accept leadership are vulnerable to criticism and sanctions from envious neighbors. He concludes, "Viewed in the light of Limited Good, peasant societies are not conservative and backward brakes on national economic progress, because of economic irrationality nor because of the absence of psychological characteristics in adequate quantities. They are conservative because individual progress is seen as—and in the context of the traditional society in fact is—the supreme threat to community stability, and all cultural forms must conspire to discourage changes in the status quo" (p. 310).

Wolf (1966) points out that the peasant is usually at the wrong end of an asymmetrical power relationship, where someone outside the community usually exercises power over his production. He adds that in highland Latin America peasants also have to bear the excessive cost of ceremonial activity in order to maintain the social order. The outside payment, cost of ceremonial, and his own subsistence use all his production. Some of the highland countries such as Guatemala and Ecuador (and parts of all of them) fall into

Wolf's category of societies where "peasants who cultivate the land with their traditional tools not only form the vast majority of the population, but also furnish the funds of rent and profit which underwrite the entire social structure" (p. 12).

There are two peasant traditions in most of the area, again Indian and European, but both have common elements. Both paid tribute outside the community, although tribute in labor was more common among Indians, tribute in produce and various sharecropping and feudal arrangements among Europeans. Both involved large expenditures for festive and religious activities and had complicated agricultural calendars marked by religious holidays. Many Indian "great traditions" have been incorporated by Catholicism and other European institutions but, in many areas of life, especially in remote sections, the veneer is thin.

The failures of many technical aid programs can be traced in part to the conditions described by Foster, and in the literature one comes upon examples of the "limited good" orientation too frequent to mention. As I said above, my own field work has turned up many examples that would also fit. But I have some reservations about applying the idea too generally. It seems to me that it ignores the impingement of outside forces on the peasant community and the position of peasants in relation to more powerful members of their society. We found in Vicos, for example, that the Indians were willing to change their agricultural technology and were blocked from doing so by middle-class Peruvians. They were unable to buy fertilizer or crop spray because they were Indians. They had no access to the government's extension service for the same reason. Once those things became available through the outside pressure of the Cornell-Peru project, many Vicosinos willingly improved their economic position.

In other parts of Peru where there was no outside protection, Indians have found that if they acquired too many animals or too much land it would be stolen from them. Ciro Alegria's novel *Broad and Alien is the World* (1941) was not overdrawn, and the abuses of peasants to each other cannot compare with the abuses of outsiders to peasants. All too common is a case reported by Marvin Harris (1964) of the introduction of Merino sheep much better than the local variety raised by the Indians in an Ecuadorian community. When suspicion was overcome and the sheep were accepted by the local Indians, wool production improved so much that the local mestizos came and stole all the sheep.[4]

Change has occurred in some areas and not others, and many people have tried to figure out why. A few generalizations seem possible. If the local value system is such that the aspirations of most of the members of a community can be realized through local resources with little threat to outside, then change does not always appear attractive. Many highland peasant communities are, to some extent, in that situation. The aspiration level is relatively low compared to middle-class, upper-class, and even lower-class urban dwellers, and many important rewards are available in the fiesta system and in holding local political office.

If some factor such as encroachment on land by outsiders, a natural disaster, or overpopulation enters to make the desired goals unavailable, or if some local or outside leader or some planned or chance exposure to new ideas makes a different set of aspirations seem more desirable than the old one, then change can seem attractive. In fact, such negative and positive events occur together, and peasant communities are constantly subject to pressures and are constantly changing. A common response to pressure is migration to a plantation or a city. Another, sometimes accompanying migration, is to draw back as the Indians do in Alegría's novel, but unfortunately the dogged resistance he describes often gives way to disorganization and resignation as, for example, in Carcas, Peru (Castillo, Castillo, and Revilla, 1964).

A third response is to acculturate strategically (Mangin, 1957)

---

[4] There are many reasons for peasants to think that they are exploiting their area as efficiently as possible. One of the reasons is that they often are. Davenport (1960), in an analysis of a traditional fishing pattern in a Jamaican village where techniques had long been tested and where the boats and the waters were well known to the fishermen, shows that they behave in a manner that can be predicted in terms of a minimax test used in game theory. In other words, they do about as efficient a job as they can given the circumstances. I suspect the same could be said about peasant agriculture in much of the highlands. In my own experience in the Andes I often have found that Indian and mestizo peasants have very sensible ideas about more efficient ways of farming and that they knew the limitations of their systems. The blocks to change were in many cases either because a landlord or employer did not want them to improve their positions or because internal distrust prevented them from joining together in a cooperative project.

by developing new ways of coping, often based on old ways presented in a new, and sometimes distorted, form, as in nativistic movements. There have been no large-scale nativistic movements in Latin America, but there have been many social bandits and primitive rebels, many of whom had small-scale milennia in mind (Hobsbawm, 1965). Indians and cholos still sing of the brigand band of Atushparia in Ancash, Peru, and two guerrilla bands operating in the central Andes of Peru in 1965, made up largely of white, Negro, and mestizo university students, that took the names Tupac Amaru and Pachacutec after a leader of a rebellion against the Spanish in Cuzco and a highly successful Inca imperialist. They were unable to attract large numbers of Indians, but the syndicates in the south have attracted thousands. Personalism plays a large role in mobilizing highland peasants but, as Hobsbawm shows for peasant movements in Andalusia and Sicily (1965), political organization and strategy are less common than manipulative charisma and anarchistic appeals based on long standing and usually merited distrust of all governments.

INDIANISM AND POLITICAL CHANGE

Indianism (*indigenismo*) goes back to colonial times in Latin America. It was part of colonialism and, to a large extent, continues to reflect colonial attitudes. The romantic *indigenista* literature is enormous, and there have been Indianists from all walks of life and all nationalities with one exception. There has never been an Indian *indigenista*.

At one extreme of Indianism is the view that the old, old Indians who are no longer around to bother anyone (the Incas, Aztecs, and Mayans, all noble) had wonderful cultures and that no effort should be spared to discover all the folktales, songs, costume variations, and ceremonies surviving. Contemporary Indians are considered unfortunate degenerate remnants of past glorified civilizations. In Peru the result is a large body of songs and tales, many Spanish in origin, published as Indian, a considerable amount of "Spanish" poetry written in Quechua, and some folk-dance troupes that reflect white, upper-class "artist conceptions" of Inca dances. Such groups perform in the United States, at French binational centers, and at the Cuzco tourist hotel. Contemporary singing and dancing groups are condemned by the *indigenistas* as having been corrupted by modern influences.

At the other extreme is the kind of *indigenismo* described by Adams (1964, p. 3).

This concern with the Indian as a whole man, a contributing citizen with a noble heritage, began principally in Mexico and Peru. There were clear rumblings in Mexico before the Revolution. It became clearly formulated in the work of Sáenz, Gamio, Caso, and others. In Peru it became apparent with the works of Mariátegui, Valcárcel, and Castro Pozo. Moises Sáenz worked, additionally, in Peru and Ecuador, promoting the ideas. What started as a partially nationalistic, nativistic, and socialistic movement, became formalized into a reputable international organization.

Although *indigenismo* has involved a variety of people, it has had a particular effect on anthropologists. The leading anthropologists of Mexico have been a part of the movement: Gamio, Caso, Aguirre Beltrán, de la Fuente, Pozas, Villa Rojas, Camera Barbachano, to name but a few at random. In Peru, Luis Valcárcel, from an *indigenista* background, has for years led the Institute of Ethnology. *Indigenismo* has been the political vehicle by which many students have been motivated to enter the profession, and modified goals of the movement still provide the rationale for much of the anthropological activity in the Indian areas of Latin America.

Indianist institutes exist in several countries. Journals are published by these institutes in Mexico and Peru, and they have produced a large amount of ethnographic material.

The one thing both extremes (and most of those in between) have in common is that they act upon and study Indians. In the case of the institutes and the UNESCO training program in Mexico for Latin American community developers (CREFAL), they tell Indians what to do. They do not ask Indians what they want to do. Until recently few people knew much about Indians and cholos in terms of their future aspirations. As shrewd and competent an anthropologist as Weston LaBarre said as recently as 1948, after stating that six other foreigners did not like the Aymara: "And in the end, if the Aymara at large do have some unattractive traits, they are those of all altiplano natives, and are shared by the Uru, Chipaya and plateau Quechua alike. As for unattractive traits of temperament, no one of these groups, not even the Aymara, is any kind of a match for the Bolivian cholo, who unites in himself the treachery, stupid cupidity, morbid distrust, hostility, and fantastic brutality of both his ancestries."

At times when the Indians' aspirations are made known, non-Indians are not always pleased and one can understand why so many *indigenistas* go back to separating Indian from Spanish traits. At a meeting of Indian and cholo peasant syndicates in Cuzco in 1963, a speaker was loudly cheered when he said, "We will kill all those who wear ties." Indianists are inveterate tie-wearers and, as a rule, solidly upper- and middle-class whites and mestizos. The Indianist political parties, particularly the Peruvian based APRA party founded by Haya de la Torre, have been white and mestizo parties and have had more success among city workers and farm workers on large commercial plantations than among Indians.

The communist Indianists of Peru have had similar difficulties. The numerous white and mestizo lawyers and doctors from Lima and Cuzco who travel the countryside exhorting the Indians to revolt against the oligarchy have some success because of the tremendous fund of resentment that exists, but their essentially paternalistic attitude comes across with much the same result as that displayed by a Republican politician in a U.S. city who campaigned hard in Negro wards. When he lost he said, "The jigs wouldn't vote for me" (Kopkind, 1966, p. 17).

It seems to me that the time is passing rapidly for the white and mestizo Indian leaders. Peasant syndicates, urban squatter invasions, urbanization and industrialization, improved communication and transportation systems, and the general involvement of Latin America in the cold war have combined to increase awareness of Indian status among Indians and cholos. There are many signs of nativistic political movements, at least in Ecuador, Peru, and Bolivia. When a popular country-music singer in Peru, El Jilguero de Huascarán, singing before a large audience in a weekly tent show in Lima, sings, "Even though I wear a poncho and sandals I am as much of a gentleman as he who wears a suit and tie," the roar from the crowd is enthusiastic, understanding, and angry. It doesn't matter that most know that El Jilguero drove there in his large automobile bought from radio, TV, and record earnings and that there are few ponchos in the largely rural migrant audience.

I would venture to predict that Indianism is dead and that in its place a new kind of Indian nativism will arise. The emphasis will be on their coping with the modern world, with land reform, industrialization, urbanization, bilingualism, education, and politics as Indians. Whites and mestizos may play a part in the organization and leadership, as in the Peruvian and Guatemalan guerrilla attempts, but the bulk of the leadership will come from Indians and cholos.

The Peruvian guerillas under Hugo Blanco in 1962 and under Lobaton and De la Puente in 1965 were not able to move large numbers of peasant supporters, although Blanco had support of a sort from some peasant federations.

Indian resentment is high and becoming more united. Perhaps one of the reasons for the limited success of the guerillas is their domination by white and mestizo students. The movements may become more powerful and popular if and when Indian leaders arise. At a time when many Latin American governments and opposition parties are concerned with freeing themselves from U.S. economic and political domination, the demands of Indians for freedom from local white and mestizo domination is a diversion many political leaders are impatient with. National parties and foreign interests from Russia, China, Cuba, and the United States are aiding and opposing various Indian factions, but none of them has penetrated deeply into Indian culture. The rise of Christian Democratic parties seeking gradual reforms is of little interest to peasants. Communist parties are factionalized and mainly based in the upper and middle classes. The U.S. efforts are generally too conservative or too baldly commercial. One meets and hears about peasant and student leaders who have made clandestine visits to Cuba, East Germany, or Russia, but my own experience in Peru leads me to believe that the United States might well finance such trips as a way of discouraging potential communists, particularly visits to Europe. Very few peasants and usually only "safe" students ever visit the United States because of visa problems. In any case, the cold war is playing an increasingly strong role in highland Latin American politics.

The reason for such a lengthy digression is that it appears appropriate in a project of this kind to sound a cautionary note to U.S.

scholars. The uproar about Project Camelot (Horowitz, 1965) is much more significant than the arguments about whether or not scientists should work on sensitive political issues financed by the Departments of Defense or State. It shows an increasing sensitivity toward the consequences of research done by foreigners in general. I have encountered bitter resentment on the part of Latin American professionals and students over differential salaries and being assigned peon roles by North Americans, as well as widespread criticism, often unjustified, of North Americans for not publishing in Spanish and not making their data available. It seems to many to be mainly a taking relationship with an occasional Latin American scholar being trained in the United States. The problem is recognized by most anthropologists, however, and is, I believe, much less serious than the political problem. Academic colonialism is really not congenial to most of us, and it is within our power to change the situation.

More serious is the increasing involvement of anthropologists and other social scientists in governmental and university contract programs that also have "public safety" and "counterinsurgency" programs operating from under the same umbrella. I think it is quite proper for the U.S. government to finance research and to employ whomever it wants, but we should all keep in mind the anthropologists from Michigan State University who were involved in a project in Vietnam that also employed CIA agents and that had as one of its main purposes training and equipping the police (Scigliano and Fox, 1965).

I don't think it too alarmist to suggest that, regardless of the political ethics or morality of the situation, if a few social scientists become so involved in highland Latin America it will jeopardize and perhaps make impossible any effective work by North Americans.

I conclude this section by referring to conversations I had with a man in Huaraz, a city in Ancash in the Peruvian Andes. The quotations appear somewhat dramatic, but the man is eloquent and Spanish lends itself drama. The man is a cholo who saved money and worked his way to buy a small hotel and store in the city. When I talked with him in 1952 he had his small children in school and seemed prosperous and content. He said he was not and that he wanted to go to Lima or, preferably, the United States. I asked why, since he seemed well off where he was. His answer stuck with me for the next ten years. He said, "I want to go so that I can participate in the passion and storm of my time. Here the movement of the world passes us by." In 1962 I visited him again and recalled the conversation to him. He said, "Maybe my children will be able to enter the storm and passion without leaving Huaraz."

QUECHUA IDENTITY AND THE COLD WAR

Indians, mostly Quechua speakers, make up close to half of Peru's population. Half of those speak little or no Spanish and live as Indians by their own and others' definitions. There are probably as many Quechua speakers now as there were at the height of the Inca Empire and they are becoming increasingly aware of themselves as Indians.

Through advanced methods of transportation and communication, particularly cheap truck rides and transistor radios, many now know the coastal region, Lima, and other mountain valleys. Many men have seen the country and talked with other Indians during their army experience. The army uses press gangs to recruit Indians, but during their terms in the army they learn Spanish and a trade, and they find out about other Indians. The many peasant syndicates formed or infiltrated by Maoists, communists, CIO, CIA, and Cubans have also raised the level of Indian political consciousness and made people more aware of their numbers and identity. There is still shame and uneasiness on the part of many Indians about their status and many do not want their children to learn Quechua in schools. My own experience has been that such feelings have declined during the last twenty years and that many more Indians are unashamed of their language and status.

During several years in Peru I have suggested to various U.S. embassy officials, particularly in AID, USIS, and the Peace Corps, that they have special programs in Quechua and that they work directly with Indians. In 1958–1959 the response was laughter or ignorance. One AID (then called Point 4) official said that he had been told by Peruvian colleagues in the Ministry of Education that Quechua only had four hundred words and was a dialect, not a language. He saw no point in fooling around with such an inadequate tool. In 1962–1964 there was more interest but still a reluctance.

The Peruvians wouldn't like it if the Peace Corps trained a group in Quechua rather than Spanish. An official of the Fulbright program (Peruvian) said, "Quechua, Indianism, Communism, they go together."

Most U.S. officials seem to have been largely uninterested in Indians except as rural Peruvians, and this policy has been satisfactory because it has been the Peruvian government's policy. Some embassy people who became involved with Aprismo became interested in the rather romantic "Indoamerican" concept of Haya de la Torre, but the Apristas have been far more active on the coast and with Spanish speakers, many of whom are racially Indian but culturally cholo or mestizo. The thrust of both past and present governments and practically all political parties including APRA has been to integrate "the Indian" into the national culture as a modern Peruvian "Western" man (or woman, but none mentions women). The feeling is that the time of Tupac Amatu has passed and that talk of separatism is divisive. I agree that it is divisive, but I think there is ample reason to expect a strong separatist movement, and that it will not matter whether one likes it or not, or whether one talks about it or not.

Nationalism and separatist movements are still strong in France (Bretons), Spain (Catalans and Basques), Belgium (Walloons and Flemings), Britain (Scotland, Wales, Northern Ireland), Yugoslavia, Russia, and other parts of Europe. Nigeria, Burundi, Kenya, Congo, Ghana, and other African states are torn by nationalist and separatist movements. Indochina has the same phenomenon (Vietnamese, Meo, Khmer, other hill nations). Malaya, China, Burma have minorities wanting autonomy. Canada has a serious separatist movement, and on and on. It seems short-sighted to me to think that one of the largest, contiguous, culturally similar nations (tribes, peoples, whatever you want to call them), namely, the Quechua nation, will not seek its day. Peruvian governments, both colonial and republican, civilian and military, have tried to abolish the Indians by pronouncement (for example, the present government has declared them all to be *campesinos*) but, for better or for worse, the Indians don't get the message. The various attempts of the last four hundred years to kill them, integrate them, or move them to the jungle to get malaria, have not been successful. The Quechuas (and the Aymaras) are tough and have continued to grow in numbers even as they also contributed their intelligence and energy to the cholo and mestizo groups in large numbers.

I will outline briefly some possible events and some possible U.S. responses. I realize that there is a certain arrogance in assuming that there can be a U.S. response independent of a Peruvian response, so I will try to put the U.S. response in the context of Peruvian actions:

1. The first possibility is the most unlikely. Let us assume that through the emergence of political leaders of great ability, a Quechua-Aymara state emerges or tries to emerge in the Andes, stretching from Bolivia to Ecuador. The opposition from the Western governments of the three countries to internal separatists is so strong that the combined opposition would be enormous. The U.S. response would probably be military aid to stop such movements, and they would be embroiled in cold war politics. I will not dwell on this possibility longer, except to say that I do not think it is outside the realm of possibility in the distinct future.

2. The second, which I consider almost as unlikely as the first, is the complete integration of Quechua and Aymara Indians into the Peruvian national culture as Spanish-speaking *campesinos*. Many white and mestizo Peruvian political leaders and many North Americans are counting on this possibility. Most U.S. policy has been predicated on the assumption that integration was taking place and that it was desirable and should be assisted. In the event that this possibility becomes reality, and it might, there would be no particular need for a change in policy.

3. The most probable series of events will occur within the general framework I have presented. The centuries of gradual and abrupt change have led to a complex social structure with overlapping groups who have different social and economic positions and aspirations. Some Indians live in separate communities, but more often they live in communities with non-Indians. As with most nationality groups, some want to mold into the general society, some want to become Peruvians as Indians, some want to separate, but most probably don't think much about it.

Depending upon political circumstances some people will identify as Indians in one context and not in another. The first two possibilities are presented as ideal types. The Peruvian and U.S. governments will be responding to actual events that will never be clear-cut examples of Quechua nationalism or separatism, but, rather, they will be complicated, multi-caused events with Quechua identity being only one facet. If I am correct in assuming that it will increase in importance as a political phenomenon, however, it will be necessary for interested governments to have a policy toward or at least to be aware of the existence of Indians as a distinct culture precisely because their concerns will become a factor in controversies and will be used by others. In fact, as many observers have pointed out, mestizos and whites in Peru have used local Indian protests against abuses as political leverage in their disputes with other whites and mestizos for generations. As the idea of Quechua independence moves into the international political arena, it will become a factor in the cold war.

Since the United States has already been associated with a military operation against two guerilla bands, a policy is beginning. U.S. planes, bombs, napalm, and U.S.-trained troops were involved in the operation in 1965, and the accusation has been made that U.S. special forces present in Peru also took part. Many local Indians, some involved in the movement, most not involved, were killed, and it is still difficult to evaluate the impact on the area. In 1960, after the Guardia Civil wounded ten and murdered four Indians on the hacienda Huapra near Vicos, the United States seemed to many to be involved on the side of the Indians. The siding was more apparent than real. Edward Kennedy, on a chance visit to Vicos, heard about the shooting from Vicosinos and from strongly pro-Indian North Americans, and he was able to pressure the then president Prado to begin expropriation negotiations to secure Hacienda Vicos for its Indian residents.

During the peasant syndicate uprisings in La Convencion area in 1962 and 1963, the United States was minimally involved with both sides, and the situation there was further complicated by the presence of a large U.S. company, Anderson-Clayton. Conflicts with Indian *comunidades* have taken place in the central Andes where Cerro de Pasco interests were involved, and, to a lesser extent, in Pararin and the Colca valley where Grace and Company has claims. There have been many other incidents with U.S. involvement and many more without, for example the incident near

Anta (June, 1969) where police fired on Indians who were apparently protesting a real or imagined consequence of the new government's land reform that they thought would deprive them of land. I mention this Anta (Ayacucho) incident to introduce the idea that Indians in comunidades have different economic interests from Indians who own small farms and/or Indians who work on other people's lands. Thus, a policy toward "Indians" that would operate in a situation where nationalism or Indian identity was involved might cause a split reaction in situations where land reform, land redistribution, small loans, and co-ops are involved. There is no automatic Indian response to land reform or to anything else.

Given the present situation of numerous incidents involving Indians, even though in different ways and occasionally with contradicting interests, and an increasing self-consciousness among Indians, a number of scenarios suggest themselves where Peruvian governmental positions and U.S. governmental positions may agree or disagree. I will not go through the logical possibilities for response with various public and private interests, and cold war interests except to say that the United States is so deeply committed in Peru that its position is always a factor.

Governments pass away and, Chiang Kai-shek, Haile Selassie, and Franco to the contrary, no chief of state serves forever. The present Peruvian and U.S. governments will change, and anthropologists are no more capable of predicting future forms of government than political scientists, politicians, businessmen, or astrologists. I agree with Albert Hirschmann, who says that the United States should disengage as much as possible from trying to influence policy in Latin America. My immediate recommendation would be to examine the three types of situations I have outlined (not necessarily as formulated by me, but the situations I refer to) and make explicit the extent of U.S. commitment to position number two while the actual situation in Peru is much more akin to what I have described in position three (see p. 231). To the extent that it is proper for the United States to be involved in the affairs of Peru, I think it highly necessary for U.S. officials to have an understanding of the presence and varied interests of millions of non-Spanish-speaking Peruvians who will not go away in spite of pronouncements from Lima, Washington, Havana, Geneva, Moscow, or Peking.

It is difficult to take a pro or con position with regard to what policy should be. In part the difficulty is due to the internal nature of the problem, as I pointed out in the beginning. In part it is due to the conflicts within the United States over what proper foreign policy should be pursued. My own position on questions of cultural identity should be obvious by now. I think that the world is a better place when diversity flourishes.

In the early fifties a friend of mine was working on African cultural identity within new states, and when I said that I thought Nigeria had to hold its nationality groups together he said, more or less, "You might think that but it doesn't mean it is going to be that way. Diversity is our only defense against the cultural imperialism of the United States and Russia." I think that idea is behind much of the rhetoric of the Third World, and I believe it has merit. The U.S. view that the melting pot has worked for us influences our view of other nations. We are generally against "Balkanization." Revisionist historians and anthropologists are beginning to question the success of the melting pot in the United States in terms of its social cost, and even to question whether there has been much of a melting pot. Ethnic identity in much of the United States is European (Italian, Irish, German-American), Asian (Japanese, Chinese, Philippine-American), Spanish-speaking, and racial. The melting-pot idea, however, has a strong hold on many of us and plays a role in our view of other countries.

I have heard U.S. officials, particularly rural southerners, compare Peruvian Indians with U.S. blacks in terms of their social position and conclude that the situation in Peru is more optimistic because physical differences are not as important in differentiating people. The implication of such a comparison is that integration is the solution and that it will be easier in Peru. My impression is that such a position is fairly widely held among North Americans who work in the Andes. I think it is a false analogy because U.S. blacks, in spite of resentment and political nativism, are, as Malcolm X said, "one thousand percent American." They are physically visible as different, but culturally they are one of the oldest American groups. Peruvian Indians are physically indistinguishable from much of the rest of the population, but they are culturally different. The consequences of supporting a policy based on integration in Peru would at least involve the risk of misjudging the situation. At most it could involve alienation of millions of Andean Indians from the United States.

The consequences of a policy supporting Quechua separatism in any form would, at least, involve the risk of misjudging the situation. But, assuming that I am partially correct in my analysis, the roots of separatism are there. In that case, such a policy would involve the risk of alienating any foreseeable Peruvian government and hundreds of thousands of Peruvian citizens. The feeble efforts of private U.S. groups to assist Ibo nationalists in Nigeria to prevent starvation resulted in the alienation of the Nigerian government from the United States. Nationality problems are extremely delicate politically and are not especially amenable to outside influence.

There is a weak but growing position in the United States (called "creative" by its proponents, called "neo-isolationism" by its critics) that would suggest disengagement from other nation's internal problems. The United States has been involved in the war in Indochina since 1943 with very little to show for it, and supporters see disengagement as a way to prevent future similar involvements. The consequences of a disengagement policy also could involve misjudging the situation. Since there is little we can do about Andean Indians anyway, I suggest that disengagement would give us a chance to devote some of our resources and energies toward solving some of our own internal problems. Being a conservative anarchist in my own politics, I believe that solutions muddled through in local areas are usually better than muddled solutions imposed from outside.

REFERENCES

Adams, Richard M. "Politics and Social Anthropology in Spanish America." *Human Organization* 23 (1964):1–4.
Beals, Ralph L. "Social Stratification in Latin America." *American Journal of Sociology* 58 (1953):327–339.

236   *William P. Mangin*

Castillo, Hernan, Teresa Castillo, and Arcenio Revilla. *Carcas: The Forgotten Community*. Ithaca: Cornell Peru Projects, 1964.

Davenport, William. *Jamaican Fishing: A Game Theory Analysis*. New Haven: YUPA, No. 59, 1960.

Foster, George M. "Peasant Society and the Image of Limited Good." *American Anthropologist* 67 (1965):293–315.

Harris, Marvin. *Patterns of Race in the Americas*. New York: Walker Paperback, 1964.

Hobsbawn, E. J. *Primitive Rebels: Studies in Archaic Forms of Social Movements in the 19th and 20th Centuries*. New York: Norton, 1965.

Horowitz, Irving Louis. "The Life and Death of Project Camelot." *Trans-action* 3, no. 1 (1965):44–47.

Kopkind, Andrew. "New Hope for Republicans." *New Republic* 5 (1966): 15–18.

LaBarre, Weston. *The Aymara Indians of the Lake Titcaca Plateau, Bolivia*. Memoir of the American Anthropological Association, No. 68, 1959.

Mangin, William. "Haciendas, Comunidades and Strategic Acculturation in the Peruvian Sierra." *Sociologus* 7, no. 2 (1957):142–146.

Mariátegui, José Carlos. *7 Ensayos de Interpretación de la Realidad Peruana*. Lima: Biblio Amauta, 1957.

Neira, Hugo. *Cuzco: Tierra y Muerte*. Reportaje al sur. Problemas de Hoy, Lima, 1964.

Scigliano, Robert, and Guy H. Fox. *Technical Assistance in Vietnam: The Michigan State University Experience*. New York: Praeger Special Studies, 1965.

Wolf, Eric. "Closed Corporate Peasant Communities in Mesoamerica and Central Java." *Southwestern Journal of Anthropology*, 13 (1957):1–18.

———. *Peasants*. Englewood Cliffs, New Jersey: Prentice-Hall, 1966.

Charles T. Goodsell

7. DIPLOMATIC PROTECTION OF
U.S. BUSINESS IN PERU

In an address before the Business Council in 1962, Secretary of State Dean Rusk discussed, among other aspects of U.S. foreign economic policy, diplomatic protection of American business abroad. He reiterated the longstanding doctrine that the U.S. government will intercede on behalf of American business firms when they suffer "economically unjustified expropriation or harassment." Also he pointed out that various forms of investment guaranties are available from the government. Then, using metaphors refreshingly extravagant for a high government official, the secretary made the following additional point:

A good fire department and fire insurance coverage are indispensable, but basic prevention of fires—natural or political—stems from sound, fireproof construction and extreme care in handling flammable materials. American firms in developing nations often operate in a volatile political atmosphere. You cannot handle liquid oxygen in the same way you handle pig iron. . . . A primary responsibility for avoidance of political risk, therefore, rests with the firm.

I am confident that American firms can, through their own efforts, avoid a large part of the political risk inherent in operations in developing nations.[1]

[1] *Department of State Bulletin* 47 (November 5, 1962):687.

It is to this matter of "sound, fireproof construction and extreme care in handling flammable materials" that this paper is addressed. I warmly endorse the position that U.S. firms can, by enlightened behavior, avoid some of the political squabbles that lead them to appeal for diplomatic intervention. But my thesis goes beyond stating that largely self-evident proposition. I will argue that U.S. diplomats, both in Washington and the embassies, need to reorient *their* behavior so as to encourage American businessmen to act in their *own* self-interest. At the same time, I urge that traditional forms of diplomatic protection be reoriented so as to have some chance of success in this age of rising nationalism in the developing lands. Although the concepts developed are, I hope, applicable to foreign investment in many contexts, the specific illustrations and recommendations concern Peru.

ALTERNATE MODELS OF ASSISTANCE

All social models are oversimplifications to a greater or lesser extent, but they are sometimes useful to heighten differences for comparative analysis or—in this case—to lay out clearly various options for U.S. foreign policy. The organization of this paper rests upon three models of diplomatic assistance to foreign investment. Two are essentially past and present protection activity. The third is, by and large, a form that is not actively pursued at the present time.

1. *The "good offices" model.* This is the more mild of the two traditional forms. It involves careful inquiry into the company's complaint for factual substantiation. In warranted cases, appeals are made to appropriate officials of the host government for explanation, and, hopefully, correction of the problem. Mediation or negotiation may ultimately develop. The diplomat's style is informal, personal, and courteous.[2]

2. *The "forceful interposition" model.* Much stronger than the first form, this concept emphasizes the filing of formal, official protest rather than informal inquiry. Included also is the notion of pressure on the host government. This may be achieved by threats, direct or implied, or the actual invocation of sanctions. These may

[2] The "Good Offices" concept, including the name, is known in the literature on this subject (although not necessarily defined in this way). The other two concepts and names are original with this paper.

include traditional actions such as trade retaliation, embargoes, blockades, or armed intervention; in the current era of "aid" diplomacy, however, the severance of foreign assistance is a possible sanction.

3. *The "self-preservation" model.* This proposed third alternative refers to encouraging firms to take steps on their own initiative that would lead to their own political self-preservation or at least to protection of their monetary interests. Unlike the first two models, diplomatic assistance in this case does not respond to events but attempts to anticipate them. As already noted, it is directed to the companies themselves rather than to the host government and is intended to modify their behavior and only indirectly that of the host government.

Several caveats are in order before discussing the application of these models or alternatives. First, the assumption is implicit that the United States government *should* endeavor to protect American business interests in other countries. Many would no doubt question the moral or political validity of that assumption. But regardless of one's value judgment on this matter, the ancient character of the concept of diplomatic protection and—more importantly— the internal realities of American politics prohibit serious consideration of a nonprotection alternative. Hence a possible fourth model, that of "no intervention," has not been included in this analysis.

Second, diplomatic protection is not the only means available to U.S. investors in their dealings with foreign governments. In fact, my research on the politics of American business in Peru reveals the unmistakable conclusion that the vast bulk of transactions between U.S. firms and the Peruvian authorities are direct, with little or no involvement by the American Embassy or State Department.

A third caveat is that the following discussion is limited to the protection of American property in Peru, not persons, and that in treating the protection of property I deal only with existing investments or interests and not potential future projects.

Finally, a special word of caution is necessary in interpreting the self-preservation model. I am not limiting that concept to preservation of the status quo or of situations preferred by the companies. Rather, it is protection of their long-term interests, which in certain situations may involve very substantial changes in their behavior. Ultimately, in fact, company interests may best be met by phased withdrawal or even sudden departure. In the latter case "protection" would constitute seeking suitable arrangements for compensation for properties acquired by the host government.

GENERAL U.S. PRACTICE

Instructions in the *Foreign Affairs Manual* make it clear that U.S. diplomatic officers abroad are generally expected to intervene on behalf of American companies that get into difficulty. The *Manual* states, "the protection of American interests, both public and private, which are threatened or prejudiced is normally undertaken by the post concerned, either through representations to local authorities or through other appropriate measures."[3]

The precise nature of the intervention is not stated. In fact, the *Manual* specifically stipulates that "the nature and extent of post intervention depends in each case on the degree of prejudice to the American interests concerned." The official rules, then, would not limit protection to any single one of the three models—they appear broad enough to allow all three.

Certainly wide discretion and flexibility in handling actual problems has been a hallmark of U.S. diplomatic protection. Cases tend to be handled individually rather than according to set formula. The State Department gives the impression of being more interested in the effects of protective acts than the form.

A few somewhat repetitive features of this activity can be identified, however.[4] One common precondition to intervention is exhaustion of local remedies. Another, stated in the *Manual*, is "substantial, though not necessarily majority, American ownership and some contribution to the national wealth of the United States through the promotion of American foreign trade or the remittance of earnings to the United States." It is noteworthy that a precondi-

---

[3] This and the following manual quotations are from the Foreign Affairs Manual, volume 10, *Economic Affairs*, chapter 900, "Trade Promotion and Protection" (December 18, 1961).

[4] J. Gillis Wetter, "Diplomatic Assistance to Private Investment: A Study of the Theory and Practice of the United States During the Twentieth Century," *Selected Readings on Protection by Law of Private Foreign Investments* (Albany: Matthew Bender & Son, 1964), pp. 787–864; and Eugene Staley, *War and the Private Investor: A Study in the Relations of International Politics and International Private Investment* (Chicago: University of Chicago Press, 1935), pp. 109–177.

tion not required is the actual occurrence of damages—only the threat of injury is needed.

A number of types of situations can be identified that are commonly viewed by the U.S. government as warranting action. These are discrimination against U.S. firms (by special taxes, for example), denial of procedural rights normally granted by the host government, injury arising from violation of treaty or international comity, breach of contract or revocation of concessions or other privileges, and seizure or destruction of property without prompt and adequate compensation. In all these situations, however, a "rule of reason" operates—the host government's action must be "unreasonable."

This, of course, is once again merely reference to the fact that wide discretion exists. Indeed, the U.S. government does not accept the view that is ever *bound* to intervene under any circumstance—the choice is always open. Higher considerations of foreign policy are always accepted as sufficient grounds for nonaction in an individual case. The *Manual* in fact states that "when representations would be inappropriate because of political considerations or the possibility of reprisals against the American interests concerned, posts should so report to the department and defer action until instructions are received."

Has historical U.S. practice conformed more fully to one or more of our three models? It has already been suggested that the self-preservation model is not in meaningful use. Perhaps the educative function it encompasses is largely confined to generalized appeals for enlightened business practices, as exemplified by the Rusk speech quoted above.

As for the traditional models, one is tempted to assume that the good offices approach is the more frequently employed. Very likely it is often used initially as a matter of course for settling the more routine problems. One is further tempted to speculate that forceful interposition is then sometimes applied when the milder approach fails.

If the "imperialist" image of the United States in Latin America is considered as having historical validity only, the idea suggests itself that forceful interposition was actively employed in decades past but is not today. Indeed, classic cases of it could be described in Venezuela, Mexico, and elsewhere during the first two decades of this century. But interestingly, Cordell Hull, a spokesman of the Good Neighbor Policy, made sweeping economic threats against Spain as late as 1940 over possible annulment of an ITT telephone concession in that country. Moreover, the 1960 trade embargo against Cuba—resulting officially, at least, from the seizure of U.S. property—is comparatively recent history. Since vivid examples have occurred in relation to Peru in the very recent past, any notion that forceful interposition is dead must be set aside.

Under the Good Neighbor Policy of the 1930's, a general and important attempt was made to renounce force and to emphasize noninterventionist approaches in diplomatic protection of business in Latin America. But this did not include pressing business to take advance initiatives on behalf of their long-run interests, as is incorporated in the self-preservation model.

DIPLOMATIC PROTECTION IN PERU

True, historical examples of forceful interposition in Peru can be cited. From 1826 to 1861, according to one student of the subject, the American envoy in Lima made exceptionally aggressive representations on behalf of American claimants on an almost daily basis. With the advent of the Lincoln Administration, oddly enough, this behavior switched to what we are calling the good offices approach.

But prior to this change some remarkable events occurred. In 1852, for example, the aging Secretary of State Daniel Webster actually dispatched a U.S. naval vessel to the Peruvian Lobos Islands on behalf of an American who had made the preposterous claim that the islands were American territory. The U.S. navy beat a hasty and embarrassing retreat after New York newspapers exposed the basis and reason for the claim.[5]

With the advent of important U.S. mining investments in Peru at the turn of the century, more serious pretexts for diplomatic intervention arose. Very active assistance was given, both at the legation level in Lima and at the State Department level in Washington, to the future Cerro de Pasco Copper Corporation in its legal battle with a rival mining firm, largely Peruvian-owned. And in

---

[5] Louis C. Nolan, "The Diplomatic and Commercial Relations of the United States and Peru, 1826–1875," Ph.D. dissertation, Duke University, 1935.

1930, during the tumult following Sánchez Cerro's overthrow of Leguía, Cerro de Pasco workers rioted and dynamited company property. The U.S. Embassy not only appealed to the Peruvian government for protection but discussed with Washington the possibility of sending gunboats down from Panama. This was not done, but, interestingly enough, when the American ambassador paid his first official call on President Sánchez, he took with him the Cerro de Pasco general manager.[6]

Before discussing recent uses of forceful interposition in Peru, it is important to stress that the good offices model also occupies a very significant place. In fact, a good guess would be that it is employed literally scores of times annually, on a routine basis without publicity. John Wesley Jones, the American ambassador to Peru from 1962 to 1969, is a diplomat whose style lends itself to the good offices approach. To those who worked with him in Lima he was considered unusually judicious and fair, and unfailingly polite. It is unfortunate that during his last months in Peru he was publicly identified as "Mister IPC," which, as we shall see, he was not.

A couple of examples of relatively mild diplomatic behavior during Jones's tenure are instructive. President Fernando Belaúnde Terry's land reform program included plans to expropriate several livestock haciendas owned by Cerro de Pasco. The company wanted very much to retain the properties even though sheep raising was an auxiliary service operation not integral with its mining activities. Jones did not try to convince the Peruvians not to take the lands. Also he did not support the company's claim that this action was illegal. Rather, he merely encouraged negotiations over compensation. The lands were eventually taken and compensation was made.

In another instance, Sears Roebuck del Peru, when exhibiting at a 1963 international trade fair in Lima, was embarrassed by the fact that Peruvian trade unions (which have not successfully organized Sears) picketed their exhibit. Sears asked the U.S. Embassy to put pressure on the fair management to get the picketing stopped. The embassy refused, however, to intervene in any way, much to the company's chagrin.[7]

6 James C. Carey, *Peru and the United States, 1900–1962* (Notre Dame: University of Notre Dame, 1964), pp. 22–23, 62–65.

7 The company's resentment also grew from the fact that outside attempts

The Fishing Rights Dispute

The longstanding argument between the United States and Peru (and also Ecuador and Chile) over offshore fishing rights is one of two major areas in which forceful interposition has been manifest in U.S.-Peruvian relations in recent years. The controversy is reviewed by David C. Loring in chapter 3 of this volume, and thus the background details may be eliminated here.

Technically, the fishing dispute could be said to be beyond the scope of this paper, since fishing is not a fixed foreign investment in the usual sense of "U.S. business in Peru." But, of course, it is a private business, and it occurs "in Peru" if one accepts the Peruvian position that national jurisdiction extends out two hundred miles from shore. Moreover, we cannot fail to consider this highly significant instance of attempted diplomatic protection on narrow definitional grounds, especially in that it constitutes an excellent example of forceful interposition.

In early 1967 a flare-up of ill feeling between the United States and Peru occurred as a result of a publicly implied retaliation for fishing seizures. In January and February of that year, Ecuador seized six American tuna clippers, and Peru two. On February 23, during a Hemisphere foreign ministers' conference in Buenos Aires, the State Department issued a stern note. The United States was "increasingly concerned over the continuing seizure" of vessels, it said. Although the American government was desirous of settling the matter "in a friendly manner," the statement continued, the governments of Ecuador and Peru had been "informed of the implications of the Kuchel amendment."[8]

This wording was interpreted as a thinly veiled threat by the Latin American governments concerned. At the closing session of the Buenos Aires conference, the Peruvian foreign minister publicly declared that President Belaúnde might not attend the upcom-

---

were being made to unionize their Peruvian work force, which had consistently voted down unionization proposals. These pressures were from an American AFL-CIO organizer and also, oddly enough, the U.S. Department of Commerce.

[8] P.L. 680, August 27, 1954, 68 Stat. 883. It is of particular interest to our subject that this law further requires that the secretary of state "shall as soon as practicable take such action as he deems appropriate to attend to the welfare of such vessel and its crew while it is held by such country and to secure the release of such vessel and crew."

ing Punta del Este meeting of presidents of the American states. In Lima the press and popular reaction was extremely antagonistic. The Peruvian government, instead of weakening under the implied threat, had of course to take the strongest possible position. The Ministry of Foreign Affairs issued a communiqué stating that it was the "unalterable intention" of Peru to continue maintaining sovereignty over the disputed waters. A few days later the State Department backed off; it issued another statement expressing regret that the earlier note had been "widely misunderstood" as a threat and that "the fullest and most friendly relations" were still desired. Belaúnde subsequently attended the Punta del Este conference.[9]

In a more serious series of incidents in 1969, U.S. diplomatic behavior was only slightly less heavy-handed in style. Early 1969 was, of course, generally a troubled time for Peruvian-American relations. The IPC dispute and threats to invoke the Hickenlooper Amendment were in the air. To exacerbate the situation further, a rash of vessel interceptions was occurring. The outraged California tuna industry insisted through its congressional spokesmen that the U.S. government take immediate and forceful action, even to the point of providing armed protection to tuna boats. Representative Pelly arranged meetings between industry leaders and State Department officials, including Undersecretary of State Elliot Richardson.

Although the fishing interests felt that the Department of State was more interested in the IPC dispute than the fishing problem, the department's reaction was stronger than it first appeared. Secretary of State Rogers summoned Peruvian Ambassador Fernando Berckemeyer immediately after the incident to express "serious concern" over the attack. On February 19 Ambassador Jones in Lima presented a formal protest to the Peruvian government. On February 25 additional pressure was applied in Washington when a State Department spokesman strongly hinted that the U.S. destroyer on loan to Peru would be withdrawn if the Peruvians did not pay compensation for the $50,000 in damage suffered by one clipper.

But already a sanction had been confidentially invoked. On

9 P.L. 90-482, August 12, 1968, 82 Stat. 729–730.

February 14 U.S. military sales to Peru had been provisionally suspended, in accord with the Pelly Amendment. No publicity had been given to the move, however. On April 3, according to the State Department, the Peruvian Embassy in Washington was informed of the action. But the action did not break in the press until late May, when congressmen disgruntled over additional tuna seizures leaked the story.

The consequence was a tremendously hostile reaction in Lima. The Peruvian government, in fact, claimed that it had heard of the cutoff only by the May press reports. It had little choice but to request the departure of the forty-one U.S. military mission personnel then in Peru. At the same time President Juan Velasco Alvarado made it clear that Governor Nelson Rockefeller was not welcome to stop in Peru on his Latin American tour for President Nixon.

It took almost a month of patient negotiations between Jones and the Peruvian foreign minister, Edgardo Mercado Jarrín, to repair this severe rift between Lima and Washington. The impasse was broken by a Peruvian suggestion that a *quid pro quo* be effected by which Peru would agree to enter into fishing negotiations if the U.S. would withdraw the sales ban. This was done, and in July and August of 1969 a conference was held in Buenos Aires on the fishing question. But the Latin Americans made no concessions on their two-hundred-mile position and, from the standpoint of California fishing interests, the present impasse must represent a failure in diplomatic protection.

Boats are still being seized and their owners fined. The real point of this case may be, though, that a forceful interposition type of diplomatic protection—which this was in almost every respect—is almost inevitably counterproductive. In an atmosphere of growing nationalistic and possibly anti-American feeling within Peru, threats of retaliation and economic sanctions simply will not work. They create ever greater resistance to U.S. objectives, and may make even compromise impossible.

The IPC Dispute

In many ways, although not entirely, U.S. diplomatic behavior in the course of the long controversy surrounding the status of the International Petroleum Company in Peru is also in accord with the forceful interposition model. This protection too, has failed, in the sense of avoiding injury to the business interests involved.

IPC, registered as a Canadian corporation but 99.9 percent owned by the Standard Oil Company of New Jersey, has operated in Peru since 1914. In 1924 the firm purchased from a British oil company the La Brea y Pariñas oil fields in northwestern Peru, previously leased by IPC. The fields were owned outright and not held in concession. The La Brea complex was expropriated on October 9, and in February, 1969 all of IPC's remaining properties in Peru were seized.

Before discussing the U.S. diplomatic response to these events it is necessary to note expressions of policy on foreign expropriation of American business made by the U.S. Congress, parallel to those in the fishing field.

In 1962 hostile congressional reactions to expropriations of U.S. companies abroad lead to passage of the famous Hickenlooper Amendment. This law, named of course after the Senator from Iowa, was enacted over State Department objections. It requires suspension of foreign assistance to any government that expropriates U.S. property and that does not, within six months, "take appropriate steps" to make "equitable and speedy compensation."[10] The amendment has been invoked only once, against Ceylon.

In 1965 a similar provision was attached to the Sugar Act, requiring suspension of the U.S. sugar quota for any country in which American property is taken without compensation.[11] It should be emphasized that no escape clause exists in these provisions, although the phrase "appropriate steps" would be open to interpretation.

In addition to action by Congress, the context of the IPC dispute includes a number of attempts by the Kennedy and Johnson administrations to attempt to apply pressure on Peru by turning foreign aid on and off. In 1962, following the military coup in July of that year, the Kennedy administration showed its dismay by making no development-loan commitments for the 1963 fiscal year and by deobligating $5.8 million in existing loan authorizations. In fiscal 1964, to support the new Belaúnde administration, the Agen-

---

[10] P.L. 87-565, August 1, 1962, Sec. 620(e), 76 Stat. 260.
[11] P.L. 89-331, November 8, 1965, Sec. 408(c), 79 Stat. 1280.

cy for International Development committed $30.8 million in new loans, of which $24.1 million was not later deobligated. Technical assistance grants also were accelerated in fiscal 1964, and actual aid expenditures rose to $10.4 million.

But loan commitments to Peru fell drastically again in fiscal 1965. Although the State Department has never admitted it, this was a bald attempt to force more conciliatory negotiations with IPC. Between October, 1963, and April, 1964, talks on the question were suspended. During this time (probably about February, 1964) a slowdown order was issued on loan commitments, probably instructed by Ambassador Jones and Assistant Secretary of State Thomas C. Mann. This was continued until February, 1966.[12] The effect can clearly be seen in the deobligation of part of fiscal 1964 loans, very small 1965 loan commitments, and loans for 1966 that are considerably below those for 1964 and 1967. Grants and actual AID expenditures continued unabated, however.

The ploy, predictably, did not work. As stated, negotiations resumed in April but came to naught. The action succeeded in stirring up considerable anti-American sentiment, however, both in Peru and elsewhere in the Hemisphere. The interests of IPC were in no way served. Although there had no doubt been support for the action in the U.S. Congress, it is important to note that the reduction had not been mandated by the Hickenlooper Amendment since IPC's surface properties had not yet been expropriated.

Once more in the 1960s economic assistance to Peru was reduced for political reasons, with equally unproductive results. In May, 1968, the Peruvian government announced its intention to purchase several Mirage V jet aircraft from France. Many influential persons in Washington, including members of the House Appropriations Committee, believed this was intolerable for a developing country receiving U.S. assistance. At the instigation of Congressmen Clarence Long and Silvio Conte, the 1968 foreign assistance appropriation bill was amended so as to require deduction from the assistance to a country that buys "sophisticated weapons systems, such as missile systems and jet aircraft."[13] Application of this prin-

---

[12] *Washington Post*, September 5, 1965 and February 11, 1966; *New York Times*, September 28, 1965 and February 10, 1966.

[13] P.L. 90-581, October 17, 1968. Sec. 119, 82 Stat. 1141. The 1968 Foreign

ciple to Peruvian loans for fiscal 1968 and 1969 resulted in virtual cessation of these credits. Also grant commitments were greatly curtailed. Once again, the only result was to make the Peruvians furious; their aircraft purchases went through without hesitation.

In the midst of these abrupt on-again, off-again turns of the foreign-aid spigot, the IPC problem continued unsettled. Yet, at the level of everyday diplomatic activity in Lima, Ambassador Jones labored arduously to get some kind of solution worked out. Quite prophetically, he worried that if the problem were not solved soon, an expropriation would occur that could force a fatal application of the Hickenlooper Amendment. Consequently Jones kept in constant and close touch with the local IPC general manager, Fernando Espinosa, and the appropirate Peruvian officials, including Belaúnde. Perceiving his role as that of encouraging and facilitating an agreement, Jones did not make substantive recommendations as to a solution but rather urged that some solution be worked out—any solution—by the parties themselves. This activity, mediative and informal, was within our good offices category. Later, after the expropriations, Jones was charged by many Peruvians as being rabidly pro-IPC.[14] This accusation is unfair, however, inasmuch as his foremost desire was settlement of the conflict, not settlement in favor of Standard Oil.

August 13, 1968, the Act of Talara was signed between the Belaúnde government and IPC. It represented the results of long negotiations and was hoped by many to constitute a lasting solution. The coup of October 3, 1968, however, destroyed this temporary *modus vivendi*. With the subsequent nationalization of the Talara complex the IPC issue, from the U.S. viewpoint, was no longer protection of an existing investment, but rather the securing of compensation for a seized investment. The Talara installations were worth, according to the company, approximately $120 million. The Peruvian government maintained, however, that IPC owed Peru as much as $640 million for the value of crude oil and gas extracted during more than four decades of operation under an

---

Assistance Act says no military assistance funds shall be used for this purpose. See P.L. 90-554, October 8, 1968, Sec. 201(a), 82 Stat. 962.

[14] The May 1969 issue of the leftist magazine *Oiga* had Jones on its cover, with the inscription "Mister IPC."

invalid title and tax regime. The obvious implication was that no payment to IPC would be forthcoming, and it has not been to date.

At first the State Department approached the compensation issue cautiously. On November 8, about two weeks after the United States recognized the Velasco government, a note was delivered by Ambassador Jones in Lima in which it was maintained that the United States had the right to make diplomatic representations on behalf of an American firm. In late November the Peruvian government replied, pointing out that IPC could defend itself in Peruvian courts and that, moreover, the company was registered in Canada and hence did not concern the American government. The United States answered back on December 12, saying that the seized property was appropriate for its diplomatic protection since it had been almost entirely owned by Standard Oil.[15]

Meanwhile the Lima government began to warn that it would not succumb to American or international financial pressures on the IPC case. On December 3 General Angel Valdivia Morriberón, then minister of finance, stated that Washington had been increasing its "futile pressures against Peru, and all Latin America is watching the spectacle." He referred to AID, the International Monetary Fund, the Inter-American Development Bank, and the World Bank as being involved. Valdivia repeated his accusations on December 11.[16] Subsequent events bear out these statements; since the revolution the agencies named have extended almost no new credits to Peru.

But the Hickenlooper Amendment presented most tangibly the specter of economic sanctions. According to it, U.S. economic assistance would cease on April 9, 1969 (six months after the Talara seizure) if "appropriate steps" were not taken with regard to compensation. At first the State Department leaned over backward to avoid giving the impression that Hickenlooper was being used as a club. On October 25, 1968, a department spokesman in Washington side-stepped the question, calling it "a complicated issue involving legal points." On December 18 the Peruvian foreign minister, General Edgardo Mercado, took the trouble of saying publicly that

[15] *Peruvian Times,* December 6, 1968; *New York Times,* December 14, 1968.
[16] *New York Times,* December 8, 1968; *Peruvian Times,* December 13, 1968.

the U.S. note of December 12 had contained no threats, direct or implied.[17]

Beginning in latter January, 1969, however, the atmosphere worsened. Statements in the press attributed to State Department sources indicated that the United States had every intention of suspending on April 9 both aid and the sugar quota if steps toward compensation were not taken. In a public speech on February 6 General Velasco accused the United States of using unjustified and unjustifiable threats against Peru, and that Peru would not be intimidated by them. This defiant attitude was backed by countless resolutions, public statements, and newspaper editorials throughout Peru. Washington continued to press, however; in a March 4 news conference President Nixon said that if compensation were not forthcoming "we will have to take appropriate action with regard to the sugar quota, and also with regard to aid programs."[18]

The Peruvians never backed down, of course. They did, however, consent to direct talks between the two governments. On March 11 Nixon announced that John N. Irwin II would go to Lima as his special emissary to discuss outstanding issues. From March 13 to April 3 Irwin was in Lima conferring with Velasco and other officials. April 7, four days after Irwin's return and two days prior to the deadline, Secretary of State Rogers announced that invocation of Hickenlooper was being "deferred" inasmuch as IPC had available to it a Peruvian administrative appeal process that constituted "appropriate steps" in the context of the amendment.[19] The final deadline on this appeal was August 9, 1969. This date came and went with no formal announcement that Hickenlooper had been invoked. Meanwhile the foreign aid program to Peru simply died quietly.

Although formally Standard Oil management did not advocate invoking Hickenlooper, privately it seemed to have. Internally the company was divided on the question. A "hawk" group argued that nonapplication of the amendment would be interpreted as a sign of weakness that would precipitate oil nationalizations all around Latin America and elsewhere. A "dove" segment of the

17 *New York Times*, October 26, 1968; *Peruvian Times*, December 27, 1968.
18 *New York Times*, March 5, 1969.
19 *New York Times*, April 8, 1969.

management, on the other hand, felt that invocation would actually strengthen Velasco's political position and lead to a new wave of anti-American feeling within Peru. Neither viewpoint became public company policy, however.

To assess this example of diplomatic "protection," we find here what is essentially another series of forceful interposition measures that were totally counterproductive. Perhaps no diplomatic action could have saved IPC interests in Peru. But the aid slowdown of 1964–1966, the lending agency pressures in 1968–1969, and the blatant threats in early 1969 did nothing but worsen the situation. Ambassador Jones's continuous attempts to encourage a settlement were at least not counterproductive; but an attempt by him to seek earlier concessions by IPC might have helped more. This would have been behavior in accord with what I am calling the self-preservation model. Although some of the oil company's executives were dead set against giving up La Brea y Pariñas prior to late 1968, the Esso management had been divided on this question just as it was on Hickenlooper. Perhaps Jones could have strengthened the hand of the more "liberal" faction by aggressively calling for a more conciliatory stand at an earlier date. This *might* have protected the firm's properties in the long run.[20]

THE SELF-PRESERVATION MODEL

The fisheries and petroleum disputes provide ample evidence of the inadequacy of forceful interposition in a country like Peru in the present era. In both cases economic sanctions against Peru may be said to have "worked" sufficiently to have precipitated talks between the two governments—the four-power fishing conference, the resumption of IPC negotiations in 1964, and the Irwin mission in 1969. But also each of these negotiations, even if we can credit hard-line pressure for creating them (which is doubtful), resulted in no tangible progress. Although in the IPC case a temporary settlement was reached with the Act of Talara it did not last. In both the IPC and fisheries cases the inherent objective of diplomatic protection—serving the vital interests of American business abroad

[20] Richard Goodwin makes a similar point in hearings of the U.S. Senate Subcommittee on Western Hemisphere Affairs of the Committee on Foreign Relations, *United States Relations With Peru*, April 14–17, 1968, p. 92. See also his "Letter from Peru," *The New Yorker*, May 17, 1969, p. 102.

—was not ultimately met. In fact, one is tempted to conclude that the interests of both the California tuna industry and Standard Oil were actually damaged by the type of diplomatic behavior employed.

Of course, the blame cannot be directed to single individuals or even to the Department of State alone. Congress has been a most powerful advocate of getting "tough" with Peru, or at least certain members of that body. Obviously diplomatic protection operates within a restricting web of legislative provisions that are difficult to get around. Without doubt the Hickenlooper Amendment, Sugar Act Amendment, Conte-Long Amendment, Kuchel Amendment, Ship Loan provision, and Pelly Amendment should immediately be repealed. It is encouraging that the Rockefeller Report advocates such; it is doubtful, however, whether Congress will follow this recommendation.

But even without legislative changes it would appear that more effective methods of diplomatic protection of business could be developed. Certainly effective methods will be *needed* by American businessmen abroad in the coming years; the currents of anti-American nationalism that make forceful interposition nonviable create an even greater requirement for adequate protection.

Good offices is not enough. It is sufficient for handling routine, noncontroversial problems. But "nice guy" type intervention will seldom help a company that is in deep trouble with a foreign government. This form of representation must obviously continue, but it must be supplemented.

The alternative offered here approaches the problem in a nontraditional way. According to the orthodox methods of protection, one waits for trouble to occur, and when it does they are called into operation. The self-preservation method is actuated prior to this time. It is designed to help the firm avoid trouble, or at least part of it. Essentially the idea is to assign to the diplomats a persuasive, consultative function. It is not a "hands off" relationship to businessmen, but just the opposite—a positive, assisting relationship that would encourage business behavior that would, in the long run, serve the foreign investor's own interests.

To give this idea more meaning, consider these possibilities in the fishing and IPC disputes. The United States government, without renouncing its present stand on the twelve-mile limit, could urge the tuna fisherman to *pay* Peru's nominal fees. At the same time that payments are made (at least initially) public statements could be issued both by Washington and the tuna industry to the effect that such payments do not constitute acknowledgement of Peru's two-hundred-mile claim. The Peruvians would presumably be satisfied with fulfillment of their legal requirements and permit fishing to proceed. To sell the idea to the tuna interests, the U.S. government could arrange to have reimbursements made for the fee payments. If Congress could not be convinced to provide for this through appropriated funds, the voluntary insurance program created by the 1968 Fishermen's Protective Act could be used as a vehicle for reimbursement, from the pool of premium payments.

The same basic idea of convincing businessmen to act in their own enlightened self-interest could be applied to the IPC case, although this is now an academic point. It is too late to do anything, probably, about IPC in Peru. But five to ten years ago something constructive could have been done. It is unfortunate that the company did not make its 1968 offer in the 1963 or 1964 negotiations with the Belaúnde government. It is also unfortunate that the U.S. State Department was not at that time actively urging IPC to make such an offer. Instead, as we have seen, the Embassy was concentrating on promoting a settlement per se rather than a settlement that would maximize the chances of achieving a lasting solution.

Such diplomatic behavior would, however, require changed attitudes. This would be true both for the diplomats and the businessmen. The diplomats would have to abandon any pretense of neutrality and any condescending attitude toward the business community. They would have to be willing to seek a constructive, working partnership with the American executives. Ambassador Jones enjoyed excellent relations with the U.S. business community in Peru but, I suspect, he tended to listen too much at times when he should have been doing more of the talking. As for the overseas businessmen, their attitudes may need revision in the direction of shedding a "striped pants" image of the Foreign Service. There is much distrust toward and misunderstanding of the State Department on the part of U.S. business executives. I talked with the board chairman of a major company with investments in Peru who felt, quite bitterly, that the State Department was spreading a "welfare state" philosophy in Latin America by championing "radical forces" there. If the beleaguered American executive is to receive any real assistance from Foreign Service personnel, he must be prepared to set aside these hang-ups and put his problems frankly on the table, together with whatever alternative strategies he can propose, even if he is not particularly comfortable in mentioning them.

As for implementing the self-preservation model, the main requirement will be continuous and candid communication between businessmen and diplomats. In many instances these communications would, no doubt, most properly be confidential discussions between the general manager of a single company and the ambassador. Other useful conversations might be through the medium of periodic meetings involving the executives of several firms. Ambassador Jones conducted such meetings monthly at the Embassy. The purpose of the conferences was twofold: briefing the companies on U.S. policy and soliciting from the companies their current problems. Generally the meetings did not include the offering of specific advice to companies, particularly on delicate subjects with competitors present. But the ambassador would, if asked, gladly advise individual firms in confidence.

What, in the context of our proposal, should be the content of such "advice"? The possibilities that come to mind fall into three categories.

First, the firms could be reminded to practice the "enlightened behavior" tenets of foreign investment whenever they neglect to do so. This would not necessarily be often; in fact, most large U.S. companies in Peru are quite careful to avoid monopolies, maximize local purchases, train and promote nationals, pay taxes fully, avoid large-scale bribery, and so on. But occasionally improvements can be made in company behavior, and the ambassador could appropriately take the initiative in suggesting them.

Second, firms could be alerted to what the Embassy considered political threats that need early action to avoid later serious consequences. The IPC case, as we have said, illustrates this need. The latter problem may not be avoided, but it may be lessened in intensity and degree of danger. Another illustration might be Southern Peru Copper Corporation's long resistance to negotiating a new Toquepala contract, even though legally (in the company's opinion) it still had some years to run. The issue was the tax rate. Eventually SPCC accepted the political realities and agreed to negotiations over a new contract with a higher rate. This decision was probably very fortunate from the firm's standpoint. According to the self-preservation model, the Embassy should have been urging SPCC all along to accept the change; it was not actively involved, however.

Third, every attempt should be made to convince overseas investors and their political friends in the United States to be discreet in requesting diplomatic protection. Any attempts to obtain intercession should be kept out of the hands of the press and members of Congress if possible. This would appear to be a common-sense matter. Yet on October 30, 1969, the chairman of the Gulf Oil Corporation, E. D. Brockett, publicly discussed invocation of the Hickenlooper Amendment against Bolivia for its nationalization of Gulf properties. Such an action can only be counterproductive. It may intensify probusiness support in Congress, but it will infuriate all Latin Americans, and Bolivians most particularly.

In Peru an unfortunate situation of publicity surrounding diplomatic protection occurred in February, 1967. At that time the Peruvian Congress was considering legislation to permit competitive bidding for telephone expansion contracts in Lima. This was contrary to the interests of the Peruvian Telephone Company, 69 percent of which was owned by International Telephone and Telegraph. The night before President Belaúnde was to determine the fate of the bill, President H. S. Geneen of ITT sent an open wire to Secretary of State Rusk requesting urgent representation in Lima by Ambassador Jones. A copy was sent to Jones via All American Cables, owned also by ITT. A company employee in Lima saw the cable, stole or copied it, and took it to a leading Peruvian senator. Soon the wire was on the front page of *El Comercio*. A seige of very bad publicity followed for the telephone company; in fact, the local general manager, extremely overwrought over the incident, was killed alone in a one-car accident a few days later. The point is not that Geneen had no right to send such a message; rather, it is that the communication should have been sent confidentially to Washington, and then to Lima via diplomatic pouch.

SUMMARY

In this time of intense nationalism in the developing countries, American investments in these lands will be increasingly subject to various forms of political and governmental harassment and difficulty. Their political problems cannot be eliminated. However, appropirate actions by the U.S. government may help to lessen their seriousness.

Such actions will only be counterproductive, however, if they involve public threats and economic sanctions, or what I am calling here forceful interposition. This form of diplomatic protection may have had some usefulness thirty years ago, but it has none today.

Informal inquiries and quiet negotiation will probably always be of assistance to American companies abroad. This good offices form of diplomatic protection is often effective in less controversial matters. It should become, by and large, the only form of intervention after problems arise.

A new concept of diplomatic protection, a self-preservation model, aims to reduce the frequency and seriousness of political problems by encouraging company behavior that will, in the long run, help the company to survive politically. Under this concept the diplomat is not so much a counselor in time of trouble as a trusted political adviser. He tries to help in the "basic prevention of fires," to refer to Secretary Rusk's words quoted at the beginning of this article.

Bruce A. Blomstrom
W. Bowman Cutter

8. THE FOREIGN PRIVATE SECTOR IN PERU

Foreign investment is generally viewed as important both to economic development and to business growth. Both businessmen and public officials necessarily bring different perspectives to foreign investment. The purpose of this paper is to comment on the implications of these differing perspectives and to apply them to the Peruvian situation.

The country receiving foreign investment is felt to benefit from higher employment, increased capital, new technology, and a better trained, more experienced work force. Business gains new markets, diversification opportunities, and increased profits. As the living standards of these nations benefiting from foreign investment rise, the American government benefits from a supposed increase in international stability.

Foreign investment can also involve enormous problems, for the parties involved have substantially different interests. Many writers on foreign investment have recognized this implicitly by asserting that successful foreign investment must satisfy two major objectives: (1) for the host country, a constructive contribution to the local economy; (2) for the investor, fair profitability and reasonable security.

The often unrecognized problem is that these objectives may be mutually exclusive. For example, the recipient country may perceive the infusion of capital not as a benefit, but as an unwelcome restriction on national independence and sovereignty. Business may fear the greater uncertainty and new risks. To the American government, or to the diplomat on the scene, foreign investment can mean apparently uncompromisable conflicts between the investing company and the host country.

During the last few years some of the most interesting and controversial problems involving foreign investment conflicts between business and government have concerned Peru. They start with the emergence of the Velasco government and include the IPC case, the swirls of controversy about the Hickenlooper Amendment, and contradicting statements and actions concerning foreign investment and its place in Peru.

THE CURRENT SITUATION

The Private Sector

Virtually no inflow of private funds occurred in Peru during 1969. This ended the annual increases that had been taking place at the rate of 5 percent and had resulted in total foreign private investment of $620 million by the end of 1968.

Of the 1969 commitments that have been announced publicly the dollar amount is over $500 million, surprisingly large given the multitude of antibusiness actions by Peru. This becomes more understandable when one realizes that there were long and complicated negotiations between the mining companies and the government for projects like the $355 million Caujone deal. It also takes on a different complexion when one realizes that most of the investments referred to were announced intentions. Whether projects like Caujone and its associated refinery (80 percent of the total) will ever take place is another question. Over 90 percent of the commitments are in mining and oil, areas that are inherently sensitive to nationalistic pressures. Very few have been announced in manufacturing, the sector in which Peru is ostensibly most interested. Ninety percent have been made by companies that have a well-identified, long-term commitment to Peru (Southern Peru

Copper Co., Belco, ITT, Marcona). Those firms new to Peru (like Homestake) seem to have made their commitments prior to the coup.[1]

One must conclude from this that most potential new U.S. investors to Peru are adopting a "wait and see" attitude. Even those firms with a long-term commitment to Peru are trying to lessen the risk of future investments. For example, Cerro is attempting to interest various European companies in joint exploration of some of their unworked property in Peru.

Peruvian Government Action

On October 9, 1968, less than one week after the Velasco government took power, part of Standard Oil's International Petroleum Company (IPC) was expropriated. This was done in the name of national pride. Ignored was the fact that only two months earlier, the Belaúnde government and IPC had arrived at a settlement of this longstanding problem.

The remainder of IPC's operations were taken over in January, 1969. On February 6, 1969, President Velasco announced that the government had delivered a bill to IPC for $690 million.[2] It was arrived at by calculating profit made by IPC on the crude oil, natural gas, and other products that it had extracted between 1924 and 1968. The amount demanded is considerably larger than the value of all of IPC's properties in Peru. In fact it is 10 percent greater than the total foreign private investment recorded in Peru at the end of 1968. Since then, no meaningful negotiations have taken place between the two parties. In the eyes of the international investment commmunity, there has been no serious effort by the Peruvian government to arrive at fair and prompt compensation for the IPC properties.

Subsequent statements and actions by the new Peruvian government have varied from outright encouragement of new foreign private investment to suggestions, by word and deed, that further investments were not wanted. The cumulative attitude has seemed

[1] Although this is not an exhaustive list, it is reasonably representative of 1969 foreign investment intentions. Virtually none of these funds flowed into Peru during 1969.

[2] The basis for the bill was that IPC did not own the land it exploited and therefore owed the profits to the rightful owner, Peru.

to suggest hostility to foreign investment; at least foreign business has interpreted the signs as being unfavorable.

Some of the negative actions noted by businessmen over the last year have been the following:[3]

1. Expropriation of the Cerro de Pasco ranch lands in December, 1968.

2. Changing the law governing expropriated land to eliminate the necessity of cash payments.

3. Arrest and confinement of the local Xerox manager over a technicality.

4. Expropriation of W. R. Grace's sugar lands in June, 1969 with no agreement yet on the compensation to be paid or its value.

5. Forced sale of ITT's 69 percent owned telephone company.

6. Antibusiness statements by many government leaders including one from General Velasco that a "conspiracy of oligarchs and foreign business interests was trying to topple his regime."[4]

7. Limiting foreign banks to a maximum 25 percent holding in local banks.

8. Price controls that made the supply of such staples as potatoes so scarce that they were available only on the black market.

9. The government takeover of meat importers.

10. A decree that all automobile plants must be 51 percent Peruvian owned by the end of 1970 and that the local content of assembled autos must be 70 percent by February, 1973, up substantially from the 30 percent current average.

11. General Motors fined $25,000 for a minor infraction of regulations.

12. Rumors that foreign mining companies would be stripped of their concessions and that the banking, power, and fish-meal industries would be nationalized.

13. Increased taxes on corporations from 35 percent to a maxi-

[3] The Peruvian attendees at the Conference felt that each of these actions could be defended on their own and were not part of a planned antibusiness/foreign investment program. For example, the Xerox manager was confined to a hospital instead of being put in jail. Local sugar owners were affected far more than W. R. Grace when sugar lands were expropriated. This still does not change the fact that, taken together, this series of actions shows a definite anti-foreign investment bias.

[4] John Goshko, *Washington Post*, December 14, 1969.

mum of 55 percent, with foreign companies bearing the brunt of this change.

14. Increased export taxes on the fish-meal industry.

15. A decree that all owners, editors, and shareholders of newspapers and periodicals published in Peru must be Peruvian.

16. An April, 1970, statement by President Velasco calling for foreign investors to turn their businesses over to the government after recovering their investment and an acceptable profit.

17. An April, 1970, statement that the government would take over the sale and pricing of copper and all other metals produced in the country. Future mining development could take place only in partnership with the government.

18. A decree in April, 1970, that all fish-meal marketing would be controlled by the government.

19. Introduction in May, 1970, of foreign exchange restrictions that did not adequately take into consideration the interests of foreign investors, including their expatriate employes.

Interspersed between these actions have been attempts to establish a favorable business climate. General Velasco himself has made repeated statements that the government will encourage foreign investment in Peru. In late 1969 he made a lengthy speech to businessmen to the effect that the government wanted to develop the economy on capitalistic lines. Other positive aspects have included (1) a continuing program of stabilizing the economy through tight government budgeting and other programs; (2) assurance to the Belco Petroleum Co. that its growing investments in the country were welcome and appreciated; and (3) investment commitments by a few U.S. companies in 1970.

These bright spots in Peru have been too few and far between to overcome the apparent antibusiness actions. Thus, short-term capital left Peru in substantial amounts in 1968 ($107 million) and 1969 ($56 million), mainly through withdrawals by the private sector.[5] Only by the imposition of foreign exchange controls in May, 1970, has the government been able to arrest this outflow.

---

[5] A. R. Abboud. "Commentary on J. P. Powelson's Paper on International Lending Agencies" (unpublished), February 1970, p. 9. Prepared for the Peru Policy seminar of the Adlai Stevenson Institute.

Past U.S. Government Policy

From the beginning of the Alliance for Progress, one of the U.S. government's guiding principles has been the preservation of a climate favorable to private investment. To most Peruvians and Americans the focus of these efforts in Peru seems to have been IPC. In fact, a leading Peruvian magazine featured a cover picture of the U.S. ambassador to Peru with the captain "The Ambassador from IPC." According to Richard N. Goodwin, most Peruvians believed "that the dominant goal of United States [Peruvian] Policy was to advance the interests and desires of Standard Oil of New Jersey." This was borne out by a suspension of U.S. aid during the first two years of the Belaúnde regime in an apparent effort to compel agreement between Peru and the company.

Goodwin reports that there was no evidence that the United States ever tried to persuade IPC to modify its terms, although "we constantly reminded Belaúnde that any action resembling expropriation would call down the wrath and retaliation of the U.S. in the form of the Hickenlooper Amendment. . . . IPC's natural and warranted impression that it was backed by the full weight of the United States undoubtedly stiffened the company's attitude, just as it restrained, and perhaps intimidated, the Peruvians."[6]

Shortly after IPC's expropriation, the conflicting points of view of the participants were highlighted by Richard Goodwin as follows:

IPC: "We were the largest taxpayer in Peru and our labor practices were a model for the country."

U.S. Embassy: Over the last several years "IPC was always very generous, and honestly worked hard to reach a settlement."

General Velasco (Dec. 4, 1968): "No people can live in dignity and with respect for its sovereignty . . . when it tolerates the insolent arrogance of another state within its own frontier."[7]

Since the IPC seizure, U.S. government policy has varied from uncertainty over how to act to a current "low profile" policy of waiting for Peru to come to its senses. The first policy phase lasted from October, 1968, to April, 1969, and ties into the six months

6 Richard N. Goodwin, "Letter from Peru," *The New Yorker*, May 17, 1969.
7 Ibid.

waiting period required by the Hickenlooper Amendment before the mandatory application of economic sanctions. During this period there was a change of U.S. administrations and a delay in appointing an assistant secretary of state for the Alliance for Progress. At the beginning of 1969 President Nixon was preoccupied with other matters and seemed to have little time for Latin America.

As the April, 1969, Hickenlooper deadline drew near, the president dispatched a prominent New York lawyer to Peru to resolve the IPC question. This led to a postponement of the required economic sanctions until August, 1969. This deadline has since passed quietly with little progress made in solving the IPC compensation problem or in improving overall relations with Peru.

Expropriation per se is not questioned by the United States, because it recognizes that states have the right to take such action. What the United States opposes is lack of prompt and fair compensation. Deviation from such compensation is construed to be either an attack upon the U.S. government or a property protection situation that requires government intervention. Appropriate action is taken, depending on the size and importance of the company nationalized, to force an acceptable settlement. In the Peruvian case, this has led the U.S. government to the following actions:

1. Suspension of new aid, officially explained by congressional cuts in the AID budget.

2. Elimination of the U.S. AID director and most of his staff.

3. A noticeable reduction in the embassy staff.

4. Unwillingness by the Export-Import Bank to help provide financing for the $355 million Cuajone project of the Southern Peru Copper Co.

The United States has been no more consistent in its actions than Peru. For example, despite the IPC case, the secretary of agriculture allocated Peru a 5 percent increase over 1969 in its sugar exports to the United States. They will now total 370,000 tons, almost 75 percent of Peru's production, making it the fifth largest supplier of sugar to the United States. With the United States paying roughly double the world price for sugar, Peru's income from this revenue source is approximately $45–50 million per year, about 50 percent more than the average financial aid provided by the United States during the 1963–1968 period. This increased quota comes in the face of the Hickenlooper requirement that a country's sugar quota should be cut off if adequate compensation is not made in six months for any expropriated U.S. properties.[8]

Perhaps the primary reason for the conflict between the United States and Peru rests on the fact that U.S. policy, particularly as it concerns business, has been narrowly defined. In general, it is U.S. policy to support all U.S. companies that are "in trouble" with the government where they are doing business. There is no attempt made by the embassy to determine which party is in the right. In the IPC case, the embassy policy was to avoid a confrontation with Peru by urging the parties involved to arrive at a settlement.

The Results of U.S. Policy

The policy that was followed had the following results:

1. Although a bi-lateral accord was reached between IPC and the Belaúnde government in August, 1968 (with a large assist from the U.S. government), the agreement was overturned just two months later by the new military junta. The expropriation or forced sale of a few other U.S. companies occurred shortly thereafter.

2. It has put our ambassador in the position of being as much identified with a particular company interest as with the overall U.S. interest. This is an untenable position with no graceful exit.

3. It has strengthened the belief that a major goal of U.S. foreign policy is the extension of this country's influence through the spread of U.S. foreign private investment.

4. Peruvian economic development has been slowed.

5. By not applying the Hickenlooper Amendment, many have charged that the United States has lost its credibility and somehow been weakened in Latin America. If this has not in fact happened in Latin America, it certainly has occurred in the United States in the minds of those who support a "hard-line" policy.

6. It has appeared to be a leading element in driving Peru away from a pro-West stance. At the very least it has contributed strongly to the poor relations now existing between the United States and Peru.

One aspect is clear. All parties have lost something. Of greatest significance is the fact that the U.S. government seems to have made little attempt to evaluate the IPC situation in light of other,

---

[8] EDITOR'S NOTE: Cf. different statistics in Strasma article, pp. 202–203.

broader foreign policy considerations. This type of analysis might have led to a different course of action. This is ample grounds for a general look at foreign investment problems.

BUSINESS-GOVERNMENT CONFLICT

Government officials and businessmen approach foreign investment with fundamentally different objectives in mind. These differences mean that the possible area for agreement between a business and a host country on investment procedures or objectives is inherently limited; they further mean that disagreements, when they occur, are difficult to resolve.

The Peruvian Policy Maker

Latin American government policy makers, like other public officials are concerned principally with national goals. In developing countries, nation-building and economic growth are likely to be given substantial priority. Often there is strong feeling about the directions along which national development should proceed.

It is these goals that policy makers hope to achieve by encouraging private investment. They are disinterested in the profits of any one corporation. They are extremely interested in the impact of foreign investment on the structure and level of national wealth. They expect and want foreign investment to function within certain constraints—constraints that will help to advance national independence, national social health, and the particular direction of development upon which the government has decided.

This national orientation of host-country policy makers is the most important point to be understood about their view of foreign investment. At any given time, in any given government, policy makers may be for or against foreign investment in principle, they may understand business or find it incomprehensible, or they may be willing to exploit the political vulnerability of foreign businesses. But in the long run they will all evaluate specific businesses according to their contribution to the long-run goals of the nation.

The American Foreign Investor

The stance of the business decision maker is, of course, totally different. To him, national goals are important only as they constitute part of his investment environment. They are not the ends for which he invests. As businesses are economically self-centered, they expand and invest abroad for profits and to maintain market shares or growth rates. Their decisions are related to the ends of the firm, not to economic development.

The basic decision of the businessman to invest or withdraw depends upon profits and returns. In arriving at a stance, businessmen are guided by the combination of risks and opportunities they perceive. Cultural differences and corporate citizenship (good or bad) may exacerbate or help to smooth relationships between a foreign business and its host government, but they do not determine the basic nature of these relationships.

The U.S. Government Policy Maker

The nature of the foreign investor/government relationship—one seeking economic gain, the other attempting to maximize national development—minimizes the possible influence of the American policy maker. But insofar as he does participate actively in the affairs of American foreign investors, he is inevitably torn in several different policy directions.

By training, by education, and by bureaucratic structure the American policy maker is inclined toward a view of foreign investment that is similar to that of the Peruvian policy maker. He sees its value in its contribution to economic development. In addition, the probable orientation of the ambassador's staff advisors and the importance to his own success of getting along with the host government tend to lead him to respect and agree with the point of view of the host nation.

On the other hand, the pressures of the ambassador's foreign investor constituency are very specific. They are the problems of individual businessmen. And because these are the Americans with whom he works most frequently, with whom he and his staff have social contacts, and who have access to his superiors, he becomes, at least in a small way, an instrument of American business.

There is nothing inherently wrong with this. As the president's representative, the ambassador exists as much to serve Americans as to interpret U.S. policy to the government to which he is accredited. In this sense, the ambassador is every bit as much used by tourists and students as by business. The major difference is the far more serious consequences that can result when business interests are served. When conflict does occur, the ambassador is torn by his general orientation and his specific allegiances. In the end, the long-range interests of the American government seem to become lost.

The Foreign Investment Process

What has been described is a process in which there are three actors with entirely different interests. The area of agreement is obviously limited. If this area is to be sufficiently defined to make any agreement possible, then the foreign investment process must be well understood.

Fortunately, the investment process is fairly mechanistic. Businesses invest according to certain risk and return criteria. For each level of risk, businesses associate (at least implicitly) a rate of return that is required before investment will take place. In addition, businesses must normally expect to receive a certain minimum level of return before they will invest regardless of risk. Finally, there is almost certainly some level of risk at which businesses will not invest regardless of return.

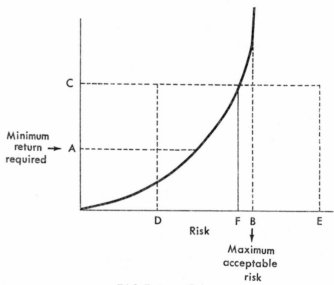

Risk-Return Curve

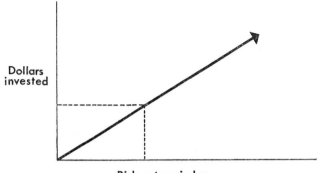

Risk-return index
Amount of Investment

The graph on p. 268 describes the risk-return point. The curve it-self represents the criteria against which investments are measured. *A* is an arbitrarily selected minimum return: the business will not accept any investment that returns below *A*. *B* is the maximum acceptable risk: the business will not accept a project with risks greater than *B* regardless of the possible returns. If a project is expected to return *C* percent, it could also have several associated risks. If the risk is *D*, the company will invest. The risk *F* is all the risk the company will accept with a return of *C*. If the risk is *E*, the company will not invest.

In addition, one can also graph the relation of a risk-return combination or index to the amount of foreign investment made in any particular country.

This is highly impressionistic and is intended only to suggest that the amount of investment made in any country is directly related to the overall conditions of risk and return as perceived by private investors. Although the *process* of investment is relatively mechanistic, governments can and do affect the elements entering into the calculations; and, therefore, the end result. Thus, if any government wishes to know the impact of its decisions on investment, it must understand this process.

Two points are of particular importance here. The first is that a major potential source of conflict is the difference between the rate of return a government may think is sufficient and nonexploitive and which a company may perceive as necessary. If government establishes a maximum allowable rate of return less than the minimum rate demanded by business, then foreign investment will not occur. If the government's rate is higher than business's minimum rate, then investment is possible.

The second point is that changes in the rules established by government probably have major effects upon the investor's perception of risks. A business can adjust—with a particular level of investment—to any one set of rules, but if they are changed repeatedly the business can make no adjustment. A government, therefore, can have some positive effect upon investment solely by determining its rules and then not changing them.

Peru has been a classic case of how to generate continued uncertainty. While professing to welcome new investment, the government has taken a series of drastic antiforeign investment steps, beginning with the IPC expropriation in October, 1968. This alone would not have been so damaging because of the extenuating circumstance. But the continuation of similar activity ranging from the Grace and Cerro expropriations to the various industry decrees continues to create uncertainty.

The limited amount of capital (and its associated technology) available for investment in the developing world suggests that one way to assure a fair share of this investment is to develop a program for capturing it. This would include public statements, published philosophy, economic incentives, or business-oriented actions. These assurances of moral support combined with the creation of a political climate receptive to private foreign business reduce the risk perceived by a foreign investor. Signing of intergovernmental expropriation and other political risk guarantees add to the attractiveness of a country.

Potential Areas of Conflict

Enough experience has been gained in the less-developed world to guide U.S. policy makers in identifying potential U.S. business–foreign government problems. They center on three characteristics: the nature of the business; the relative size of the business and country; and ownership and control.

THE NATURE OF THE BUSINESS

The fact that a business is foreign is always a source of potential conflict. But more specifically, the kind of business that is developed can be a good predictor of potential conflict. Recent experiences in underdeveloped countries indicate that problems are likely in industries that are oriented toward resources, national security, and low value added. Conflicts are less likely in businesses that are high value added, export oriented, import substituting, high technology, service oriented, and labor intensive.

Resource-based industries, such as mining, oil, sugar, and other agricultural products, are increasingly regarded by host countries as theirs to develop by right. The profit should go to the people, not to the foreign manufacturers. The land and surrounding water with its contents belong to the country. Emotional involvement of patriotic fervor is typical. The experience of foreign mine owners in the Congo and Rhodesia, and of oil producers in Indonesia, Algeria, Bolivia, and Peru are typical of the conflict that can be expected. No amount of good corporate "citizenship" activities, no amount of company financing of worthy projects can overcome this problem. It exists by the very nature of the business.

National security industries in less-developed countries are of a different nature than those in developed countries. Frequently, the economy is too small to support aircraft, munitions, and similar industries. Food, power, and communications are more likely to be in this category. ITT has gone through a series of forced nationalizations of the telephone companies it has operated in Latin American countries and probably anticipates them in countries where they are still operating freely.

Low value added industries, such as the assembling of parts made in other countries, are coming under increasing pressure to manufacture more of their components locally. For example, auto assemblers in Peru have been told that future operations will be possible only if they increase the percentage of locally made products they use from the current level of about 30 percent to 70 percent by February, 1973.

Manufacturers of high value added products are much less likely to find themselves in conflict with local government. They can clearly demonstrate that they have contributed substantial value to the economy and are not exploiting a resource. Manufacturers of consumer and industrial goods fall into this category.

High technology businesses are closely related to high value added industries. The key thing is that policy makers consider the import of technology beneficial in the long run. In fact, a recent foreign investment conference of the Inter-American Development Bank suggested that Latin American governments should deliberately set out to attract technologically oriented industries.

Export-oriented businesses improve the balance of payments and are therefore encouraged by policy makers. The same is generally true of import substituting industries.

Service industries generally do not involve a very large investment and therefore are not sensitive on the grounds of visibility. Expansion of tourism, one of the leading service industries, is often a primary goal of policy makers. If foreign companies can help, so much the better. Consulting businesses fall either into this category or that of high technology.

Labor intensive companies are favored in underdeveloped countries with a high degree of unemployment.

RELATIVE SIZE OF THE BUSINESS AND COUNTRY

In a small country, foreign investors are likely to play a substantial and highly visible role. Plants and offices generally stand out in the minds of policy makers. Where quasi-monopolistic positions are obtained, either through government agreement or because of the smallness of the market, questions of public policy are likely to result in government-business relations that are far closer than in larger countries. Thus, businessmen can have a tremendous influence on government policy.

Large foreign businesses or a sizeable concentration of foreign investment creates a set of negative reactions. They threaten local businesses by their sheer size and the mystique of foreign "infallibility." Large, concentrated foreign investment sectors can be seen by policy makers as limiting their control over their economy.

Large businesses can intimidate foreign governments by their sheer size or their importance to the local economy. This causes hidden resentments that erupt in unforeseen ways. The threat by IPC to stop gasoline imports as a device for obtaining a price increase is one of these instances. The fact that the price increase was justified due to devaluation was not understood by the public policy makers. Nor did IPC understand the public policy implications of its threat. Because they are so big, large U.S. companies are identified with the U.S. government. What affects one, tends to affect the other.

International companies are often felt to be making various internal adjustments that lower their rate of taxation or enable them to evade currency or other restrictions. Intercompany pricing changes and switching of manufacturing from one plant to another can result in a shift in profit source. High charges by headquarters for administrative expenses have the same effect. Insofar as these methods are used as an "evasion" device, they run the risk of generating conflict if detected. The tax departments in most countries are generally aware of such actions and are able to take appropriate counter measures.

OWNERSHIP AND CONTROL

To an investor with a sizeable chunk of money about to be sunk in a project, control of the project is crucial to its success. International companies generally opt for 100 percent control. Lack of capital or high risk may make them willing to accept less. Government restrictions can also result in changes from this position, depending on the resulting profit and risk. Fifty-fifty joint ventures, licensing, management contracts, and investments of less than 50 percent generally result from the desire to spread risk, from lack of capital, and from government or political requirements. Political efforts to force a change in ownership will lead to a slowdown in private foreign investments. New money will flow again only when the situation stabilizes and the government's course is clear enough for investors to judge risk.

If U.S. policy makers bear these possible conflict points in mind, they can do much to assist U.S. investors in their initial decision to invest and the way this is carried out. They can also provide guidance to existing U.S. business on actions to be taken to lessen the possibility of a conflict with their host government.

ALTERNATIVES AND RECOMMENDATIONS

Foreign private investment is important to the investing nation, to the host nation, and to the investing business. However, public policy affecting foreign private investment has led—particularly in the developing nations—to controversy and crisis. These can only be avoided if policy makers truly understand private investment. Several characteristics of foreign private investment seem particularly important.

First, the private investment process is relatively predictable and is subject to easily ascertainable economic facts. Businesses invest where the potential returns are highest. Significant uncertainty of any kind enters into the risk-return calculations of business investors. And if risks are high, high returns will be demanded by business.

Foreign investment, therefore, responds directly to economic incentives and disincentives. The flow of foreign investment becomes quickly related to conditions within any particular country; and, consequently, policy regarding foreign investment is never made without fairly immediately affecting the amount and type of foreign investment a nation receives.

Second, a host country can have significant influence over the amount and type of investment it receives. In the long run, of course, investment is determined largely by the economic potential of a nation. But in the short run, with many nations competing for capital, investment is determined, at least in part, by ease of entry, by the nature of regulation, and by the degree of uncertainty involved. All of these factors a nation and a government can affect.

Third, the investor nation can have only a limited effect upon the flow of investment to less developed countries. It can, by its own policies, retard or stimulate the total amount of investment, but it cannot dependably and predictably alter the policies or economic potential of any one nation. It cannot alter significantly the receptiveness of a particular foreign government toward investment. It cannot easily turn on and off the amount of foreign investment going to any one nation. Should a controversy arise involving a potential expropriation, the investor nation can have a decisive voice only by bringing an excessive amount of power to bear on the problem.

And fourth, many U.S. companies are so big and powerful that their fate abroad is often intertwined with that of the U.S. government and vice versa. While it is understandable that certain U.S. government policies could lead to retaliation against U.S. companies operating abroad, it does not seem appropriate for one U.S. company to seriously affect relations between the United States and another country. Yet this is what IPC (Standard Oil) did in Peru, to the detriment of other U.S. businesses as well as the United States government.

These points, we believe, suggest a range of general policy alternatives that might be followed with respect to foreign investment.

Alternative U.S. Policies and their Anticipated Result

The United States government has both traditional consular responsibilities to protect the life and property of U.S. citizens and long-term foreign goals. The encouragement of private investment is part, but only part, of these long-term goals.

The principal problem of U.S. foreign policy is to find a strategy that does not make these differing responsibilities mutually exclusive and that enables as many of them to be accomplished as possible. Likewise, U.S. government policy toward foreign investment must encourage it *without* rendering other goals impossible to achieve.

There would seem to be at least three alternate kinds of U.S. policy toward foreign investments: to encourage and protect, "carry on" as in the past, or to adopt a policy of general restraint. Only one of these truly suits both the special characteristics of foreign investment and the goals of U.S. policy, as we have stated them. The possibility of discouraging U.S. investment abroad has not been considered because it is not a realistic alternative.

The first alternative implies a close identification between the American government and U.S. business interests abroad. Supporters of such a policy would vigorously apply sanctions in the event of expropriation, perhaps of an even greater magnitude than called for in Hickenlooper and the various other foreign-assistance act amendments. They would, perhaps, also call for close involvement by U.S. officials in the day-to-day problems of U.S. business abroad. They often point to the fact that other governments seem to provide their businesses with much more protection and support.

The IPC experience points out the danger of this type of approach. If the IPC case has had any effect, it has probably been to make long-run U.S. foreign policy goals more difficult to attain and to complicate enormously in Peru the exercise by the U.S. government of its consular responsibilities. It is far too easy to

create a business crisis that adversely affects our diplomatic relations and alliances throughout the world. This is particularly so
when many nations are eager to seize upon any excuse to tweak
the giant's nose.

In short, a policy of vigorously protecting U.S. foreign investment seems to involve more risks than gains.

A second possibility is to continue as we have been. This ad hoc
approach has increased the uncertainty faced by private investors
and has brought the U.S. policy maker to crisis after crisis. It
makes American foreign policy the end result of a series of acci-
dents rather than a carefully considered effort to maximize U.S.
interests.

The "restrained" approach is more in keeping with the tenor of
the time. It enables the U.S. government to continue to service and
support its business constituents while lessening the possibility of
foreign-policy crisis. In adopting this approach, the government
could take the following specific actions:

1. *Encourage the development of an International Expropriation
Agency.* To lessen the possibilities of nationalization as well as to
smooth out the resulting frictions, the U.S. government should seek
increasing participation from international agencies. They should
be made the focal point for discussion, eliminating direct identification between an individual U.S. company and the American government.

Setting up an effective international mechanism to assist in eas-
ing expropriation problems is not an easy task. Although the
World Bank's International Centre for the Settlement of Investment Disputes (ICSID) has been operating since 1966 and now has
over sixty members, it has yet to hear a single case. All Latin
American countries have refused to join. Defenders of the Centre
say there have not been enough disputes or that the World Bank
has not been forcefully suggesting that it be used. Perhaps it is too
early for this type of instrument to be effective. Alternately, this
may be a sign that the Centre is not likely to be a useful force in
expropriation matters and needs to revise its modus operandi.

Having ICSID plus a policy of encouraging a healthy climate
for private investment (while not assisting governments who have
failed to equitably settle expropriation incidents) makes the World

Bank the logical international body to develop an international expropriation agency.

2. *Help institute an International Investment Insurance Program.* The Peterson Commission report has called for the U.S. to support actively the World Bank's proposal for expropriation insurance. Unfortunately, many countries, both developed and underdeveloped, are resisting it. Some are locked into their own schemes. Others have no interest because they do not export capital. Recipient country attitudes range from complete hostility, as in Latin America, to dislike over the potential cost if they should be asked to shoulder some of the premium load. Despite these problems, the United States should work vigorously for agreement on this subject, because multinationalization can lessen the kind of problems encountered in the IPC situation.[9]

3. *Repeal the punitive clauses of the Foreign Assistance Act.* In rejecting the alternative of vigorous application of sanctions, repeal of the Hickenlooper Amendment along with the other punitive clauses of the Foreign Assistance Act is required. This avoids tying the hands of the Administration in its efforts to reach an appropriate solution, while still enabling it to adopt this policy if it seems appropriate. As we have seen in the Peru case, there has been a de facto application of Hickenlooper-type sanctions as far as further foreign aid is concerned. The point has undoubtedly not been missed by the Peruvian government.

There is another, even better incentive for foreign governments to pay a fair and prompt compensation. Without compensation, additional investment will be more difficult to obtain from international business. It should be noted that the Hickenlooper Amendment (Sec. 620e of the Foreign Assistance Act of 1961) has been used only once. In the early 1960s aid was terminated to the Ceylon

[9] Frank Tannenbaum made a similar suggestion some years ago. He argued that the United States government should answer confiscations with a temporary repayment tax on the imports of the confiscating country until the expropriated property is paid for. He further argued that the United States should couple such a tax with a clear statement of support for the efforts of Latin American governments to improve the social and economic conditions of their country. Frank Tannenbaum, *Ten Keys to Latin America*, pp. 232–237. Alfred A. Knopf, New York, 1962.

government after its refusal to pay compensation for some petroleum marketing facilities that it took from several international
oil companies. After a change of government, compensation was
negotiated on a mutually acceptable basis, and the U.S. aid program was reinstated.

4. *Broaden and streamline the U.S. expropriation insurance program.*[10] The U.S. government should concentrate—in the absence
of a vigorous International Foreign Investment Protection Agency
—on completing the negotiation of expropriation agreements with
other nations, particularly the five Latin American World Bank
members who have not yet agreed to this approach (Argentina,
Chile, Mexico, Peru, and Uruguay). This will not be an easy task
as all are convinced that this type of agreement is not necessary to
attract private investment. The nature of the U.S.'s expropriation
insurance should be revised along more traditional insurance lines,
such as:

a. Making it possible to buy expropriation insurance at any
stage of the investment's life. Currently, only new investments
are insurable and application must be made prior to a final
commitment.

b. Relating cost to risk. Where the chances of expropriation
are limited, rates should be low; where they are high, the cost
should be increased. Currently, the United States has a fixed
annual fee of $\frac{1}{2}$ percent per year for this insurance. The only
adjustment mechanism is to deny insurance in high risk cases.
This would be changed if premiums could be adjusted according
to the size, nature, and risk of the investment. For example, rates
might rise as the size of the investment increases, on the assumption that high visibility investments in industries sensitive to
nationalistic feeling are more likely to be expropriated. On large,
sensitive projects, AID has recently tried to incorporate risk
management analysis by providing a declining coverage tied to
the payout of the project. Indeed, the U.S. government's—or an
international agency's—most effective policy regarding foreign
investment might be to provide a risk rating service similar to
the many commercial services that rate public and private

[10] Some businessmen felt that passing risks on to the government could lead
it into participating in their decision-making process. To them, this is a situation
to be avoided even if expropriation insurance has to be foregone.

bonds. Such a service would better enable business to evaluate the risks of investing and would allow recipient countries to see how their policies are perceived. The only mechanism available now is to deny coverage on countries, like Peru or Bolivia, deemed too risky.

c. Relating premiums to the length of time for which the insurance is taken out should be considered. Currently, there is a limit of twenty years (twelve years on large natural resource projects) and a minimum fee of 1/10 percent for the guarantee period.

d. Any investment where the host country has indicated its approval of the project should be automatically supported by the United States. Currently, the United States makes all sorts of judgments as to the nature of the investment. For example, if the United States judges that the project does not further the economic development of the country, then an investment guarantee is not possible. Agricultural projects are also forbidden if they are for the export of commodities in surplus in the United States.

e. Lowering premiums. Fee income at the ½ percent rate for political risk insurance including expropriation has consistently made a handsome profit for the United States. Over the twenty-year history of the program, fee income has totaled $58.4 million, and claim settlements pending or issued have amounted to a paltry $7 million. Either the rates should be lowered or more risk investment insured. Unfortunately, current thinking in AID is that rates are too low given the fact that there is $8 billion of insurance outstanding, 75 percent of it written in the last four years. If a Cuba-type situation should occur in a country with a large number of loans, this kitty would be quickly depleted.

5. *Adopt a policy of encouraging U.S. business to work out "expropriation type" issues and "compensation" questions directly with the government concerned without involving the U.S.* Expropriation generally results from political change or from inappropriate corporate behavior. Neither of these is particularly susceptible to U.S. government control. By avoiding the kind of intimate involvement in expropriation crises that occurred in the IPC situation, the United States retains flexibility of action, avoids creating

crises, maintains ongoing relationships, and enables other foreign policy objectives to be advanced. For these reasons, the United States should let it be known that larger foreign policy aims make it impossible to support a U.S. company to the hilt in any expropriation crisis. In support of this, it can point out that those companies who reach a mutual settlement get rewarded financially (*à la* ITT) and those who do not risk losing all (IPC, for example). The handling of the Grace situation, where the United States was not involved to any great extent, is the model that should be followed.

As a general principle, any government will have to pay compensation upon expropriation if it wants to continue to attract private foreign investment. The U.S. government should not be involved in determining what is fair compensation. Any effort to do so seems likely to involve the United States in endless and fruitless entanglements.

By maintaining that fair compensation should take place but retaining distance in specific negotiations, the U.S. government incurs less risk of any particular issue becoming a full-blown foreign policy crisis. The IPC affair makes manifest the folly of the U.S. government in overidentifying with a specific American company. Many would agree that it is unrealistic to expect the U.S. government to adopt this kind of policy. On the other hand, the advantages in so doing seem to suggest that the administration would be wise to find a way to present this course of action in a politically palatable manner.

These policy recommendations seem to us to reflect reasonably the limits of any U.S. foreign-investment policies. Conceivably, the United States could also suggest alternate investment forms and encourage appropriate corporate behavior, but neither suggestion seems to us to be near the core of the foreign-investment problem.

Recommended Corporate Foreign-Investment Policies[11]

Foreign corporations should not try to affect the broad national policies of the countries in which they invest. Should a nation de-

---

[11] The authors recognize that there are alternatives to the corporate foreign-investment policy they have suggested. However, we feel strongly that the whole model of business-government perspectives points strongly to the general policy outlined here.

cide upon public ownership of all basic industries, for example, a foreign business can do little to alter the decision. But a business can attempt to insure that it does not become an individual target through its own behavior or mode of operation. Business does not have to invite attack, and it can help to avoid it by:

1. *Generating as much local ownership as possible, including government participation.* Local equity participation lowers the size of individual investment and gives local partners a stake in the success of the venture. Thus, in two ways wider equity participation reduces a business's visibility.[12] Government partnerships should not be ignored. This is one way to lessen the possibility of future conflict with the authorities. It may be the only sector with sufficient financial resources to take an ownership position.

Agreements to sell in a fixed number of years may be appropriate in some cases. As the ITT experience indicates, this is not likely to mean the end of U.S. company involvement but rather shifts in *how* it is involved. There are many good arguments from business which suggest that this type of policy cannot work. They include:

a. There is insufficient capital available in the government or private sector of most economically lesser-developed countries.

b. Local investors demand a constant dividend stream once an investment is made. This is often not possible in the start-up years where losses are quite freqently the rule or earnings must be ploughed back.

c. Preservation of technical secrets is required, i.e., IBM.

d. Decision making and control are so complicated in a joint venture that timely action, particularly for the long term, is not taken.

e. With myriad opportunities elsewhere in the world, it is better to invest in areas where 100 percent control can be maintained.

---

12 One Peruvian businessman felt that an ideal combination would be a ⅓, ⅓, ⅓ formula. That is, one-third owned by the foreign private investor, one-third by the Peruvian government, and one-third by a Peruvian entrepreneur. Alternatively, one-third might be distributed to several thousand small investors. The U.S. company is important to give the little man confidence in the success of the enterprise.

While these arguments have merit, the examples of IBEC and ITT, plus the political realities of much of the less-developed world, suggest that increasing local partnership may be the best possible solution. In doing this, it would be helpful if the Peruvian government were to concentrate on creating a vigorous stock market. This would include an SEC-type agency to assure stockholders that their money would be safe.

2. *Creating local competition or other businesses.* To avoid charges of monopoly, every effort should be made to create effective, local competitors. While not encouraging direct competition, Sears has successfully helped develop local suppliers. This is another way to give local interests a stake in the success of the venture.

3. *Identification with the country of investment.* Country identification activities can range over the following: being sensitive to local needs and aspirations; working closely with local government officials to educate them on the company's role; employing as many local nationals as possible in all levels of management; being a good corporate citizen, providing good working conditions and wages; and working quietly and unostentatiously in the pursuit of normal business objectives.

The IPC experience suggests that this kind of philosophy must be present from the moment a company invests, otherwise the bad feelings engendered in the early days can overshadow later years of good will. IPC has tried hard over the last ten to fifteen years to identify with Peru. Unfortunately for them, they suffered for their actions of even earlier years, actions which Peruvians have never forgotten.

Company policy should be based on an understanding that U.S. Embassy protection and support for a particular business will be limited. Should an individual company create a foreign policy problem, the broader ramifications must dictate its handling. Relatively narrow business objectives will have to bow to more important ends.

The fundamental point is that if a business is fulfilling a needed role in the economy and if it has successfully identified with the country, then this is a better assurance of longevity than any protection that could be provided by the U.S. government.

Recommended Peruvian Government Policies[13]

Recipient nations can influence significantly the amount and type of foreign investment they receive. They can do this by altering the investment risks perceived by business. This point is perhaps made most clearly by the results of Peruvian policy, which has been anything but clear.

Foreign investment has been directly, indirectly, and simultaneously encouraged and discouraged by the Peruvian government. The impact of this on business, as we have seen, has been a slowing of investment in, paradoxically, all but the most sensitive areas. These latter have shown activity because of government pressure and the heavy financial commitment of existing resource-based companies in Peru. Other investors are waiting and will continue to do so until the situation is stabilized.

Stability can be anything the Peruvian government desires, from complete nationalization to unabashed encouragement of foreign investment. But *if* foreign investment has a place in the Peruvian government's plans, then there are certain requisites that should be taken into consideration:

1. *Investment flows when the rules of the game are well known.* Investors are concerned with the preservation and growth of their funds. Uncertainty is not welcome because it makes risk prediction difficult. Changes in the rules for investor behavior and participation create this uncertainty. This is the situation that now exists in Peru. Change will require clear indications from the Peruvian government of new policies that encourage foreign investment. The "rules" under which businesses are to operate in the future should be spelled out in as much detail as possible. These might include defining sectors where investment is most wanted, indicating the form of investment desired, suggesting allowable returns, and explaining how profits can be repatriated.

2. *Public statements encouraging foreign private investment*

13 The recommendations contained here are strictly those of the authors. The Peruvian Conference deliberately avoided discussing future Peruvian policies on the grounds that this was a Peruvian matter. The Conference discussion centered only on the alternatives for U.S. foreign policy, and the authors have confined themselves to describing the general kind of policy toward foreign investment that emerges from their model.

should be made. These should be coordinated at all levels of government. Deviations should be publicly denied. Presumably, good use can be made of the advantages of a military government, namely its "party" members can be controlled.

3. *Harassment of foreign private investors should end.* Having won the battle of national pride, harassment of business should end. The imprisonment of the Xerox manager as a *contrabandista* and the $25,000 fine of General Motors for a minor rule infraction are examples of irritants that salve national pride, but defeat the larger purpose of economic development. They drive away foreign private investments.

4. *Fair compensation should be promptly determined for IPC and others.* Delays in arriving at the amount and kind of compensation prevent the establishment of a favorable investment climate. Although a settlement with IPC is hard, it is necessary to develop the confidence of international agencies, the international financial community, and foreign business. It also removes an important point of tension with the U.S. government. It would give congressional supporters of U.S. assistance to Peru a base for having it renewed. The settlement need not be a giveaway to IPC, although it could be reasonably generous given the great boost to national pride that has already taken place in Peru. The fact that IPC property would remain in Peruvian hands should be a source of satisfaction to nationalists. Magnanimity can come from this strength.

5. *An appropriate formula for investment in high-conflict industries should be developed and publicized.* Given the lessons of 1969–1970, the Peruvian government should have sufficient ownership of any new "high-conflict" foreign investment to satisfy nationalist sensitivities. The proposed Southern Peru Copper investment does not yet contain any measures of this sort. Until it does, trouble can be predicted with a high degree of certainty.

6. *Incentives for foreign private investment should be developed.* These are well known. They include tariff and quota protection, subsidies, and tax benefits. Incentives will probably not have a great impact. But they might indicate a change in investment climate, serve as a means of reducing investor risk, and stimulate particular kinds of investment.

CONCLUSION

One of the principal practical problems of foreign investment is that it involves sectors with different motives and different perspectives on the process. The host country views foreign investment as it affects national goals. The investor views foreign investment as one of many means of earning a return on capital. The investor's own company should—but rarely does—view foreign investment only in the light of its long-term interests.

If these differing outlooks are clearly understood, then policy alternatives can be presented that might lend to more fruitful and less disruptive investment relationships on all sides. This paper has tried, first, to set out these different perspectives and, then, to apply the analysis to the case of the United States–Peruvian relationship, which has in recent years been anything but harmonious. Basically, we conclude that erratic, but generally antibusiness actions of the Peruvian government and overidentification with U.S. private investment on the part of the U.S. government have both been inappropriate. And we suggest a set of policies that (1) require the host country—in this case Peru—to establish a predictable investment environment; (2) require the investing business to live within the constraints established by this environment; and (3) suggest that the investor nations—in this case the United States—endeavor, in its long-run interest, to remove itself from the process.

EDITOR'S NOTE

While the emphasis of this chapter is on the role of government in protecting business, it should be noted that the two sectors are at times quite interdependent, with each needing the other's help to accomplish goals of mutual interest. The following story, a concrete example of this, was related to the editor by one of the corporate representatives invited to the Conference.

In February, 1969, the Hickenlooper Amendment was about to be applied on April 9th, 1969 (cutting off all foreign assistance, the lucrative U. S. sugar quota for Peru, etc.), six months after the expropriation of IPC. Official communications between the two governments had virtually broken down. A few weeks earlier, for example, when the U. S. ambassador to Peru requested an audience with President Velasco before flying to Washington to brief President Nixon, the request was denied.

Several individuals from the U. S. and Peruvian private sectors in Peru, who had known each other before, had informal but close relations with their respective governments and were committed to preserving U. S.-Peruvian diplomatic relations and the avoidance of the application of the Hickenlooper Amendment if possible.

At the instigation of a Peruvian lawyer and a U. S. businessman, a private meeting was arranged for them with a member of President Velasco's cabinet on Wednesday, February 19, 1969. This cabinet officer arranged for a meeting alone between the U. S. businessman and President Velasco two days later (Friday, February 21, 1969). At that meeting, the businessman elicited from President Velasco a statement of his willingness to receive a personal envoy from President Nixon to have discussions regarding the IPC case, the Hickenlooper Amendment, and related matters.

This was an indication that formal diplomatic meetings between the two governments had not produced and was the one missing ingredient required to avoid the application of the Hickenlooper Amendment on the date of the six-month deadline—April 9th. If that date could be passed by, with meaningful negotiations underway, the prospects for permanently avoiding a confrontation via the formal application of the Hickenlooper Amendment were greatly enhanced.

With this indication from President Velasco of a willingness to receive an emissary from President Nixon in hand, the U.S. businessman went directly from the presidential palace to the residence of the U. S. ambassador to describe the meeting he had just had alone with President Velasco. The U. S. ambassador responded immediately by saying that this was the one missing link they had been waiting for. He requested the businessman to stop off in Washington the next day (Saturday, February 22) to meet with the acting assistant secretary for Latin American affairs and the undersecretary of state to relay to them what had transpired. This was done during the afternoon of February 22 in considerable detail. The undersecretary indicated that the planning for and designation of the personal envoy of President Nixon had already been largely done and that, with this new information and statement from President Velasco of his willingness to receive such an envoy, the machinery for sending such a representative could now be put into motion. This was done and shortly thereafter the president's envoy, John Irwin, in fact arrived in Lima. Peru had commenced the talks that avoided the necessity of an open confrontation between Peru and the United States on April 9, 1969, the date by which many observers had felt the United States would have had to put the Hickenlooper Amendment into effect. But what was required to bring this about, as is so often the case in Peru, was an informal relationship and channel of communication based on personal friendships and confidence. This was provided by individuals from the U. S. and Peruvian private sectors.

DECLARATION MADE BY THE REPRESENTATIVES OF THE PERUVIAN PRIVATE SECTOR

The Peruvian citizens from the private sector participating in the Peruvian-North American Conference organized by the Adlai Stevenson Institute of Chicago consider it to be of interest to express the following:

1. The image that Peru has in the United States has suffered a process of deformation that we trust can be corrected in some measure thanks to the analysis of the realities and situations undertaken at this conference.

2. As do the organizers and United States participants, we believe it to be of the utmost importance that the formulation of future decisions on the part of the U.S. government relating to Peru, should correspond to a proper evaluation of the realities and expectations of our country.

3. We also consider it to be important to stress our profound adherence to democracy and our faith in its future in Peru, and at the same time we recognize that the profound and rapid changes of the economic, social, and political structures of the country were necessary and desired by the great majority of our population. These changes, inspired by a peruanista trend, coincide with previous proposals made by various political sectors of the country. This gives a sense of continuity to the present process of modernization of Peru.

4. During this conference we thought it also necessary to point out coincidences and discrepancies with some Government decisions and with the evaluations of those decisions by international public and official opinion. We think that the fundamental reasons for uncertainty and retraction on the part of the private sector, both Peruvian and

foreign, are the consequence of the difficulties of communicating appropriately with the government authorities, a situation that fortunately seems to be now on the road toward favorable change.

5. We have also pointed out those actions taken by the government and some private enterprises in the United States, and of the international financial institutions, that in our opinion have impaired the efforts of our country to move beyond its present stage of underdevelopment, and we have proposed alternatives that we believe necessary to modify the situation.

6. We are grateful for the opportunity that has been given to us to contribute to a better understanding between the U.S. and Peruvian public and private sectors, being convinced as we are, that a country like ours, blessed with great human and natural resources, only requires the positive action of all the internal and external sectors acting together to rapidly move beyond the present situation, to improve the quality of life of our population, and to restore to all Peruvians the right to decide our own destiny.

Wingspread, May, 1970

Carlos Zuzunaga-Flórez   Ramón Remolina   Alejandro Tabini   John Watmough   Patricio Ricketts   Ricardo Saettone D.   Samuel Drassinower   José Valle-Skinner

William J. McIntire

9. U.S. LABOR POLICY

The longer draft of this paper, which was presented at the Racine meeting in May, was accepted as being factually accurate, but criticized by some participants as being imbued by the strong subjective bias of the author. It was said that "loaded words," whose meaning is not very well understood in the United States, were used. Also the paper's conclusion that past and present U.S. labor policy is largely irrelevant in the emerging "new Peru" was distressing to some.

At Racine, the friendly but sharp debates I had previously had in Lima with Mr. William Douglas, director of the American Institute for Free Labor Development (AIFLD) programs in Peru from 1967–1969, were brought up to date. At first the thought was to try to combine in the final paper the differing points of view and the policy suggestions that flow from them. But Mr. Douglas suggested, and I concurred, that it might be best on this "labor" topic for him to present his own ideas in a short separate paper. This is what Mr. Douglas has done, and this is why the usual format for papers in this volume has not been followed here.

I have tried in this final version to accept criticisms and to change or explain words or sections that were unclear or "unobjective." But I should warn the reader that, for any person who is involved in the fascinating reality that is Peru today, it is probably impossible (and maybe undesirable) to be completely dispassionate. I also apologize for the use of a number of initials, confusing to the nonspecialist but necessary to keep from repeating lengthy trade union names.

PERUVIAN LABOR HISTORY

Until the post-World War II period, the Peruvian labor movement was very weak. Guilds and other benevolent associations of workers had existed since Spanish colonial times, but the first "trade union," which was more a benevolent association than a class instrument, was the Federación de Panaderos (Bakery Workers) Estrella del Perú, founded in 1887. As in other Latin American countries, anarchosyndicalists, many of them immigrants from Europe, were active in Peru from 1900 on. The first textile unions were formed in 1911, and in these and other trade unions in the years immediately following there were numerous incidents of bloody repression by Peruvian government authorities. A Federación Obrera Local (Local Worker Federation) was founded in the Lima area in 1918, but this was put out of operation by the second Leguia regime (1919–1930). Concurrent with the Marxist-nationalist movement of José Carlos Mariátegui in the 1920s, there was established in 1929 a Confederación General de Trabajadores del Perú (CGTP, General Confederation of Workers of Peru), which from the beginning was under communist control.

The Alianza Popular Revolucionaria Americana (APRA, American People's Revolutionary Alliance) of Victor Raúl Haya de la Torre gained control of some trade unions after being established in Peru in 1930–1931, but both these efforts and the CGTP were crushed by General Sánchez Cerro in 1932. Other Marxist and Aprista efforts did not get very far until the World War II period because of the political atmosphere of the time, generally repressive of leftist thought and activity. But in the World War II period, when Peru became an important producer of raw materials, including minerals for the Allied war effort, the Peruvian economy surged and with it the Peruvian labor movement.

The Confederación de Trabajadores del Perú (CTP, Confederation of Workers of Peru) was founded in 1944, and since then has been the largest, most important, and most representative Peruvian trade union national organization. In its first year the CTP was under far leftist control, but in 1945 APRA political forces took control of the Confederation. It is interesting that the Confederación Interamericana de Trabajadores (CIT, Inter-American Confederation of Workers), the first post–World War II, anticommunist, inter-American labor grouping, was founded with strong CTP influence, and that the first CIT Congress was held in Lima in January, 1948. But the growing influence of the CTP under APRA control was cut back by the coming to power in October, 1948 of the dictatorial and then violently anti-APRA regime of General Manuel Odría. General Odría was paternalistic toward labor: the Ministry of Labor was established, and labor made economic gains and slightly improved its position with Peruvian society during the Odría regime (1948–1956). But the regime was anti-CTP, and Confederation leaders were driven into hiding, jailed, or exiled.

The "modern history" of the Peruvian labor movement dates from 1956 and the coming to power of President Manuel Prado, a government (1956–1962) that APRA backed. It will probably be seen in retrospect that APRA influence in the trade union movement and its control of the CTP reached its apogee during the period from 1956 to October, 1968, the latter date being when the present military government took over.

The APRA party had its history of martyrs and of sincere and hard-fought struggle for its ideals during the 1930s. The CTP also points with pride to its record from the middle of the 1940s of conquistas (conquests), the better wages and working conditions it secured for its own workers, and the advanced labor legislation it secured for Peruvian workers in general. But by 1956 the APRA party (not unlike the Mexican "revolutionary" PRI group) had gone through ideological changes. Instead of *lucha* (struggle) for power and for its earlier ideals, it seemed far more ready to compromise. From severe condemnation of "imperialism" and U.S. influence in the 1930s, and of the way capitalism operated in Peru, APRA had moved to the right, making ever more adjustments with its former enemies in its quest to take power. Although some Apristas said and believed it was all a stratagem, Victor Raúl Haya de la Torre and APRA leadership acted as though they thought liberal capitalism and free enterprise were the best of all possible worlds.

APRA collaborated from 1956 to 1962 in the regime of the gentlemanly but oligarchical Manuel Prado.[1] The very conservative Lima newspaper *La Prensa* and its owner Pedro Beltrán Espantoso, who after the death of his APRA-assassinated predecessor Francisco Graña Garland in January, 1947, had pledged "a struggle that would not end until *aprismo* had been wiped out as a political force,"[2] now performed the extraordinary about-face of supporting APRA. More radical elements in APRA split off, and some went very far over to the left to form APRA-Rebelde. APRA still had more support among Peruvian workers (even the blind allegiance of many of them) by far than any other Peruvian political party. APRA often continued in the 1960s to be regarded abroad as the leading proponent of liberal democracy in Peru. The CTP emphasized collective bargaining and better labor legislation, always within the context of the presumed continuance of a capitalist, free-enterprise economy.

In the 1962 elections at the end of President Manuel Prado's six-year rule, the vote was split three ways (between APRA, the Unión Nacional Odriista [UNO] of General Manuel Odría, and the Acción Popular of Fernando Belaúnde Terry). But APRA had a slight plurality, and it appeared that finally and for the first time APRA might be able to assume full power in Peru. But various factors, including that APRA for the moment was unable to form a coalition with General Odría's UNO, and the Peruvian military's traditional grudge with APRA (dating from the "Year of Barbarism, 1932," when APRA and the army had engaged in bloody strife), prevented this from happening. The Peruvian military intervened in a coup. Interesting as an illustration of the continuing close ties between APRA and the CTP is the following passage from the late Serafino Romualdi's memoirs:

Then I took [Arturo] Sabroso [secretary-general at the time for the CTP] aside:

"Why did you call for a general strike, when it was obvious that the

[1] Oligarchical or oligarchy, literally meaning the "rule of the few," is in common, current Peruvian usage used to refer to the small group of landed and wealthy Peruvian individuals and families with international financial connections who, at least until recently, were reputed to dominate Peruvian society completely.

[2] Frederick B. Pike, *The Modern History of Peru* (London: Weidenfeld & Nicholson, 1967), p. 286.

unions would not respond, because it was too late and the issues were confused? After all, it was a general strike to protest the Army's intervention that had prevented not *Haya's* but *Odría's* accession to the Presidency."

"Perhaps you are right, Serafino, but the pressure was too strong. The order came, and we had to obey it."

"From whom, from the Party, from Haya de la Torre himself?"

Sabroso did not answer. He was visibly embarrassed. At times, silence is more eloquent than words.[3]

The APRA-CTP strike did not get very far, and a year later in 1963 Fernando Belaúnde Terry of Acción Popular was elected president to rule Peru until October, 1968. The political lineup during the next five years was such that an alliance of AP and the Christian Democrats ruled the executive branch and a coalition of APRA and UNO (who had been archenemies until seven years previously) ruled the National Assembly. With certain limitations, during the Belaúnde period the CTP was recognized by the Peruvian government as the most representative voice of Peruvian labor.[4] The strong APRA-UNO majority and opposition in the Assembly was one of the factors that prevented some of President Belaúnde's program from going into full effect, and which perhaps gave some of the military and others pause as to whether the traditional "democracy" could ever be effective in Peru or move the country out of its underdevelopment and dependence.

At the time of the military coup that overthrew President Belaúnde on October 3, 1968, Peru had a population of 12.7 million and a labor force of 4 million. Of this labor force, some 12.5 percent (500,000 workers) were organized into trade unions. We may estimate that, of these, about half were members of the CTP. The CTP was strong in the regional federations except in Cuzco and Arequipa (where the communist influence was probably stronger); it was strong among bank workers, chauffeurs, graphical workers, petroleum workers, sugar workers, textile workers, and white-collar workers, and had some strength among agricultural workers through the Federación Nacional de Campesinos del Peru

---

[3] Serafino Romualdi, *Presidents and Peons: Recollections of a Labor Ambassador in Latin America* (New York: Funk and Wagnalls, 1967), p. 319.

[4] Ibid.

(FENCAP, National Federation of Agricultural Workers of Peru).

Of course by the 1960s the CTP was not the only current in Peruvian labor. Far left and communist-oriented trade unionists and political leaders have remained active in the labor field in Peru. An Executive Committee for the Reorganization and Unification of the Peruvian Confederation of Workers was founded in 1962 by unions that had broken away from the CTP, and by independent trade unions. These unions were for the most part of communist, APRA-Rebelde orientation, and included some chauffeurs, civil construction, maritime, port, and metal workers. Because of the strength of the CTP, growing ideological divisions among the communists and other leftists, and Peruvian government surveillance, this effort did not get very far. A new Confederación General de Trabajadores del Peru (CGTP), in which Moscow-line communists were the strongest group, was formed at a Congress in Callao in June 1968. But it did not have the ten Federations needed to form a legal Confederation, and, for example, the Chimbote fishermen among whom Peking-line influence was present and other non-Moscow-oriented groups refused to become full members.

The third important grouping of Peruvian labor in the 1960s was the Movimiento Sindical Cristiano del Perú (MOSICP, Christian Trade Union Movement of Peru), established in 1955, an outgrowth at first of Young Christian Worker (JOC) groups in Lima, and in close contact in its first years with the Catholic Church and the new Christian Democratic party in Peru. MOSICP was affiliated internationally with the Latin American Confederation of Christian Trade Unionists (CLASC according to its Spanish initials; now headquartered in Caracas) and with the International Federation of Christian Trade Unions (IFCTU or CISC, headquartered in Brussels and now renamed the World Confederation of Workers, or CMT). MOSICP by the early 1960s, especially on the basis of extensive funding from the Solidarity Fund of the CISC in Brussels and from German Christian Democratic (CDU) sources, showed promise of going places, but the promise never seemed to be realized. However, the German-financed training programs for MOSICP were impressive in that they were oriented toward giving the workers *mística* (mystique), solidarity with all Peruvians who suffered exploitation, and an understanding of the basic, underlying causes of Peruvian and Latin American under-development.[5]

By the middle 1960s, reflecting CLASC policy, MOSICP was attacking U.S. "imperialism"[6] and rejecting virtually all U.S. government and trade union influence and "interference" in Latin America. MOSICP was especially interested in *campesino* affairs, and as of 1970 still has some influence among fish-meal workers in Callao, railroad workers in Arequipa, and in sections of the altiplano. Perhaps twenty to thirty thousand members would be a generous estimate of its 1968 and present strength. It makes frequent use of its good training facilities at Cieneguilla outside Lima, and in 1970 was seeking to get ten federations affiliated so that it will have the legal basis to form a confederation. An earlier tendency to flirt with the far left now seems superseded by the willingness to collaborate even with APRA and the CTP's FENCAP in protest against alleged lack of trade union and *campesino* participation in the current agrarian reform process.

There were also in 1968 and are now important unions including teachers, postal and telegraph workers, stevedores, and newspapermen who were independent of the three national centers.[7] But as will be spelled out further in the sections of this paper on U.S. labor policy in Peru, the Peruvian trade union movement was extremely politicized, with each of the three principal trade union centers closely linked both to a domestic political party, and for funds and ideas to a foreign patron: the CTP to APRA and the United States, MOSICP to the Christian Democrats and to Germany and Western

[5] The Germans, through the Social Democratic Friedrich Ebert Foundation, assist also APRA and the CTP, but their programs with the CTP would in no sense be comparable to the U.S. programs, which will be described in the following section.

[6] Neither here in this paper nor in current Latin American usage is the word "imperialism" used in its classical Marxist or Leninist sense. Many contemporary Latin Americans would not accept Lenin's thinking from the early 1900s about imperialism being "the last stage of capitalism," although they perhaps would regard some of his analysis as being valuable. Instead, "imperialism" refers to the conscious or unconscious mechanisms by which the countries of the rich and developed world (including both the United States and the Soviet Union) are alleged to try to maintain and extend their political, economic, and cultural domination of the Third World.

[7] Some of these independent trade unions were or are now linked internationally to an International Trade Secretariat.

Europe, and the CGTP to the Moscow-line Peruvian Communist
party and to the Soviet Union. It may be debated whose fault this
was, and the Peruvian trade unionists themselves share some of
the blame along with the foreigners. The key fact being emphasized is that as of 1968 the main groups of Peruvian organized
workers were highly dependent, without much evidence that they
were becoming more independent. The Peruvian trade union movement in recent years has been a classic example of a colonialized
and dependent trade union movement.

PAST U.S. LABOR POLICY IN PERU

A conscious effort has been made to avoid mentioning U.S. labor
policy in Peru until this point in the paper. This was done in order
to compartmentalize this paper along the lines requested by the
Adlai Stevenson Institute for all papers in this book. This was difficult to do, and constitutes an incomplete and perhaps even false
view of Peruvian labor history. For since the middle 1940s, and in
an increasing manner up until at least October, 1968, U.S. government foreign policy in general, and the U.S. government's and the
U.S. trade union movement's labor policy in Peru have had an
enormous influence on the Peruvian labor movement.

The United States had little contact with the Peruvian labor
movement until the post–World War II period. But perhaps it is
advisable to mention briefly the contacts the United States had with
the Latin American labor movement generally until 1945–1946.
Let us recall that the principal organization in the U.S. labor
movement in the early part of this century was the American
Federation of Labor (AFL), founded in the 1880s. Because of the
strong influence of AFL founder Samuel Gompers, the AFL quickly adopted a pragmatic, nonsocialist viewpoint. This reduced the
range of AFL contacts with the only other trade union movements
then fairly strong, the Western European. Certainly by the 1920s
the AFL, by the then existing international trade union standards,
was already a conservative movement, primarily interested in getting "more, more, more" for the comparatively privileged workers
in the craft unions that were AFL members. However, Samuel
Gompers from an early date was interested in Latin America, and
the AFL backed Cuban independence in 1895, condemned U.S. an-

nexation of Puerto Rico in 1899, and supported the Mexican Revolution of 1910. In 1918, with only Mexican, Central American and Caribbean area trade unions participating in addition to the AFL, the Pan American Federation of Labor (PAFL or COPA) was established. Peruvian workers never participated, and with the death of Gompers in 1924 and growing isolationism in the AFL (and in U.S. society), PAFL grew weaker and weaker and had disappeared for all practical purposes by the time of the crash in 1929.

The next chapter of important U.S. trade union involvement in Latin American labor (U.S. government interest through this time continued minimal or nonexistent) dates from 1938. By this time in the United States, the Congress of Industrial Organizations (CIO), to the left of the AFL and then including communist influence, had been established and made great gains in organizing U.S. industrial workers. The CIO was one of the founding members at Mexico City in September, 1938, of the Confederation of Latin American Workers (CTAL). Peruvians were among the delegates from some thirteen countries who participated. CTAL, under the leadership of Vicente Lombardo Toledano, a Mexican Marxist, quickly became communist dominated. CTAL was an important instrument of communist penetration of the Latin American trade union movements, in complete accord at any particular moment with the Russian foreign policy line. By the early 1940s, with few exceptions and still with little U.S. government influence or interest, the trade union movements in general in Latin America were under communist or leftist control.

This did not present special problems for the United States government or trade union movement during the World War II period, for it was in the interest of the communist-dominated trade unions to support the Allied war effort (which included their Russian mentors after June, 1941). The first (in the world) U.S. government labor attachés, career Foreign Service officers, were placed in U.S. embassies in Latin America in Rio de Janeiro and La Paz about 1943, and in Lima soon after. The purpose of these first labor attachés was primarily to maintain contact with and report on labor and trade union movements, so that the shipment of vital war materials to aid the Allied war effort would not be obstructed.

But with the beginning of the "cold war" in 1946, both the U.S.

government and trade union movement realized there was a serious problem in Latin America, in that the trade unions, one of the
few mass organizations in the still largely feudal Latin American
societies, were under communist control. This constituted a serious
threat to U.S. political, strategic, and economic interests. The case
can be made quite strongly that if the U.S. government and trade
union movement had not stepped up the contacts with Latin American trade unions, communism by now and many years back would
have taken control in many more than one Latin American country.

In the first post–World War II years, the late Serafino Romualdi
of the Inter-American Affairs Office of the AFL (after 1955, of the
AFL-CIO) began his trips through Latin America including
Peru. Mr. Romualdi, born in Italy and a socialist during his youth,
had migrated to New York after Mussolini came to power. During
the Second World War he was a U.S. government OSS functionary. His earlier radical views had mellowed during his years in the
States. Like various other ex- or mellowed socialists who in this
era were influential in U.S. government and private labor policy
overseas, he continued in contact with the Socialist International
and with the now moderate socialist parties in Europe and persons
of similar orientation in the United States.

Also active in AFL international and Latin American policy was
(and still is) Jay Lovestone, secretary-general of the U.S. Communist party until 1929, who had been driven out of the party because of ideological feuds, and later became a doctrinnaire anti-
Communist. Mr. Lovestone in particular, and others also, have
been charged with labeling any force for social change not in their
good graces or under their control as "communist."

When Dubinsky discovered Lovestone, there was a market for informed veterans of the left who knew the tactics and ideology of fight-
ing the left, both Communist and non-Communist. The unlikely joining of the careers of Meany and Lovestone, who by then had become
head of the Garment Workers' international affairs department, was
consummated. From that time, the doctrine of anti-communism and
the foreign posture of the American Federation of Labor became one
and the same. With little difficulty it became also the policy of the
merged AFL-CIO after 1955. . . . Thomas Braden, then Allen Dulles'

deputy director in the Central Intelligence Agency, would later write that Lovestone had "an enormous grasp of foreign intelligence operations."[8]

In Europe in the first years of the cold war, according to a multitude of published revelations that leave little room for doubt, Mr. Lovestone learned to work closely with the U.S. government and to use U.S. government and intelligence funds for various overt and covert work with trade unions.

In 1947 an Office of International Labor Affairs (OILA, now the Bureau of International Labor Affairs, or ILAB) was established in the U.S. Department of Labor. In the Labor Department, in the State Department where similar offices existed, in aid programs, and in other U.S. government agencies, there was growing interest in the labor and trade union factor in Latin America as in other parts of the world. There was constant movement of trade union functionaries in and out of U.S. government labor positions. U.S. government Labor Attachés either came out of the labor movement or were civil servants, but Mr. Lovestone and his colleagues had an important say in whether or not they got the jobs.

Until the middle 1950s, the U.S. trade union movement had some important differences with general U.S. foreign policy in Latin America. While the Eisenhower administration from 1953 was giving full support to General Odría in Peru, General Pérez Jimenez in Venezuela, and to other Latin American dictators, the AFL was backing the opposition parties: in the case of Peru the support went to APRA, Victor Raúl Haya de la Torre, and the CTP. These "days of struggle" set up strong and even emotional ties between the AFL and APRA, ties which in a number of cases endure to this date. The AFL also very strongly pushed from the start of the post–World War II period the idea that international trade union organization in the Western Hemisphere must be based on an Inter-American or Pan American organization basis. They thought Latin Americans were misguided or falling into a communist trap if they wanted to form Latin American organizations. The fact that there was an impressive difference between the

---

[8] Joseph Hill (pseudonym), "Labor's Establishment: Stop the World . . . AFL-CIO plus CIA-ICFTU = 0," *Commonweal*, March 21, 1969, p. 5.

power and money of U.S. trade unionists, with their fifteen million members, and the relatively weak Latin American trade unionists, some fifteen million in all split among more than twenty countries, never seemed to suggest to the AFL people that it might be best if the Latin Americans had some separate identity. Serafino Romualdi in his memoirs mentions with apparent horror the suggestion made in 1957 by Charles Millard, a Canadian who was then director of Organization of the International Confederation of Free Trade Unions (ICFTU) in Brussels "to split ORIT [Inter-American Regional Organization of Workers] in two by creating a regional office for North America (United States, Canada, and possibly the English-speaking Caribbean Islands) and another for all of Latin America."[9]

The AFL's labor policy toward Latin America and Peru, which I would maintain has been the basis also in recent years for U.S. government labor policy, is spelled out in the following quote from Mr. Romualdi. The policy was and largely is "to help the wage earners of Latin America to raise their living standards by assisting in the organization of stable and strong unions; to strengthen the cause of freedom and representative democracy; to combat and defeat Communism and other totalitarian movements; and, above all, to assist in the development of a new type of Latin American labor leader who would reject the stale concept of class struggle in favor of constructive labor-management relations in a democratic, pluralistic society."[10]

Since 1957 I have known personally a great number of U.S. citizens, in official or private positions, working in the labor field in Latin America. With a few notable exceptions, their basic policy was and is anticommunism, collective bargaining as the essential thing for trade unions, and the promotion of free enterprise. From the middle 1940s in the case of the U.S. trade unions, and from the later 1950s in the case of the U.S. government, this policy in Peru was primarily directed at and through the Peruvian political movement considered most likely to achieve these goals: APRA and its trade union expression, the CTP.

As has been mentioned, the Confederación Interamericana de

[9] Romualdi, *Presidents and Peons*, p. 132.
[10] Ibid., p. vii.

Trabajadores (CIT, Inter-American Confederation of Workers) had its founding meeting in Lima in 1948, with the CTP acting as host. But the CTP was soon severely curtailed in its domestic activities by General Odría's government. However CTP leaders, in exile or through clandestine means, had close contacts with the AFL, with the CIT and with CIT's successor the Organización Regional Interamericana de Trabajadores (ORIT, Inter-American Regional Organization of Workers), founded in 1951 as the Western Hemisphere branch of the ICFTU. APRA and CTP people got along very well in ORIT circles and with the Latin American parties and trade unions of similar ideological orientation which (aside from the constant presence of the AFL and CIO) were dominant in ORIT. These included the Mexican PRI Party and CTM trade union movement; in Venezuela Acción Democrática and the CTV trade union movement.

ORIT's image as an expression of Latin American trade unionism was tarnished by the fact that three-fourths of its members and even more of its funding came from the United States and the AFL-CIO. There was also the embarrassment that much of its leadership in the pre-Castro (and as exiles, in the post-Castro) epoch came from the Confederation of Cuban Workers (CTC), which had worked out a modus vivendi with the dictatorship of General Batista. Although the Inter-American Office of the AFL-CIO and ORIT were loud in their protestations of being against dictatorships, and they did oppose General Odría in Peru and General Pérez Jiménez in Venezuela in the early 1950s, their position on this matter became less clear by the 1960s. They seemed to have little difficulty getting along with repressive regimes so long as these regimes were "anticommunist," not antagonistic to U.S.-style trade unionism, and favorable to U.S. political and business interests. They continued their opposition to Duvalier in Haiti and to Stroessner in Paraguay. But, for example, it does not seem altogether a coincidence that when the Goulart government was overthrown in Brazil in April, 1964, the U.S. government within a matter of hours recognized the anticommunist, right-wing regime; and within a couple of days AFL-CIO Inter-American Affairs director Andrew McLellan was interviewing President (General) Castelho Branco and bargaining for an expansion of AFL-CIO activities. By the early 1960s also, Arturo Jauregui Hurtado of APRA

and the CTP became (and continues to this date) secretary-general
of ORIT, and the CTP was receiving small but regular subsidies
from ORIT.[11]

As has been mentioned, U.S. Labor attachés were almost continuously attached to the U.S. Embassy in Lima from the middle
1940s. By the middle 1950s, especially from the start of President
Prado's government in 1956, there were at times also an assistant
labor attaché and one or more AID (or its predecessor organizations) technicians who specialized in technical labor matters or
assistance. USIS also had its labor program in Peru. All these functionaries were working closely, especially from 1956 on, primarily
with CTP trade unionists. This was perfectly natural: the CTP
was (and is) the most important trade union organization, and
under APRA control the most friendly to the United States. Of
course also these Embassy functionaries had close contacts with U.S.
business interests, as part of the general Embassy policy to promote
U.S. business. Numerous CTP functionaries were brought to the
United States on exchange programs ranging from a couple of
weeks to several months. Over a period of years virtually all first
and second-level CTP functionaries, as well as those of CTP affiliates, had the opportunity to visit the United States. In all, my estimate would be that up to five hundred Peruvians have visited the
U.S. on publicly financed labor programs. While this figure would
include some Ministry of Labor functionaries and members of independent trade unions, by far and away the majority were CTP
people. The U.S. trips were as much geared toward tourism and
propaganda as to straight trade union training. Many a Peruvian
trade unionist had the opportunity to visit Disneyland, Niagara
Falls, and other U.S. tourist spots, as well as to have impressive
personal contacts with U.S. trade union counterparts and their
standard of living. I recall, on my first visit to Lima in 1964, being
driven around town by an official of the Trade Union Central of
Private Employees (CSEPP, CTP), who was extremely proud of
the passenger car he had recently acquired. He could not praise
enough U.S.-style free enterprise and collective bargaining as the
answer for Peru, and praised to the skies what U.S. official and

---

[11] James L. Payne, *Labor and Politics in Peru* (New Haven and London:
Yale University Press, 1965), p. 200.

private trade union policy had done for the CTP and its affiliates.

International Trade Secretariats, groupings of workers in a particular occupational field, headquartered in Europe for the most part but strongly dependent upon U.S. funds and personnel for their Latin American activities, also entered strongly on the scene in Latin America and Peru by the middle 1950s. Thus the Postal, Telegraph and Telephone International (with strong backing and personnel from the U.S. National Association of Letter Carriers and the Communications Workers of America), the International Federation of Commercial, Clerical and Technical Employees (backed by the U.S. Retail Clerks' International Association), the International Petroleum Workers' Federation (backed by the Oil, Chemical and Atomic Workers of Denver), the International Transport Workers' Federation (backed by the U.S. transport and maritime worker unions); the Inter-American Federation of Working Newspapermen's Associations (backed by the American Newspaper Guild[12]) and other groups, were all on the scene in Lima by the late 1950s, and had established Latin American Regional Offices or other activities there. Lima and Peru, because of the central location and the strong contacts with the CTP and its affiliates, were clearly by this time a prime focus of U.S. official and unofficial labor interest in Latin America.

In 1961–1962 the American Institute for Free Labor Development (AIFLD or IADSL), for the development of "free and democratic labor" in Latin America, was established by and in Washington. With extensive funding from the U.S. government, 90 percent as it was eventually forced to make clear, and 10 percent from the AFL-CIO and from various big U.S. corporations such as Grace, Cerro de Pasco, and Standard Oil of New Jersey that had interests in Latin America and Peru, AIFLD began extensive activities in trade union training and "social projects" all over Latin America. The best students from AIFLD courses held in individual countries were invited to advanced courses in the United States.

---

[12] The Inter-American Federation of Working Newspapermen's Associations (IAFWNO) was apparently backed also by the CIA, to the tune of $1,000,000 routed through "dummy" foundations—according to reports published in the *New York Times* and elsewhere in early 1967. IAFWNO quickly went out of existence, and so far as I know, the allegations of CIA funding were never denied.

The Peruvian branch of AIFLD, the Centro de Estudios Laborales del Perú (CELP, Center of Peruvian Labor Studies), was established in Lima in 1962–1963. In the years since CELP has trained thousands of Peruvian trade unionists through its centers in Lima and Arequipa, and with frequent courses and contacts also in the Peruvian provinces. Until 1966 the U.S. government signed the CELP contract with the Peruvian government *and* the CTP; in 1966 the Belaúnde government insisted that the CTP no longer be a signatory to the contract (*convenio*) on CELP, and the CTP has not been since then. But there has been, through all the years of CELP history, CTP control of the organization, and especially in Lima few professors or students who were not approved by APRA and the CTP could participate in CELP programs.

In the 1962 elections the U.S. government, through its ambassador in Lima, James Loeb, and the U.S. trade union movement did everything possible to achieve an APRA victory. Mr. Loeb, appointed by President Kennedy, and former president of Americans for Democratic Action (ADA) in the United States, was to an extent almost unparalleled in Foreign Service history, unabashedly pro-APRA. After the military coup in 1962, he became *persona non grata* and was removed. Through the Belaúnde period (1963–1968), U.S. influence in the labor field in Peru continued strong, with extensive U.S. government and private trade union assistance being given the CTP. The AIFLD maintained its high level of activity, through the CELP labor education programs (with a budget of about $200,000 U.S. per year) and the AIFLD Social Projects Department (community development, housing cooperative ASIN-COOP, school buildings, and other projects). But U.S. government economic aid to the Belaúnde government was never high. It was quite clear in the first years that this was in reprisal against President Belaúnde's threats (which never materialized during his regime) to take strong action up to nationalization against the International Petroleum Company (IPC). Until 1967, Peru and Peruvian labor did make strong economic progress under the Belaúnde regime. Times were relatively good for the organized worker: the leadership of the CTP seemed to become ever more moderate in its demands against capitalist society, and seemed to have become co-opted by that society. It became difficult to get CTP solidarity in the case of strikes, and CTP leaders talked of close labor-business collaboration as the way to achieve a better Peru.

The U.S. citizens, government employees, and trade unionists active in the labor field in Peru were sincerely interested in making the CTP and CELP less political, less under APRA control. But they underestimated the politicization present in CELP and in every aspect of Peruvian society, and how valuable an asset CELP was in APRA's quest for political power. Perhaps some progress *was* made toward less APRA control in CELP. For example, the CELP office in Arequipa (directed by a Paraguayan trade unionist) succeeded in including may non-CTP and non-Aprista people in their courses (APRA was not at all strong in Arequipa). But such efforts were always subject to pressure by the CTP and APRA, by their strong supporters in the AFL-CIO and AIFLD in Washington. It was also clear during the closing years of the Belaúnde administration that the Peruvian government would have liked to see the CTP become less APRA-controlled, or as an alternative set up an Acción Popular–controlled confederation, but these efforts did not have time to come to fruition either.

In justice, it must again be mentioned that both MOSICP and the communist-oriented trade union groupings were also receiving extensive funds from overseas, conceivably more in all than did the CTP. Also there were a few trade union contacts from the U.S. which were not altogether a part of the now virtually identical U.S. government and trade union line. The International Trade Secretariat–International Metalworkers' Federation (IMF), which had much backing from the late Walter Reuther's United Automobile Workers (UAW), was active in Latin America and followed a line somewhat independent of the U.S. government, ORIT, and the AIFLD. But aside from occasional visits by IMF functionaries, this group was not very active in Peru.

PERUVIAN LABOR HISTORY SINCE OCTOBER 1968

For a variety of reasons, including what was thought to be a new giveaway to the IPC, the Peruvian military headed by President (General, now retired) Juan Velasco Alvarado took power on October 3, 1968. CTP Secretary-General Julio Cruzado Zavala, who succeeded Arturo Sabroso in 1964, was away in Mexico, but while rushing back and considering the possibilities of a general strike against the new military regime, realized that the CTP rank and file were not particularly distressed by the military takeover. The attitude of the average worker was, "Belaúnde was a nice man, but not such a good president, and maybe this new man will be better." Señor Cruzado was one of the very few Peruvian public figures who criticized the military for having taken power.

The military government's first important move, the nationalization of IPC's properties in Peru as of October 9, 1968, was tremendously popular, and resulted in a tremendous surge of nationalism and pride in being Peruvian all over the country. The CTP-affiliated petroleum workers' union at Talara had shown little interest previously in getting Peruvian petroleum away from U.S. control. But APRA and the CTP could not and did not oppose the IPC expropriation once it had taken place, clearly supported as the measure was by the Peruvian majorities. APRA and the CTP entered a period of confusion that has continued to this day, as little by little the military government (which by now has certainly earned the title "revolutionary government") began putting into effect a series of radical measures that promised basically to change structures in Peru and go far beyond anything the CTP had been thinking of for at least twenty years past.

The CTP position after October, 1968, was and is that they will not stand for repression of "democratic trade unions" or of "trade union liberty." Along with the APRA party, and almost all the press, they called for "free elections" and the return of "representative and democratic government." Instead of beauty contests, bingos, raffles, fiestas, and other fund-raising activities, which had become increasingly common expressions of CTP "trade unionism," especially in the provinces, the CTP sought to concern itself more with basic issues and the common good. For example, in April, 1968, before the coup, *Revista Central Sindical,* organ of CSEPP-CTP, the white-collar workers' affiliate, referred mainly to worker conquests such as "trade union education, social security, protection of the *campesino,* more schools, better transport, cheap food, laws for the worker, better salaries, and one's own house," with little indication of a need for basic structural changes in the society, or that it would not be possible under the then-existing Peruvian capitalism to improve indefinitely the organized worker's situation.[13] An editorial prepared for *Cetepé*, organ of the CTP, in preparation for May Day, 1969—several months after the coup, was much more militant, referring to the "odious privilege and insulting riches of a certain few, and the sordid, wounding misery and desperation of the rest." The same editorial, as did almost all Peruvians, reacted against the "threats to apply the Hickenlooper Amendment."[14]

In the twenty months now since the military coup, the CTP among the trade union organizations has found the going especially rough. Its former influence in the Labor Ministry is being whittled away, as people who are thought to be APRA sympathizers or "counterrevolutionaries" either change their attitudes or are removed from positions of influence. The fact the CTP is regarded as being controlled by APRA makes it subject to suspicion by the government and all groups supporting the present government. The government's desire to hold the line economically, the emphasis now being put on agrarian reform and national industrial development, and the suspicion that basically political motives may be in back of CTP worker demands makes the government rather unresponsive to what the CTP and its unions request. With the rapid succession of Decree Laws now being issued by the military government to completely change the pattern of Peruvian society, it often seems that it is generally difficult for organized labor even to keep pace or mentally to catch up with the reforms the government is instituting.

In general the government's desire to achieve and maintain fiscal and economic stability, and the discipline required in what is seen as being a period of domestic and international threat, has made the government very firm in dealing with worker requests for higher wages or other benefits. The one exception was in the case of a CGTP-backed march to Lima in March 1970 by Cerro de Pasco miners, who pledged support of the government and whose complaints were directed against Cerro Corporation. The miners' complaints were personally settled in their favor by the government. It is the CGTP and its for the most part Moscow-line leaders

[13] *Revista Central Sindical*, cover, April 1968.
[14] *Cetepé*, April 1969, p. 3.

who have tried to profit from the whole situation in Peru, and indeed in recent months it has made gains in membership and influence. The CGTP still has little or no *campesino* strength, although it would certainly like to acquire this strength. The CGTP now strongly backs the present government, and its activities are fully reported and favored in the cooperativized and worker-controlled Lima newspaper *Expreso*. But May Day, 1970, celebrations both by CTP and CGTP groups in Lima were poorly attended. The Peruvian government is now spelling out its ideological "line" ever more clearly, indicating that it seeks a new solution for Peru which is neither communist nor capitalist, that "communist" advisers within the government do not exist and would not be tolerated, and that there must be an end to foreign dependence in any sphere. Thus it is highly unlikely that such a Moscow-line controlled group as the CGTP will be allowed to expand their activities very much or be able to take control of the labor situation in Peru.

Although predictions are always risky, there are indications as to what is likely to occur on the labor scene in Peru. One such indication came when the former antigovernment newspapers *Expreso* and *Extra*, owned largely by Manuel Ulloa, one of the last ministers of economy under the Belaúnde administration and now living in exile, were expropriated by the Peruvian government in early March, 1970, and turned over to worker cooperative control. Provision has been made for compensation to the former owners. Cooperativism and the concept of an integral cooperative movement are now tremendously popular in Peru. Now that the example has been given by *Expreso* and *Extra*, other workers who consider themselves oppressed are raising the possibility that they also may take over their industries or factories and turn them into worker cooperatives. But the Peruvian government is not encouraging such possibilities, because of the lack of worker cooperative training and mentality, and also because of the chain reaction this would cause throughout the country and the consequent discouragement to foreign and domestic private investment. As regards trade unions in cooperatives of production, they are seen by the workers as continuing to be necessary so long as the cooperativization process continues, so long as there is extensive government supervision and cooperative concepts have not reached maturity. But the eventual result may be that trade unions in such cooperativized economic entities will change their nature radically.

In an article in the new Peruvian magazine *Rikchay Perú*, Edilberto Rivas, secretary-general of the trade union in the former sugar hacienda Cayaltí (now Cayaltí Agro-Industrial Complex), near Chiclayo in Lambayeque, gives an interesting anaylsis of the initial steps in setting up the agrarian cooperative there. The hacienda had been wretchedly mismanaged by its former owners, Aspillaga Anderson Hnos., S.A., and there were some 240,000,00 soles (U.S. dollar = approximately 43 soles) in debts at the time the Peruvian government intervened and began the process of expropriation of the hacienda in June, 1969 (immediately after the new Agrarian Reform Law). The Cayaltí trade union was in an attitude of struggle, not dormant and paternalized as in the case of other haciendas where better conditions had prevailed, and had organized several protest marches and even the symbolic seizure of the Chiclayo Cathedral in the months just prior to the government takeover. At first, after the announcement of the Agrarian Reform Law, Rivas and his union were skeptical: "When the Agrarian Reform Law was announced, at first we said: Just one more law. [After a discussion on the pros and cons of the law] we said that this law is not such a good instrument but it is an instrument, and it will depend upon us with our experience and work that it be converted into a good thing. We remarked that it is the Government which is making the Revolution possible, but that it is the people who are going to bring it to fruition."[15]

When I talked with Señor Rivas at a meeting on agrarian reform in early May, 1970, at Chiclayo, he told me the trade union leaders and workers at Cayaltí are not interested in short-run benefits in the form of consumer goods. Rather they considered themselves to be working for their children and grandchildren, and that profits these next years must be ploughed back mainly into improving the infrastructure of the hacienda and not into consumer goods. The Cayaltí workers seem determined that they themselves not be converted by economic progress merely into another bourgeois

---

[15] Edilberto Rivas, "Cayaltí: De la hacienda capitalista a la cooperativa de los trabajadores," *Rikchay Perú* (Lima) 1, no. 1, (March 1970): 4.

class,[16] and that the struggle will not be ended until all Peruvians, especially those now most disadvantaged, share in the benefits of the new society. In this and in other cases, I have been impressed by the way the Peruvian worker with good leadership responds to really noble ideals. There is the desire by Señor Rivas, shared among a growing sector in Peru, that the current process lead to a new type of communitarian society, based on humanistic, Christian, and specifically Peruvian elements. When I asked Señor Rivas what the relation of the trade union in Cayaltí is now to the National Federation of Sugar Workers (a CTP affiliate) and to the CTP itself, he said they were still nominally affiliated but commented that if they had paid attention to CTP functionaries, the agrarian reform process would never have taken place. In the Santa River Valley near Chimbote this past year, it has also been most interesting for me to observe the growth in the *campesinos'* own sense of dignity, and their disillusionment with the traditional political parties and trade unions.

The Peruvian government in recent months has put into effect stiff penalties for "sabotage" of the agrarian reform process. Several FENCAP and CTP–National Federation of Sugar Worker officials, who had been active on the big sugar haciendas of the north, have been arrested and charged with this "sabotage," and are still under confinement. The Peruvian government throughout the country has been encouraging the past couple of months the organization of Comités de Defensa (Defense Committees) of the Revolution and of Agrarian Reform, while warning at the same time that these committees must serve positive and not merely political purposes, and that they not be allowed to fall into extremist hands.

What may happen within the next couple of years is that pro-government workers will try to take over control of the CTP. If the present government remains in power for any substantial period of time and continues its reform program, this effort will prob-

[16] It should be understood that the word *burgués*, in its current common usage in Peru, indicates a person selfishly concerned with his own material comfort and individualistic self-expression, with little or no concern for the disadvantaged masses.

ably succeed. APRA control in trade union and worker circles may be progressively diminished. But—on the basis of existing government policy—it is very unlikely that communists or other extremists will be allowed to take over the movement's leadership. It may happen also that when this process has been completed, there will be a movement to disaffiliate from ORIT (although the withdrawal last year of the AFL-CIO from the ICFTU leaves open the possibility that ORIT itself may become more independent of the AFL-CIO and/or become a Latin American movement). The Peruvian trade union movement that may emerge will probably back closely, and perhaps even impel, progressive government policies. Already the Peruvian government is insisting that, if it is to sign a contract renewing CELP's existence in Peru, it must be able to name a Peruvian subdirector.[17]

On April 22, 1970, at Punta del Este, Uruguay, General Francisco Morales Bermúdez, minister of economy and finances, defined what the present Peruvian government is seeking: "Neither Communism, which destroys the liberties which are the essence of a democratic regime; nor Capitalism, which recognizes them in a restricted form, on condition there is submission to capitalist interests and unilateral pressures; can be acceptable models for the national majorities of a less-developed country." It appears that the new Peru will have important State, cooperative and private sectors of the economy, with private enterprise being fully encouraged on the condition that it truly serve the common good and not only profit interests.

RESULTS OF U.S. POLICY

This paper has made the case, and I have yet to find evidence to the contrary, that there was almost complete uniformity and coordination since 1956 in the labor policy toward Peru of the U.S. government and of the main elements of the U.S. trade union movement and of U.S. business. I believe that until October, 1968, the U.S. government and private interests achieved a high degree of success in their labor policy goals for Peru:

[17] In recent years, according to the contract, the Peruvian government has given CELP the use of a building and a small percentage of CELP operating expenses.

1. Communism made little progress in Peruvian trade unionism, and the CTP, the most important Peruvian labor confederation, became and remained a fervent ally of the AFL-CIO's "cold war" approach and anticommunism.

2. The CTP became financially and ideologically dependent upon the AFL-CIO and the U.S. government. The CTP largely accepted the idea that "what is good for U.S. labor must be good for Peru."

3. The CTP progressively lost its sense of class consciousness or general solidarity, and instead of revolutionary methods or basic changes of structure in Peru, emphasized reformist methods such as collective bargaining and labor-management collaboration. The CTP accepted the idea that free enterprise and liberal capitalism were the best economic approach for them personally and for Peru's development.

On the other hand, U.S. policy did not make very much progress on its goal in the later 1960s of making the Peruvian trade union movement less political, and specifically of making the CTP more independent of APRA.

In large part as the result of U.S. policy and programs since 1946, CTP officials became well-traveled and well-trained in the technical aspects of trade unionism. The CTP officials acquired a middle-class approach and attitudes. However, the CTP people were also subject to widespread criticism even before the October, 1968, change of government on the basis that they had become alienated from general Peruvian reality and even from much of their own rank and file, and that they were too closely identified with or even the "puppets" of the U.S. government and of conservative U.S. trade unionists and business interests.

There is a serious problem now for the continuation of past U.S. labor policy in Peru, in that the Peruvian government is rejecting aspects of the free enterprise approach that U.S. policy tried to strengthen, and that the Peruvian government is trying to eliminate all forms of dependence and alienation in Peru.

Alternative Future Policies

The options now open to the United States government in its labor policy toward Peru are perhaps five: (1) maintaining the past policy; (2) making minor changes in past labor policy; (3) making major changes in past labor policy; (4) stopping all labor programs and activities in Peru; and (5) having no labor policy in Peru.

PROBABLE RESULTS OF EACH ALTERNATIVE

The possible options for U.S. policy makers are limited by general U.S. foreign policy and relations with Peru, political and other pressures within the United States, and the willingness of the Peruvian government to permit U.S. labor programs. It is in the light of these factors that the probable result of each alternative must be examined:

1. *Maintaining the past policy.* This is probably what the AFL-CIO and its leaders want, and there is no question but that the AFL-CIO has had and now has strong influence over any U.S. president and over U.S. foreign policy. But in terms of present Peruvian government policy, which is running counter to traditional AFL-CIO and APRA attitudes and programs, this option is not feasible unless there is a change in the present Peruvian government.

2. *Making minor changes in past labor policy.* This is in fact what is happening now. The Peruvian government will name a subdirector for CELP, but basic U.S. labor policy in Peru, the content of courses and programs, has so far not much changed. This situation of making only minor changes could continue indefinitely if the Peruvian and U.S. governments concur that there is real value in the programs as they now exist and/or the Peruvian government decides the general interests in maintaining friendly relations with the United States is more important than trying to secure drastic changes in U.S. labor policy and programs in Peru.

3. *Making major changes in past labor policy.* This is probably what the present Peruvian government would prefer: that it receive technical and financial assistance from the U.S. in the labor field, but that it be Peruvians and Peruvian ideas directing the programs. Any tendency of State Department or U.S. Embassy, Lima, officials to go along with Peruvian overtures in this direction would now be countered by AFL-CIO pressures. It could happen, although it would be unusual, that the State Department

would decide that overall U.S. foreign policy interests and good relations with Peru are more important than particular U.S. trade union and business lobbying and pressures.

4. *Stopping all labor programs and activities in Peru.* Neither the Peruvian or U.S. governments would want this, since it probably would harm general relations between the two countries. This alternative could occur, however, if either the AFL-CIO is resistant to all changes or if the Peruvian government decides the programs constitute too much "interference" in Peru or too much "dependence" on the part of Peruvian labor upon the United States.

5. *Having no labor policy in Peru.* It is highly unlikely and probably impossible that the United States, with its multiple strategic, political, and economic interests in Peru and Latin America, should cease to have a policy toward so vital a factor as Peruvian labor.

CONCLUSIONS

My personal wish, as has probably been very evident in the preceding exposition, is that the United States make major changes in its labor policy toward Peru. I see the changes of structure that the present Peruvian government is trying to institute in Peru as necessary and extremely positive. At the very least Peru has the right to expect that U.S. policy not put obstacles in the way of these Peruvian developments. President Velasco and other Peruvian officials are tireless in expressing the hope that the traditional ties of friendship and basic respect between the U.S. and Peruvian peoples can be strengthened, and it is my feeling that the blame will fall basically upon the United States if they do not. If the past almost complete identification between U.S. government and private U.S. trade union policy in Peru continues, the U.S. government has the obligation to maintain careful vigilance over AFL-CIO and AIFLD financing and activities in Peru so that the general foreign policy interests of the U.S. do not suffer. What Peru is seeking is a dialogue with the United States based on man, not just commodities or technical skills, so that when aid programs have terminated, the relationships thus established will endure. Such a dialogue can be achieved and will always be important for the peace and development of the world.

REFERENCES

Alba, Victor. *Historia del movimiento obrero en América Latina.* Mexico, D.F.: Libreria Mexicanos Unidos, 1964.
Alexander, Robert J. "The Taming of Peru: Behind the Coup." *Commonweal,* December 6, 1968, pp. 340–343.
Aportes: una revista de estudios latinoamericanos (Paris). No. 16, April 1970. See articles by Jorge Bravo Bresani, "Naturaleza del poder peruano," pp. 6–12; and François Bourricaud, "Los militares: ¿por qué y para qué?" pp. 13–55.
Chaplin, David. "The Peruvian Industrial Labor Force." Princeton, 1967.
Fajardo, J. V. *Sindicalismo Libre en el Perú.* Lima: Editorial Mercurio, S.A., 1965.
Hill, Joseph. "Labor's Establishment: Stop the World . . . , AFL-CIO plus CIA-ICFTU = 0." *Commonweal,* March 21, 1969, pp. 5–6.
Lajo L., Manuel. "Perú: ¿prensa libre o libertad de prensa?" *Mensaje* (Santiago, Chile) 19, no. 187 (March–April, 1970):129–133.
Landsberger, Henry A. "The Labor Elite: Is it Revolutionary?" In Seymour Martin Lipset and Aldo Solari, *Elites in Latin America,* pp. 256–300. New York: Oxford University Press, 1967.
———. "International Labor Organization." In Samuel Shapiro, ed., *Integration of Man and Society in Latin America.* University of Notre Dame Press, 1967.
Malpica, Carlos. *Los Dueños del Perú.* 3rd edition. Lima: Ediciones Ensayos Sociales, 1968.
Payne, James L. *Labor and Politics in Peru: The System of Political Bargaining.* New Haven and London: Yale University Press, 1965.
Pike, Fredrick B. *The Modern History of Peru.* London: Weidenfeld & Nicolson, 1967.
Rivas, Edilberto. "Cayalti: De la hacienda capitalista a la cooperativa de los trabajadores." *Rikchay Peru* (Lima, Perú) 1, no. 1 (1970):2–5.
The Rockefeller Report on the Americas. Official Report of a United States Presidential Mission for the Western Hemisphere, by Nelson A. Rockefeller. Chicago: New York Times Edition, Quadrangle Paperback, 1969.

Romualdi, Serafino. *Presidents and Peons: Recollections of a Labor Ambassador in Latin America.* New York: Funk and Wagnalls, 1967.

U.S. Department of Labor. *Directory of Labor Organizations, Western Hemisphere.* Chapter 32, Peru (revised May 1964). Washington: U.S. Government Printing Office, 1964.

U.S. Senate, Committee on Foreign Relations. "Survey of the Alliance for Progress, Labor Policies and Programs." A study prepared at the request of the Subcommittee on American Republics Affairs by the Staff of the Committee on Foreign Relations, U.S. Senate, together with a report of the Comptroller General, July 15, 1968. Washington: U.S. Government Printing Office, 1968.

U.S. Senate, Committee on Foreign Relations. "American Institute for Free Labor Developments, Hearing before the Committee on Foreign Relations, United States Senate, Ninety-first Congress, first session, with George Meany, President, AFL–CIO." August 1, 1969. Washington: U.S. Government Printing Office, 1969.

William A. Douglas

10. U.S. LABOR POLICY IN PERU— PAST AND FUTURE

U.S. LABOR POLICY IN PERU IN THE DECADE OF THE SIXTIES

At the beginning of the decade the U.S. government affirmed that it was in the U.S. national interest to assist the growth of economic, social, and political democracy in the nations of Latin America. The expression of this policy was the Alliance for Progress. The U.S. labor movement had long shared the ideals that came to expression in the Alianza and sought to play its proper role in the overall effort, namely to assist the labor movements in Latin America in becoming powerful forces for democracy in all three of its dimensions. U.S. labor organizations had begun training and cooperative programs for Latin American unions in the late 1950s and sought to expand this effort to match the scope of the new Alianza. Lacking funds of its own sufficient to mount a

NOTE: The author was in Peru from 1966 through 1969 with the American Institute for Free Labor Development, the last two years as AIFLD Country Program Director in that country. The views in this paper are his own; the paper is not an official statement of AIFLD policy, but is rather an insider's personal attempt to describe, explain, and evaluate that policy.

labor technical assistance effort on the scale required, the U.S. labor movement arranged contracts with the U.S. government to fund programs in Latin America falling within the wide areas of agreement between government policy and the labor movement's policy. On the initiative of the AFL-CIO, the American Institute for Free Labor Development was created as a specialized organization for Latin American labor programs under contract with the AID. Building on the cooperation achieved in the union-to-union programs of the late 1950s, U.S. labor invited the Latin American unions to become partners in the new Institute. The cooperation of the American business community with interests in Latin America was also solicited for this effort. As a result, the AIFLD operates under policies set by a labor-dominated, tripàrtite board of directors from U.S. labor, Latin American labor, and U.S. business. As in the case of AID contracts with other U.S. private-sector institutions such as the Credit Union International (CUNA), the Cooperative League (CLUSA), the National Farmers' Union (NFU) and many U.S. universities, government funding of AIFLD contracts was from the beginning on a completely overt basis. The wisdom of the open approach to government funding of private-sector technical assistance institutions as stipulated in the Foreign Assistance Act, has been dramatically confirmed by events during the decade.

The U.S. labor movement viewed U.S. assistance to the growth of economic, social, and political democracy in Latin America as urgent for two complementary reasons. One was the imperative of cold-war security requirements. If communists came to power in Latin American countries, this would have an adverse effect on the world balance of power and hemispheric security. If communists came to power in Latin American labor movements, this would greatly facilitate communist efforts to win government power also. The other imperative was that of development. It would be neither feasible nor moral for the United States to continue as an island of wealth in a sea of world poverty, even if no communist threat existed. If economic, social, and political democracy could be built in Latin America, this would have the double effect of defeating the communist challenge and facilitating the rapid industrialization of Latin America.

The goal of U.S. labor programs has thus been a positive one:

assisting the growth of democracy in all its forms. The negative task of simply stopping communism would not be sufficient to accomplish the goal to which labor has committed itself. Supporting anticommunist elements that were also opposed to social, economic, and/or political democracy would make impossible the achievement of the broad positive goal. U.S. labor, like the U.S. government, therefore saw the proper course for the United States under the Alianza as being to support the democratic left in Latin America, as those political forces were the ones striving for all three dimensions of democracy.

In Peru, social and economic democracy were lacking, so social reforms were required to create full democracy by breaking down ethnic and class barriers to equal opportunity and by achieving and maintaining a fair distribution of the wealth. Reforms were needed in land-holding, taxation, education, the wage structure, and the price structure. U.S. labor and the AIFLD saw their role in the general effort as that of strengthening the Peruvian labor movement as an effective force for promoting these reforms. To be a strong reformist force, Peruvian labor would have to be equipped to carry out three main functions, two of them economic and one political. The most basic function was that which is the economic *raison d'être* of any trade union: *to get better wages and working conditions for its members.* This would contribute to a continual process of redistributing the wealth in Peru from the owning class to the working class. In the private-ownership economy existing in Peru, the way for the workers to improve their wages and working conditions was by increasing their capacity for effective collective bargaining with management. Whether one advocates socialism, cooperativism, free enterprise, or a mixed economy as the eventual goal for Peru, there was and still is an immediate crying need for union strength in collective bargaining to get more for the workers under the system of ownership which prevails to date in Peru.

For a socialist worker in Peru, there is no necessary contradiction between strengthening union collective bargaining power vis-à-vis private management now, and, at the same time, working for a subsequent transition to a socialist system that would eliminate private management.

To strengthen unions and improve their collective bargaining skills, the AIFLD during the 1960s carried out a program of trade-union education, including such topics as union organization, labor legislation, collective bargaining, social security, and union finances. These and other topics are taught in introductory evening courses in Lima, two-week seminars in the provinces, and ten-week residential courses for the best graduates of the initial Lima and province courses. A few Peruvians are sent each year to the regional AIFLD school in the United States.

The second function for Peruvian labor as a force for social reform in Peru was also economic: *the creation of worker-controlled economic institutions.* With all economic power concentrated in a thin crust of institutions controlled by the owning class, there could be no pluralistic balancing and decentralization of economic power, which is the basis for social justice as well as for full and secure political democracy. Peruvian workers needed their own institutions such as cooperatives, credit unions, and banks. Building such institutions was another service the union could offer its members, in addition to the collective bargaining function.

To help build such worker institutions, the AIFLD sought to channel assistance from such Alliance for Progress sources as AID, private investment, and the IDB directly to the workers. In AIFLD's view, providing all aid on a government-to-government basis promotes centralized statism in the economy, and this would run counter to the social goal of a decentralization of economic power. Government-to-government aid also relies upon the "trickle-down" mechanism to get the aid to the lower-income groups who need it, and this mechanism does not work. Since Peruvian unions lack both the expertise to prepare complex project submissions in Peru and representatives in Washington to push the submissions through the lending bureaucracies to approval, AIFLD's Social Projects Department undertook these functions. AIFLD in the 1960s helped Peruvian workers create a worker-controlled housing bank (ASINCOOP) and many trade-union housing co-ops in the provinces. An AID/GOP $10 million loan was obtained, half for ASINCOOP, which functions in Lima, and half for the co-ops in the provinces. Most of this loan has now been used, with almost two thousand worker families now living in new houses. A large number of trade union consumer and credit co-ops have also been aided by AIFLD's Co-op Advisory Service in Lima, and by loans and grants from the AFL-CIO's own Impact Projects Fund.[1] Finally, AIFLD/Peru has been a strong supporter of worker-owned industry in Peru. Loans and grants have been made to a worker-owned printing firm in Piura, a sewing production co-op in Lima, and a worker-owned bus line in Arequipa. A $50,000 loan was recently made to the first large worker-owned textile factory in Peru. This factory is the largest industry in Huancayo.

The third function of Peruvian unions in promoting social reform is a political one. The unions have to work actively in national politics, pushing reform by pressuring executive and legislative branches of the government, teaching the rank-and-file the necessity for reforms, organizing support for reformist political parties, and carrying on agitation and propaganda for reform among the general public. The AIFLD believes that if a union is not politically active, it is failing its membership. Obtaining gains through collective bargaining with management is necessary but not sufficient for successful unionism. In Peru, where economic and social power is concentrated in a few hands, it is particularly important that basic national reforms be instituted. Without them, in the figurative poker game that constitutes a collective bargaining session, management in Peru has the advantage of sitting down at the table with a stacked deck. There is no place for nonpolitical unionism in Peru.

Ideally, trade unions should enter the political arena as autonomous forces, forming alliances with reformist political parties rather than being dominated by parties. Most U.S. labor leaders believe that if a particular interest group controls a party, or vice versa, both organizations are hampered in the effective performance of their respective roles. The interest group is inhibited from freely articulating the demands of its members, and the party is not free to play its proper arbitrating and integrating role among the various interest groups.

In Peru there are formidable obstacles both to effective political action for reform by trade unions and to autonomy of unions vis-à-

---

[1] As this article was being completed, a disastrous earthquake struck Peru. AFL-CIO funds are being used to purchase relief supplies and support an innoculation campaign organized by the Peruvian Hospital Workers Federation. Faced with the immensity of the tragedy, some of the political issues treated in

vis parties in the political sphere. As many recent books on political development have pointed out,[2] the organized industrial working class in Latin America tends to be politically passive, trying to find a satisfactory niche within the existing socioeconomic balance of power rather than being a major force for reform. This is a natural tendency in the early stages of development that reflects the objective short-run class interests of the workers. Keeping the bird in the hand, namely a fairly secure job at a wage somewhat above the mass of the work force, appears safer than trying for the multiple birds in the bush, namely social reforms. The economic position of the organized worker, while superior to that of the *campesinos* and the *Lumpenproletariat*, is still so precarious that it provides no margins for risk taking. It is easy for well-fed U.S. social scientists and labor aid technicians to urge the Peruvian workers to take those risks. It is hard for the worker, who cannot provide his family with adequate food, medical care, and education, to assume risks that might throw him back into the growing *Lumpenproletariat*, by which he feels constantly threatened.

The economic reasons why the working class must take the risks, hard as that course may be, is that the workers' long-range interests can be satisfied only by a growing, industrializing economy that can be built only if social reforms remove the structural obstacles to development. The political reason why the workers must be re-

this paper seem petty indeed, and perhaps will be resolved by the need for all labor organizations in Peru to work together in aiding those stricken by the disaster.

[2] See Lauchlin Currie, *Obstacles to Development* (East Lansing: Michigan State University Press, 1967), pp. 7–8; Samuel P. Huntington, *Political Order in Changing Societies* (New Haven: Yale University Press, 1968), pp. 283–288, 298–300; Anibal Quijano Obregón, "Tendencies in Peruvian Development and in the Class Structure," in James Petras and Maurice Zeitlin, eds., *Latin America: Reform or Revolution?* (Greenwich, Conn.: Faucett Publications, 1968), pp. 316–319; Rodolfo Stavenhagen, "Seven Fallacies about Latin America," in Petras and Zeitlin, *op. cit.*, pp. 28–31; Torcuato Di Tella, "Populism and Reform in Latin America," in Claudio Véliz, ed., *Obstacles to Change in Latin America* (New York: Oxford University Press, 1965), pp. 50–51, 58, 60; Osvaldo Sunkel, "Change and Frustration in Chile," in Véliz, *op. cit.*, pp. 129–133; Celso Furtado, "Political Obstacles to Economic Growth in Brazil," in Véliz, *op. cit.*, p. 153; Anibal Pinto, "Political Aspects of Economic Development in Latin America," in Véliz, *op. cit.*, pp. 25–28, 45; Abraham F. Lowenthal, "Alliance Rhetoric versus Latin American Reality," Foreign Affairs, April 1970, p. 497.

formist is that if they are not, forces hostile to organized labor can appeal to the *campesinos* and the *Lumpenproletariat* over the heads of the unionized minority, and use the marginally employed as a base for political power. In such a case, the labor movement is usually suppressed and then remade into an organ of the government, as happened in Argentina with Perón and in Cuba when Castro suppressed the post-Batista labor leaders from the 26th of July movement.

For these reasons, a labor movement that looks inward only to the narrow interests of its own membership in Latin America is doomed. The workers must be made conscious of the contradiction between their objective short-run interest in the status quo and the long-range necessity for labor to lead the fight for social reforms and make itself the spokesmen for the masses rather than being viewed by those masses as a hostile "worker aristocracy."[3] The deep-seated nature of the forces making workers passive on national social issues in Peru is shown by the fact that many independent unions have been particularly inward-looking and narrow in their views. Only by giving the unions an integral social philosophy can these forces be overcome.

The AIFLD in Peru, through its worker education program, has tried to help the Peruvian unions educate the workers to their social tasks, so that through a better grasp of the broad social picture they can surpass their immediate class instincts. In a sense, labor's Centro de Estudios Laborales del Peru (CELP) in Lima has tried to do for the trade union movement what the CAEM has tried to do for the middle-class army professionals, who also had to rise above their traditional conservative view of their own class interests before they could become a key force for reform. In addition to the basic trade union subjects listed earlier, the Peruvian unions have from the start insisted on including in the standard CELP curriculum several courses on social doctrines and economic development. The workers are taught that economic, social, and political democracy must form an integral system, and are made conscious of the minority position of the stably employed, organized workers within the work force as a whole. They are taught that only social reform

[3] See William A. Douglas, "La Importancia de los Sindicatos en el Desarrollo Nacional," *Revista Central Sindical*, Lima, May 1968, p. 6.

and economic development can provide long-term prospects of improvement in the life of the organized workers, and that the labor movement must therefore spearhead reform.

The AIFLD has also assisted Peruvian unions in building ties to the community, so that the unions look outward to a wider constituency than their own members. Groups of trade union volunteer instructors have been trained to carry on simple educational activities in the *barriadas* (shantytowns) of Lima, initially in civic education for prospective leaders of community organizations. In the 1970s it is hoped that these teams can also move into consumer education and nutrition courses. In some *barriadas*, trade unionists resident in the *barriada* itself have organized committees to bring the skills and influence of their unions to bear on community problems. These committees, and also trade unions as such, can draw on loans and grants from the AFL-CIO Impact Projects Fund, which was set up specifically to support union projects serving the wider community. In these ways the U.S. labor program in Peru has tried to assist trade unions in their efforts to become the spokesmen for the masses.

In regard to the control of trade unions by political parties in Peru, this problem also results from deep social and historical forces, as is true throughout Latin America. Many union movements were originally formed by political parties so as to build a mass base of political support. Many trade unions have needed the protection of political parties against hostile governments or business interests. Many trade unions lack the financial base to stand alone without the party tie. For these and other reasons the majority of unions in Peru have partisan leadership. By far the largest group is with the APRA, and smaller groups are connected with the Communist and the Christian Democratic parties.

Most Peruvian union leaders, including many who are now actively partisan, view union autonomy vis-à-vis parties as a desirable long-range goal. While agreeing with this desire, U.S. labor has also recognized what the Peruvian unionists know from experience: the Latin American reality is very different from the U.S. scene. Consequently, the AIFLD realizes that the transition to union autonomy can be made only gradually, and only as fast as the unions can be strengthened enough to overcome the objective conditions that have made the party ties necessary. In Peru, the AIFLD-supported education program has taught the distinction between unions being active in politics on an equal basis with allied parties, and unions being subordinate to parties. It has taught techniques for strengthening union dues structures, such as the check-off and the setting of dues on percentage rather than absolute quotas. In this way the CELP has tried to make workers aware of the need for a gradual transition to greater independence, and to help them build the financial base for autonomy.

The AIFLD does not provide financial subsidies to the budgets of union confederations or federations. This would lead to the creation of artificial constructions that could not stand alone and that would tend to represent the interests of the foreign donors rather than the local membership. Instead, the AIFLD provides services to the unions, giving them supplementary programs in worker education and social projects that the unions could not finance themselves. The strengthening of the dues structure to allow larger union administrative budgets is a task for the Peruvian workers themselves. The paucity of funds available to many unions in Peru, and especially to the confederation level, makes clear how much remains to be done on the dues problem.

The above discussion summarizes the three basic roles that Peruvian labor must play to become a stronger force for social reforms leading to economic, social, and political democracy, and what AIFLD has done to assist the unions in taking on those three roles. In carrying out labor technical assistance along these lines, U.S. labor policy has faced some political choices as to which groups to assist and what course to steer between them. Since democracy is the goal, AIFLD should logically work with the democratic left in the trade union movement. In Peru this eliminated the communist unions as possible recipients of AIFLD assistance, since the communists advocate a reformist totalitarianism for Peru rather than a reformist democracy. In any event, the communists are bitterly hostile to the United States, and no relation with them was possible. (AIFLD, while not assisting communist union organizations, does sometimes provide training or social projects assistance to workers whose unions have communist leadership, in the belief that the rank-and-file should not be cut off from help just because of the political coloration of their leaders. Such aid is provided directly to the workers, as giving it through communist-controlled union structures would be neither possible nor desirable for the reasons mentioned above.)

The Demo-Christian unions associated with MOSCIP in Peru are also bitterly hostile to the United States and U.S. labor, and thus a technical assistance relationship with the MOSCIP has never been a practical possibility. However, AIFLD in Peru has given education courses and housing assistance to a number of union locals that are sympathetic to MOSCIP but that do not share its radical anti-American viewpoint. This assistance has been concentrated in the Arequipa area.

With the CGTP and the MOSCIP either nondemocratic and/or hostile to U.S. labor, this left the CTP affiliates and the independent unions as possible candidates for assistance. The CTP is under APRA control at the confederation level, and most of its affiliated unions, though by no means all of them, have APRA leadership. To adopt a doctrinaire stand and refuse assistance to CTP unions because of their ties to a party was not a feasible course for several reasons. First, with the CTP the only legally recognized confederation and being by far the largest force in Peruvian labor, to work with only the independent unions would have confined labor technical assistance to such a minor segment that the program would have had little overall effect. Second, foreign labor groups must be impartial in dealing with the various currents within the democratic labor sector. Favoritism to the independent unions by U.S. labor would have constituted unwarranted meddling in internal Peruvian affairs, and would have aroused effective opposition by the CTP to the program. Third, the U.S. labor movement has historical ties to the CTP as part of the democratic left in Latin America, and the CTP would have correctly viewed refusal of assistance as a betrayal of democratic labor solidarity. Because of these factors, the AIFLD has worked with both the independent unions and the CTP, trying in the ways discussed above to help the CTP build the basis for greater independence vis-à-vis the APRA party, and providing technical assistance to aid the CTP unions in fulfilling the three basic roles already discussed in the fight for social reforms in Peru. AIFLD has tried to provide assistance to democratic unions in Peru approximately in proportion to their strength within the movement. In the northern and central areas, where the CTP affiliates predominate, they have received the lion's share of the help. In the south, where the union political picture is fragmented, most aid has gone to independent unions.

While aiding both CTP and independent unions, the AIFLD had to consider the interests of both groups as well as those of the Peruvian Labor Ministry. To aid independents in excess of their proportion of the organized workers would understandably make the CTP resentful that its affiliates were not getting their rightful share. To give too much program control and aid to the CTP unions would constitute Aprista favoritism and antagonize the independents. The latter course would also have put the Labor Ministry in a difficult position, and AIFLD can work in Peru only with the approval of that Ministry. Throughout the 1960s, the Ministry was under the control of non-APRA governments: the military in 1962–1963, the Acción Popular party of Belaúnde from 1964 to 1968, and the military again in 1969. AIFLD therefore has made an extra effort to work with every non-Aprista union it could find, especially in the Lima-Callao area, and uses several Labor Ministry officials as instructors in core courses at the CELP including labor legislation, social security, and economic development. By careful concern for the interests of each, the AIFLD was able to carry out its technical assistance programs in the 1960s while keeping the Ministry, the CTP, and the independent unions all tolerant of the program.

Another issue that required some tact to manage and that looms larger in the 1970s is what line, if any, AIFLD should take on the proper economic system for a future Peru building economic, social, and political democracy. The triple democratic goals can be approached, according to various strands of Western thought, through a socialist, a private-ownership, a cooperative, or a mixed economy. U.S. trade unionists, because of the success of the private enterprise system in the United States and the particular history of U.S. trade unionism, are personally strongly biased in favor of a free-enterprise system of regulated capitalism with a strong but minority sector of worker-owned production cooperatives. Within this system U.S. labor seeks social justice through continuous adjustments in the distribution of the wealth. These adjustments are to come about through collective bargaining within a responsible labor-management relationship plus legislation for social reform obtained from government through support by lower-class interest groups for reformist political parties or politicians.

U.S. labor programs abroad have reflected an ambivalent set of attitudes as to whether U.S. labor technicians should proselytize for such a U.S.-style system in the developing countries. At times U.S. labor has talked as if not only social, economic, and political democracy in general should be the goal, but also a U.S.-style free-enterprise system as the particular economic vehicle by which to reach that goal. At other times, labor officials have recognized that the different cultures and economic conditions pertaining in developing countries may require economic systems greatly differing from the free-enterprise model. They have also recognized that the choice of an economic system is a country's own business, and is not a proper area for U.S. pressure, so long as the system works toward the economic, social, and political democracy that is the only goal U.S. labor can support without violating its own deepest values.

In general, U.S. labor abroad has adopted the stance of recommending the free-enterprise system when asked for advice, but working loyally with socialist and other democratic, noncapitalist labor groups when it encounters such forces. The approach has been neither to conceal the American bias, nor to impose the U.S. view on other nations' unions as the price for obtaining U.S. labor technical assistance. Certainly in Peru, proselytizing for free-enterprise has not been a major thrust of the AIFLD program. The AIFLD-supported education courses at the CELP have rather stressed collective bargaining as a necessity in the existing Peruvian situation, proclaimed social reform as a necessity for the future, and described the alternative economic systems on which full democracy can be built, but without hammering home a particular endorsement of any one such system. The courses have pointed out that in point of fact most developing nations are ending up with mixed economic systems, and, extrapolating from that trend, the probabilities are that Peru will do the same. With the present Peruvian government stressing the question of the country's future economic structure, AIFLD will have to be even more careful than in the 1960s to avoid the appearance of trying to impose a foreign economic model on Peru.

Another difficult issue for AIFLD in terms of Peruvian public opinion has been the fact that many of the workers taught by AIFLD go back to the job to bargain against U.S.-owned companies. Since AIFLD is a U.S. organization, to suggest that workers should be more moderate in their demands on U.S. companies than on Peruvian-owned companies would have been a fatal mistake that would have quickly united the Labor Ministry, the CTP, and the independent unions in a concerted effort to expel the U.S. labor mission. Consequently, AIFLD endorses the CELP doctrine that in collective bargaining the union team's role is to get "more" from management (within the practical limits set by the size of the "more" that is there to be gotten) without regard to the nationality of the management. The AIFLD's attitude on this matter was well-expressed in a May Day speech given in Lima in 1968 by William C. Doherty, Sr., representing the AFL-CIO. Brother Doherty stated:

The AIFLD's Communist critics like to point out that many large employers in Latin America are U.S. companies. The Communists ask if the AFL-CIO and its right arm, the AIFLD, will be as firm in their support of unions dealing with U.S.-owned companies as compared with locally-owned. The answer, brothers, is yes, we will. We believe in a fair share for the workers in the proceeds of every industry, everywhere, regardless of whether it is owned by Europeans, Peruvians, Germans, North Americans, or the state. That is our position. J. Peter Grace and his friends in the U.S. business world know it is our position, they respect that position, and they would have contempt for us if we, as labor leaders, took any other position.[4]

U.S. companies in Peru have respected AIFLD's role as part of the labor sector, and have avoided using AIFLD/Peru as a channel of influence. Not once in the author's two years as AIFLD director in Peru did a U.S. company, directly or by implication, ask for AIFLD to urge moderation of demands being made by workers on the company. This restraint must have required some effort to maintain. In the 1970s, with nationalism even stronger in Peru than in the past decade, great care will have to be exercised to avoid even the impression that AIFLD tries to moderate worker demands on U.S. companies in Peru.

In summary, U.S. labor policy in Peru in the 1960s has given education and social projects technical assistance to CTP and independent unions to strengthen them as forces for social reforms that

---

[4] See *Noticiero Sindical*, Centro de Estudios Laborales del Peru, Lima, May, 1968.

can produce social, economic, and political democracy in Peru, the unions acting in the three areas of making gains through collective bargaining for their own members, building worker-controlled economic institutions, and working in the national political arena on behalf of reform.

A BRIEF LOOK AHEAD TO THE 1970s
Evaluation of Past Policy

To decide on the future course of U.S. labor policy in Peru, it is appropriate to take stock of the efforts made so far. On the first goal of improving wages and working conditions through collective bargaining, much progress has been made. The number of trade unions in Peru increased greatly during the 1960s, the initial increase coming after the Prado government issued a decree in 1961 clarifying the conditions for official recognition of unions .The policy of promoting union formation begun by Prado was continued by the Belaúnde government, even though most of the new unions were led by that government's Aprista opposition.[5] During the years of AIFLD's operation in Peru, the number of unions continued to grow steadily.

With more bargaining units in existence, the number of collective agreements signed yearly in Peru has also increased, rising by at least 30 percent during the first four years of the Belaúnde government as compared to the six years of the Prado administration.[6] The complexity and sophistication of agreements have also improved. Many agreements now are the thickness of a small book, indicating a great expansion in the different matters covered. The gains in wages, fringe benefits, and working conditions have also been considerable. Unfortunately, in view of Peru's economic troubles, those gains have served more to keep the worker's standard of living from declining rather than to increase it very much. While a number of factors worked together to improve the collective bar-

[5] See Larry Larson, "Labor, Social Change and Politics in Peru," mimeographed. Political Science Department, University of North Carolina, Chapel Hill, North Carolina, 1967, pp. 93–97. For a table showing the sharp increase in the number of unions during the early 1960s, see *Acción del Gobierno en el Campo Laboral*, Ministerio de Trabajo y Asuntos Indígenas, Lima, May, 1965, p. 21.

[6] Larson, "Labor, Social Change and Politics," p. 120.

gaining system and to increase the gains workers made under it, one of those factors was U.S. labor technical assistance. As in any phase of development, such foreign assistance can have only a marginal effect. The real job must be done by the people themselves, in this case, Peru's unions and its Labor Ministry, together with labor's negotiating partners across the table. The Peruvians did make progress, and the U.S. can take satisfaction that its aid helped them achieve what they did.

In the other economic goal, that of building worker-owned economic institutions, progress has also been good. ASINCOOP, the worker housing bank, exists and functions as well or better than the average *mutual* in the Peruvian system. Many housing cooperatives have been founded and others strengthened. About two thousand houses have been built for workers, with an investment of $10,000,000. Many consumer and credit cooperatives associated with unions have been strengthened. In the social projects field, the aid *has* been brought directly to the workers, and it has built new institutions to help fill in the empty core within the oligarchic shell of the economy Peru inherited from its colonial past.

In the third goal, the political one of making the labor movement a force for social reform, the U.S. labor assistance program did not produce dramatic results. In this sector, attitudes and institutions change more slowly, and the marginal effects of foreign aid take longer to appear. Despite exhortations from the national leadership, many Peruvian union locals remain concerned mainly with the narrow interests of their members. The unions have not been able to reduce their isolation from the masses as much as they had hoped. Independence of unions from political parties did not greatly increase. (However, the CTP made considerable progress in becoming the voice which *makes* APRA labor policy, rather than receiving policy guidance on labor issues from professional politicians who are not themselves from the labor movement.[7] In this sense the CTP moved closer to the influential role wielded by the CTM within the PRI in Mexico.) Dues structures, the Achilles heel of much of Latin American labor, have not dramatically improved, although definite progress can be seen in many individual

[7] See James L. Payne, *Labor and Politics in Peru* (New Haven: Yale University Press, 1965), p. 120.

unions.[8] As to social reforms, the democratic sectors of Peruvian labor have favored them, and the unions thus do not constitute an *obstacle* to reform. However, in the 1960s neither did the labor movement become the primary force in the struggle for reforms, as was hoped. In fact, at the end of the decade Peruvian labor found that role preempted by its traditional enemy, the military.

The results of U.S. labor assistance on the unions' performance in their political role will clearly become apparent only over the long run. Teaching eleven thousand participants in AIFLD-supported CELP classes that labor's future depends on its leading the reform fight cannot help but change attitudes as the younger trainees move up in their unions. Helping the unions put even a few teams of volunteers and a dozen community impact projects out into the towns, *barrios*, and *pueblos jovenes* of Peru at least provides some models and some experience on which future community-service efforts can build. The AIFLD's efforts to help Peruvian unions improve their political role have not been wasted, even though their full benefits will come only in the future. The record is basically good progress on the unions' two economic goals, and a start, but not a payoff yet, on the political goal.

Policy Options

Having evaluated the past program, we must now briefly consider the alternatives for U.S. labor policy in Peru in the 1970s. One of these would be to terminate the labor technical assistance program. This might be suggested from several viewpoints. First, some might maintain that by giving extensive assistance in the 1960s, the U.S. labor movement and the U.S. government have fulfilled their obligation to aid Peruvian labor's development, and now the time has come for Peruvian labor to advance on its own. Second, termination of the program would be consonant with the present mood of neo-isolationism that prevails in many circles in the United States, partly in reaction to the Vietnam war and partly from a feeling that active U.S. involvement in development abroad was overrated in the 1960s in terms of what it could accomplish,

---

[8] By 1967, for example, two-thirds of the trade unionists in the Lima-Callao area were paying their dues under the checkoff system. See *Union Membership in the Lima-Callao Area*, CISM, Servicio del Empleo y Recursos Humanos, Ministerio de Trabajo y Communidades, Lima, 1968, p. 19.

and underrated in terms of the difficulties in which it could enmesh U.S. policy. Third, ending the program would be in line with the views of those who have always opposed foreign aid as an unwarranted program that gives away U.S. funds for no useful purpose. The basic anti-aid view has been strengthened as U.S. domestic crises have multiplied and the need for funds for domestic problems has thus become more acute (or at least better perceived). Fourth, ending the program would implement the view of those who feel that, because of U.S. labor's free-enterprise bias, it can make no useful contribution to the Peruvian labor movement, and that in fact any U.S. labor presence in Peru is inherently harmful to the growth of a militant and socialist Peruvian movement.

A second possible alternative would be to continue the program but to confine U.S. labor technical assistance only to the independent unions, thus ending aid to unions with Aprista leadership. Those supporting this alternative would argue that Peruvian workers are tired of seeing their labor movement divided mainly among politicized sectors, each with special foreign relationships with the USSR, Communist China, West Germany, or the United States. This view would maintain that with the increasing political maturity of Peruvian workers, plus the present constellation of forces in Peruvian politics, the moment is ripe to create a single, unified Peruvian labor confederation, which would be tied to no political party, but would function purely as an interest group expressing the demands of the workers as a class rather than as a set of political groups. Limiting U.S. labor aid now to only the presently independent sector would in this view facilitate the unification and partisan neutralization of the labor movement, allowing U.S. aid then to be expanded later to help the new unified confederation through its initial problems.

A third possibility would be to continue and possibly expand somewhat the U.S. labor assistance program along basically the same lines as have been followed in the 1960s, moving on from first-generation to second-generation labor projects as former needs are filled and new opportunities open up. This policy would be a reaffirmation of the original Alianza commitment to give U.S. aid to Latin America and to provide active U.S. encouragement of social reform there. It would be in line with the recent appeals of such expert bodies as the Pearson Commission that world stability requires continued aid from the industrialized nations to the under-developed countries. It would also be an application of the recent emphasis on institutional development as the key to both economic growth and political stability. This view is found in legislation such as the original Humphrey Amendment on cooperatives and the more recent Title IX addition to the U.S. Foreign Assistance Act, and in theoretical writings by such leading experts as Samuel Huntington and Dankwart Rustow.[9]

A fourth possibility would be not a policy alternative, but rather a course of events that would in themselves necessarily determine the fate of the U.S. labor assistance program in Peru. This would be a sequence that would begin with a direct confrontation between the Peruvian military government and the Peruvian labor movement, with the government then winning out and suppressing trade unionism. By eliminating the aid receivers, such a course of events would effectively also wipe out any U.S. labor aid program. Political events in Peru since 1968 indicate that neither the military government nor the unions wish such a showdown, but some outside observers have suggested that the dynamics of Peruvian politics make such a confrontation inevitable, no matter how hard each side tries to avoid it.

Evaluation of the Alternatives

Taking the fourth possibility first, chances appear good that Peruvian labor can continue functioning under the present regime, and will thus exist as a potential aid recipient as we move into the early 1970s. First, there is the evident desire of both sides to avoid a showdown. Second, the reformist nature of the present junta

---

[9] On the results of the Humphrey Amendment, see *Development of Cooperative Enterprises—1967*. Subcommittee on International Finance, Committee on Banking and Currency, House of Representatives, U.S. Government Printing Office, 1968; for the proceedings of a major AID/private-sector conference on Title IX, see David Hapgood, ed., *The Role of Popular Participation in Development*, Center for International Studies, MIT, Cambridge, Massachusetts, November, 1968; for the thesis that institutional development is the key to political stability, see Samuel P. Huntington, *Political Order in Changing Societies*; for a view that institutional authority is required to support an integrated national identity and a social order of equality, see Dankwart Rustow, *A World of Nations*, The Brookings Institution, Washington, D.C., 1967, especially pp. 91, 126–129.

makes a confrontation much less inevitable than it proved to be in the past when the military governments in Peru were basically favorable to the elite and opposed to the changes needed by the lower-income masses. Third, the junta has already at least promised that its policy will encourage the growth of trade unions and prevent their domination by extremist elements with foreign ties. Survival of the union movement in the 1970s in Peru is thus probable enough to warrant serious consideration of the three policy alternatives suggested above on the assumption that a labor-aid recipient will be available.

Terminating the labor assistance program on the theory that it has already accomplished its tasks would be a very premature action in view of the continuing weaknesses in the labor movement that have been discussed in this paper. While the progress made (mainly on the two economic goals) has been gratifying, much remains to be done, especially in helping labor strengthen its political role. Cutting out the Peru labor program as part of a general turning-inward of U.S. attention in a spirit of neo-isolationism would risk seeing the United States commit the same error on the international scene that the Latin American workers have long been criticized for making vis-à-vis the community in which they must function. Just as Peruvian workers are bound to the fate of the Peruvian masses, the fate of the United States is bound up with that of the international community in this modern age of interdependence. These considerations overrule both the traditional opposition of some conservative U.S. groups to foreign aid, and also the more recent swing to isolationism in liberal circles. Finally, the view that U.S. labor contacts with Peruvian labor are inherently harmful because of U.S. labor's bias toward capitalism and collective bargaining has been shown above to overlook the need for immediate improvement in collective bargaining regardless of Peru's future economic system, plus the sometimes belated but historically proven flexibility of U.S. labor in dealing with democratic socialists. If the above considerations have merit, the alternative of terminating the labor assistance program to Peru must be ruled out.

As for continuing the labor program but confining aid only to the independent unions, the same objections to this policy that existed seven years ago still prevail today. The CTP and the Aprista unions within it are still such a large part of the total movement that aid only to the independent sector would amount to a small side show and would probably be effectively opposed by the CTP in any event. The goal of a unified, nonpartisan labor movement in Peru can still be advanced best by working with the existing major confederation and helping it build the strength it requires to move toward greater independence. Mere removal of U.S. relations with and aid to CTP unions would not in itself contribute much to the partisan neutralization of Peruvian labor. The forces for partisanship lie deep within Peruvian society and history, not in the existing international contacts of the CTP. To think that the U.S. contact is the major reason for Aprista strength in CTP unions is to grossly exaggerate the effect of foreign aid, which is now generally recognized to be only marginal. A labor aid program in Peru in the 1970s, as in the 1960s, is possible only if both the independent democratic unions and the Aprista unions receive assistance.

This leaves the option of continuing the basic pattern of the program as in the 1960s, improving it where it remains weak, and shifting from first-generation to second-generation programs as opportunities arise. The practical experience of the 1960s points in this direction, as does the theoretical approach to institutional development that has appeared in development literature as a reflection of that experience. Transfer of resources and skills from the developed to the underdeveloped countries is a process that will be needed for at least a generation, not just for ten years, if the world is not to be fatally divided between rich and poor countries. The U.S. labor aid program to Peru still has many defects in application which remain to be overcome. Also the mix of projects must be modernized lest the program do the same old things year after year out of habit rather than conscious planning. Basically, the provision of services by the United States (the approach that prevailed in the 1960s) must be replaced by an institution-building approach in the 1970s that will help Peruvian unions build their own education and social projects departments so that they can perform these services themselves. In carrying on the labor program in this new direction, the same old frustrations, petty political crises, and stubborn historical and social obstacles will continue to be encountered. In facing these problems, however, the U.S. trade union movement can be strengthened by the knowledge that it is living up to its responsibilities toward *los demás*.

Robert G. Myers

11. PERUVIAN EDUCATIONAL DEVELOPMENT

Education means many things to many people. Similarly, policy has many guises. To frame our topic, therefore, several contextual comments seem appropriate and necessary at the outset.[1]

First, in this paper *education is not regarded as synonymous with schooling*. To equate education with schooling would be to narrow our analytical perspective and our options unnecessarily. Past United States educational assistance programs have emphasized schooling; consequently, schooling will be emphasized in this exposition. However, the reader should remain open to the very real possibility that other forms of education outside the traditional system of schooling are more closely related to policy success or failure than is schooling.

Second, *education will not be presented as a cure-all*. There is a current tendency to regard education as a kind of miracle drug and to disregard neutral or negative results of past educational policies.

[1] Although such cautionary comments about schooling and about the impact of investments in education will seem obvious or commonplace to some readers, I believe they must be made at a time when international organizations, foundations, and the United States government all seem to be particularly disposed toward investment in education as one of the most beneficial and/or "safest" forms of assistance.

In our policy appraisal, let us try to avoid thinking about education as unquestionably "good." Let us make explicit the fact that the-more-the-better is only one orientation to educational investment. (Miracle drugs can be taken for the wrong disease with unfortunate results, or they can be taken in overdoses.) Let us recognize that it may be as naive in the present to predict dramatic economic and social results from reforms in education as it was in the past to expect dramatic economic growth from an infusion of physical capital without associated inputs of human capital or without changes in values and attitudes.

Third, *education of all kinds takes place within a broad social context.* Thus, policy decisions pertaining to agriculture, taxation, and industrial organization all have an impact on education. Sometimes the impact is direct; more often than not it is very indirect. Consider, for instance, the indirect influence of a new mining or industrial law on education in Peru and on North American involvement in Peruvian education. To the extent that the law influences technologies, it will influence the type of training that industry will need for its labor force and the type of training that the industry itself will be willing to offer its workers. To the extent that North American firms opt to leave Peru or are forced out, a potential source of training will have been eliminated. Or, consider the possibility that minimum-wage legislation could lead to substitution of machines for men, which would also lead to investment by industry in upgrading skill levels of the work force. There are thousands of linkages that might be made. It is not inconceivable, therefore, that policy decisions in other areas will have a greater effect on education than will educational policy decisions.

Fourth, as we approach the discussion of policy alternatives, we should be explicitly aware that *education is expected to serve several (and often competing) goals simultaneously.* This is a critical point in our discussion: the fact that education serves multiple goals can produce conflict (if goals do not overlap) or can provide a pleasant meeting ground for policy makers who support similar investments but for different reasons.

In the Peruvian Development Plan (1967–1970) for instance, we note that education should be directed (1) toward increasing production and productivity, (2) toward a better distribution of income, (3) toward an appropriate occupational distribution (presumably tied to 1 or 2), and (4) toward reducing vulnerability from abroad.[2] The goal of efficiency implied by 1 may conflict with the equity goal implied by 2. Number 4, which might be relabeled as a goal of independence or freedom or self-determination, may require sacrificing gains in either efficiency or equity or both, at least in the short run.[3] To further complicate the picture, education in the form of schooling is looked upon as a natural right, as a means, if not *the* main means of transmitting culture and as the vehicle for integrating marginal groups into the dominant culture. In addition, education acts to both enhance and to deter social mobility.

As educational programs are developed, it is difficult enough to balance conflicting goals or to set priorities intranationally. But when options are significantly influenced by external forces as well, the task may become even more complicated depending upon the degree to which goals and priorities of the external influence correspond to those established internally.

In the past decade, Peru and the United States have found their primary meeting ground in a commitment to increasing efficiency and to economic growth. Political and economic redistributional goals of the Alliance for Progress were also endorsed by both nations but were probably taken more seriously by North Americans charged with carrying out the intent of the Alliance than by Peruvian leaders (in spite of Belaúnde's local elections). Ever present, however, were competing goals such as the protection of U.S. property abroad, which, though missing from official lists of U.S. policy considerations, have served on occasion as the fulcrum for U.S. foreign assistance policy. The Peruvian government did not mount an effective challenge to the United States's more blatantly self-interested uses of foreign assistance. That has changed.[4]

Although economic growth has not been discarded as a goal by the present Peruvian government, it has been muted—at least in

[2] República del Perú, Instituto Nacional de Planificación, *El plan de desarrollo, 1967–1970* (Lima: Instituto Nacional de Planificación, 1967), pp. 11–47.

[3] For an excellent statement of conflicting goals and their implications, see C. Arnold Anderson. "The Social Context of Educational Planning" (Paris: International Institute for Educational Planning, 1967).

[4] Consider, for instance, the leading role of Peru in the Viña del Mar declaration as well as the standoff between Washington and Lima over IPC and the fishing issues.

the short run—in order to emphasize self-determination and redistribution.[5] Freedom from external domination is desired for its own sake, but it is also useful as the present government attempts to build a viable and lasting nationalism. Furthermore, the Peruvian government, in emphasizing independence, adheres to the position that "domination" is a major impediment to "true" economic growth, an alternative to the view most commonly accepted within the North American community.[6]

Conflicting goals must be taken seriously, but the tenuous nature of both North American and Peruvian goals is easily illustrated by noting obvious contradictions as each government acts out policies based on the goals. While the United States, under the Alliance for Progress, strongly endorsed policies to promote greater social equality and a redistribution of power within Peru, the same principle did not seem to apply at an international level to reducing inequalities among nations. The United States retained an extremely paternalistic posture toward most developing nations, including Peru, and was not unwilling to use power politics when pressed. On the Peruvian side, while the military is pressing for independence and freedom of action vis-à-vis other nations, it carries the burden of having taken and retained power at home by force (or the threat of force). Such obvious contradictions will continue to undermine "development" efforts and to complicate the dialogue between nations.

Finally, I should make clear that simply by discussing U.S. policy toward education in Peru I am not assuming the United States should or has a right to influence priorities guiding allocation of resources to and within Peruvian education. That is an internal matter. But the fact remains that *by making resources available in varying amounts, under varying conditions, for selected programs, a force has been and is exerted on Peruvian educational policy from*

[5] See, for instance, the statement by General Francisco Morales Bermúdez, Peruvian minister of economy and finance at the annual meeting of the Inter-American Development Bank, 1970. Reported by J. N. Goodsell in *The Christian Science Monitor*, April 25, 1970, p. 14.

[6] For one treatment of the theory of domination, see Fernando H. Cardoso y Enzo Faletto, "Dependencia y desarrollo en América Latina" (Mexico: Siglo XXI Editores S.A., 1969). For application to the Peruvian situation, see Julio Cotler, "La mecánica de la dominación interna y del cambio social en el Perú," in *Perú Problema* (Lima: Moncloa, 1968).

abroad. Our task is to examine that force and to try to anticipate influences that alternative policies might have in the future. In that effort, attention must be given to the question "who controls decisions?"

With the above in mind, let us turn to an overview of education in Peru and of U.S. involvement in Peruvian education, past and present. As an organizational device, let us consider U.S. educational assistance in the periods 1909–1924, 1944–1962, 1963–1968, and 1968 to the present. In the overview emphasis will be placed on U.S. government programs. Special attention will be given to higher education, in part because the field of education is so broad that it is unmanageable, in part because the Peruvian government expressed interest in higher education when topics were being considered for the Peru Study Project, and in part because my own interests currently incline in that direction.

PERUVIAN EDUCATION AND U.S. POLICY—PAST AND PRESENT[7]
1909–1924

Direct United States involvement in developing the Peruvian educational system dates from 1909, when Leguia called in North American educators to write and oversee implementation of a Peruvian educational law. It is doubtful that the United States had at that time anything that might be labeled a "policy" toward involvement in Peruvian affairs in general or toward involvement in Peruvian education. The apparatus of modern technical assistance did not exist, the preoccupation with hemispheric defense was not present, and the term "cold war" had not been coined.

From 1909 to 1912 and again from 1919 to 1924, a North American team of Protestant, mostly non-Spanish-speaking educators worked as administrative officers in the Ministry of Education. The highly visible team (at peak, twenty-four members) was given a strong hand by Leguia but encountered considerable resistance

[7] I am deeply indebted to Rolland Paulston for his assistance in developing this section of the paper. The section draws heavily from his "United States Educational Intervention in Peru, 1909–1968," a chapter in his forthcoming book. For a more detailed and documented history, the reader should consult Rolland G. Paulston, *Society, Schools, and Progress in Peru* (Oxford: Pergamon Press, forthcoming, spring 1971). Interpretations and error are, of course, my responsibility.

from Ministry officials whose positions were threatened, from the church, which was not ready to accept such institutions as coeducation and sex education, from the press, and from political figures. North American efforts to reform Peruvian education along North American lines were effectively constrained and little of a lasting nature was accomplished. From the early experience, we see a need for support below the presidential level and for support from outside as well as inside the educational establishment if advice about reform is to be accepted. Furthermore, we can point, as others have done, to the ineffective policy of imposing U.S. institutions on other nations. Finally, we are made painfully aware of the problems caused by cultural insensitivity among advisers.

1944–1962

From 1944 to 1962, the United States again became enmeshed in Peruvian education, principally through SECPANE (Servicio Cooperativo Peruano-Norteamericano de Educación), a Point IV and ICA technical assistance program. As such, the program was related to stated policy goals of Point IV. My impression is that the United States was much more active in seeking involvement than previously, largely stimulated first by immediate concern for hemispheric defense growing from World War II and later by anti-communist fears.

During the eighteen years of SECPANE tenure, U.S. government policy seems to have been one of nudging gently in the direction of social change. Stability was also important to the United States both from a diplomatic and economic vewpoint. Consequently, there was no particular aversion to working with a military regime that provided the desired stability. The SECPANE program continued —in fact thrived—under the Odría dictatorship. Nor was there an attempt to push social change to the extent that it would threaten stability.

U.S. advisers and their Peruvian counterparts constituted a *servicio*, only informally linked to the bureaucratic structure of the Ministry of Education, through which U.S. funds were channeled into various educational projects. U.S. personnel were employed by an AID predecessor, the Institute of Inter-American Affairs, controlled by the U.S. State Department. Although Peruvians and North Americans were "equal" in the SECPANE organization,

Peruvian counterparts seldom initiated programs and tended to rubber-stamp North American suggestions. The SECPANE team was involved in all major areas of Peruvian primary, secondary, and normal-school education. Little attention was given to education outside the schools.

SECPANE was extremely active in the field of rural education, establishing a system of *nucleos escolares* (nuclear schools) in which as many as eight or ten three-year rural primary schools were formally linked to a six-year primary school in a nearby town.[8] The larger school theoretically provided assistance to the smaller rural schools, including agriculture and health instruction by qualified people. Well conceived in theory, the *nucleos* encountered difficulties in practice. The Ministry, controlled by urban mestizo middle-class Peruvians, was not willing to extend schooling to the rural Indian in a form that might disturb existing sociocultural distinctions. Rightly or wrongly, nuclear schooling was regarded with suspicion. Although the Peruvian government was contributing approximately two-thirds of the SECPANE budget, it was not in a position to block the program, and it forged ahead as, in effect, a North American program lacking moral support within the Ministry. In spite of impressive efforts to create special training programs for rural teachers and to produce special teaching materials, most teachers still had only a primary education and few students in the nuclear system progressed beyond the first year or two in school. When SECPANE was phased out in 1962, the Ministry did not pick up the administrative and financial burden dropped upon it and the *nucleos* have, since then, been dying a slow death.

In the area of technical education, SECPANE contributed by developing curriculum materials and by helping to organize technical programs in comprehensive schools called *grandes unidades escolares* (GUE), and in separate technical schools. Although there was a growing demand for technically skilled workers, it became clear that the demand could not be met by graduating more people from more schools. Training in the schools had little relation to the job and employers soon learned that technical school graduates had to be re-taught. A study done about 1961 showed that only 11 per-

[8] An excellent description of the *nucleos* may be found in John Baum, *Estudio sobre la educación rural en el Perú: Los nucleos escolares campesinos* (Mexico City: RTAC, 1967).

cent of the industrial school graduates found (or sought) employment in industry.[9]

Through the rural education program and technical schooling, SECPANE sought to respond to growing pressures from what today would be called the "disadvantaged" or "marginal" sectors of the population. In the same vein, an extensive program of school expansion and construction was funded; it would presumably bring in more individuals from the lower sector of society. School lunches were provided to upgrade health and increase attendance. Also, pressure to eliminate secondary school fees was applied, and several of the GUE were located in the provinces, presumably to provide "quality" public education at the secondary level outside Lima.

One might easily argue that SECPANE programs, aimed at disadvantaged groups in the Peruvian society, served simply as a means of heading off discontent, thus reinforcing the status quo. While giving the appearance of increasing educational opportunity (and therefore economic opportunity?), the net effect, it might be argued, was to provide only minimum schooling so that the competitive advantage of disadvantage groups was not raised. At the same time, lower socioeconomic groups became committed to schooling as the main path to success, a path that upper socioeconomic groups could continue to control effectively. The stratified system of schooling linked to sociocultural distinctions remained intact.[10]

A major portion of the SECPANE budget was spent for participant training, usually in the United States. In spite of the inevitable boondoggling and some poor programing, a large number of

[9] The percentage comes from Fernando Romero, *La indústria manufacturera y su mano de obra en 1962* (Lima, 1963). Romero's estimate is probably unduly pessimistic. A follow-up study of public secondary technical school graduates, 1950–1958, by Aristides Vega N. shows that 16 percent of the graduates were employed in the specialty they had studied but another 37 percent were in related occupations, while 13 percent did not specify their occupation. Aristides Vega N. and Edward A. Parker, *Informe sobre los problemas de educación industrial*, Ministerio de Educación Pública, Servicio Cooperativo Peruano-Norteamericano de Educación (Lima, November, 1959), p. 3.

[10] For an analysis of the linkages between educational organization and social stratification in Peru, see Rolland Paulston, "Estratificación social, poder y organización educacional: El caso Peruano," *Aportes* 16 (April, 1970): 91–111.

Peruvians were trained and did return to serve actively in SEC-PANE or in the Ministry. I know of no evaluation of SECPANE participant trainees per se, but in a larger evaluation of the Peruvian participant training program, "education" trainees were found to be "utilizing" their training at a relatively high level.[11] Nevertheless, a net result of the training may have been frustration because utilization was principally within existing social structures and did not lead to changes.

The need for quality educators also led to plans for an "ideal" normal school to groom talent locally. The result, La Cantuta, became highly politicized and quickly rejected its North American foster parents, but it also channeled some very capable individuals into education—individuals who are now entering decision-making positions in the Peruvian Ministry, the National Planning Institute, and other governmental agencies concerned directly and indirectly with education.

Although SECPANE was independent from the Ministry and had special access to outside funds, Ministry officials were still in a position to thwart programs if not decisions. For instance, one set of primary school textbooks, created and printed by SECPANE at considerable expense, was never moved out of warehouse storage because they were never approved by the Ministry.[12]

Any overall evaluation of SECPANE would, of course, depend on the standard applied. It was probably a positive force in Peruvian education: some organizational improvements can be traced to SECPANE, and some curricular materials are still used in Peruvian schools today; considerable work was done in areas (geographical and educational) to which the Ministry was committed in word but not in deed. Whatever the standard applied, it is probably fair to say that results during the eighteen years were not overwhelming. On the other hand, in fairness, we might also ask rhetorically, "Could more, realistically, have been expected, given the social context and the painfully slow changes occurring in other social institutions?"

[11] International Research Associates, Inc. *A Survey of the Peruvian Participant Training Program*, prepared for the Department of State, AID (New York, July, 1965).

[12] This may serve as a warning to those U.S. policymakers considering interventions in "civic education" under Title IX.

As political changes occurred in both Peru and the United States in the early 1960s, as the Alliance for Progress became a reality, as multilateral agencies took on increasing significance, and as technical assistance was reorganized under AID, changes in the form and substance of U.S. involvement in Peru were inevitable. And even in the early 1960s relatively direct involvement by North Americans in Peruvian affairs, as had occurred with SECPANE, was becoming difficult to defend.

It is not particularly surprising, then, that SECPANE was phased out as the military junta took over in 1962. Discarding its former reluctance to rock the boat, the United States agonized over recognizing the new military government that had acquired power by force. In true "liberal" Kennedy style, support for the military government was withheld, a symbol of U.S. objection to nondemocratic military rule. Aid was cut at the same time. Although diplomatic recognition was subsequently given, the flow of aid did not pick up at the same time—the gap left by the SECPANE departure was not filled immediately.

1963–1968

At this point, I will divide the discussion in order to distinguish U.S. involvement in schooling from involvement in education outside the traditional system of schools.

SCHOOLING AT THE PRIMARY AND SECONDARY LEVELS

The political picture changed again with the election of Belaúnde in 1963. Conditions for renewed foreign assistance in the field of education appeared to be propitious. Negotiations led to the arrival of a team of educational advisers from Teachers College Columbia University (TCCU) contracted by AID to work with the Peruvian Ministry of Education. The TCCU team was the principal U.S. government-sponsored organization working directly with primary and secondary schooling in Peru from 1963 to 1968. Contracting a university presumably permitted access to a wider spectrum of resources and presumably muted objections arising from direct government-to-government contact. TCCU advisers were to have no direct decision making power.

Projects and responsibilities ranged widely. In addition to the chief of party, TCCU advisers were provided at various times in elementary education, educational administration, educational research, educational planning, teacher education, trade and industrial education, rural elementary education, and educational materials. Short-term advisers were brought in as needed. The following table, taken from the 1968 AID program book, gives an idea of pro-

TABLE 1: PERUVIAN EDUCATIONAL ACTIVITIES PROJECTED
FOR FISCAL YEAR 1967–1968

Target Area	Continued Emphasis	New Initiatives
I. Improving the administrative structure and procedures of the Ministry of Education	Completion of regulations for Ministry officials Completion and final approval of regulations for regional offices Implementation of rural education offices in primary division and in teacher education Participant training scholarships for young potential administrators	Region-by-region analysis of administrative problems and recommended procedures Gradual development of training program for regional and Ministry administrators Experimental program of training for Ministry accountants and auditors Creation of administrative office to deal with regional colleges
II. Planning an educational program geared to Peru's economic and social needs	Analysis of implications of manpower study Refinement of five-year educational plans Participant training scholarships for potential planners, statisticians, and researchers	National Conference on Educational Planning Organization of data gathering services Development of Educational Research bureau, staff, or institute

Target Area	Continued Emphasis	New Initiatives
III. Improving teacher education	Refinement of new year teacher preparation curriculum Refinement with Catholic University of its program in education as per study by TCCU technician	Development of 3 regional normal schools as model teacher training institutions (loan) Development of standards for normal school staffs
	Completion of standards for normal schools Continued assistance with CRECER program for teachers in service Participant training scholarships for potential leaders in teacher education	Assistance to universities in the development of programs for preparing normal school teachers Reorganization and development of teacher-training program at La Cantuta
IV. Developing a modern system of secondary and post-secondary vocational education in Peru	Completion of loan application to World Bank Continued work with technical and vocational division of Ministry on vocational education programs Assistance with development of industrial arts and home and family life components of general education in comprehensive secondary schools Participant training scholarships for potential leaders in technical education	Assistance in development of regional colleges and 5 technical secondary schools administrative organization, instructional programs, buildings, equipment, staff, teaching materials, etc. (World Bank loan funds and AID finances) Assistance with development of vocational offering in proposed comprehensive secondary schools

Target Area	Continued Emphasis	New Initiatives
V. Increasing the effectiveness of rural education in Peru	Assistance to Ministry ing nucleo schools officials in develop- and rural education Implementation of new rural education offices in Ministry Occasional small loans through AID Special Projects Office Establishing of budget in the Ministry for the two rural education training centers Participant training scholarships for potential leaders	Development of 3 rural education training centers (loan) Assistance in school construction east of the Andes (loan) Assistance in development of experimental vocational training programs in rural schools (loan) Revolving fund for starting self-supporting projects in rural schools (loan)
VI. Improving the quantity of teaching materials	Assistance, in cooperation with Peace Corps, with Ministry educational T.V. program Participant training scholarships for technicians in educational T.V. and instructional materials	Development of instructional materials production center (loan) and in-service personnel training program Feasibility study of educational T.V. in Peru (loan)

SOURCE: Department of State, USAID *Country Assistance Program* FY 1968. Peru, Part II. Washington: USAID. The description reflects thinking as of October 1966.

jected activities as of October 1966 and provides a reasonably good outline of the U.S. involvement in Peruvian education through TCCU. Note the participant training component in each area.

The TCCU team encountered difficulties getting started, not the least of which related to personnel problems within the team. Establishing proper lines of communication with Ministry officials also proved difficult at the outset. More important, however, was the upsetting fact that an educational sector loan (for nine million dollars), promised to the Peruvian government at the time the TCCU contract was negotiated, was subsequently withheld. Freezing technical assistance (not only in education) was used to put pressure on Belaúnde not to expropriate IPC.

As early difficulties were overcome, the U.S. advisers settled into their relatively unproductive routine. Much of the energy of team members was consumed in the preparation of loan requests to such organizations as AID and the World Bank. Ministry officials felt they had already made an agreement with AID and that further proposals were not necessary; that was a game for the TCCU technicians to play. A World Bank loan to be used for regional *colegios* was requested and apparently approved, then withdrawn in the wake of Peru's purchase of Mirage airplanes from France.

In part, TCCU ineffectiveness was related to political problems, but there were other reasons why the Ministry of Education was unable to utilize the technical personnel wisely. Absorptive capacity of the Ministry was, and still is, an important constraint on the amount of technical assistance that can be rendered effectively. Indeed, the difficulties inherent in any technical assistance endeavor linked to the Ministry of Education with its immense bureaucracy (whether indirectly linked and on a government-to-government basis as in SECPANE or directly linked and channeled through a "private" U.S. institution as in the TCCU case) should not be underestimated. Money and men with expertise are thinly spread throughout the Ministry. The political labyrinth within the Ministry is very confusing to an outsider. (The same comments can be made about the United States Office of Education.) The promised sector loan might have been denied on other than political grounds. If it had been granted, it would not have solved the problem of absorption although part of the funds would have been earmarked for upgrading Ministry personnel.

In 1967 the TCCU team was reduced to five members. The sector loan (now requested for ten million) was again withheld and actively continued at a frantic but unproductive pace. One of the hopeful developments during the 1967–1968 period was initiation of an educational research program organized within the Ministry. Several good pieces of empirical research emerged from the program.

Several other means of U.S. involvement in primary and secondary education from 1963 to 1968 deserve mention. The U.S. government provided school lunches on a massive scale under PL 480, Title III, according to the 1968 program book, approximately twelve million dollars was budgeted for the four years 1965–1968. (There is little doubt that the food program had a major impact on enrollments.) Peace Corps workers were involved in the distribution of food, in the construction of schools, and occasionally in teaching, usually in rural areas. The "U.S. community" operates one of the best schools in Peru (K-12) for North Americans and Peruvians (most of whom are from upper socioeconomic backgrounds). The Instituto Cultural Peruano-Norteamericano offers English and other classes to Peruvians.

Church groups from the United States have also made their educational presence felt.[13] Roman Catholic orders have been particularly active. Among other educational concerns, the Catholic church operates several of the most prestigeous secondary schools in urban Peru and is responsible for a system of radio schools in rural Peru. For approximately twenty-five years, the Wycliffe Bible Translators, usually referred to in Peru as the Summer Institute of Linguistics (SIL), has been working, in conjunction with the Ministry of Education, with Indian tribes in the Peruvian jungle, writing down previously unwritten languages and developing syllabuses to teach Spanish as a second language (using the tribal language as the first). The SIL is also experimenting with bilingual education (Quechua-Spanish bilingualism) in the sierra.

North American church and nonchurch groups are deeply involved in a wide range of programs for residents of the Peruvian *pueblos jovenes* (previously called *barriadas*) that ring Lima and other major cities. Most of the programs have an educational component. Some, such as ALFALIT (a literacy technique with a religious underpinning) are directly concerned with education. Others, such as birth control or public health programs, not only involve educating people, but will also have an effect on enrollments.

Before leaving the primary and secondary level, I should note that during the post–World War II period, the Peruvian educational system did make enormous quantitative gains. From 1958

13 See chapter 12.

to 1968, for example, combined primary and secondary enrollments increased by 114 percent (as compared with a population
growth of 40 percent),[14] an expansion rate surpassed only by Mexico and Nicaragua among Latin American nations in that period.
The expansion was clearly related to a major financial commitment by the government, as indicated by the fact that investment
in education grew from less than 3 percent in 1958 to approximately 6 percent of the gross national product in 1967 (one of the highest percentages in the world). Meanwhile, the percentage of the
national budget devoted to education rose from approximately 18
percent to 26 percent.[15] As I have pointed out earlier, expansion
does not necessarily mean an improvement in quality, nor is it
necessarily an index of major social reform.

SCHOOLING AT THE HIGHER EDUCATIONAL LEVEL

Until the 1960s, Peruvian universities received little foreign assistance; U.S. involvement was largely restricted to exchange programs (Fulbright and others). Early in the decade, however, attitudes changed; the university was rediscovered by Peruvians and
North Americans alike. The realization that universities have an
important place in society is not new, of course. Peru boasts a long
and strong tradition of universities. However, only since World
War II, and primarily in the last decade, has pressure been placed
on Peruvian universities to serve national economic and social as
well as intellectual and political ends. The Peruvian government
began to view the university as a powerful force in society that
could be more constructively utilized to prepare individuals for
"needed" occupational roles (note goal 3 of the 1967–1970 plan, p.
338). In addition, increased demand for the limited university
places created strong pressure for expansion as well as for university reform. The U.S. government, the foundations, and multinational agencies stimulated and responded to the internal pres-

----

[14] Cited in Paulston, p. 101. See also, the Inter-American Development Bank,
Social Progress Trust Fund, *Ninth Annual Report, 1969*, "Socio-economic Progress in Latin America" (Washington, D.C.: ADB, March, 1970), p. 143.

[15] República del Perú, Instituto Nacional de Planificación, *Diagnóstico Nacional de Educación, 1955–1965* (Lima, December 1967), pp. 2–104; also, IADB,
p. 440.

sures for expansion and for redirection of Peruvian higher education.

Responses to pressure for change in the university system were both quantitative and qualitative. Before Belaúnde took office in 1963, university enrollment had already started its dramatic climb. From 31,900 students in eight universities in 1958, the numbers increased to 53,000 in twenty-six universities (including two branch affiliates) in 1963, and then to 123,100 in thirty-two universities in 1968.[16] Among South American nations, no other country could claim a higher rate of expansion during the ten years. Uncontrolled and uncoordinated growth led to lower-quality education on the average. At the same time, however, particular institutions displayed marked improvement, at least as indexed by such standard indicators as the number of full-time professors employed or the number of advanced-degree holders on the faculty. Foreign assistance was more directly associated with attempts to improve the quality of Peruvian higher education rather than the quantity.

The greatest numerical growth within universities occurred in education and humanities faculties, leading some observers to suggest that aspirants prefer and demand nonscientific and nontechnical fields. But relative enrollment is not a good indicator of student preferences or of the strength of demand for university places. If one looks at the relationship between the number of applications and the number of students admitted by field of study, there is less basis for the contention that students avoid "modern" fields.[17] Enrollments, then, are as much a function of supply (places available) as well as of demand. The fact that it is much less expensive to expand education or humanities offerings than engineering of-

[16] "Reflexiones en torno a las opportunidades educacionales," *Boletín del Instituto Nacional de Planificación*, no. 93 (February 30, 1970), p. 2.

[17] In 1967, for instance, 370 students enrolled in *ciencias* at San Marcos and 1,126 enrolled in *humanidades*. However, only one in five applicants was accepted into *ciencias* as contrasted with one in three applicants accepted in *humanidades*. Medicine continues to be the most selective career—only one in ten applicants gained admission in 1967. Oficina Nacional Inter-Universitaria de Planificación, Consejo Inter-Universitario, Departamento de Estadística, *Boletín No. 2* (Lima, December, 1968), pp. 9, 10).

ferings affects the supply and through supply the relative enrollments.

Increased university enrollment in education faculties was not
only associated with availability of places; in addition, demand for
such training was high and had sparked improvements in the relative earnings position of teachers during the first half of the
decade.[18] Also, secondary school teaching is a relatively realistic
career goal for many upwardly mobile students who lack the social
status and related connections to establish themselves in other
professional fields.

During the period of rapid expansion, external assistance was
made available to Peruvian universities in a variety of ways. The
largest inputs were soft-loan monies obtained through the IDB.[19]
The University of San Marcos received a 1.5 million dollar loan in
1962 to establish a postgraduate department of basic sciences; the
Agrarian University and the Engineering University received 2
and 2.5 million dollar loans respectively in 1964 to be used for
construction and equipment. All three loans were made from the
IDB Social Progress Fund. In 1968 the University of Trujillo received a 1.8 million dollar loan from the Fund for Special Operations of IDB to expand and improve general studies and chemical
engineering. The foundations were also actively involved in higher
education through grants to San Marcos, Agrarian University,
Engineering University, the Catholic University, and Cayetano
Heredia, among others. Heavy emphasis has been placed on basic
science, but funds have also been available for improvements in
other areas.

The U.S. business community in Peru has had little contact
with higher education, preferring to send trainees abroad and/or
to recruit U.S. trained Peruvians whenever possible. Each year
firms make funds available for scholarships and some firms contribute to the Instituto Peruano de Fomento Educativo (IPFE).

Assistance efforts by private and public institutions alike were

[18] Shane Hunt, "Distribution, Growth, and Government Economic Behavior
in Peru," Discussion Paper No. 7 (Princeton University, Woodrow Wilson
School, March, 1969). The zenith was reached in 1965 with the passage of Law
15215 guaranteeing teachers a 25 percent increase in salary each year for the
next four years. The promise could not be kept.

[19] Inter-American Development Bank, *Tenth Annual Report* (Washington,
D.C.: IADB, 1970), pp. 116, 117, 142.

concentrated in science and technology. Probably emphasis has been conditioned not only by the weak character of existing programs and by a growing faith in objective science as an important answer to underdevelopment, but also by a basic mistrust of the social sciences as dispensed by the United States.[20]

The policy orientation of both U.S. and multilateral organizations converges in an emphasis that might be labeled "institution building." That is, assistance has been concentrated within relatively few institutions rather than dispersed across institutions. In the institution-building efforts there seems to have been at least informal coordination among organizations effecting transfers of resources. The Engineering and Agrarian Universities have been favored recipients for assistance. In part, the institutional basis for making grants and loans resulted from the fact that there was no effective administrative structure tying the universities together in the 1960s.

The U.S. government has supported the development of Peruvian higher education in many ways. In the Agrarian University, for instance, PL 480 funds have been used to finance construction; a textbook lending library has been established with Alliance for Progress monies; scores of university professors have been sent abroad for advanced degrees in a wide range of academic areas, from forestry to agricultural economics and sociology; personnel from U.S. universities have been imported to work in an advisory capacity as the university restructures along departmental rather than along traditional "faculty" lines; and some teaching has been carried out by U.S. personnel both under technical assistance and under Fulbright programs.

Although the amount of assistance given by the United States for higher education in Peru is relatively small, the U.S. presence in higher education in Peru is sometimes overpowering. The universities seem, on occasion, to be overrun with technical advisers, Fulbrighters, Ford Foundation consultants, and U.S. graduate students doing their doctoral research. There is a tendency to forget

[20] The "functionalist" and "free market" models so deeply entrenched in U.S. sociology and economics are viewed as apologies for maintaining U.S. domination of less-developed nations and for maintaining existing inequitable social structures within Peru. Stress is on equilibrium in the models; conflict and changes are not treated adequately in the eyes of the reform minded.

that the entire university system of Peru enrolls only slightly more students than New York University.

The most direct involvement by the United States in Peruvian higher education has occurred through an AID contract with Stanford University to establish a graduate school of business administration, the Escuela Superior de Administración y Negocios (ESAN). Although the school does not have official university status, it offers a master's degree sanctioned by other Peruvian universities. ESAN is well equipped and well run (originally by U.S. personnel, increasingly by Peruvians as the U.S. attempts to phase out). Criticisms have been leveled at ESAN because it tends to serve only the sons of wealthy Peruvian families. It does not seem to have lived up to expectations in terms of turning out entrepreneurs who then generate new businesses and new employment; rather, it trains for existing positions in family or foreign businesses. An evaluation of the effectiveness of ESAN depends heavily on the perspective brought to the evaluation.

Another form of U.S. government assistance to Peruvian higher education has been to provide continuing support for the Instituto Peruano de Fomento Educativo (IPFE), a nongovernmental agency that also receives support from Peruvian and North American businesses. Decisions about the use of IPFE monies are made by the Peruvians charged with administering the funds. Disbursements have been made for student loans (both for study at home and abroad), for educational projects such as a seminar on instructional methods for science teachers, and for small research projects. IPFE also administers the Latin American Scholarship Program (LASPAU), a carefully designed program of study abroad in the United States linked to future employment in Peruvian universities upon return. The support for IPFE constitutes an important exception to the general university-by-university mode of transferring resources to Peruvian higher education.

U.S. assistance to Peruvian higher education through programs of training abroad deserves more detailed treatment. From 1960 to 1968 the number of Peruvians studying in the United States in institutions of higher education increased from approximately four hundred to approximately twelve hundred.[21] One-fourth of the stu-

[21] Institute of International Education, *Open Doors* (New York, various years).

dents are registered at the graduate level. There is a heavy emphasis on "modern" subjects. The largest numbers of students are in engineering and business. Although it has been pointed out painfully by the Peruvian government that study abroad results in an outflow of funds,[22] we should keep in mind that approximately 40 percent of the Peruvians studying in the United States are sponsored in part or entirely by U.S. universities, international organizations, foundations, U.S. businesses, or the U.S. government. Others finance their education by working in the United States while attending a university. Furthermore, study abroad relieves some pressure on local Peruvian institutions, provides a huge educational subsidy (even when students pay their own way the institution also contributes because fees never cover university costs), and gives access to expensive technical and scientific offerings both needed and demanded in the development process. Thus, even when allowance is made for the fact that some Peruvian students do not return home following study abroad,[23] there is little doubt that Peru gains, on balance, from study abroad in the United States. Indeed, when U.S. university subsidies are added to the direct investment by government, foundations and international organizations to which the United States contributes, study abroad may be the largest single source of U.S. involvement in Peruvian education.

EDUCATION OUTSIDE THE TRADITIONAL SCHOOL SYSTEM

School systems need other educational institutions to supplement offerings and to compensate for ingrown defects that are hard to remove, given the inflexibility of schools. It would not be surpris-

---

[22] República del Perú, Instituto Nacional de Planificación, *Desarrollo económico y social: educación, "orientaciones para el desarrollo del sistema nacional de educación"* (Lima, September, 1968), p. 48.

[23] Robert G. Myers, *Education and Emigration* (New York: David McKay, forthcoming), chapter 7. Among students who are sponsored to study in the United States, the rate of nonreturn is less than 5 percent. A higher percentage, probably between 15 and 20 percent, of the nonsponsored students remain abroad in the United States. Evidence indicates, however, that the decision to emigrate to the United States is made prior to, or at the same time as, the decision to study abroad in most of the non-returnee cases. Hence, study abroad does not *cause* emigration. Furthermore, if jobs are available, Peruvians do return home and often at salaries far below those that could be obtained abroad. The one area in which Peru seems to be experiencing a talent drain is in the field of medi-

ing to find that the number of people trained outside traditional school settings—in industrial courses, on-the-job training, in apprenticeship programs, in military education programs, and in improvement courses offered by government—exceeds the number trained in schools in Peru. Such extraschool programs are usually directed toward fulfilling a specific demand for skills by employers. One of their virtures lies in their ad hoc nature and their limited life.

In the period 1963 to 1968, the U.S. government sponsored several nontraditional, extraschool projects. One of the more interesting commitments was to education offered by and through the Peruvian military. Funds were supplied to give Peruvian conscripts, almost exclusively from the lowest social levels, literacy training throughout their tour of duty and, prior to discharge, vocational training for three months (in one of twelve trades). The programs were expensive and results have not been adequately evaluated. I hesitate to hazard a judgment of their effectiveness.

On quite a different plane, the U.S. government has supported educational programs in sales and management. In addition to developing ESAN, funds were allocated for seminars, workshops, and conferences sponsored by the Peruvian Management Association (IPAE) and the Peruvian Sales Management Association (ADV). In 1965/66, approximately fifteen hundred individuals participated in IPAE training courses and another seven hundred in marketing courses.

At the same time, the U.S. government promoted a workers education center for trade unionists (through the American Institute for Free Labor Development and the Confederation of Workers of Peru),[24] established small libraries in rural areas (under a Special Projects category of technical assistance), trained Peruvians in survey research and demography techniques (through CISM, a sample-survey organization in the Ministry of Labor), sent Peruvians abroad for practical experience and supported Peace Corps members in, for instance, community development activities with a large educational component. In brief, the scope of extraschool

---

cine. The drain is related to an internal brain drain and to an oversupply of doctors relative to "effective demand" (as distinguished from "need") for doctors.

[24] See chapters 9 and 10.

involvement in education was broad and the institutional arrangements were varied. Programs were not coordinated; there was no recognizable policy toward education outside the schools.

One of the most successful extraschool educational developments in the 1963 to 1968 period was the growth of SENATI, an apprenticeship training program modeled after similar programs in Brazil and Colombia. SENATI included literacy training, trade instruction, and some secondary vocational training tied to employment in industry. U.S. firms in Peru were among those that were assessed 1 percent of their payroll to support SENATI, but the U.S. government declined to contribute funds directly despite several such requests, largely because foreign assistance at that time was frozen.

Unfortunately, I know of no data accumulated on training in industry in Peru and cannot comment on the extent to which U.S. business has provided education for employees. My impression is that if the informal and formal training given (or supported) could be quantified it would turn out to be considerable at all levels— from stockroom to management. On one hand such investment in human resources, if substantial, would provide a counterargument to those who contend that foreign enterprises only extract resources; on the other hand, the direct link to North American training would provide fuel for those who would like to interpret education as a means of making Peru ever more dependent upon the United States by emphasizing U.S. technologies.

One of the most noteworthy extraschool programs developed during the Belaúnde period was located within the Central Bank. Supported by the Ford Foundation, selected students were given sound instruction in "modern" economics. The Central Bank training program is an excellent example of an educational investment made outside the traditional school system that seems to have yielded well even if in a somewhat different manner than that anticipated. Although many program graduates left the Central Bank, a large proportion continue to utilize their training effectively within Peru.

Undoubtedly, the list of U.S. organizations participating in education in Peru could be drawn out to a much more impressive length. However, I think the foregoing should be enough to make the general point that U.S. involvement takes many forms and is, to say the least, extensive. When all educational forms and programs are brought together, the Peruvian charge of "domination" does not seem quite as exaggerated as it might have appeared before.

1968 to the Present

With the change of government in October 1968, the status of TCCU members became unclear. For a period after the turnover, advisers remained in Peru but reported to AID rather than to the Ministry. Meanwhile, attempts to renegotiate the contract with the new government snagged, in spite of support for the TCCU team from within the Ministry at the middle levels. An idealized pattern on how technical assistance should work was apparently postulated in which U.S. advisers would not only be restricted from the fringes of decision making, they would also be asked to refrain from taking any program initiatives. "Advising" was to mean just that and was to take place only upon request. The Peruvian view of technical assistance seemed closely linked to preoccupation with independence from external influence.

Had there been a strong desire to renegotiate the contract on either side it could have been done. Education officials in AID and in the Ministry were, however, locked in by the respective political positions of their governments in early 1969. The pretext for discontinuing the contract and for sending TCCU personnel home became default by the Ministry on an obligation to pay relatively minor supporting costs for the TCCU group.

In May 1970 the USAID mission in Peru included one man whose primary responsibility was education. His task was to keep channels of communication open. The withdrawal of the TCCU team was probably wise; under the best of circumstances, performance had been spotty and successes had been tied more to individual relationships and initiatives than to the efforts of a smoothly functioning organization. Ironically, however, there was a feeling among some TCCU members that obstacles to effective assistance were finally being removed—just at the time the contract was terminated. AID can, of course, still call in individuals if requested by the Peruvian government.

It does not take long for "successes" to wither. For instance, the highly praised system of nuclear schools built up over many years by SECPANE reverted to a system of traditional one-teacher schools. The decline began during the TCCU tenure as available resources declined. To cite another example, the potentially successful research program started within the Ministry by TCCU has been converted into an unimaginative office concerned more with educational inventories than with empirical educational research.

Other U.S. government involvement in Peruvian education was not so dramatically affected by the change in government. Some U.S. advisers working in Peruvian universities were sent home but others remained. ESAN continues to function with U.S. support and the blessing of the current regime (which is contributing 50 percent of costs and which chose ESAN for a governmental contract that might have been handled elsewhere). Programs of study abroad continue at approximately the same pace as pre-1968. Peace Corps members still perform educational tasks.

Nongovernmental U.S. institutions including foundations, church, labor, and business continue their educational support in varying degrees. As U.S. businesses adjust to the new rules of the game, the amount of on-the-job training is reduced, at least temporarily, perhaps permanently.

Viewing the broader picture, then, U.S. withdrawal from involvement in Peruvian education following the military takeover in 1968 has been more symbolic than real.

A commission focusing on primary and secondary education is presently laboring diligently to come up with recommendations for improving the Peruvian educational system. On one hand, the commission has served to provide a needed delay for a reform-minded government that could not possibly handle reform in all areas at once. On the other hand, the commission has taken its charge seriously. From the extensive probing by fourteen subcommissions, a wealth of information should appear and an integrated set of programs and priorities should take shape. Presumably the process will establish areas in which external assistance would be welcome.

According to a press conference given by the Minister of Education in January, 1970, at least two priorities are evident—reform of teacher training and renewed efforts in agricultural education, particularly as associated with the Agrarian Reform.[25] In addition, preliminary releases by the Reform Commission point to major structural and curricular reorganization, to incorporating children under five into the educational program, and to a de-emphasis on traditional formal schooling in the upper high school years, perhaps through coordination of SENATI and the Ministry of Education.

The "renovation" of higher education was, and is, seen as a crucial element in the revolutionary government's program.[26] Among the changes in the now famous Decreto 17437 (as modified by 17833) are the following:

1. A reorganization of the academic structure. Academic departments organized by academic discipline replace "faculties" organized by career sequences.

2. A curriculum reform. Basic studies programs are envisioned for all universities. The curriculum within each university is to be made "flexible," giving each student more freedom to choose courses.

3. A reorganization of the governing structure. Under the reform, students and faculty are represented on the University Assembly that elects the rector and determines broad policy. Student representation in the Assembly is reduced from one-third to one-fourth. Policy implementation, however, is to be carried out by a university council in which students have no representation and in which faculty members are represented only by their department head. In addition, a restriction is placed on eligibility for the position of rector (he must have been in the university for ten years) and restrictions are placed upon student eligibility for election to the Assembly (they must be in the top 20 percent of their class).

4. Cost of education. No longer would public university education be free. A graduated scale of fees based on ability to pay is to be established by each university. Most universities have managed to neutralize this provision to date.

5. Academic freedom. The right to enter university campuses has been given to civil authorities, but the decision to call civil

25 See chapter 5.
26 Leopoldo Chiappo, "Estructura y fines de la universidad peruana," *Aportes* 16 (April, 1970): 68.

authorities lies with each university. Political activity on campuses is presumably prohibited.

6. Coordination at the national level. The Consejo Nacional de la Universidad Peruana (CONUP) is given data-gathering, planning, and accreditation functions as well as control over distribution of funds allocated to Peruvian universities by the government. At the same time, CONUP is supposed to arbitrate conflicts among institutions, has the power to consolidate institutions, and can remove officials for mismanagement.

As might be expected of any drastic changes, there has been opposition. The 1969 school year was filled with student disturbances. The law was tested with the election of rectors. The Agrarian University and the Engineering University, the two main recipients of foreign assistance and probably the most up-to-date universities in Peru, were closed for part of the year; Engineering students lost a semester of work. The fact that opposition to the new law centered in these two universities has led some observers to question the effect of foreign assistance to higher education.

Increased politicization of the universities could undercut effectiveness of almost any technical assistance offered, either directly through a student attack on foreign assistance programs, or indirectly as the universities are immobilized and unable to absorb assistance. But the long-term effect of the 1969 university reform on student politicization is not clear. The government has shown some responsiveness to student pressures and the university system seems to have survived a first round of disturbances. Whether or not student leaders will be forced into more radical positions and will acquire a significant following in their new positions remains to be seen.

Criticisms of the reform come from many quarters, sometimes from individuals who are concerned about the imposition of what seem to be North American values and structures on the Peruvian system.[27] While such values and structures might be appropriate for the United States, and while they might make the Peruvian universities more efficient, their applicability to the Peruvian situation and goals is not clear. In promulgating the law, the new gov-

[27] Based on my conversations with various Peruvian university students and faculty members.

ernment seems to have endorsed as critical the role of the university in providing manpower for economic development—a slant critics feel is too closely linked with North American desires.

Critics of the reform also argue that lower socioeconomic groups in Peruvian society will be placed at a greater disadvantage than before the reform because they will have to pay.[28] Again, there is a conflict of goals. Education is expected to promote equity while fostering economic growth and encouraging freedom.

Not all of the current strains within the Peruvian university system stem from the reform law. The government has reduced the relative funding for universities, putting a squeeze on budgets. In addition, the moderately favorable salary position of university professors (in some universities) has been threatened by a separate reform decree (17834) regulating salaries and linking professors to the civil service scale. The result may be a return to multiple employment, a change of occupation, or emigration.

CONUP is being severely tested as it attempts to bring marginal universities up to standard and as it is called upon to moderate mounting cross-pressures among the major universities. The degree to which U.S. assistance to higher education can be effectively used may depend in large part upon the success of CONUP in dealing with its present political difficulties.

Categorizing the Alternatives

Broad policy alternatives may be categorized as follows: (1) total detachment; (2) make resources available but on a general budget support level, i.e., without stipulating whether resources should be allocated to education or not; (3) make funds available for education only, but for general use within education, i.e., without stipulating specific projects or agencies; and (4) make funds available for specific educational projects or agencies. Each alternative implies a different degree of choice for the United States and Peru in managing and allocating resources.

Rather than pursue each of the four alternatives directly, I prefer to treat them indirectly and to organize the discussion about several cross-cutting considerations. From answers to the following

[28] Alberto Escobar, "Las paradojas de la ley universitaria peruana," *Aportes* 15 (January, 1970): 8.

five questions, one or another broad policy tends to emerge. However, the reverse procedure, choosing a broad policy first, may or may not provide answers to the questions, all of which must be dealt with in some way when discussing foreign assistance:

1. To what point should resources be made available, if at all?

2. What institutional mechanism for transfer of resources should be utilized?

3. Under what conditions should resources be made available? Are there specific preconditions that should be met? Should strings be attached, and if so what are they? What terms of repayment should be included, if any?

4. Who should receive the resources? Should public or private institutions in the receiving country be favored? Should particular subpopulations receive disproportionate amounts? Are there specific institutions that should receive the resources?

5. What are the priorities governing resource allocation? What purposes will be served by the transfer of resources?

POLICY ALTERNATIVES

In this section, I will concentrate on U.S. government involvement in education and will not attempt to delineate alternative policies that nongovernmental institutions might follow. However, many of the same sorts of decisions about the form and substance of involvement will have to be made by other organizations as well. Although governmental policy obviously influences educational involvement by nongovernmental institutions such as the foundations, business, and the Church, I will not treat the influences explicitly. In part, my reluctance to explore effects of governmental policy on other institutions stems from my feeling that the more government controls or manipulates nongovernmental responses, the greater the monolith and the greater the policy risks will be.

Within education, I will deal mainly with U.S. involvement in higher education. Almost inevitably, the discussion of educational assistance will be, at the same time, a discussion of foreign assistance in general and, to a lesser degree, of U.S. foreign policy goals.[29] Rather than discuss foreign policy goals in the abstract, I

---

[29] For an excellent discussion of the shifting context within which I am discussing educational policy, see Abraham F. Lowenthal, "Alliance Rhetoric

prefer to look at policy operationally. By answering operational questions, the impact and intent of foreign assistance is often more clearly delineated than in a discussion of goals. Let us keep in mind, as noted earlier, that there are multiple goals for foreign policy and for education to serve. Conflict and overlap among the expressed goals frame the problem.

Questions but not Answers

What amount of resources should be made available? At the moment, we find a minority who feel that the U.S. should increase its overseas involvement by increasing the level of resources committed to international assistance, regardless of the form of assistance and regardless of the project. The argument for increases is usually phrased in apolitical, "humanitarian" terms and as often as not is based on the assumption (probably false) that the modest results associated with international assistance to date could be improved upon by providing development support on a larger scale. There is even evidence to indicate that the effectiveness of foreign assistance does not relate to the scale of the assistance (unless there is an inverse relationship).[30]

Let us turn, then, to the arguments of those who feel that disengagement from foreign assistance is the most appropriate course for the United States to follow. Although the extreme position—withdrawal of all aid from Peru—is taken by relatively few, the same arguments used for the extreme position are also marshaled to support more moderate reductions as well.

One line of argument derives from a strong liberal, antimilitary stance. Many liberals feel that under no condition should the United States support a military regime in Peru (or elsewhere); that all are basically totalitarian and will therefore do more harm than good in the long run (perhaps even in the short run). It is not difficult to find examples supporting liberal preconceptions in the current Peruvian context. In the field of education, for instance, we have noted cutbacks in "academic freedom" embodied in the

---

versus Latin American Reality." *Foreign Affairs* 48, no. 3 (April, 1970):494–508.

[30] K. B. Griffin and J. L. Enos, "Foreign Assistance: Objectives and Consequences," *Economic Development and Cultural Change* 18, no. 3 (April, 1970): 313–327.

university reform. The military move against the opposition news-paper *Expreso* might be cited by liberals to prove their point. But the argument is ideologically based. It has little to do with whether or not the Peruvian military government can bring about economic growth or social change more rapidly than would occur through a traditional system of political parties. Whether or not the govern-ment is military or civilian may have little to do with the positive or negative effects U.S. resources could have if provided to support specific development decisions.

Another argument for withholding foreign assistance to Peru is that Peru lacks sufficient absorptive capacity. Until there is evi-dence that resources can be effectively used, it makes little sense to release the resources. Indeed, many examples can be cited of ineffi-cient administration and allocations of money or people to projects that collapse immediately once the money has been used up or once the foreign advisers have left. Thus, the argument has sur-face validity.

But the lack of absorptive capacity can be exaggerated and the argument overdrawn. The fact that resources have been improper-ly utilized in the past does not lead in an obvious manner to a policy of withholding resources. We should first recognize that at least part of the blame for misallocation of foreign assistance must lie directly at the feet of the U.S. administrators and advisers. Often projects were pressed upon Peruvians that were not wanted or requested, projects for which the society was not yet prepared. Where such was the case, there is a question whether it was low absorptive capacity or failure to identify the appropriate areas for investment that caused foreign assistance to flounder.

If absorptive capacity is indeed low, what may be called for is a policy stressing investments that are directly aimed at building up the absorptive capacity. For instance, insufficient training for in-dividuals in key positions has often been identified as a deterrent to effective use of foreign assistance. Rather than withhold resourc-es, a policy of rechanneling resources into training might be ap-propriate.

In the specific case of higher education in Peru, we encounter an argument that U.S. involvement inevitably breeds conflict, hence is counterproductive. Ubiquitous "Yankee go home" graffiti on university walls are cited to show that the U.S. presence provokes university disorganization and that therefore support should be withdrawn. In Peru, the argument is weak. It could become stronger if students become even more politicized as they react to reforms of the military government, but generally, student protests have not been directed against the presence of U.S. citizens working or studying in Peruvian university settings. Rather, protest is against the U.S. economic presence in Peru. Even though the governments have been at odds, U.S. individuals have been able to continue their work in Peruvian universities on a person-to-person or institution-to-institution basis. True, there is suspicion that the U.S. money and U.S. scholars are tied to the CIA, and a link is often made between academic and economic goals; but there is also a pragmatic and personal side to relationships within the university community that works to overcome that suspicion. If, on the other hand, suspicion is fed by a Camelot or by unnecessary, boastful advertising of U.S. programs to the point where the programs appear to be motivated by political self-interest rather than humanitarian or scholarly concern, the United States can legitimately expect problems. (Perhaps one of the errors of the Alliance for Progress has been the inordinate public-relations overtone that has pervaded Alliance projects from the beginning.)

Related to the argument that infusions of U.S. funds can be counterproductive because they are disruptive is another, less obvious point. Resources are scarce, and there is competition for the scarce resources among institutions and within institutions. Inevitably, some institutions and departments will be placed at a disadvantage because they have not received foreign funding. In Peruvian higher education, U.S. assistance has favored two universities. Even though the reasons for the choice may be economically sound, political repercussions could offset the economic advantages. More specifically, as norms are established by CONUP for accrediting universities (norms that emphasize the very factors for which some but not others have received extensive external assistance), political infighting within CONUP will probably intensify. Disputes will influence, as well as reflect, patterns of distribution from abroad of men, money, materials, and training grants among universities. Whether the long-run effect will be to undermine or to strengthen CONUP remains to be seen. Again, a conclusion that resources should be withheld does not flow naturally from the discussion. What does emerge is the need to be sensitive to latent effects any educational involvement may produce, among which is conflict over resource distribution.

It is not unusual to hear another set of arguments (usually from Latin Americans) that, in the extreme, also lead to a "no support" policy conclusion. In brief, the argument is that, by its very nature, all U.S. assistance helps to perpetuate (and even to increase) dependence on the United States and that true development cannot occur until Peru achieves an independence of action that is now missing. If applied literally, there is no room to maneuver. However, as pointed out in the introduction, the fact that most societies have multiple goals provides an opportunity to seek policy in an area of overlap. The problem then becomes one of locating points at which the concern about domination gives way to competing concerns. I think there must be some skillful reading between the lines to arrive at policy implications. Cues should probably be taken from actions rather than from words.

In higher education, a charge of developing or perpetuating cultural as well as economic domination over Peru is frequently levied against the United States. The threat of cultural domination, linked as it is to influencing thoughts and long-standing patterns of behavior, is at once more serious and more tenuous than the threat of economic domination linked to control of capital and markets. To the extent that Peruvians are firmly grounded in their own culture, which I believe most are, the concern with cultural domination is a questionable issue. If cultural domination is occurring, it is not the university but the movie theater that should be examined closely.

Transplanting U.S. institutional forms within education is sometimes viewed with alarm as cultural penetration. However, the main effect seems to be that transplants are rejected or function in a different manner from that intended; that the cultural effects of institutional transfers are minimal. Indeed, the main reason for much of U.S. ineffectiveness in technical assistance is directly related to cultural insensitivity. There should be little fear, then, of the damage that North Americans can do in the cultural sphere and there should be little support for cutting off U.S. involvement in Peruvian higher education simply because of anticipated cultural encroachment. Still, the *fear* of cultural imperialism remains, rightly or wrongly, and that fear must be recognized, both in formulating policies and in implementing them. That such fears exist, however, should not prevent a search for critical areas in which both governments agree that U.S. involvement could be beneficial to Peru and in which interested groups (including students) feel cultural compromises are not required.[31]

Having examined several reasons used to support a policy of withholding or withdrawing foreign assistance from Peruvian higher education, we can assume that an appropriation for foreign assistance will continue to be made and that a flexible amount is available for investment in education in Peru. Consideration can now be given to other threads in the policy fabric.

What institutional mechanism(s) for transfer of resources should be favored? Let us consider the following alternatives: (a) transfer through multilateral organizations such as UNESCO, IDB, the World Bank, OAS, or the Zona Andina regional organization; and (b) transfer through bilateral arrangements either directly from the United States government or indirectly through a nongovernmental U.S. institution such as a university to the Peruvian government or a nongovernmental Peruvian organization.

There is a strong argument for the present U.S. policy of dividing resources available for foreign assistance between bilateral and multilateral agencies. By so doing, a choice of places to seek funding is made available. Perhaps the greatest advantage, however, is that by spreading available funds there is less chance of becoming locked into major organizational problems that might develop if funds were concentrated in a single institution. Therefore, moves to concentrate foreign assistance efforts in any one agency and to phase out bilateral programs should be reviewed with extreme care.

Still, pressures are strong for the United States to switch much or all of its foreign assistance to multinational agencies and to abandon the present bilateral structures. By so doing the United

[31] That agreement is possible is suggested by my experience at one university where several radical professors who expressed deep concerns about economic and cultural imperialism nevertheless had no difficulty coming up with the suggestion that they needed and would accept assistance in the form of a computer. Surprisingly, that assistance was not looked upon as involving cultural encroachment by the United States.

States could withdraw many of its expensive administrative personnel from the field, could presumably relieve itself from criticisms that assistance is used solely for political purposes, and could hopefully side-step charges of economic and social imperialism.

Unfortunately, a shift to multilateral agencies will probably not bring the anticipated results. It would seem, for instance, that unless the United States is willing to remain politically detached, the multilateral approach can be used as easily for political ends as the bilateral approach. As illustrated by the Powelson paper,[32] the temptation to manipulate international agencies is present, particularly in the IDB, where the United States may exercise its "veto." Whether or not loans are cut off as a result of U.S. political problems with a country or whether loans from a multilateral agency are halted in response to changing economic conditions in a country, criticisms will be forthcoming.

By putting educational investment decisions in the hands of international organizations, priorities and projects would theoretically originate with the potential recipient; there would be less chance of an "imposed" program from the United States. But I think we can question whether shifting from bilateral to multilateral transfer of resources does assure a greater voice for the recipient country in setting its own priorities. The shift might give countries less leeway than before. One of the problems that could easily develop and that is incipient if not present already in most multinational organizations is the problem of political infighting over limited funds. Priorities must still be established. How? There is a tendency for funds to be allocated "by the numbers," cutting out some good projects that deserve funding and incorporating others merely because a particular country has not had a project approved before. Or, some nations are more successful than others in lobbying or in placing their own people in decision-making positions within the international organization, thus obtaining a favored position.

There is no immediate reason why Peruvian control over priorities and projects could not be as great or greater under a binational as under a multinational arrangement. As pointed out in outlining broad policies, money could be made available at the level of the

[32] See chapter 4.

national budget. Education would then get whatever share the Peruvian government decided it should get. Of course, there is the possibility that resources would be withheld until the Peruvian national budget approached a distribution that the United States thought appropriate. In such a case, resources put in at the national level would give only an illusion of Peruvian control. Note that even if, under a bilateral arrangement, funds were made generally available, a policy decision would have been made, in effect, that the government rather than the private sector should set priorities.

Alternatively, under a bilateral arrangement, resources could be made available *for* education but without stipulating priorities *within* education. There is really little difference between this alternative and the previous one, because budget monies made available for education would free budget constraints elsewhere. Just as in the above alternative, the United States could withhold funds until priorities were brought more closely in line with a preconceived "ideal." And the United States would again be implicitly making public-private choices as discussed above.

Another method of treating funds made available for education in general through a bilateral agreement might be to handle the funds through a special commission created to review projects in the field of education. The commission, which could be all Peruvian or joint Peruvian-U.S., might both review past projects and make recommendations for future projects. Research funds for carrying out the review might be built into each project from the start and the commission might even have a small research staff at its disposal. By creating a commission, members from the private as well as public sectors could be represented in the decision-making process.

Throughout the SECPANE era, a joint U.S.-Peruvian commission existed in effect, but, as pointed out previously, the control was with the North American members. My impression is that the same dominance could not occur as easily today. Furthermore, the commission could include members from outside the Ministry of Education (which the SECPANE group did not do), much as is being done for the current educational reform commission. The same scheme might be used exclusively for higher education.

Although it is probably true that the bulk of United States assistance to Peru cannot now flow through bilateral channels, it is also worthwhile to explore ways in which bilateral channels might be made more "respectable." One alternative would be for the U.S. government to loosen up on its grudging attitude toward turning funds over to private national institutions in Peru, which would then administer the funds. A model for such an arrangement exists in the Instituto Peruano de Fomento Educativo.

Under what conditions should resources be released? I will consider three sets of conditions briefly: conditions related to political sanctions (Hickenlooper and others), conditions tying purchases of goods and services to particular markets, and repayment conditions.

At present, the many political conditions that are attached to bilateral agreements tend to make a mockery of U.S. assertions that the government is seriously interested in supporting the continuous economic and social development of Latin American nations. Assistance can be (and has been) cut off solely on political grounds in Peru and elsewhere.

In the political world in which we live, sanctions may be necessary. But should all programs be candidates for use as sanctions? There has obviously been an effort to distinguish areas in which to apply sanctions. In education, for instance, a distinction seems to have been made between university and other educational programs. Although the TCCU team was pulled out, other U.S. advisers remained in universities. The principle is there, however, and unless education is formally exempted, it will be subject to the same conditions as all other forms of assistance. Even if one accepts the principle of applying sanctions it does not follow that because a fishing vessel involves the United States and Peru in an international dispute, an ongoing educational program developed at great expense over several years should be threatened. If the United States is strongly convinced (as it seems to be) that educational improvement is a key to more rapid development in Latin America, perhaps educational programs should be exempted from serving as points of political pressure and should not be subject to cutoffs under Hickenlooper or other conditions that presently pertain to all forms of technical assistance.

U.S. bilateral assistance has been conditioned in the past by balance-of-payments considerations. Recipient countries were required to use most of their grant monies to purchase U.S. goods and services. The condition not only prevented local purchase but also symbolized U.S. domination. This is no longer true: purchases may be made in other Latin American countries if desired. One of the advantages in removing the condition is that there is now greater freedom to hire nationals for formulating, administering, and evaluating programs of foreign assistance. In the past, even though talent existed locally, it was difficult to contract. But the question arises, "Should the United States open up the purchase option to a broader area than Latin America?" Then, for instance, it would be possible for Peruvian educators to hire with U.S. money an expert on educational television from, let us say, Germany.

Turning to repayment conditions, a paper on education is not the place to try to detail whether soft or hard loans or grants are preferable and under what circumstances. Let me simply note one or two problems with soft loans and grants—favored forms of educational support. If the return to education is as high as governments seem to think it is, then a case might be made for charging higher rather than lower rates on educational loans. A problem with giving education a preferred status in the loan market is that governments (including Peru) apply for loans that would normally be financed from the regular budget, thus freeing budget money for another project that is lower on the priority list that would require hard financing, or that is politically sensitive and therefore not fundable.

To whom should resources be directed? If a multilateral path to transferring resources is chosen, there would be no need for the U.S. government to consider choices among recipient institutions in Peru; that would be determined by the multilateral agency. If bilateral assistance is continued, however, the U.S. government will be faced with difficult choices. With respect to future support for higher education, for example, a major question will be whether or not to channel all, or part, or none of the foreign assistance through CONUP. As indicated earlier, CONUP has the force of law but is also subject to political pressures from the universities, which may weigh more heavily than legal status. Failure to support CONUP at this juncture might hasten its demise. Yet if only CONUP is selected, private universities will be at a disadvantage.

One might argue that if CONUP does not care to or is not able to draw up a request for U.S. assistance, then the United States should seek (or be open to) alternative channels for funding the development of higher education (which would, in effect, mean returning to previous policy). It should not be difficult for a request to be formulated by CONUP dealing with data gathering and processing, or research, or textbook procurement, or overhauling the admissions procedure on a national scale or coordinating programs of foreign study by university professors. The problem may be, however, that a vicious circle is operating. The organization cannot find time to draw up a request for help, and without help, it cannot deal with the problems that are filling the limited time and sapping talent available to the organization.

At the secondary and primary levels, the U.S. government might be more open to requests from agencies outside the Ministry of Education than it has been in the past. When discussing multilateral and bilateral assistance above, I suggested establishing a commission to make allocations comprised of non-Ministry as well as Ministry people.

What are the priorities governing resource allocation? From one perspective, we have arrived at the really crucial set of questions to be answered. Policy should depend on the educational "needs" identified. The amount, conditions, mechanisms for transfer, and receiving agencies may differ depending on whether literacy training or equipment for a science laboratory in a university is deemed more important.

From another perspective, decisions about the final disbursement of foreign assistance funds are second-level or third-level decisions. Policy goals must first be clearly established within which identified needs are to be judged. Another previous decision involves whether or not to channel all assistance through an international agency or through a Peruvian organization that will then make decisions about the investments. If the latter choice is made, the implication is that the United States would be willing to live with allocation decisions of a multilateral or Peruvian agency handling U.S. money, even though the United States might disagree with the use to which the funds were put. Such a posture might seem naive, but might be defended on at least two grounds. First, there is little evidence that the U.S. "experts" have been able to avoid mistakes;

they have no monopoly on the wisdom of allocation. Second, learning to allocate funds wisely may be a trial-and-error process. The most important result of assistance, then, may be to help Peru and Peruvians discover themselves and to arrive at a better policy through trial and error.

Wherever the decisions are made, the first and most important level at which the question "for what?" must be attacked is that of choosing between allocating funds to educational or noneducational projects. As indicated by my analogy between education and a miracle drug, my own feeling is that education should not be overdone; that massive injections of education will have little effect unless other features of the social setting are changing at the same time. Perhaps the United States would perform a service for Peru at this point in time by refusing to give educational aid, thus providing an excuse for decreasing the relative investments in education by the government until the social and economic social structure brings expectations and opportunities more closely in line or until an evaluation can be made. But Peruvian investment in education cannot stop altogether. Hence, a series of choices must be faced (whether by Peruvians, multilateral agencies, or the United States) concerning the manner in which those resources to be devoted to education will be allocated within the broad field of education.

Consider, for instance, the choice between investing in formal versus nonformal education. If it is decided that emphasis should be placed on education outside the schools, we should be led to consider such a possibility as creating incentives for U.S. and other industry in Peru to invest beyond the level that they might ordinarily invest in the training of Peruvians.

Rather than try to elaborate on a long list of projects, let me simply round out the discussion by listing several major areas of choice: public versus private education, rural versus urban education, primary versus secondary versus higher education, and technical versus general education.

Conclusions

First, policy might *emphasize the decision process* rather than the results of the decision process. That is, resources might be directed toward improving the ability of people and institutions to make decisions rather than toward a series of specific outcomes such as increasing primary enrollments to a certain percentage of the age group. Such a policy orientation might lead to Peruvian-U.S. agreement concerning the following kinds of requests: money for CONUP (or other organizations responsible for making allocation decisions) to improve the information base from which decisions are made; resources for training decision makers, particularly in the art of evaluating information that is (or could be) made workable; or funds for short-term researchers and consultants on specific issues that the organization does not feel are within its specific competence and for which training is out of the question.

Second, this is *a time for listening*. Listening is an active process, but it does not necessarily lead to additional initiatives. Indeed, this is a time *for communicating*, not for taking initiatives.

Third, if there is to be effective communication between Peruvians and North Americans regarding the desirability of one versus another form of cooperation for Peruvian development, it will be essential for U.S. policy makers to admit that independence from foreign vulnerability is indeed an existing and legitimate Peruvian goal. It will also be necessary to establish to what degree the goal is sought for its own sake (even though it competes with economic growth) and to what degree it is seen as a prerequisite to economic growth or redistribution.

One of the most obvious means of dealing with the desire for self-determination would be to withdraw from *all* forms of providing assistance, noting that the Peruvian desire for independence requires withdrawal and that the desire coincides nicely with the growing neo-isolationist sentiment that characterizes much of the United States today. It does not follow, however, that the best interests of either the United States or Peru would be served by a neo-isolationist posture, even though that might be the easiest position to take at this time.

To react too strongly to the Peruvian drive for international independence would be to respond in terms of only one goal. It is highly probable that the government of Peru, as it pursues multiple and conflicting goals, does not feel massive retreat by the United States would be in its best interest. Presumably, the Peruvian desire for both economic growth and for redistribution can still provide a meeting ground as goals that are in the best interests of both parties. And education seems to be one area that can serve both growth and redistribution goals simultaneously. The problem, then, becomes one of exploring alternatives to bring mutual benefit with the limiting consideration that such alternatives should also serve to reduce Peruvian dependence on the United States or, more positively, to enhance Peruvian self-determination.

Finally, the inevitable uncertainty associated with efforts by societies to change themselves dictates *flexibility*—both institutional and intellectual flexibility—from those responding to that change. Institutional flexibility might include simply cutting red tape so that existing mechanisms can work more easily, or it might require elaborating entirely new forms for responding to Peruvian initiatives. Intellectual flexibility within the field of education implies a broad view of education as linked to other social institutions and a freedom from our contemporary preoccupation with schooling and with the "goodness" of all education. Intellectual flexibility also implies an acceptance of uncertainty, of instability, and of conflicting social goals, not the least of which is the goal of self-determination.

Dan C. McCurry

12. U.S. CHURCH-FINANCED MISSIONS IN PERU

THE SEARCH FOR A USEABLE FUTURE

The world's political forecasters traditionally overlook the power of organized religion. Like other major institutional powers, the Church is beset by dissent and demands for change, yet it remains firmly wedded to the existing structures of power. A discussion of U.S. missionary presence in Peru, then, cannot view the Church as a locally influenced pastoral structure, but rather as an international nonprofit corporation directed by boards of professional managers and represented by long-established branch offices in Peru.

Perhaps the most permanent political consequences affected by the U.S. missionary presence in Peru are those cultural value orientations these foreign churchmen have promoted during their stay. The primary missionary "message" is the direct or indirect stimulation of new wants, and, since over one-third of these North American clergymen are devoting full-time to "economic development" or "technical assistance" projects, the social attitudes and goals implicit in these activities should be closely examined.

In the 1960s a large migration of U.S. Catholic missionaries and the continuing expansion of U.S.-initiated Pentecostal groups in

Peru have brought to the religious situation the same developmental models that the Alliance for Progress brought to the economic order. Both were ahistorical structures directing Peruvians toward a U.S.-model working class that supported the continuing power of Peru's herodian elites. Mission dollars were funneled into an educational system far beyond the aspirations of the majority of Peruvian children—a system which suffices only to teach the little-schooled the superiority of the better-schooled and trains the elite in those skills necessary to maintain their control of the institutional ties between external and internal colonialism.

U.S. missionary participation in the "developmental" process has been narrowly defined as the teaching of values of hard work and high consumption, and of the attainment of modest skills to improve industrial or agricultural performance. This production-model ignores basic questions about the quality of life in Peruvian society and the *relation between goods and the "good life."* Developmental concepts centered on affluence cannot possibly deal with the Peruvian problems of structural legitimacy, identity, and freedom, and most U.S. missionaries are culturally blind to these qualitatively different patterns of possibility.

Through a politics of humanitarian relief, missionary societies have conducted massive give-away programs in a "welfare department" solution to the poverty endemic to Peruvian political structures. The indirect effect of this "charitable" activity has been the preservation of a dependency system within the Peruvian Church and of reinforcing the structural relationships of an external imperialism that has bound the human needs of Peruvians to an image of esteem and freedom intolerably threatening to the present position of the United States.

The following analysis indicates that U.S. missions have traditionally been an integral element of U.S. policy in Peru. There is little, however, to indicate that this missionary effort will find a useable Peruvian future.

THE ROMAN CATHOLIC CHURCH IN PERU

In the 1960s the impact of the Alliance for Progress has produced several perceptive studies of the Latin American Church. These investigations, conducted by both North and Latin Americans, have developed a general emphasis that the Latin American Church achieves its influence and social control not on its capacities as a Christian religious system, but from the support Church leaders give to the existing powers and from their multiple involvements in education, social welfare, and administration. This is an equally appropriate description of the United States religious establishment and its representative bodies in Peru.

Unlike nineteenth-century mission efforts that portrayed a world of social conflict and disorganization, we have now entered a period of structures and operations in which an emphasis on "consensus" and missionary "organization" is premised on the unquestioned legitimacy of the existing political order. The conceptual frames of reference for most studies of the Latin American Church are, then, devised so as to demonstrate this balance in society. "Objective criteria acknowledge an equilibrium and any opposition becomes a 'value judgment.' "

This methodology overlooks the dialectical and Manichean nature of life and is totally inadequate in explaining the states of real conflict and societal flux in Peru. In attempting to transplant an equilibrium model, a vision of orderly change in Peru, United States Protestant and Catholic missionaries have served to reinforce the power of the governing elites. The impotence of such a world view is manifest in the internal struggles of contemporary Peruvian Catholicism.

In his recent study, Ivan Vallier has discerned four patterns of development within the Latin American Catholic Church that are immediately applicable to the Peruvian situation.[1]

1. During the seventeenth century, an unbridgable gap developed between the institutional church and the "Catholic" religion. A shortage of clergy and the hierarchy's fusion with ruling elites brought a structural impotence to hold the formal loyalties of a people who turned to a "Catholicism" grounded in brotherhoods, feast days, and devotional groups.

2. Emerging from this cleavage as a series of isolated units, structurally undeveloped and divided, the Church's elite rulers have yet to articulate a unified stand as *religious* leaders.

3. With its energies primarily directed to political maneuvering

[1] Ivan Vallier, "Religious Elites: Differentiations and Developments in Roman Catholicism," in Seymour Martin Lipset and Aldo Solari, eds., *Elites in Latin America*, (Oxford: Oxford University Press, 1967), pp. 180–223.

in other power groups, the Church has seldom initiated or responded to the emergence of new values within the society.

4. This continuing tie between political power and moral legitimacy has rearranged the differentiation process through which
cultures create the value orientations about the nature of the "good
society" and the mechanisms for its attainment.

In their 1969 assembly, the Peruvian bishops furnished a par-
ticularity to these insights in their acknowledgment that the Peruvian Church's primary goal of institutional survival had precluded
a significant response to the basic life-needs of its adherents.

With a population increase of 3–3.5 percent and a projected 1970
population of over 13.5 million Peruvians, these fundamental needs
find many new expressions. Over half of all newborn Peruvians
will live in the coastal areas where there is but one priest for every
4,160 Catholics. The Church's greatest structural growth has occurred in these coastal cities into which have poured large numbers
of U.S. Catholic missioners.

The 1955 papal call for North American Catholic organizations
to send 10 percent of their personnel to Latin America by the end
of the sixties has changed the complexion of U.S. missionary involvement in Peru. What before had been the relatively small-scale
task of such professed missionary groups as the Maryknoll Fathers
became the divinely commissioned duty of every religious congre-
gation, regardless of the training or aptitudes of their members.[2]

Peru received a disproportionately large number of these foreign-
born priests, but the bureaucratic beneficiaries of this largesse continued to search for more donors in this massive give-away program.

Conceived in surprise, executed in haste, and now abandoned in
frustration, this missionary invasion "was governed more by
strategy and tactics than by anything resembling policy criteria.
. . . The most glaring error was that it took place with the Peruvian
laity and clergy as passive bystanders."[3] Without the orientation of
even a provisionally defined policy, many U.S. missioners with-

[2] Edward R. Sunshine, S.J., "The Peruvian Church and American Missionary Work," prepared for the Peru Policy Project, Adlai Stevenson Institute, p.
13.

[3] David Farrell, C.S.C., "The North American Missionary in Peru," prepared
for the Peru Policy Project, Adlai Stevenson Institute, p. 5.

drew into their newly constructed enclaves and soon returned to the United States. For those who still remain, the personal crisis engendered by this aimless invasion of Peru has brought a commitment to find a new Peruvian identity and is one of the major characteristics of the U.S. missionary community.

That some of these U.S. missioners will be politically active is apparent in the March 1969 statement by 135 religious workers in Peru urging a careful consideration by the U.S. government of the crisis involving the International Petroleum Company's confiscation by the Peruvian military government. Asserting that property rights are not absolute and that property may rightly be subjected to the needs of the common good, these missionary migrants further maintained that the present complex form of economic, political, and cultural domination by the United States in Latin America, for the most part unconscious, has not been solving Latin America's development problems; in my view it has been aggravating them.[4]

Such a prominent presence of U.S. missionaries in Peruvian affairs has a strong tradition in the work of two Maryknoll priests, Dan McClellan and Robert Kerns. Since their arrival in 1943—detoured from China by World War II—the Maryknoll Fathers have been oriented toward the creation of a New England–model working class among Andean and coastal peasants, a task in which Fathers McClellan and Kerns found some significant success.

Dan McClellan came to Peru in 1950 and was assigned to the altiplano. Five years later his work in the San Juan parish of Puno had initiated a workers credit union that soon expanded into a unique financial cooperative movement throughout Peru. With the 1964 passage of the national cooperative law, Father McClellan came to Lima where he started the Mutual del Pueblo, a savings and loan association for worker housing. Recently awarded the Peruvian government's Order of the Golden Condor, Father McClellan represents the most successful practitioner of the socioeconomic, neocapitalistic emphasis of Maryknoll during the 1950s.

The previous policy of Peruvian missioners was a strong emphasis on "native vocations" and its best representative is Father

[4] "Statement by a Group of United States Religious and Lay Volunteers on the IPC Case—An Appeal for Justice," (Lima: Centro de Información Católica, March, 1969).

Robert Kerns. Known as "Mr Puno" Father Kerns lived in the altiplano from 1943 to 1959 as the founder and director of Indian radio schools in Puno. Broadcasting daily to an estimated twenty thousand Quechua and Aymara, these radio schools are the most visible Maryknoll missions in Peru. (A brief experiment with a television station in Puno has recently ended with its sale to a large commercial chain in Lima).

Without special relationships with dioceses in the United States, the initial work of both McClellan and Kerns would have received far less publicity and financial support. Other U.S. dioceses with priestly ties to Peru are from Ogdensburg, New York; Buffalo, New York; Bridgeport, Connecticut; and Jefferson City, Missouri. The major U.S. orders in Peru are the Marianist Fathers, the Maryknoll Fathers, the Holy Cross Fathers, the Jesuit Fathers, the St. James Fathers, and the Augustinian Fathers.

Financed mainly through small contributions from the United States, the work of these U.S. orders and dioceses priests is greatly assisted by periodic gifts from large U.S. corporations in Peru. As in the United States, the major Peruvian Catholic universities culti- vate these wealthy benefactors in Grace & Company, Marcona Mining, and International Petroleum Company. One of the most prominent of such gifts was the donation by I.P.C. of an entire building to the Catholic University in Arequipa.

The U.S. missionary effort in Peru has passed through three dis- cernible stages: (a) the Marianist presence in the 1930s was direct- ed to the provision of a "liberal education" to those elite groups whose future was tied to the United States; (b) the Maryknoll arrival in 1943 brought a professional sociocultural emphasis on "native vocations" with the establishment of radio schools and agri- cultural cooperatives; and (c) the 1960s missionary migration that emphasized free-floating staff positions within the Church institu- tions. Presently, however, the defining action of Peruvian Catholi- cism is not occuring through official Church structures, but rather in the deliberations of a highly skilled group of social analysts, priests, and labor leaders organized in 1968 as the National Office of Social Information (ONIS). Hindsight informs us that only when faced with ONIS demands for which it had no institutional replies was the U.S. missionary hierarchy clearly aware of its own lack of policy orientation.

The Catholic Church in Peru, like other Latin American churches, began a process of modernization only in the 1960s. In 1937 Archbishop Pascual Farfán of Lima reminded Peruvians that "poverty is the most certain road to eternal felicity. Only the state which succeeds in making the poor appreciate the spiritual treasure of poverty can solve its social problems."[5]

This position was not officially challenged until 1958 when the Peruvian hierarchy composed their first important joint pastoral letter attacking social problems and demanding an increased application of the principles of distributive justice.[6]

Soon after this 1958 bishops' letter, a few Lima priests associated principally with student and worker groups began regular discussions on the pastoral and theological priorities promoting social justice. The principal figures in these discussions were the Alvarez Calderón brothers, Carlos and Jorge, and a brilliant theologian, Gustavo Gutiérrez Merino.

At the same time, another more politically oriented group of clergy and other religious, including Romeo Luna-Victoria, S.J., was organized. The orientation of this caucus is well illustrated in Luna-Victoria's 1966 work entitled *Ciencia y práctica de la revolución* and published with the imprimatur of both the Jesuit order and the archbishop of Lima.

The impact of these discussions was felt mainly within ecclesiastical circles until early March 1968, when Romeo Luna-Victoria brought together at Cineguilla many priests and laity connected with the Movimiento Sindical Cristiano (Christian Trade Unions). This site east of Lima was purchased by the German Adenauer Solidarity Foundation for the use of the Instituto Nacional de Formación Trabajadores (INFT) as a training center for Peruvian Christian trade unions. The participants spanned the Peruvian Catholic labor movement from the young North American dominican Henry Camacho to the older leader of Catholic Social Action in Peru, Augusto Camacho, who in 1955 was an early advocate of

---

[5] *Carta pastoral de Pedro Pascual Farfán con motivo de la proxima festividad de Santa Rosa de Lima*, Lima, 1937, cited by Fredrick B. Pike, "The Catholic Church and Modernization in Peru and Chile," *Journal of International Affairs* 28, no. 2 (1966): 287.

[6] See Fredrick B. Pike, "The Modernized Church in Peru: Two Aspects," *The Review of Politics* 26, no. 3 (1964): 307.

the clerical approach to trade unionism offered by the new Christian Democratic party.

Coming out of the Cineguilla meeting was (1) the establishment of an organization—ONIS—to maintain regular weekly discussions and (2) a strong declaration documenting and condemning social injustice in Peru. This "Declaration of Cineguilla" was drafted by a committee headed by Luna-Victoria and released during the last week in March 1968 to a mixed reception by the Lima press. *La Prensa* ignored it, but *El Comercio*, strongly campaigning against the government's position on the International Petroleum Company, gave the Cineguilla declaration full coverage. Peruvian churchmen had never spoken so loudly and corporately against the maldistribution of wealth.

The reaction of Cardinal Juan Landazuri Ricketts, a Franciscan from an old family of Arequipa oligarchs, could not be anticipated. Upon the receipt of an honorary doctorate from the University of Notre Dame two years previously, Cardinal Ricketts proclaimed that "we are totally aware of the course of the social revolution. We identify with it."[7]

From this position, the cardinal gave weak but encouraging support to the ONIS statement. In turn, members of ONIS have been instrumental in the socially progressive statements issued by the Peruvian hierarchy at Medellin, and most importantly, in the January 1969 declaration of the Peruvian bishops.

Not present at the March Cineguilla meeting was the group of clergy including the Alvarez Calderóns and Gustavo Gutiérrez, who considered that their theological and pastoral concerns would be lost in the political debate of ONIS. However both pastoral and political concerns came together in July, 1968, for the first national ONIS meeting in the Center for Social Action at Chimbote. Including many more politically conservative churchmen than were present at Cineguilla, the hundred registered participants elected Jorge Alvarez Calderón as the first president of ONIS's four-man executive board.

Both the pastoral and political emphasis of ONIS claimed nation-

[7] "Discurso del Cardenal Juan Landazuri Ricketts, Primate of Peru," University of Notre Dame, Indiana, June 5, 1966, in *Signos de Renovación*, compiled by Comisión Episcopal de Acción Social Lima, 1969, p. 81.

al attention as events within the Church and government reached a climax. At the end of July, Luna-Victoria, who had lectured at the CAEM (Center for Higher Military Studies) gave the major "Fiestas Patrias" speech to the army. (The present military government acknowledges that the social philosophy informing their political goal has its source in the CAEM, and Luna-Victoria's writing continues to find a receptive ear from the government.) Likewise, the Second General Conference of Latin American Bishops (CELAM II) meeting in Medellin, Colombia, August 24–September 6, echoes much of the work of Gustavo Gutiérrez, the aide of Cardinal Ricketts.[8] Particularly in those documents on peace and justice that legitimize an ideology of radical social change is Gutiérrez's influence clearly evident.[9]

The Medellin statements found immediate interpretation in the Peruvian context, and in September ONIS issued a paper strongly criticizing the Peruvian government for signing a secret "eleventh page" agreement with International Petroleum Company. While the existence of this "eleventh page" has yet to be determined, its rumored reality was sufficient to lend support to the October 3 military coup.

With the expropriation of IPC and other social reforms enacted by the new military government, ONIS was organizing for comparable ecclesiastical changes at the January, 1969, conference of Peruvian bishops. Weekly columns appearing in *Oiga* and other periodicals urged the bishops to strongly condemn the structural and class exploitation in Peru. The bishop's response was an invitation for clerical and lay advisers to attend the assembly, and Jorge Alvarez Calderón and Gustavo Gutiérrez attended as the most prominent exponents of the ONIS position.

Few bishops were comfortable in signing the final assembly statement, which officially acknowledged that "these unjust conditions (of poverty) are not isolated facts in time and space: they are the consequences of a process of world dimensions characterized by

[8] See David Albos, "The Medellin Conference," *Cross-Currents* 19, no. 2, pp. 112–133.

[9] See also Gustavo Gutiérrez Merino, "From Colonial Church to Medellin," prepared for 1970 CICOP Conference, Washington, D.C., and published (mimeograph) by Latin American Department of U.S. Catholic Conference.

a concentration of economic and political power in the hands of a very few, and an international imperialism of money which cooperates in complicity with the Peruvian oligarchy."[10]

ONIS observers and advisers, however, found an official sanction of their efforts in the bishop's call for "concrete acts" of identification with the poor. Within the month, priests meeting in Chimbote approved the organization of ONIS Norte to concentrate on the social-pastoral problems of northern Peru. A number of these priests soon found themselves involved in a controversy that split the hierarchy and led to the recall of the aristocratic papal nuncio, Romolo Carboni.

Strikers in the steel mill at Trujillo had enlisted the economic and propaganda support of several foreign and Peruvian priests in the area. To focus attention on their struggle, the strikers' wives and children occupied the cathedral of the conservative archbishop of Trujillo. While this three-day occupation of the cathedral was in progress, another symbol of oligarchical power was also under attack by Trujillo priests.

At the dedication of an expensive new building for the Trujillo Country Club, priests and students issued newspaper declarations and demonstrated against this blatant example of oligarchical wealth. Citing the recent bishops' statement as well as the Medellin and Vatican II positions of the Church, and in line with the ONIS position, these young clerics called for the destruction of the oligarchical class in Peru.

Two priests were arrested at the country club, and the archbishop quietly ordered them to leave their parishes. However, with the ensuing publicity and plans for a large demonstration of laity in front of the archbishop's home, civil authorities persuaded the archbishop to allow these ONIS priests to remain in their positions.

A few weeks later, an Italian priest, who had vehemently opposed the ONIS priests, was appointed auxiliary bishop of Trujillo, and in angry response many priests and workers walked out of the cathedral during his official designation. The Italian papal nuncio, Romolo Carboni, was outraged at this challenge to the nomination of an Italian auxiliary bishop and to the authority of his good friend the archbishop of Trujillo. In both secret and open letters to

[10] *Signos de Renovación*, p. 256.

officials in the Church and in government, the nuncio denounced the protesting ONIS priests as clowns and disruptive elements. The frequency and vehemence of these attacks finally forced Cardinal Ricketts to publically remind the nuncio that ecclesiastical discipline was the responsibility of the Peruvian hierarchy. The papal delegate had openly challenged the hierarchy to punish these "rebel priests," but his intervention had the effect of forcing the hierarchy to reaffirm their support of such social activism by the clergy.

Carboni had been a major figure in the Peruvian Church since his arrival in 1960. Maintaining an incredible correspondence with the United States, he was the man most responsible for attracting the huge U.S. invasion of personnel and money into Peru during the past decade. While accustomed to meddling in Peruvian Church affairs far beyond the scope of his office, the cardinal's public rebuke of the nuncio's attack on the ONIS priests led to the rather rapid replacement of Rome's representative.

Other foreign clergy in Peru have likewise been the focus of ONIS attention. Of the approximately 150 U.S. priests now working in Peru, around forty are active participants in ONIS discussions. In July and August of 1969, the U.S. Dominican priest Henry Camacho was instrumental in calling a series of meetings to concentrate on the role of foreign Church aid in Peru. These assemblies urged a public accounting of all foreign Church funds spent in Peru as well as a reevaluation of the role of foreign clergy. One of the major goals of ONIS, particularly of ONIS Norte, has been the "integration of foreign clergy into the Peruvian reality." Non-Peruvian Church personnel are continually challenged by this examination.

The second national ONIS meeting was held in Lima in October, 1969. At this crucial point in its development, the organization faced two options: it could enlarge its base to include other groups that were not so pastorally oriented, or it could remain small and maintain and refine its theological and pastoral concern. The presence of several bishops, foreign clergy, and a number of highly qualified social analysts was reflected in the assembly's conclusions, calling for a *concientización* and popular participatin in the process of structural change, continued clerical assistance in the struggles of labor unions, the periodic and public disclosure of all Church properties, and the renunciation of all privileges and legal ties to the State. These ONIS delegates opted for a continuing pastoral focus but with a political analysis of the social reality, which is the principal object of Church concern.[11]

With this decision to expand its constituency, ONIS has acquired a political power unavailable to any other group of Latin American priests. Unlike the explicit Church support for the Chilean Christian Democrats in the 1964 elections and, due to the openness of Cardinal Ricketts, far less polarized against the hierarchy and government than are the Golconda priests of Colombia, ONIS has emerged at the fortuitous juncture of a radical reorientation of the Church's social policy and a comparably revolutionary political activity by the present military government. Within the *ambiente* created by this new ideological convergence of political and ecclesiastical structures, ONIS has found a sympathetic audience. However, power is never willingly surrendered, and it is very unclear that the power of decision in Peru is, indeed, changing ideological hands.

A major function of organized religion remains the legitimation of governmental activity. ONIS has effectively performed this role for the present military junta. President Velasco gave specific mention to ONIS in his June, 1969, promulgation of the new agrarian reform, and due both to history and constituency, ONIS is the most apparent ideological voice in the Christian trade union struggles. The social policies of the military government may have muted the Medellin warning that the Church's tendency is to dissuade people that there is any radical error in the way society is structured and that, in time, these institutions will correct the present imbalance.

ONIS now poses a significant challenge to those official agencies of U.S. policy whose survival depends on sterilizing organized opposition to their Peruvian activities. But in both State and Church, the ONIS challenge may well be co-opted in colonialist structures' seemingly endemic ability to absorb opposition. This realism (or pessimism) must finally be tempered by the spirit of hope that emerged at Medellin—a spirit that may yet empower a revolution in Peru.

[11] *Conclusiones del Segundo Encuentro Nacional de Sacerdotes de O.N.I.S.*, mimeographed.

THE PROTESTANT PRESENCE

The history of Peruvian Protestants began with the 1821 visit to Lima of Reverend James Thompson of the British and Foreign Bible and School Societies.[12] Reverend Thompson remained for only two years to establish two Lancasterian schools for mass literacy training, and was followed in 1825 by Reverend John C. Brigham touring Latin America for the American Board of Commissioners for Foreign Missions. This initial period of Protestant interest ended abruptly with Dr. Brigham's recommendation that no further initiatives be encouraged in Peru for several years.

Various U.S. merchants sold bibles and held small Protestant services in Peruvian coastal cities, but the establishment of regular Protestant worship was left to the British commercial interests of Lima and Callao. In these cities, the guano trade had attracted a colony of several hundred English artisans, traders, and technical men who requested from their consulate a place for Protestant services. So as to circumvent the constitutional prohibition against "cults," the Anglican church established services in the British consulate under the Consular Chaplaincy Act of England. As this church, founded in 1849, was solely for the English-speaking community and did not engage in overt proselytizing, it was allowed to exist without harassment by Catholic officials.[13]

The U.S. government was first involved in Protestant missionary activity in Peru with the 1890 arrest of an American Bible Society agent, an Italian Protestant, Francisco Penzotti. Imprisoned in Arequipa for his aggressive proselytizing, Penzotti was soon released under the direct order of President Manuel A. Caceres. Arrested again in Callao, this Italian colporteur was jailed on the grounds of holding a constitutionally prohibited *public* Protestant service. The case wound its tortuous way through the Peruvian Supreme Court where, despite strenuous efforts by the Peruvian Catholic hierarchy to obtain a conviction, Penzotti was finally freed. (The American Bible Society, through its influential board of directors, appealed directly to Secretary of State Blaine, who then sent word to Consul

[12] James Thompson, *Letters on the Moral and Religious State of South America* (London: British and Foreign Bible Society, 1827), p. 45.

[13] Wenceslao Oscar Bahamonde, "The Establishment of Evangelical Christianity in Peru (1822–1900)," Ph.D. dissertation, Hartford Seminary Foundation, 1952, pp. 120–135.

Hick in Lima to work immediately for the release of Penzotti from prison.)

This liberal constitutional decision opened the national borders to numbers of Protestant missionaries. Catholics strongly resisted this Protestant presence, but an armed attack on a missionary service by the bishop of Puno so aroused the liberals in Congress that a constitutional amendment was approved in 1915 that abolished the restrictions on non-Catholic worship. With the exception of local skirmishes, this congressional action effectively removed the Protestant presence from the arena of national conflict.

A present crisis centers on the assumed abuse by the rapidly growing Pentecostal groups of the duty-free privilege granted by the Peruvian government to all goods imported "for religious purposes." Under the threat that Peru will revoke this privilege, Church World Service—the major Protestant conduit for U.S. church-financed food shipments into Peru—is attempting with little success to preserve this duty-free license.

An expansion of the U.S. church has been a major consequence of its abuse of tax-free privileges. In Peru, this parasitic exploitation finds expression as Protestant policy alternatives turn from articles of faith to matters of finance. The following examination of past missionary policies clearly indicates this economic undergirding and ideological orientation.

Past Policies of U.S. Missionaries: 1960–1968

The "idea of mission" that brought U.S. Protestant and Catholic clergy to Peru during the 1960s was strategically different from the impulse to spread the U.S. national cult that had governed past missionary efforts. Issued in Rome as a "papal call for Latin American service" and in Washington as an "Alliance for Progress," this new and more sophisticated mission strategy successfully promoted an increase in all areas of U.S. activity in Peru.

These expanded ecclesiastical relations brought large numbers of men and funds, particularly from the U.S. Catholic Church, into Peru. To report on these meanderings of this missionary migration throughout Latin America, the Maryknoll Fathers established in Lima a regular English publication, *Noticias*, of the Catholic Information Service. The following account by a Maryknoll journalist, Joseph Michenfelder, who was associated with *Noticias* through most of the 1960s, is illustrative of the policy patterns active among U.S. Catholic missioners in Peru during the 1960s.[14]

U.S. Catholic Presence

In the wake of radical theological renewal sponsored by Vatican Council II (1962–1965) and the Medellin Bishops Conference (1968), profound ecclesiastical reforms have swept across Latin America, all but obliterating previous "policies" of the 750 North American missioners working in Peru. While significant vestiges of the pre-Conciliar, pre-Medellin Church surely remain, the overwhelming thrust of the present and future generations of North American religious personnel in Peru is 180 degrees removed from the rationale, mystique, and "policies" of the immediate past.

There is a problem of nomenclature—specifically, with the word "policies." The use of that term vis-à-vis the North American mission effort in Peru from 1960 to 1968 is a misnomer. For the fact is that North American Church authorities in Peru never really fashioned, much less articulated, a body of policy in the classical sense. If they and their subordinates related in any sense at all to policy, it would have been solely in reference to a centuries-old principal, universally revered by all Roman Catholics, namely, the Gospel-derived mandate "to establish the Church" throughout the world.

Forced, therefore, to perform apostolically without a body of policy, North American priests, sisters, brothers, and lay volunteers contrived a *modus operandi*. Although essentially intuitive in origin and involving diverse groups of missioners separated by great distances, this *modus operandi* embodied common, interlocking components, all oriented toward *expediency*. Predictably, these components molded into a sturdy rationale, induced among the missioners a heady, contagious mystique, and, in the existential order, evolved rapidly into surrogates for a body of policy. The most comprehensive approach to this phenomenon is to identify the major surrogates, describe them operationally and permit the reader to evaluate them from his own empirical sources. In effect, such a schematic, albeit subjective, overview illustrates what was neither policy nor nonpolicy, but rather, *un*-policy. The un-policy statements (only space limitations prevent their being documented) that follow will be readily recognized by most North American missioners who served in Peru during the 1960–1968 period, as well as by a considerable number of Peruvians who either observed or were directly affected by the phenomenon.

[14] Joseph F. Michenfelder, "The Policies of the United States Catholic Church in Peru 1960–68," Peru Study Group, Adlai Stevenson Institute, mimeographed.

In the absence of a clearly defined, publicly articulated policy, the following missionary *practices* were both the substance and intent of U.S. missioner activities in Peru, 1960–1968. Their continuation should be rejected.

1. *Triumphalism.* Commit and deploy a maximum of North American religious personnel and monies to those remote "mission areas" of Peru deprived of pastoral ministry in order to balance priest-to-people ratios and to radically augment the number of baptisms, confessions, valid marriages, etc. Over the past two centuries, the preoccupation of missioners with numerical indices and construction of churches and schools as tangible evidence of "*establishing* the Church" is regarded as triumphalism.

2. *Enclavism.* Assert virtually total autonomy within the "mission area" (parish, prelature, diocese) and negotiate as much freedom of action as the situation permits in order to construct physical plants, assign personnel, develop apostolic works, allocate monies, generate funding abroad—with minimal interference from local, regional, or national authorities of the Peruvian Church or government.

3. *Paternalism.* Expedite the "establishing of the Church" according to North American norms, experiences, and structures. Then, as soon as possible, transfer the enclave enterprise to the "native clergy" and move on to other areas where the Church is "unestablished," i.e., in dire pastoral and economic circumstances. (In point of fact, this seldom if ever occurred in Peru. Instead, North American missioners began to perceive their enclaves as a network of power bases from which "fresh new ideas" could be launched, pastoral and socioeconomic "experiments" tested, social commitments (especially to the supposedly a-borning middle class) deepened and modular example displayed for the edification of the "native clergy.")

4. *Corporate executivism.* Create regional and national entities theoretically responsible to the Peruvian hierarchy but financed, staffed, and directed by North Americans for the purpose of "modernizing" the Peruvian Church vis-à-vis public relations, communications, funding, training, and formation programs by borrowing norms and guidelines developed by successful business corporations. (This component, still much in evidence in Peru, is often described as neo-Triumphalism.)

5. *Pan/Pax Americanism.* Avoid contacts or collaboration with indigenous organizations, movements, unions, media, political parties, and personalities regarded as "unfavorable" by the United States Embassy. (More often than not, an Embassy appraisal of "unfavorable" was a euphemism for Marxist or leftist and was conveyed to the North American missioners via the apostolic nuncio, Embassy political offi-

cers, USIS staff, and senior members of the U.S. business community in Lima.)

6. *Elitism*. U.S. religious maintain minimal social and professional contact with the Peruvian clergy, as missionaries consider the majority of Peruvian priests to be culturally and intellectually inferior to North Americans. (A small minority of Peruvian clergy, products of European training in pastoral and social sciences were regarded as dreamers, idealists, or leftists.)

7. *Ecclesiastical interventionism*. Cooperate closely, though not always openly, with the apostolic nuncio and his staff in maintaining Roman Curia hegemony at the expense of the authority and responsibility of the Peruvian hierarchy. (The cooperation between North American missioners and the apostolic nunciatura evidenced itself in a highly pragmatic fashion: the unilateral creation of new ecclesiastical jurisdictions [prelatures and diocese] and national offices, the soliciting of non-Peruvian personnel to staff and fund such entities, the nominating of bishops and prelates, the selection of scholarship candidates for studies abroad, and the suppression of indigenous social and political action movements of Peruvian priests and laity.)

8. *Anti-intellectualism*. Learn the languages of Peru and become familiar with the more obvious traditions and cultural traits in order to communicate adequately and perform ministerial tasks; but refrain from introducing sociological and anthropological studies or research into the pastoral programs directed by North Americans. Unable to speak to Peruvian cultural values and socioeconomic structures through the traditional forms of sacramental ministry imported from the United States, most missioners refused to search for a new analysis appropriate to the Peruvian reality.

9. *Frontierism*. Maintain priorities of action, funding, and personnel in the remote provinces or urban slums and avoid proportionate commitments to other sectors of national life such as labor unions, university community, military, artists, and oligarchs.

Without pretending to a full explanation, something should be said here about the basic homogeneity of the North American missioners— a quality that readily assured the viability of the *modus operandi*, and its major components as just described. Apart from their origins (middle class, heavily Irish Catholic, and largely from the northeastern United States) they possessed much in common by way of religious and cultural formation. The Roman Catholic schools, seminaries, convents, and institutes that trained them bequeathed an almost identical dependency upon credal faith, dogma, legal structures, and authority. As Catholic Americans they quite typically, though by and large unconsciously, reflected Anglo-Saxon prejudices vis-à-vis ethnic and national origins. Finally, they possessed all of the negative and positive characteristics (beginning with a naive esprit de corps) endemic to the materialistic, bourgeois, preconciliar North American Roman Catholic Church that dispatched them to Peru. Thus their *modus operandi* in Peru was but an extension of their *modus vivendi* in the United States.

Had a body of policy existed, certainly much of what transpired never would have occurred at all. Further, it is agonizing to contemplate "what could have been" given the enormous human and financial religious resources that appeared on the Peruvian scene during those erratic years of nation building, resources concentrated for the most part in critical socioeconomic zones of the country. (The Maryknoll fathers and sisters, by way of their numerical strength [170], diversity of "apostolic works," twenty years experience in Peru, and remarkable prestige among Latin and North Americans alike, tended quite naturally to be pacesetters for the smaller, less-experienced communities of religious.) The latter were not, in point of fact, "professional missioners." Rather, they came to Peru during the late fifties and early sixties in response to Pope John XXIII's urgent appeal (1958) for North American religious personnel to offset the serious shortage of Latin American clergy and religious—especially in the provinces of the continent. (They would not have come otherwise.) Without implying that Maryknollers *consciously* promoted the body of un-policy outlined above, much of the onus rests with them. Indeed, their recent impressive internal reform, based on the documents of their 1966 General Chapter, is a kind of admission that their *modus operandi* in Peru and elsewhere was thoroughly incompatible with the signs of the times, and that authentic mission policy is indispensable to their own future and the future of the people they hope to serve as instruments of liberation. [End of Michenfelder quotation]

U.S. Protestant Presence

In contrast to the 750 U.S. Catholic clergy and other religious working in Peru at the opening of the 1960s, Peruvian Protestantism's 94,000 members were served by only 168 U.S. missionaries and 258 native clergy.[15] For the most part, this Protestant community remains within the cultural orientation and ideological influ-

---

[15] Prudencio Damboriena, S.J., *El Protestantismo en América Latina*, vol. 2 (Fribourg: FEPES, 1963), p. 18.

ence of United States missioners, almost one-third of whom were associated with Pentecostal, Adventist, or independent churches.

Protestant missioners, unlike their Catholic counterparts, found no large body of adherents in Peru, and thus, instead of attracting a wayward membership to an active participation in their churches, these Protestant clergy sought to convert citizens to their own denominational stance. To be sure, the "mainline" Protestant groups sought much missionary support in their internal struggles with *los pentecostales*, but the main thrust of missionary efforts was an increase in urban membership.

Rather than face the difficulties of rural or small-town Peruvian life, the missioners of "traditional" denominations have most often preferred the urban life of the upper-middle-class Peruvian. In the past, this urban ministry has entailed staffing the mission's schools, clinics, and churches with a bit of discreet proselytism and colportage on the side. In the main, the small clusters of urban converts preserved a U.S.-financed and missionary-guided Protestant outpost, which viewed its lack of growth as due more to Roman Catholic strength than to its own defined impotence.

The power of the U.S. missioner is by far the most significant factor in Peruvian Protestantism. The missionary organization contributed the founding, the form, the fundamentals of faith, and, most important, the funds on which the churches' existence depended. Periodically threatened by "native dissension" to those imposed ecclesiastical patterns, and most often under the direct administrative control of U.S.-based denominational headquarters, the Protestant missionary church in Peru was circumscribed in the following protective policy patterns:

1. *Messianic colonialism.* The first significant U.S. Protestant missionary presence appeared in Peru at the beginning of the twentieth century in conjunction with the expansionist period of U.S. "dollar diplomacy." With ideological support from the developing American empire, with a theological mandate from the biblical exhortation to "go forth into the entire world, preaching and baptizing," and with the financial backing of large U.S. businessmen living or operating in Peru, the missionaries naturally brought a style of U.S. church life congenial to all these interests. In program and architecture, through administration and exhortation, the mis-

sioner erected a North American–model church that effectively pointed the eyes of the faithful upward to the United States.

Difficulties with local officials brought instant recourse to the U.S. consul. Since local influential U.S. Protestant businessmen, as well as the Peruvian government's major financial supporters (the banks of J. P. Morgan and the International Petroleum Company of John D. Rockefeller) also had strong charitable interests in the denominational mission and American Bible Society efforts in Peru, the consul was usually able to resolve a conflict to the missionary's satisfaction. The Leguia governments were particularly vulnerable to such U.S. pressures.

After the financial cutbacks necessitated by the Depression of 1929 were partially restored, programs were greatly expanded. Those promising young national church leaders who might pose a threat to the missionary's power were sent to the U.S. seminaries for study and returned more thoroughly indoctrinated in the North American ecclesiastical mode. Likewise, the major function of local mission schools staffed by U.S. clergy and other religious was to train future exponents of basically New England–style educational methods.

In government as well President Leguia placed a highly visible team of Protestant, mostly non-Spanish-speaking North American educators in key administrative positions in the Ministry of Education. As might be expected, during their stay (1909–1912, 1919–1924) these Protestant administrators encountered stiff resistance from the Roman Catholic Church.[16]

2. *Anticommunism*. The contemporary focus of this colonial mentality and the stimulus for a frenzy of mission reevaluation during the last decade was the 1959 Cuban Revolution of Fidel Castro. A plethora of social-gospel rhetoric could not calm U.S. clerical fears of a communist power seizure in Peru, and missionary activity assumed a new importance as a "civilizing and pacifying" arm of United States foreign policy.

Under the Alliance for Progress emphasis, significant amounts of U.S. public and private funds entered Peru, with Protestant institutions, particularly schools and clinics, expanding their programs.

[16] Robert G. Myers, "Peruvian Educational Development and United States Policy," Peru Study Group, Adlai Stevenson Institute, mimeographed, p. 6. Cf. pp. 341–342.

Emerging spirits of ecclesiastical nationalism were effectively co-opted and their energies depleted through evangelistic crusades, fund-raising campaigns, and structural "reforms" designed to demonstrate the moral strength of the Church against "atheistic communist subversion." This tactic effectively retained missionary power and ideological orientation in most denominations until the struggle between "ecumenism" and "confessionalism" brought a crisis of leadership within most Protestant groups.

3. *Ecumenism.* Under this policy direction, Peruvian Protestants included not only discussions with Roman Catholics, but most especially cooperative ventures among various denominational groups. Due to a historically derived context of suspicion between the more "internationalist" and the regionally based mission foci, little interdenominational cooperation has, in fact, occurred.

Efforts by European mission organizations to brand early North American missionaries in Latin America as anti-Catholic colonialists intruding in an already Christian continent stimulated an energetic response from the U.S. Deeply resenting their exclusion from the 1910 Edinburgh World Missionary Conference, U.S. missionaries meeting in Panama in 1916 organized the New York-based Committee on Cooperation in Latin America (CCLA) to coordinate and publicize Protestant mission work in Latin America. Finally, in 1938 CCLA succeeded in seating Latin American Protestants as members of the International Missionary Council, thus obtaining a recognized legitimacy for continued Protestant activity in these Catholic nations.

With their own mission image now affirmed, the "distinctive American witness" of U.S. missioners in Peru felt little threatened by the 1948 association of their major denominations with the World Council of Churches. Ties with the U.S. home office remained strong, and Protestant churches were benefiting from the large postwar urban migrations into major Peruvian cities. However this short-lived security of "mainline" churches was soon challenged by the rapid growth of Peruvian Pentecostal groups.

Constantly on the defensive against the overwhelming Catholicity of Peruvians, the missionary's supportive relationships to the U.S. denominational hierarchy are of crucial importance. Finding his own funds reduced, faced with a seeming rejuvenation of the Catholic Church, and witnessing the progressive and costly social statements and activities of the World Council of Churches, the Protestant missionary felt that the denomination's neglect of his own work was due to an emphasis on ecumenical projects of dubious and nonbiblical character. Particularly acute was his antipathy for World Council of Churches relations with communist nations.

While inclined to agree with the necessity for many of the social initiatives urged by the World Council of Churches and his own denominational headquarters, and supportive of the ideals of the APRA and the programs of the Belaúnde Terry government, the "mainline missioner" was pushed toward a social conservatism by the rapid growth of Pentecostal groups in what had traditionally been his urban field of ministry. These autochthonous churches attributed their success to a fundamentalist teaching of the Scriptures, and in creating a strongly based local community of support they rejected the broader social involvements proposed from the United States. The Pentecostal expansion challenged the mainline missioner to a greater emphasis on his particular denominational creed, and it was just these creedal differences that the missioner maintained that international ecumenical movements had obscured.

Peru served as background and case study for this conflict when in July 1961, forty-five years after the first Panama Congress on Christian Work, there convened in Lima a Second Latin American Evangelical Conference. The findings of this Lima conference were significantly influenced by two previous Peruvian meetings: the harsh self-evaluation of the three hundred Catholic laymen at the 1958 Chimbote gathering of Inter-American Catholic Action, and the equally self-critical pre-conference meeting in Huampani of what later was known as ISAL or "Church and Society."

The findings of the Lima conference carried little of the commitment to action later present in the CELAM II meeting of bishops in Medellin. They were, however, sufficiently troublesome to many Protestant missionaries to necessitate the following reply from Dr. John A. MacKay, former Presbyterian missionary to Peru and later president of Princeton Theological Seminary: "The affirmation has been made that the Lima Conference was initiated by the World Council of Churches and was designed by the Council, in an allegedly subtle and sinister manner, to exercise a controlling influence upon the future development and policies of Latin American Churches. That affirmation is both groundless and untrue."[17]

Despite some cooperative efforts in the Peruvian Council of Foreign Voluntary Agencies in literature distribution and through other mass-communication ministries, the conspiratorial setting depicted by Dr. MacKay still hangs over the Peruvian Protestant community today.

4. *Pentecostalism and Confessionalism.* First seen in Peru with the Adventist and Methodist missions of the early twentieth century, the present "return to orthodoxy" of Pentecostal and confessional groups is more than a negative response to ecumenical pressures. This strict adherence to fundamental beliefs has always played a prominent role in Peruvian Protestantism and is now expanding due to an expressed need for clear doctrinal statements by Peruvians perplexed by rapid change. Confessionalism in Peru often looks to Europe as initiator of its movements, while Pentecostal and other independent missions are one-time appendages of the North American frontier revivalistic tradition.

Confessionalism and Pentecostalism both maintain a focus on "right doctrine" and a strong rejection of "syncretic" tendencies in Peruvian Protestantism. However the latter groups are continually strengthened through their response to and incorporation of just those localistic heritages condemned as "nondoctrinal" accretions to Catholic and main-line Protestant churches. In a growing assertion of ecclesiastical nationalism, many Protestants are attracted to these "indigenous" churches while viewing with strong suspicion the overtly paternalistic ties from the United States maintained on "main-line" churches.

Due to an increased emphasis on denominational divisions and the common pressures encouraging this isolationism, a much more directive policy is discernible for Peruvian Protestant missionaries than for their Roman Catholic counterparts. However, despite the absence of commonly articulated policies, both Protestant and Catholic missions exhibited quite similar ideological themes and programmatic orientations during the 1960s. The elite paternalism

[17] John A. MacKay, "The Latin American Churches and the Ecumenical Movement," Committee for Cooperation in Latin America, National Council of Churches, 1963, p. 2.

of U.S. Catholic missioners found sympathetic correspondence in a Protestant-variety colonialism. Furthermore, Pentecostal groups developed overt stances of anti-intellectualism and frontierism quite similar to the "un-policies" of North American Catholic clergy in Peru.

Within the U.S. missionary community in Peru, Protestants held a policy-making power that allowed for the acceptance of their social and theological positions within their own denominational enclaves, while Catholic missioners were often relegated to low-level positions in areas shunned by Peruvian clergymen. With the exception of a few priests such as Father Dan McClellan, the influence of U.S. Catholic missionaries was felt, not in the force of their individual decision makers, but in the large number of clergy and other religious who invaded Peru. In most cases, then, policy decisions were in the hands of the Peruvian Catholic hierarchy and the personalistic control of the U.S. Protestant missionary.

ALTERNATIVE POLICIES

Given our original premise that, in its policy role, the U.S. Church should be viewed as an international nonprofit corporation, those alternative goals realistically available for implementation are ideologically delimited by the actions of other powerful institutions. Rather than analyze policies for each of these structures (labor, universities, private industry/public corporations, foundations, Knights of Columbus, Protestants, and Other Americans United, etc.), this section assumes that a pragmatic, "politically conscious" governmental official will be knowledgeable of the positions of these power factors before recommending a policy directive. This first section is concerned with policies germane to the United States government, while part two is directed to those objectives possible for the North American ecclesiastical establishment.

While organized religion is maintained as a self-validating cultural faith and political palliative in both societies, Peru acknowledges a greater interdependence of the state and the Roman Catholic Church than does the United States, with its espoused heritage of ecclesiastical and governmental separation. Some foreign clergy in Peru, both Protestant and Catholic, concede a direct financial dependence on European state-supported churches or political parties.

North American missionaries, however, do not perceive that their receipt of Agency for International Development (AID) funds or their participation in Food for Peace and other United States government-financed programs is essential for their Peruvian work or in violation of U.S. constitutional traditions. While such denials find strong reinforcement in the infrequently observed North American traditions of ecclesiastical disestablishment and voluntary church financing, our cursory examination clearly indicates that the institutional church is de facto an increasingly important political element in Peruvian relations with the United States and that the activities of North American missioners in Peru have definite political implications for United States policy.

Following the 1915 Peruvian constitutional amendment permitting non-Catholic public worship, an informal "missionary policy" was developed. This full liberty of worship encouraged the arrival of many new Protestant missionaries, and conflicts between these North American Protestants and Peruvian Catholics found consular officials assuming the role of advocate and protector of the property and activities of these U.S. citizen-clergy. The utilization of ecclesiastical personnel in various Peruvian economic development projects financed by the United States government was expanded within the last decade by a large migration of North American priests and religious into the Peruvian Catholic Church. Presently, however, the economic and social reforms enacted by General Velasco's government and an increasing reduction of United States ecclesiastical and public-sector funds available to Peru have encouraged many North American missioners to seek an integration within this new "Peruvian reality" and to reject further ties of dependency on the United States.

A review of the United States missionary presence in Peru suggests a continuation of the following pattern: Both the Peruvian and United States governments will permit a relatively unrestricted interchange of ecclesiastical personnel and funds; and there will be a decrease in the United States' response and in the Peruvian Church's requests for such assistance.

In over a century of contact with North American clergy working in Peru, United States officials have developed—though not always consciously—a discernible "missionary policy." This idea of mission has remained the most active element in the United States' "civil religion" supported by both the ecclesiastical and political structures. These policy alternatives are thus directed to the financial and ideological sources of North American missionary presence in Peru—the U.S. church and other governing institutions of the United States.

Options Open to the U.S. Government

Given its traditional espousal of the separation of church and state, it would seem that the United States government should have no position or policy at all in regard to the North American missionary presence in Peru. Indeed, United States missioners should expect and demand a posture of *militant neutrality* from representatives of their government. This policy of refusing to supply AID and other government assistance to missionary-related programs should find strong lobbying opposition from some members of the Catholic and Protestant hierarchies of both nations. However, a welcoming support would emerge from those Peruvian and U.S. clergy who are sensitive to the U.S. presence—particularly its religious encroachment—and especially from other Peruvian leaders planning formal talks on the separation of the Peruvian state and church.

The present policy of *continuing collaboration* between missioners and U.S. agencies sacrifices the credibility of these clergy in exchange for the short-range benefits of information gathering, administrative skills, and for political support of other U.S. policies in Peru. This relationship also encourages missionaries to involve U.S. officials in those internal church conflicts where angels fear to tread and government risks serious entanglement.

A stance of *active opposition* to the U.S. missioner's work in Peru would probably remove the threat of this increasingly unreliable element of foreign policy, and would allow the elevation of a "benevolence and technical assistance" organization more fully in accord with the present goals of U.S. policy makers. The supplanting of this high-profile North American presence for a more sophisticated agency of U.S. policy should be quietly planned so as to avoid arousing ecclesiastical pressure groups at home.

Militant neutrality is a feasible policy objective only if the U.S. government wishes to convince Peruvians of the independence of U.S. institutions. Having adopted this stance, it then becomes imperative that North American missioners in Peru be allowed to voice publicly their *full* and *diverse* opinions on all questions of U.S. foreign poicy. The increasingly public missionary opposition to current U.S. policy in Peru should not be greeted with outrage by the Embassy, but rather supported as the right and obligation of any U.S. citizen. Such manifestations should be expected by the Embassy, and, particularly in regard to politically apathetic Protestant missionaries, public expression should be encouraged.

Attempts to use missioners as agents of information or as propaganda support for a given political line both compromises confidences given to clergy and destroys their credibility as agents of social change. Particularly in regard to the Roman Catholic faith, attempts to harness the Church to short-term U.S. policy interests would seriously weaken one of the few remaining arenas of U.S.-Peruvian conversation.

The Embassy should especially avoid any close association with Peruvian Protestantism. With the exception of groups such as the Summer Institute of Linguists and the Wycliffe Translators, Protestantism in Peru remains a symbol of North American cultural colonialism. Protestants, on the whole, reflect an enclave reaction to Peruvian social change and have offered little contribution to the revolutionary theological movements active there.

An important exception to this "hands-off" policy toward Peruvian Protestants is the necessary establishment of communication with the rapidly growing Pentecostal and Adventist groups. The denominational disposition of Protestant policy makers is toward the recognition of more traditional groups such as Presbyterians, Methodists, and Baptists, but the Peruvian Protestant community will soon be dominated by continually expanding Pentecostal and independent churches. The political strength of the large Pentecostal community in neighboring Chile demonstrates the importance of Embassy communication with their Peruvian counterparts.

A continuation of the present collaborative relationship between missionaries and U.S. agencies will entail an expansion of those individual briefings Embassy personnel informally maintain with missionaries, as well as increasing those institutional ties related to Food for Peace, technical training schools, agricultural and housing cooperatives, etc. In most cooperative arrangements, the U.S. gov-

ernment furnishes the funds and overall supervision while missionaries provide staff and daily program direction. Given the continued decline in U.S. missionary personnel, an escalation of U.S.
governmental employees involved may be necessary to maintain
even the present level of cooperative activity.

With his proper elevation to full membership on the U.S. "country team," the missionary would establish closer working relationships with Peace Corps, AIFLD, private foundations and corporations, the military advisory mission, university task forces, and
other U.S. presences in Peru. This integration with other U.S.
structures will be necessary to assure the missionaries' continued
stay in Peru. For in agreeing to a policy of further collaboration,
the missioner will be rejecting any future participation in Peruvian
struggles for liberation.

A policy of active opposition to the U.S. missionary presence in
Peru should have several carefully calculated elements—the most
essential of which is a low-profile approach. Otherwise the opposition of ecclesiastical lobbying groups would surely block its implementation.

This policy should be initiated with the reconsideration—on their
merits alone—of all funding requests from church-related missions
in Peru. Church personnel should be impressed that, in the changing Peruvian political climate, such U.S. governmental assistance
attaches the onus of colonialism to the receiving missionary agency
—a highly visible U.S. presence. The tightening of governmental
purse strings is a major tool to discourage further missionary efforts abroad.

American churches are in critical need of funds simply to maintain their present structures, and are thus highly vulnerable to
threats of an end to their tax-exempt status. In particular, the
Catholic Church faces certain termination of many of its educational, medical, and other charitable activities unless it receives
considerable federal assistance. These offer two important areas of
common concern that should be considered in the U.S. government's attempts to convince North American churches to terminate
their large outflow of dollars to Peruvian missions.

CARITAS remains another significant symbol of government-
missionary economic cooperation. In the past, it was an important
vehicle of U.S. missioner influence in Peru, but its food is now so

limited in amount, deficient in variety, and sporadic in delivery that the Peruvian government will probably cease to pay freight charges. Faced with the elimination of this program, missionaries will surely request that the U.S. government provide for CARITAS delivery. In accord with an opposition policy, this request should be denied. (Large quantities of U.S. disaster relief have entered Peru in response to the June 1970 earthquake that killed an estimated fifty thousand Peruvians. This crisis has increased the impact of humanitarian relief as an instrument of U.S. policy and thus temporarily provided the missionary administrators of this disaster assistance with the power to block any policy that threatens to terminate their funds.)

One of the major purposes of U.S. economic aid to the Church has been to effectively tranquilize militant political movements in Peru. The existence of groups such as ONIS testifies to the partial failure of this assistance, but the withdrawal of U.S. Catholic missioners might effectively neutralize this potent political force.

Radical Peruvian priests are especially vulnerable to the attacks of a conservative hierarchy. However, as ONIS membership includes leading representatives of U.S. mission societies, which contribute substantial numbers of personnel and funds to the Peruvian Church, some bishops have deemed it unwise to move against the activist Peruvian members of ONIS. Official U.S. governmental opposition to missionaries in Peru could remove them as allies of more radical Peruvian priests and thus encourage the demise of ONIS.

These tactics of governmental discouragement of U.S. clergy in Peru all presuppose that, in the long run, this North American Church presence will prove detrimental to U.S. policy goals. As in other forward-aid and relief policies, there is little likelihood that the U.S. government can maintain a consistent economic assistance program to the Peruvian Church. With the termination or decrease of such aid, the recipients are more dependent—and thus angrier—at the United States than when the assistance program was initiated. Peru is a good case of this general experience.

Finally, a multilateral policy approach to the U.S. missioner presence should prove more useful than the present bilateral perspective. Here government must incorporate and confront the interests of contending ecclesiastical systems. The Vatican and the World

Council of Churches constantly confront U.S. policy makers with diplomatic initiatives that, given the international character of the Peruvian missionary community, should be utilized to discover other "missioner policy" alternatives.

This approach has already proven effective in regard to U.S. support of Christian trade unions in Peru. Through Department of State encouragement, the German bishops and the Adenauer Foundation have donated sizeable funds for union organization in Peru. Due to this German investment the onus of paternalism has been partially removed from the United States.

Recognizing that the German bishops hold a large financial interest in Peruvian missionary activities and that many of these funds are used cooperatively in programs also financed and staffed by U.S. mission societies, the U.S. government might move indirectly through the German government to discourage this assistance to U.S. missionary work in Peru.

Likewise, the present expectation of large transfers of Vatican funds into economic development projects in Latin America presents serious policy considerations for the United States. Rome has both the funds and the power base to seriously challenge the U.S. economic hegemony in Latin America. The presence and influence of U.S. Catholic missionary societies now serving in Latin America may prove an important factor in this conflict.[18]

Options Open to the United States Church

Most of the considerations necessary to formulate alternative government policies are equally applicable for the Church's discussions and thus will not be repeated. Indeed, the character of U.S. civil religion poses interrelated consequences for bad policy decisions by either the government or the Church.

Government policy can ostensibly be articulated by a single voice, however the U.S. church presence in Peru speaks with at least three tongues: "traditional or main-line" Protestantism, Catholicism, and "ahistorical" or Pentecostal Protestantism. This characteristic of Pan American ecclesiastical anatomy strongly influences the policy control or influence that U.S.-based groups have on their missionaries in Peru.

[18] Simon Spivac, "The Vatican as a World Power," *Atlas* 19, no. 5 (May, 1970): 15–20.

For example, a unilateral policy decision by U.S. churches to immediately terminate contributions to Peruvian churches would have at least three different responses in Peru: (a) the traditional Protestant denominations, having a very weak base in Peruvian society and heavily dependent on the U.S. for financial survival, would quickly deteriorate into small enclaves of believers while most missionaries would leave the country; (b) in contrast, Pentecostal groups, which are largely self-sufficient and thoroughly grounded in a large support community, would suffer no fatal disruption and might offer to employ many of their missionaries who wished to remain; (c) Roman Catholic groups, on the whole, would be forced to withdraw from Peru. However, a significant number of priests and other religious would surely request permission to remain in Peru with the strong possibility that they could secure subsistence in programs funded from other Catholic or secular sources.

With only a few hundred U.S. priests and other religious in Peru, a determination by the missionary societies to cease sending personnel to Peru would require very little adjustment in their domestic activities in the United States. Likewise a decision to terminate personnel in Peru but to maintain other financial assistance to churches there would be no great administrative hardship. Politically, however, these decisions would cause great turmoil within both Protestant and Catholic hierarchies.

Latin America has received many missionaries who were withdrawn from the Orient in the wake of World War II and the creation of the People's Republic of China. These "old China missionaries" have also reached powerful administrative positions within U.S. churches, where they form a cohesive block to major cutbacks in their colleagues' work in Latin America. With the exception of some Pentecostal groups in Peru, the experience of the 1960s has convinced most missionaries that a larger investment of funds and personnel would not be of assistance to their work. The Catholic Church is still recovering from the massive inundation of U.S. clergymen during the 1960s and "main-line" Protestant denominations no longer have the funds to support a large missionary staff in Peru. Pentecostal groups, however, quickly establish self-supporting churches that free missionary funds and staff for other activities. In this case, a continuing U.S. missionary migration should strengthen and expand Pentecostal membership.

A policy of noninterference should be pursued by the U.S. missionary in response to internal Peruvian ecclesiastical disputes. However the internecine conflict apparent within both the Protestant and Catholic communities of Peru will have strong influence on political possibilities. In many traditional Protestant churches, anti-Catholicism and anticommunism have been replaced by anti-Pentecostalism, and the comparative decline in main-line Protestant membership has only increased the antipathy and conflict with Pentecostal and Adventist groups. While some U.S. denominational offices receive urgent requests for support in this internal Protestant struggle, only when the contending parties find their own Peruvian agreement will the Protestant community find peace.

Likewise, U.S. missioners' participation in the middle-class *cursillista* groups within Peruvian Catholicism should be reexamined in light of the hierarchy's recent decision to curtail *cursillista* activities. Unlike the social analysis/pastoral action orientation of ONIS, the *cursillista* movement is primarily a lay brotherhood sustained by a spiritualistic internationalization characteristic of many Peruvian Pentecostal groups. Their sacramental focus attracts large numbers of Peruvian faithful, including many U.S. missioners. However, an ideological struggle within the movement has created such turmoil within the entire Church structure that *cursillista* meetings have been officially forbidden. Missioner policy should respect the hierarchy's position.

A continued U.S. Church presence in Peru demands the development of selective criteria for funding recipient Peruvian Church agencies and for training U.S. missioners to work in Peru. The difficulties of establishing such criteria become evident in structuring policy alternatives for the withdrawal of all U.S. personnel from Peruvian education programs. Large numbers of U.S. religious are presently engaged in educational work that would become the responsibility of the Peruvian government if missioners were withdrawn. Such a decision would find stiff opposition in both the Peruvian hierarchy and government, and as few mission groups have clear understandings of the alternative styles of ministry needed in contemporary Peru, this policy of withdrawal could probably be revoked.

Given the relative independence with which Peruvian bishops

hunt for U.S. personnel and funds, a bureaucratic solution to the dilemma of selective criteria would be the establishment of a joint U.S.-Peruvian commission of bishops to review U.S. Church financial and personnel allocations to Peru and to coordinate the requests of the Peruvian Church. However, such a plan would require a tighter restructuring of the U.S. Catholic Church than is now evident.

The Protestant majority among U.S. policy makers in Peru should be greatly reduced. Roman Catholicism remains one of the major links between the United States and Peru, yet the majority of the U.S. government's policy analysts have not been Catholic. The limited policy perceptions and possibilities inherent with this predominance of non-Catholic policy makers is well illustrated in the American response to the 1969 papal encyclical, *Humanae Vita*. When the Vatican reaffirmed its traditional stance against any artificial birth control, AID and other U.S. government agencies were already heavily committed to birth-control programs as a policy tool in their economic assistance grants to Peru.

This conflict was quickly resolved by adopting a low-profile continuation of population control as a policy objective, with government planners demonstrating little sensitivity to the dilemma facing Peruvian Catholics. (Perhaps the designation of Henry Cabot Lodge as presidential emissary to the Vatican offers an opportunity for further U.S. evaluation of its approach to overpopulation. The Church should strongly encourage this reexamination.)

A growing number of U.S. churchmen consider any form of U.S. aid to Latin America as a form of dependency and are demanding not only the withdrawal of Church personnel and funds, but are also mounting an attack on other forms of U.S. Church-related benevolences present in developing nations such as Peru. With the view that U.S. churches, foundations, and educational missions are the unwitting or willing supporters of other forms of U.S. colonial presence in Peru, this policy alternative entails a confrontation with churchmen who also occupy major decision-making roles in corporations, government, and other private and public U.S. organizations operating in Peru to make them recognize the systematic pervasiveness of the U.S. presence in their nation. A similar self-examination is warranted by the Church in the United States.

CONCLUSION

Given our original policy presuppositions of a continued missionary access to Peru and a diminishing response to requests for funds and personnel, the major initiative for substantial changes in the American missioner presence is held by U.S. churches. In many instances, however, missionary societies are structured so as to allow the U.S. Church a very limited control over the activities of its personnel in Peru. This removes the actual formulation of policy to a Peruvian context where U.S. governmental and other private agencies have more effective influence on missioner decisions than possible back home.

Missionary policy, then, is a seldom articulated and infrequently analyzed *modus operandi* of the U.S. Church and state which, due to a traditional American espousal of ecclesiastical disestablishment, must be described as giving neither Church nor state the credit or responsibility for its implementation. With full knowledge, these policy recommendations transgress this disestablishment barrier to point out both the present realities of interrelationship and the future dangers of a continued ignorance of their existence.

The Latin American Church now sees itself in a struggle of self-authentication; however, calls for radical social changes have yet to find much concrete fulfillment. There is little the United States can do to accelerate this process of liberation, but there are many ways to arrest its growth, among the most important of which is a continuing presence of U.S. Protestant and Catholic missionaries. The politically powerful constituency of U.S. churchmen should be organized to exercise a prophetic criticism and destruction of the structure of systemic oppression that energizes U.S. policy efforts to tranquilize and subdue the forces of social change and political freedom in Peru.

ACKNOWLEDGMENTS

I wish to ackowledge the invaluable assistance and editorial comments of the following persons without whom this paper could not have been prepared; the final conclusions, interpretation and recommendations are my own.

Luigi Einaudi, Rand Corporation. See his study of U.S.-Peruvian Military Relations in this volume, chapter 2.

David Farrell, C.S.C., U.S. Catholic missionary in Chimbote, Peru; Gonzalo Martin-Mandly, C.S.C., Spanish priest working in Chimbote, Peru.

William McIntire, M.M., U.S. Catholic missionary in Peru. See his study of U.S.-Peruvian Labor Relations in this volume, chapter 9.

Joseph F. Michenfelder, former U.S. missionary-journalist in Peru.

Rev. John Sinclair, Latin American Secretary for Commission on Ecumenical Mission and Relations of the United Presbyterian Church in the U.S.

Edward Sunshine, S.J., U.S. Catholic missionary formerly in Peru.

REFERENCES

Armstrong, Roger D. *Peace Corps and Christian Mission.* New York: Friendship Press, 1965.

Burns, Edward McNall. *The American Idea of Mission.* New Jersey: Rutgers University Press, 1957.

Carey, James C. *Peru and the United States, 1900–1962.* Notre Dame: University of Notre Dame Press, 1964.

Castro, Josue; John Gerassi; and Irving Horowitz. *Latin American Radicalism.* New York: Vintage Books, 1969.

Coleman, William J. *Latin-American Catholicism.* Maryknoll, N.Y.: World Horizon Reports, 1958.

Considine, John J. *Call for Forty Thousand.* New York: Longmans, Green and Company, 1946.

———, ed. *The Missionary's Role in Socio-Economic Betterment.* Maryland: Newman Press, 1960.

———. *Social Revolution in the New Latin America.* Notre Dame, Indiana: Fides Publishers, 1965.

D'Antonio, William V., and Fredrick B. Pike, eds. *Religion, Revolution and Reform.* New York: Frederick A. Praeger, 1964.

Dew, Edward. *Politics in the Altiplano.* Austin, Texas: University of Texas Press, 1969.

Dozer, Donald Marquand. *Are We Good Neighbors?* Gainesville, Florida: University of Florida Press, 1961.

Horner, Norman A., ed. *Protestant Crosscurrents in Mission.* New York: Abingdon Press, 1968.

Houtart, Francois, and Emile Pin. *The Church and the Latin American Revolution.* New York: Sheed and Ward, 1965.

Lara-Braud, Jorge. *Social Justice and the Latin Churches.* Richmond: John Knox Press, 1969.

Latourette, Kenneth Scott. *Missions and the American Mind.* Indianapolis: National Foundation Press, 1949.

Lipset, Seymour, and Aldo Solari, eds. *Elites in Latin America.* Oxford: Oxford University Press, 1967.

McCarthy, Dan B. *Mission to Peru.* Milwaukee: Bruce Publishing, 1967.

Mecham, J. Lloyd. *Church and State in Latin America.* Chapel Hill: University of North Carolina Press, 1966.

Morgan, Richard E. *The Politics of Religious Conflict.* New York: Pegasus, 1968.

Morgenthau, Hans J. *Politics among Nations.* New York: Alfred A. Knopf, 1963.

Neil, Stephen. *Colonialism and Christian Missions.* London: Lutterworth Press, 1966.

Pike, Fredrick B. *The Modern History of Peru.* New York: Praeger, 1967.

Pike, Fredrick B., ed. *The Conflict between Church and State in Latin America.* New York: Alfred A. Knopf, 1964.

Scherer, James A. *Missionary Go Home.* Englewood Cliffs: Prentice-Hall, 1967.

Shapiro, Samuel, ed. *Integration of Man and Society in Latin America.* Notre Dame: University of Notre Dame Press, 1967.

White, John W. *Our Good Neighbor Hurdle.* Milwaukee: Bruce Publishing, 1943.

PROFESSIONAL JOURNALS

Cole, Arthur H. "The Relations of Missionary Activity to Economic Development." In *Economic Development and Cultural Change*, vol. 9, 1961.

Gannon, Francis X. "Catholicism, Revolution and Violence in Latin America: Lesson of the 1968 Guatemala MaryKnoll Episode." *Orbis* 12, no. 4 (1969).

Griffin, Clifford S. "Religious Benevolence as Social Control." *Mississippi Valley Historical Review* 44, no. 3 (1957).

UNPUBLISHED MATERIAL

Bahamonde, Wenceslao Oscar. "The Establishment of Evangelical Christianity in Peru (1822–1900)." Ph.D. dissertation, Hartford Seminary Foundation, 1952.

Sparks, Donald. "The Influence of Official Protestant Groups on the Formulation and Conduct of American Foreign Policy." Ph.D. dissertation, University of Chicago, 1959.

Voth, Alden H. "The National Council of Churches Philosophy of International Relations." Ph.D. dissertation, University of Chicago, 1959.

13. PERU'S RELATIONS WITH THE UNITED STATES AND NATIONAL DEVELOPMENT POLICY

Our position insofar as relations between Peru and the United States are concerned is mainly influenced by the problems encountered in our struggle against underdevelopment. The difference between developed and underdeveloped countries lies not only in the high level of industrialization and technological advancement of the former, but also in the subordinate position of the latter, as producers of raw materials under one sole international economic system involving production and marketing.

The underdeveloped position in which Peru and other Latin American countries find themselves gives way to a type of relationship with the industrialized countries which is not only of an economic character but also political in nature. This is known as foreign dependence. It is a type of situation that must be overcome through action undertaken in the fields of cooperation and integration.

The independence from foreign sources to be attained through development is conditioned by the growing interdependence which exists between countries; hence, it does not have an absolute meaning. It consists rather in the greater or lesser self-determination ability of a given State to orient its international relations.

In spite of the above situation, it should not be overlooked that both countries are, at the same time, involved within one sole security system, the world-wide projections of which must necessarily be taken into account. Certain characteristics peculiar to modern society have led to the adoption of security systems dominated by the interests of the great powers who lead the respective blocks. The medium-size and small powers which move along with them present within their respective systems more noticeable similarities than those that might be found in the opposite block.

The complex problem of relations between Peru and the United States should be approached in the light of the three main issues that have affected them, as follows: the International Petroleum Company affair, international economic cooperation, and maritime jurisdiction. In all these instances, the three-fold objective of our foreign policy became evident—development, independence, and security.

The first case pertains to the defense of our country's sovereign right to exploit its natural resources. The problem originated with the revindication of the Brea and Pariñas oil fields and with the expropriation of the Talara industrial complex, which put an end to a situation maintained by International Petroleum in detriment of our national interest, inasmuch as said company exploited a natural source of wealth in a privileged manner, alien to the Constitution and laws of Peru. The action of the Peruvian Chancery sought to prove the illegal basis on which IPC's position rested and to persuade the United States not to apply the Amendments, to which purpose discussions between the two governments were held.

International cooperation, the second objective of our foreign policy, has been a matter of considerable concern for the Peruvian government. The maladjustment which exists in the application of international cooperation became evident during the past few years, since it did not respond to the realities of the social and economic development process of our days. Peru realizes that it is necessary to strengthen solidarity among the Latin American countries in order to attain their own objectives and consolidate their independence.

Peru's belief that it is necessary to mobilize not only the governments but the public opinion of the Continent as well received international support during the meeting of the Special Commission for Latin American Coordination (CECLA), where the fundamental principles which group the Latin American countries together were laid out. Peru, displaying its usual initiative, played a leading role in what has been called the Viña del Mar Consensus, which represents the main contribution of the developing countries to the definition of their relations with the United States.

The Viña del Mar Consensus reflects the three basic development concepts of the American nations: self-effort, economic integration, and international cooperation. The aims which these concepts pursue are the efficiency of our own governments, the search for new ways of attaining coordinated solidarity at regional and subregional levels, and participation, on the basis of equal opportunities and advantages, in the shaping up of a new structure for the international community.

From Peru's viewpoint, international cooperation is understood to mean a commitment free of all forms of intervention in the internal affairs of the other nations, alien to any attempt to interfere with their personality and with the political, economic, and cultural elements that make them up. Peru considers the right to freely dispose of its natural resources to be an essential requirement and cannot accept a type of economic cooperation which is subordinated to political or military conditions. It cannot accept either any threats involving the application of coercive economic and political measures which exert pressure upon the sovereign will of the States in order to obtain any type of advantages. Peru also stands against the adoption of policies, actions, and measures, and against any provisions, the mere mention of which endangers the economic evolution of a country, which might result in disguised or open economic aggression.

The third problem encountered with the United States refers to the defense of our maritime jurisdiction. For the last twenty years our country has been maintaining a position which, based upon modern scientific, legal, and socioeconomic criteria, responds to the peculiar characteristics of the Peruvian sea and to Peru's development needs. The geological conditions of our national territory and the Humboldt Current, which flows along the Peruvian coast, create a favorable physical configuration which may be interpreted to represent natural compensation for the barrenness of the soil along this region. The defense of the wealth contained in our sea constitutes an ineludible commitment, inasmuch as it represents a source of employment and resources, a heritage involving a large potential for the generations to come.

Many of the above reasons, based upon principles of sovereignty, supported by sound scientific findings, and having social and economic projections, have not been adequately understood by certain fishing powers. Hence, under the banner of obsolete doctrines governing maritime rights they attempt to engage in indiscriminate and destructive fishing, with consequent damage to the species and to the exploitation possibilities of these resources by Peruvians.

The Peruvian government is confident that adequate understanding of the principles and positions maintained by Peru, and in general by the countries in the South Pacific, will prompt certain powers such as the United States to establish a clear difference in their dealings with the Latin American countries, "between the interests of its people and its government and the interests of a few of its citizens." In this connection and as a result of the lifting of the Pelly Amendment, the countries in the South Pacific considered that it would be timely to hold a four-party conference in order to explore the adoption of practical measures that would eliminate incidents and which, without involving a pronouncement on the legal position of the Parties, might in some way convey acceptance by the United States of the jurisdictional rights proclaimed by the three countries.

In Latin America, Peru maintains an attitude of collaboration with the other developing countries, seeking to attain at the same time new ways of international collaboration. Antagonism between the two prevalent ideological trends has an adverse effect upon the majority of countries which are forced into attitudes not always in agreement with their interests and expectations. Hence, the international community should collaborate in the search for approximation formulas and reciprocal understanding, holding development as a goal with a view to security and general welfare. Peru's decision to extend its diplomatic relations to those areas of the world from which it was alienated due to political and ideological considerations is based upon the belief that it is in this way that the cause of peace is best served.

Peru, a patron of the Americanist ideals of self-determination and respect to treaties, provides constant collaboration to the Organization of American States, based upon the belief that the Regional System, which is now joining a group of states sharing similar geographic characteristics and interests, will lead the United States, Peru, and the Latin American countries to a harmonious conjunction of common interests and expectations.

Peru is collaborating with the Latin American countries to meet the needs of development and to obtain fair treatment in international trade and financing. The search for physical and economic integration in which the Latin American countries are engaged represents a means to promote common interests and to effectively accelerate the development of the nations of western South America. Various regional and subregional integration systems have been adopted notwithstanding the problems presented by the geography and by the political and socioeconomic structures of Latin America. Peru is actively engaged in this task; the signing of the Andean Subregional Integration Agreement represents one of the most genuine cooperation ideals.

Well-balanced and harmonious development should be conducive to a fair distribution of the benefits derived from integration among the member countries in order to reduce all existing differences in this connection.

THE PERUVIAN POLITICAL PICTURE

The Peruvian Revolution, which began on October 3, 1968, emerged in response to the innermost demands of the people. From the very beginning it was inspired by an entirely autonomous conception seeking a solution to our problems through the efforts of all Peruvians and pursuing a new social order, fair and free.

The purpose of the Revolution is to open up to Peru the path to genuine social justice, to modify the pattern of its basically unfair traditional socioeconomic structure, to attain full independence of the country, and to overcome its present underdeveloped condition.

The present government is transforming both the appearance and the traditional structures of Peru, adopting solutions of our own which conform to the socioeconomic characteristics of the country, without importing solutions and doctrines alien to our national realities. Peruvian nationalism represents a firm decision to attain social cohesion and political unity, to strengthen the economy, and to achieve full independence. In transforming our structures and in attaining economic and social development national traditions and institutions are not being sacrificed.

We are struggling to place our sovereign rights on a firm basis, to defend our legitimate interests, and to make it possible for our people to attain higher living standards compatible with human dignity. To achieve these objectives the government has drafted and passed important laws which constitute the bases of its program:

1. A genuine Agrarian Reform, which has received the unanimous support of the Peruvian people and full international endorsement. This law has radically changed the traditional structure of land ownership and has set the basis for full economic reconstruction.

2. A Mining Law which incorporates mining activities into the national economy and which represents an effective contribution to the country's transformation process. It has established a new system which is in full agreement with the policy of the Revolutionary government to provide for greater participation by the State in the exploitation of the natural resources, based upon a rational and profitable utilization of our mining wealth. The government proposes to encourage domestic and foreign investment provided it conforms to the laws of the republic and fulfills the role which pertains to it within the social and economic development framework, ensuring recovery of the investors' capital and reasonable profits.

3. A draft of an Industrial Law which also tends to satisfy the need for general welfare of the population through the permanent and self-supported development of industries, ensuring actual economic independence.

Laws have also been drafted which will govern and regulate education in accordance with modern scientific and technological demands. Additional laws are also being drafted which involve particular significance for Peru's integral development.

EDITOR'S NOTE

This chapter was submitted to the final project conference at Wing-spread by the delegation appointed by the President of Peru, General Juan Velasco Alvarado. The delegation was presided over by General Marco Fernández Baca, president of Petroperu, and included Ambassa-dor Carlos Alzamora, undersecretary for economic affairs of the For-eign Ministry; Dr. Otoniel Velasco, technical director of the National Institute of Planning; Ing. Agustín Merea, superior director of the Ministry of Agriculture; Dr. Jorge Bravo Bressani of the Institute of Peruvian Studies, with the association of Admiral Luis Edgardo Llosa, formerly on two occasions foreign minister of Peru.

Papers covering the same subjects were not received from spokesmen for each political party in Peru, because it is this present government that the U.S. recognizes and it is their policies that condition our own. Nor, by publishing this paper, is the project losing its neutrality, be-cause opinions have been invited and secured from spokesmen of the other points of view and have influenced subsequent chapters. For ex-ample, former President Fernando Belaúnde Terry met with the study group for an entire evening to discuss all subjects considered in this book. Many of his close associates and those of other leading political leaders of Peru have been consulted throughout the project. The only real limitation involved is that, being an official government paper, no editing was done by me (or on the U.S. government portions either). The English translation was done officially by Peru and the editor was requested to make no alterations. This request was honored to insure that the official position was set out in precisely the words desired by the Peruvian government.

Submitted by the Peru Desk
of the U.S. Department of State

14. U.S. AID TO PERU UNDER THE ALLIANCE FOR PROGRESS

U.S. aid policy in Latin America in the 1960s arose out of a consensus that developed in the late 1950s among the leaders of the hemisphere that a dramatic and concerted economic and social development effort was needed. The Charter of Punta del Este articulated this consensus and called for sweeping social and economic change.

Peru, the fourth largest country in South America, plays a major role in the hemisphere. By tradition, it also has strong cultural, political, and economic ties to the United States. The U.S. aid program to Peru, under the Alliance, accordingly, was shaped as a reflection of our hemispheric policy to collaborate as a partner with Peru in finding solutions to its profound economic and social problems.

U.S. ASSISTANCE OBJECTIVES IN PERU

President Belaúnde's election in 1963 brought into office a constitutional government committed to accelerated economic and social progress, and raised great hopes for the role that Peru might play in the Alliance for Progress.

Peru, in many ways, epitomized the challenge facing the Alliance in Latin America. It was characterized by uneven income distribution. Half the population consisted of Indians living in the mountains who were not integrated socially with the rest of the country and who subsisted at or below the economic and cultural standards of the pre-Spanish era. The country lacked a tradition of stability and popular participation in the political process. A fresh start for attacking these deep-seated problems seemed to be offered by the democratic election of Belaúnde, who had run on a platform of development and social reform. To carry them out, his new government prepared an ambitious program, including development of agriculture, agrarian reform, opening up new lands in the high rain forest, together with related roads and infrastructure development and programs in rural development, industrial decentralization, and education.

The Belaúnde Administration began with relatively favorable economic prospects, at least from a national standpoint (although the greater part of the activity centered in Lima). Growth rates in the late 1950s and early 1960s had been high, averaging over 6 percent, led by a rapid expansion of the export sector. The balance-of-payments position was strong, with net international reserves of $125 million in 1963. With this background, the Belaúnde government launched a program of greatly expanded investment in roads, power projects, and other infrastructure, as well as other programs in education, health, agrarian reform, and agriculture.

The main thrust of U.S. economic assistance was aimed at supporting the government in these development programs. The U.S. program is described in the following sections. The description covers direct AID assistance of various types. It does not cover the loans or guaranties provided through the U.S. Export-Import Bank or indirect U.S. assistance channeled through contributions to the multilateral institutions, such as the World Bank, Inter-American Bank, UN, or OAS.

Agriculture

Agriculture and rural development are of key importance to the economic and social development of Peru. Virtually one-half of the economically active population of Peru earns its livelihood from agriculture, yet the agricultural sector in 1969 contributed only

14.5 percent to the gross domestic product. The annual rate of growth of food crop production in Peru in recent years has averaged 3.9 percent, which barely exceeds the 3.1 percent annual rate of population growth. At the same time, the demand for food has been growing at an annual rate of 4.4 percent. Agricultural imports increased from $67 million in 1960 to $155 million in 1969. Another aspect of the agricultural problem has been the serious imbalance in land distribution. Despite an agricultural reform law of 1964, 85 percent of the landowners still owned only 5 percent of cultivated land in 1969, while only 1 percent of the landowners owned 75 percent of the land under cultivation. A sweeping new law was promulgated in June, 1969, and was applied immediately to the sugar-growing areas along the coast. Implementation of this law in other areas is only just now taking place.

The agricultural sector, accordingly, has been the largest single area of concentration for the long-term AID technical assistance program. Expenditures totaled $12 million from 1962 to 1970. Major objectives have been an increase of the food supply and distribution, with emphasis on production of four key food staples for domestic consumption and development of institutions and the education and training of technicians. In pursuit of these objectives, assistance has been provided in agricultural credit, extension, research, marketing, sectorial planning, land reform, and university-level agricultural education.

Of first importance from the Peruvian standpoint of developing high-quality institutions is the National Agrarian University, La Molina, outside Lima. With U.S. government help, it has developed into a centrally administered university with many strong departments and staffs including a number of full-time professors trained in the U.S. Student enrollment has increased from 835 in 1962 to 2,115 in 1969. Under a joint loan program of AID and the Inter-American Development Bank, four office buildings, a library, two laboratory buildings, a maintenance building, and a college union have been completed. The faculty has been upgraded, and the curricula have been restructured toward providing graduates oriented toward scientific agriculture, including both basic and applied research. Programs attack problems of both production and distribution.

The second major institution involved in the program is the Peruvian Ministry of Agriculture. AID assistance to the Ministry has been concentrated in commodity production projects, through provision of research, teaching, and extension services on selected basic foods: potatoes, beans, rice, livestock, and forage. A major emphasis has been placed on improvement of seed quality. For example, since 1968 all farmers planting beans under the supervised agricultural credit program (partially funded by AID loans) have used disease-free seed produced under this project.

A long-term AID contract with North Carolina State University is the vehicle by which technical assistance requested by Peru has been provided both to the National Agrarian University and to the divisions of extension and research in the Ministry of Agriculture. From 1954 to 1963, six U.S.-funded technicians worked in agricultural research. The contract was expanded to a peak of twenty-nine technicians in 1964 and the program widened to roughly its present scope.

A second major effort in agricultural planning and studies is being carried out under a similar contract with Iowa State University. This project was originally conceived to provide technical services in the field of agrarian reform and agricultural credit. In 1964 the project was modified to assist the Peruvians in their development of plans and analyses of the overall agricultural sector. Since 1966 the scope was broadened to include national economic analysis, agricultural regional planning, economic and legal aspects of marketing, price policy, and project evaluation.

Substantial contributions have been made by the Iowa group to several research and planning units of the Peruvian government and through publication of over forty specific studies and recommendations. These have been used by the government for initiating a marketing news service, altering fertilizer tax and tariff policy, and arranging duty-free imports of items used exclusively in agriculture. The sweeping Agrarian Reform Law of 1969 draws heavily on studies prepared under this project; the North Carolina project's institution-building efforts have also contributed to agrarian reform and related activities.

The importance attached to agriculture is also reflected in the AID lending program. Dollar loans directly in agriculture, including supervised credit, total $30 million, and a number of additional dollar loans bear a close relationship to agriculture. For example, transportation loans totaling $23 million were made during this period for the construction of highways to open up potentially rich agricultural lands in semitropical and tropical areas lying on the eastern slopes of the Andes Mountains. Two AID loans (one in local currency) amounting to $4 million were made to the Agrarian University at La Molina, as mentioned above, and a $7.5 million loan helped set up a private investment fund to stimulate the development of agri-business. Further details of the principal loans are as follows:

Supervised agricultural credit. A special fund for this purpose was established within the Agricultural Development Bank, administered by a committee made up of representatives of the Bank and divisions of the Ministry of Agriculture. The fund has provided financing to some fifty-eight thousand small and medium-sized farmers who would not qualify for credit under normal criteria. It covers material inputs—seeds, fertilizers, and equipment—which are combined with technical and management advisory services of Peruvian technicians, and which help these farmers toward integration into the national market economy. In some cases the fund serves as a means of assisting largely ex-tenant farmers or farm laborers to become viable farm owners. The fund has received four AID loans totaling about $25 million, of which $22 million is now disbursed. This constitutes the largest single AID loan program in Peru. The fund has extended credit in a total amount of roughly $35 million.

As must be expected in any small farm credit program, some problems have arisen. They have included a shortage of well-trained credit and extension personnel, which has hampered loan supervision and technical assistance in some cases. The Peruvian government did not provide the full $5 million counterpart scheduled for 1967–1969; this slowed down the volume of subloans, but a new schedule of payments has recently been agreed to.

Private investment fund. The primary purpose of this $7.5 million AID loan, signed in 1968, is to stimulate the development of the Peruvian agro-industrial sector. Subloans are made through state development banks, investment companies, and commercial banks to private industrial enterprises that engage in processing, packing, or preserving agricultural commodities. Services that provide major inputs to the agro-industrial field may also be eligible.

The purpose is to provide medium to long-term financing for priority activities and to stimulate the growth of export industries related to the agricultural sector. Commercial banks and investment companies are being encouraged by the Peruvian authorities to undertake medium-term project lending. In addition to the AID seed capital, the Peruvian government contributed $7.5 million to the fund, and credits of $1 million from Denmark and $6 million from Czechoslovakia have been extended. Subloans are moving slowly, with only $455,000 of the U.S. portion committed to date, due primarily to the decline of interest of the Peruvian private sector in new investment.

Mantaro Valley rural electrification. This AID loan of $1.6 million was signed in 1967 to assist the establishment of a rural electric cooperative, the first in the country, and to expand Peru's capacity to develop rural electrification systems. The Peruvian government and the cooperative are contributing, in the form of cash and assets in place, the equivalent of $2,925,000 to the project. The Mantaro Valley, in the central highlands of Peru, has perhaps the greatest agricultural potential of the entire sierra region of Peru. The development of rural electrification in the valley is a pilot project for Peru and will stimulate the dairy, beef, and poultry potential of this area. The loan is financing some of the physical facilities and management and technical assistance for the cooperative. Construction is essentially complete and the cooperative is presently serving 3,500 members.

Food marketing. This loan project signed in 1968 will provide an investment of approximately $5 million U.S., to be combined with a local contribution (in Peruvian soles) of $3 million. The objective is to develop efficient, larger-scale food marketing systems to replace the traditional, inefficient Lima arrangements, which include ten thousand small retail stores and seventy thousand pushcart venders, resulting in excessive food costs to the consumer in most parts of the city. An additional $500,000 will be used for equipment and technical assistance. Conditions precedent for disbursements on this loan have not yet been met by the Peruvians.

Rural Development Revolving Fund. The Popular Cooperation (COOPOP) agency of the Peruvian government was established by President Belaúnde to promote the economic and social development of poor Peruvian rural communities by stimulating collective self-help actions by their inhabitants. COOPOP was to bring to the communities technical assistance, equipment, and materials to join with local labor and materials in the execution of community-sponsored projects. This would help to offset the concentration of power and resources in Lima.

The major purpose of the AID loan, authorized in September 1966 at $2.1 million, was to supply construction materials and to introduce a revolving loan fund. Since the government had problems in organizing and staffing the program and provided only $500,000 as its contribution, the AID loan was reduced accordingly.[1]

Public Administration

In terms of overall importance, the program in public administration probably comes second, immediately after agriculture and rural development. $7.3 million of AID grant funds were allocated during the period. The development of an efficient public administration capacity is of critical importance to the organization and administration of any government's development effort, since most of such programs rely upon the public sector for their execution, financing, or guidance. The need for public administration improvement in the early 1960s was very great in Peru (as in most other Latin American countries) due to its highly centralized bureaucracy, low levels of pay and training, rapid turnover of the small policy-making group, and the extreme scarcity of resources at local levels.

In addition to general public administration aspects of the agriculture and development activities, specific assistance in Peruvian tax administration and general public administration has been provided since 1962.

In the tax field, an advisory team from the U.S. Internal Revenue Service has worked with Peru in the modernization of tax administration, by improving organization and management, systems of processing and audit of tax returns, simplifying tax regulations, promoting taxpayer information and improving enforcement. Although improvements in the field of public administration are generally gradual, a number of significant accomplishments can be

[1] Agricultural Policy is discussed in fuller detail in chapter 5.

identified including assistance in the reorganization of the Peruvian Tax Office along functional lines, installation of a merit system of employee hiring and promotion, creation of a taxpayer identification-number system; establishment of enforcement methods, and improved tax administration.

In the general public administration field, AID has provided assistance since 1962 through a contract with the Institute of Public Administration of New York. This effort was channeled initially through a central institution, the Office of Public Administration Reform and Training, but IPA is now cooperating directly with specific ministries and agencies that have sought aid, particularly the Ministries of Agriculture and Finance. Public administration is a lively topic in Peru at the present time, and the government has reorganized many of the ministries and extended central budgetary control over autonomous agencies and abolished earmarked revenues. A new budget law has been drafted and standards set for all ministries in personnel administration, procurement and supplies, and budgeting and accounting. During the course of these changes, the IPA team has given continual assistance.

Assistance was given in customs administration from 1964 to 1968 under a contract with a U.S. management consulting firm. Emphasis was on personnel training, enforcement, appraisement and classification, and reorganization of the Customs Superintendency.

A small continuing project that has already produced very fine results consists of help to the sample survey center, CISM, in the Peruvian Labor Department. Set up with AID-funded assistance from the University of Michigan, CISM has assimilated modern sampling techniques and is now producing high-quality data for a variety of public programs in Peru at modest cost.

Education

Education represented another priority field under the Belaúnde Administration. Major attention was devoted to improvement of urban and, particularly, rural education, which had been traditionally neglected. A large school expansion and construction program was undertaken by the government. AID provided $5.2 million in education over the period. The principal objectives were to help

Peru improve educational planning and the quality of education at the primary and secondary levels. This was carried out through a contract with Teachers College, Columbia University, which provided consulting assistance to the Ministry of Education from 1962 to 1969 in the following areas: improving the administrative structure and procedures of the ministry; planning an educational program geared to Peru's economic and social needs; improving teacher education; developing a modern technical-vocational education system; increasing the effectiveness of rural education; and improving textbooks and teaching materials.

Specific accomplishments of the program during the contract period included assistance to Peru in the adoption of a four-year normal school curriculum replacing an inadequate three-year program; consolidation and improvement of normal schools; creation of an Office of Research in the Ministry; and development of broadscale training for middle and top grade educators, with 137 Peruvians trained outside the country. The Columbia findings and recommendations and the assistance of the AID education adviser continue to help Peruvian efforts and reform education.

At the university level, efforts have been made to help the most promising institutions, in addition to the Agrarian University, to strengthen their faculties, through means such as teacher seminars in basic sciences, and to focus on producing graduates in fields critical to Peru's economic development. Thus, a program for complementary development of two private universities has been worked out, including interchange of credits and course specialization in the natural sciences, mathematics, social sciences, and education. Low-cost textbook rental systems have also been set up at a number of universities with AID assistance.

A private supporting institution, the Peruvian Institute of Educational Development, has also received direct AID grant assistance. Organized in 1962 as a vehicle to obtain private financing for education, it first concentrated on a program of grants and scholarships, but has now expanded to support high-priority projects in individual universities for both technical and administrative improvement. The growing stature of this institution and its collaboration with the newly-formed National University Council is strengthening private-sector participation in educational development.

Finally, the AID technical book program, using materials produced by the AID center in Mexico as well as Latin American commercial houses, has achieved outstanding results in getting first-class written materials in large quantities into the hands of teachers, students, and workers in agriculture, labor, industry, and other AID-related fields.[2]

Private Enterprise Development

Private enterprise has been a priority field in Peruvian development, and AID support to the sector totaled $4.4 million in grant funds from 1961 to 1970.

One of the most successful of AID-supported projects during the period was the independent Graduate School of Business Administration (ESAN), established in Lima in 1963 jointly by the government and AID under an AID contract with Stanford University. High-quality teaching standards were established, and a modern curriculum centered around an eleven-month masters degree program was developed. The school is now providing top-quality training for future managers and executives in Peru's private sector, as well as related short-term training and extension programs to current managers and executives; increasing numbers of public-sector representatives are also participating. Utilizing its annual capacity of eighty full-time students, nearly three hundred students have received MBAs, and some fifteen hundred businessmen have attended executive programs in Lima and the provinces. A core of ten Peruvian professors have received advanced training. ESAN is highly respected in Peru, and it is considered one of the two or three finest schools of its type in Latin America. It also draws students from several other countries. ESAN is now well on its way to establishing financial independence.

Other AID technical assistance activities in the private enterprise field have included support to the regional development corporations, particularly in the less-developed districts of southern Peru that are trying to promote industry, to industrial management promotion, and to the private Peruvian Institute of Management (IPAE), which conducts short management training courses

---

[2] U. S. education policy is discussed in fuller detail in chapter 11.

and conferences. AID capital assistance to this sector includes the Private Investment Fund described above.

Housing

An additional area of substantial interest has been the development of housing institutions. AID provided a $13.5 million capital investment, consisting of loans of $7.5 million and $6 million, to the Banco de la Vivienda, the Peruvian Housing Bank. The $7.5 million loan, together with an equal amount from the government of Peru, provided the initial seed capital of the bank and helped establish the Peruvian savings and loan system. Since the loan agreement was signed in 1961, the Banco de la Vivienda has established twenty-three savings and loan institutions throughout Peru, which have accumulated over $86 million in savings deposits and made housing loans of $107 million. Today the bank and the Peruvian savings and loan system are among the finest in Latin America. A later $6 million AID loan for cooperative housing, with $4 million from the Peruvian government, is providing added strength to the savings and loan system and is stimulating the development of workers' cooperative housing projects through a program divided evenly between Lima and the provinces. Some 1,880 houses have been completed under this cooperative project, and another 365 are under construction.

A related activity, which does not involve direct expenditures by the U.S. government, but is nevertheless significant in stimulating private investment and in supporting the development of housing institutions and modern construction techniques, is the AID housing guaranty program. Here AID guarantees private U.S. long-term loans for investment in housing projects in developing countries. Peru has a large program under which six of these housing projects representing a total of $23.2 million are providing approximately 3,700 dwelling units for middle-income families, and the developers have built additional units without AID assistance.

Community Development

Since 1963, assistance has been provided in a joint Peruvian-AID effort to encourage the development of democratic institutions to enable groups of people who have previously played no role in government to become active participants in the national life and to engage in constructive self-help projects.

AID capital assistance related to community development has included loans to Cooperación Popular and a rural electrification program worked out with technical support from the National Rural Electric Cooperative Association. From 1967 to 1969, technical services were provided through the International Development Foundation to an important farmers' marketing organization (ALPACA). A variety of other rural and urban activities have been carried out, such as support to a cooperative revolving loan fund, and to the Cooperative Management School now being given special attention by the government. Under the AID Special Projects activity, small grants have been given to more than four hundred rural and urban communities and organizations carrying out self-help projects such as construction of schools and community facilities. Peace Corps volunteers have participated frequently in the development and review of these projects.

Labor Development

The AID labor development program was set up in 1963 to cooperate with Peruvian authorities in strengthening the democratic labor movement in Peru through education and labor-sponsored social projects in housing, cooperatives, and credit, so that organized labor could more adequately represent the economic and social interests of the workers and participate more responsibly with management and the government in national economic and social development programs.

This program is operated under Ministry of Labor auspices through the American Institute of Free Labor Development (AIFLD). Early emphasis was placed on training. Through a new Labor Studies Center, training was provided to 11,800 labor leaders, instructors, and workers in Lima, and branches were opened recently in the provinces. On the social projects side, AID in 1964 assisted the Peruvian democratic labor movement to set up the first workers' owned and operated savings and loan association in Latin America. Five years later it had 11,400 workers' savings accounts, with total savings of $3 million, and had made almost eight hundred housing loans. AIFLD has also developed small impact projects in cooperatives, school construction, vocational schools, and related union activities. AID grant support throughout the period totaled $2.2 million in this field.[3]

Public Safety

The AID public safety program in Peru from 1962 to 1969 was in response to requests from the government for help with national security needs. The purpose was to assist the Peruvian police, especially the Guardia Civil, to operate as an effective force capable of controlling internal disorder, which posed a serious threat at the time. Since then AID has helped the Peruvian government to set up an improved police communications network, establish new training standards and centers, and modernize management methods.

Training

An important element in the AID program in Peru, as elsewhere in Latin America, is the provision of out-of-country (or so-called participant) training to selected Peruvians. This takes place in the United States and other countries such as Mexico. In many cases the techniques, attitudes, and contacts offered by such training produce a significant impact on the leaders, managers, and technical specialists selected. During the Alliance period more than 1,500 Peruvians received "participant" training. The largest group came from the agricultural sector, and included a number of candidates for advanced degrees at U.S. universities. Labor, education, community development, and public administration are other programs that have sponsored sizeable groups of "participants."

Food for Peace

Sizeable cooperative programs of Food for Peace, averaging about $4 million per year, have been carried out in Peru since 1965. The largest example is the Ministry of Public Health's school feeding program, which was expanded from a local to a national basis, providing at least one hot meal per day to 750,000 primary school children. Food for Work programs of the Peruvian government covering reforestation and secondary road construction in various parts of the country have benefited about 100,000 additional Peruvians.

---

[3] See chapters 9 and 10 for a fuller discussion of labor policies of the United States.

Disaster relief was provided to drought-stricken areas of northern Peru.

U.S. Technical Assistance: Summary

The technical assistance program in Peru, averaging a total of $5 million annually during the 1960s, has been concentrated in the areas mentioned above. (See Appendix A for details.)

These funds have supported a staff that has varied from some fifty to over a hundred U.S. citizens, including contract employees and an equal number of Peruvian local hires. A large portion of the program has been contracted out to U.S. institutions, including several large universities (North Carolina State, Iowa State, Michigan, Columbia, and Stanford). Additional contracts have been made with the League of Insured Savings Associations, the National Rural Electric Cooperative Association, the Institute for Public Administration, and the American Institute for Free Labor Development, among others.

USAID Capital Assistance: Summary

U.S. dollar loans made to Peru since fiscal year 1960 total $95 million. These loans have been concentrated largely in agriculture ($30 million), transportation ($20 million), and housing institutions ($13.5 million). Appendix B shows the amounts, sectors of activity, dates of authorization and execution, and status of disbursements on each of these loans; it also includes major economic development loans made from PL 480 local currency proceeds.

U.S. Assistance for Peru Disaster Relief

A massive earthquake hit Peru Sunday afternoon, May 31, 1970; at first, it was not possible to know just how serious it was, but U.S. government preparations for relief nevertheless began at once. By Monday morning, June 1, the U.S. ambassador in Lima, Taylor G. Belcher, authorized a U.S. contribution of one million soles (about $24,000) from the Disaster Relief Contingency Fund of the Agency for International Development.

Monday evening the ambassador gave Washington the first indication of the types of assistance needed. By Tuesday morning, the first of a steady stream of relief supplies were on their way to Lima in Lockheed "Hercules" (C-130) flights from the U.S. Panama Canal Zone. The first flights also contained two helicopters to carry out relief in remote areas and a twenty-four-man disaster assistance survey team. The team included doctors, medical technicians, a veterinarian, sanitary engineer, and other relief specialists. It surveyed the disaster area and assisted the Peruvian government in deciding what emergency supplies were needed, what the order of priorities should be, and what additional assistance the U.S. might provide. Two additional heavy-lift helicopters were located in the United States and were started on their way to Peru the next day, June 4.

On June 5, a joint State–AID–Red Cross Center for Peruvian Earthquake Relief was set up in the State Department. This center served as a clearing house, filling all U.S. offers of assistance, official and private, into requirements from Peru as determined by the relief authorities of the Peruvian government.

On June 8, the White House announced that a $10 million grant had been extended to Peru for relief and rehabilitation. Of this amount, $7.4 million was for rehabilitation and $2.6 million for emergency relief. This latter figure was subsequently raised to $3.1 million, for a total grant of $10.5 million.

President Nixon also announced on June 8 that a special steering group was being set up under the direction of then Secretary of Health, Education, and Welfare Finch to coordinate all U.S. government participation in Peruvian relief efforts. The steering group included representatives from the Department of State, the Agency for International Development, the Department of Defense, HEW, and the Peace Corps. Peace Corps Director Joseph Blatchford went to Lima to organize a program in which American citizens could participate in relief and long-term reconstruction efforts.

Although supplies poured into Peru, access to the disaster area remained very difficult. To remedy this, the U.S. sent the helicopter carrier *Guam* to the disaster area. It anchored off Chimbote, and its seventeen helicopters flew more than eight hundred relief flights, carrying supplies and men into the area and evacuating the injured to a hospital set up on board the *Guam*.

U.S. private efforts were rapid and generous. CARE sent over $600,000 in food, blankets, and medicines. Church World Service sent over $200,000 in clothing, blankets, and medicines, and appealed to its members for an additional $1.5 million. The Catholic

Relief Service sent clothing, blankets, and medicines worth over $1 million and appealed to their churches for an additional $1.5 million. The Direct Relief Foundation sent $275,000 worth of medicines and a 150-bed hospital. Braniff Airlines and Pan American Airlines contributed free cargo space. The Seventh Day Adventists and the Salvation Army contributed large amounts of clothing, tents, and blankets, valued at over $200,000. The American National Red Cross sent blankets, food, medicine, and cash, worth over $330,000.

APPENDIX A

U.S. TECHNICAL ASSISTANCE PROGRAM BY FIELDS OF ACTIVITY
DURING THE ALLIANCE FOR PROGRESS* ($ thousands)

AID Grants	FY 62 9,084	FY 63 3,047	FY 64 4,551	FY 65 5,396	FY 66 5,841	FY 67 5,183	FY 68 5,416	FY 69 3,985	FY 70 (est.) 3,657	Total 46,160
1. Agriculture	2,753	434	958	1,293	1,347	1,256	1,408	1,465	1,140	12,054
2. Transportation	76	138	162	191	188	176	282	32	98	1,343
3. Public administration	1,520	315	819	804	982	917	760	669	555	7,341
4. Education	1,590	342	375	106	582	446	1,071	272	435	5,219
5. Private enterprise	1,522	112	529	837	313	283	413	221	200	4,430
6. Labor	257	235	169	336	281	244	238	240	200	2,200
7. Community development	—	50	227	455	301	404	216	232	176	2,061
8. Health and sanitation	405	148	34	—	—	—	—	—	—	587
9. Public safety	226	466	620	737	1,060	529	280	132	33	4,083
10. Housing	385	94	54	—	60	—	52	33	105	783
11. Technical support and misc.	350	713	604	637	727	928	696	689	715	6,059

* Gross obligations.

APPENDIX B

AID LOANS TO PERU SINCE 1960*

Loan (or Project)	Current Amount Authorized ($ thousands)	Date Authorized	Date Agreement Signed	Disbursements through February 28, 1970 ($ thousands)
Agriculture and Rural Development				
1. *Agriculture*				
Agricultural Development	9,000	6/12/61	9/8/61	9,000
Agricultural Development	6,600	3/5/64	7/8/64	6,599
Agricultural Development (PL 480)	1,000	—	7/8/64	1,000
Supervised Agricultural Credit Fund	9,000	6/30/66	11/23/66	6,013
Food Marketing	5,500	4/26/67	7/22/68	0
2. *Transportation*				
Aguaytia-Pucallpa Road	4,500	10/23/59	12/19/60	4,500
Munepata-Teresita Road	1,348	6/12/61	9/8/61	1,348
Panamericana-Cajamarca Road (PL 480)	1,474	—	1/9/64	1,474
Tulumayo–La Morada Road	1,900	1/27/64	4/21/64	1,838
Pomacocha-Tarapoto Road	12,100	3/3/64	5/19/64	2,610
Tarapoto-Juanjui Road (PL 480)	2,000	—	2/15/65	2,000
3. *Rural Development*				
Cooperación Popular	585	5/31/66	9/20/66	331
Mantaro Valley Rural Electrification	1,600 ·	6/21/66	1/26/67	1,389
Education				
Agrarian University (PL 480)	2,063	—	2/25/64	2,063
Agrarian University	2,000	3/10/65	8/24/65	1,820

Appendix B, continued

Loan (or Project)	Current Amount Authorized ($ thousands)	Date Authorized	Date Agreement Signed	Disbursements through February 28, 1970 ($ thousands)
Urban Development				
1. *Housing Institutions*				
Mutual El Perú (PL 480)	1,000	—	7/13/60	1,000
Peruvian Housing Bank	7,500	7/15/60	7/27/61	7,500
Cooperative Housing	6,000	6/15/64	2/15/65	5,309
2. *Health and Sanitation*				
Lima Water and Sewage	8,600	2/9/62	3/26/63	7,857
Industrial Development				
1. *Industry*				
Private Investment Fund	7,500	6/19/67	4/25/68	212
2. *Electric Power*				
Cañón del Pato Hydroelectric	2,200	8/29/63	3/12/64	2,200
Pativilca Hydroelectric	2,000	12/12/63	10/16/64	2,000
Feasibility and Prefeasibility Studies				
Feasibility Studies	2,979	6/8/62	3/15/63	2,979
National Resources Studies (ONERN)	1,800	3/2/67	6/28/67	522
Feasibility Studies (Planning Institute)	1,400	3/2/67	2/5/68	176
Supporting Assistance				
Puno Emergency Relief	1,168	12/5/61	2/8/62	1,168
TOTAL (including PL 480 projects)	$102,817			$ 72,908
TOTAL (excluding PL 480 projects)	95,280			$ 65,371

*Includes all dollar loans authorized by AID and the Development Loan Fund, plus major PL 480 economic development loans.

Notes on Contributors

Daniel A. Sharp

Mr. Sharp created and directed the Peru Policy Seminar, which produced this book. He was at that time assistant director of The Adlai Stevenson Institute of International Affairs and coordinator of the Institute's Latin American programs and its activities in the field of education.

One of the original members of the Peace Corps, Mr. Sharp negotiated some of the Corps' first treaties, took the first volunteers to Peru and directed operations in Bolivia and Andean Peru. The government of Cuzco, Peru, awarded him its gold medal and diploma of honor. He has visited fifteen countries in Asia, Africa, and Latin America to evaluate programs, conduct conferences, and start and direct operations. Mr. Sharp created and directed the Staff Training Center, preparing six hundred overseas managers to supervise fourteen thousand volunteers in fifty-seven countries.

Mr. Sharp was deputy attorney general in California from 1959 to 1961, is a graduate of the University of California at Berkeley (B.A. in international relations and political science) and of the Harvard Law School (J.D.). He served as a military police officer in the Far East, as a captain in the Judge Advocate General's Corps, and was with the United States delegation to the United Nations Economic and Social Council. He is a trustee of LASPAU and the Chicago Council on Foreign Relations.

Luigi Einaudi

Political scientist Luigi Einaudi has A.B. and Ph.D. degrees from Harvard and has taught at Harvard, Wesleyan, and most recently at UCLA, where he has lectured intermittently since 1964. He has been since 1962 a staff member of the Social Science Department of The RAND Corporation, where his research has concentrated primarily on the social and political roles of the military in different Latin American countries. In September 1967, he became head of RAND's social science research on Latin America. In 1966, Einaudi received a grant from the Rockefeller Foundation for work on the uses of Marxism by radical nationalists in Latin America. Einaudi's publications include work on university and student politics, revolutionary ideology, and military analysis. Most recently he has co-authored a study of the changing place of the Catholic Church in Latin American life. His primary research interests are summarized by two works, "The Peruvian Military" (in preparation for RAND), and *Marxism in Latin America* (revision of Ph.D. thesis for the Harvard University Press). In 1968, Einaudi contributed to the Adlai Stevenson Institute's book *No More Vietnams?*, edited by Richard Pfeffer.

DAVID C. LORING

Mr. Loring was born in Los Angeles, California, on March 29, 1942. He graduated from Pomona College in 1964 with a B.A. in economics and also received three awards in economics. He graduated from Stanford Law School in 1967, where he received the Carl Mason Franklin Award in International Law. From 1967 to 1969, he worked in Central America under a United States Agency for International Development contract, where he studied capital formation, co-authored a text and materials on Central American commercial law, and was visiting professor of law at the University of Costa Rica Law School. From 1969 to 1970, Mr. Loring conducted interviews throughout Latin America on the two-hundred-mile movement. Under a Stanford Law School/Ford Foundation grant, Mr. Loring wrote a book analyzing United States policy in relation to the two-hundred-mile question; the book will be published soon. Mr. Loring is presently in private law practice in Washington, D.C.; he is a member of the California Bar, the American Bar Association, the Inter-American Bar Association, and the American Economics Association.

LUIS EDGARDO LLOSA

Admiral Llosa has twice been minister of foreign relations of Peru in 1955 and 1962. He has held the highest posts in the Peruvian navy, been naval attaché at the Peruvian Embassy in Washington, head of the delegation of the Peruvian military to the Inter-American Defense Committee, and head of the joint command of the Peruvian armed forces. From the inception of the new Peruvian maritime doctrine, Admiral Llosa has participated in international conferences related to it. He was president of the delegation from Peru to the first Congress on Marine Biology held in Viña del Mar, Chile, in 1949, and has been president of the Institute for Marine Resources of Peru.

John P. Powelson

Mr. Powelson is professor of economics at the University of Colorado. He was formerly economic advisor to the government of Bolivia and director of the Program on National Accounts at the Latin American Monetary Studies Center in Mexico City. Mr. Powelson received an A.B. in Economics from Harvard College, an M.B.A. from the Wharton School of Business at the University of Pennsylvania, and an A.M. and Ph.D. in economics from Harvard. Prior to assuming his current position, he was professor of economic development at both the University of Pittsburgh and the School of Advanced International Studies, Johns Hopkins University. He served in the research department and as assistant chief of training for the International Monetary Fund. He is the author of *Latin America: Today's Economic and Social Revolution*, and of various articles on Latin America.

John Strasma

Mr. Strasma, who received his A.B. from DePauw University and his Ph.D. from Harvard, is associate professor of economics and agricultural economics at the University of Wisconsin. He is presently serving as advisor to the Office of Tax Research and Development, Ministry of Economy and Finance, in a Ford Foundation project in Peru. As a specialist in public finances in developing countries, Dr. Strasma was consulted on land reform in Peru in 1964, 1966, and 1968, under the auspices of the Food and Agricultural Organization and the Inter-American Development Bank. His publications include several items relevant to agrarian reform, particularly a United Nations study of compensation to former owners of land expropriated in agrarian reform programs (UN 4th Progress Report on Land Reform, 1966, Chapter 2).

William Mangin

Mr. Mangin attended Syracuse University, receiving his B.A. in anthropology, sociology, and mathematics, and his Ph.D. in anthropology from Yale University. He is currently professor of anthropology at Syracuse University, where he has been department chairman for the last four years. From 1952 to 1953, Mr. Mangin was the field director of the Cornell–Peru Project in Vicos. He received a grant from the National Institute of Mental Health to study mental health and migration to cities in Peru (1957–1959). He has been deputy director and director of the Peace Corps in Peru, training volunteers for work in urban areas and in squatter settlements, and has been co-director of the Peace Corps training program at Cornell and director of the program at Syracuse. Mr. Mangin has served as consultant to many projects, including the Harvard Center for Studies on Education and Development project on innovations in primary schools in Peru, Venezuela, and Cuba. He was a member of the Peru Study Group.

CHARLES T. GOODSELL

Mr. Goodsell is associate professor of government at Southern Illinois University. He was formerly a research associate at Princeton University and assistant professor at the University of Puerto Rico. A graduate of Kalamazoo College and Harvard University, he received a Ph.D. in political science from Harvard in 1961. He is the author of *Administration of a Revolution*, and is currently writing a book on the political impact of American investment in Peru, tentatively to be entitled *American Business in Peruvian Politics*. Mr. Goodsell was a member of the Peru Study Group.

BRUCE A. BLOMSTROM

Mr. Blomstrom is currently director of International Product Management at Libby, McNeill & Libby, Chicago, Illinois. He recently completed an assignment as assistant to the president. From 1962 to 1964 he was assistant secretary in Uganda's Ministry of Commerce and Industry. His responsibilities centered on international economic matters including trade agreements, EEC association, and GATT policy. He is a graduate of the Massachusetts Institute of Technology in Industrial Management (M.S. 1962, B.S. 1959). Articles by Mr. Blomstrom have appeared in the *Harvard Business Review*, *The Journal of Marketing*, and several books on economic development and marketing. Mr. Blomstrom also serves as treasurer of the Chicago Council on Foreign Relations, and is a director of the International Trade Club of Chicago and the International Visitors Center.

BOWMAN CUTTER

Mr. Cutter is presently special assistant to the president of Northwest Industries, Inc. He has studied economics with particular emphasis upon development, in England as a Rhodes Scholar (1964–1966) and at The Woodrow Wilson School of Princeton University (M.P.A. 1968). Mr. Cutter was a co-author of *High-Level Manpower in Colombia: A Market Analysis*, published in 1968. Both Mr. Blomstrom and Mr. Cutter are members of the Peru Study Group.

WILLIAM J. McINTIRE

The Reverend William J. McIntire, M.M., a Maryknoll priest working in social action and human development projects in Peru since 1967, was formerly an International Relations Officer in the Bureau of International Labor Affairs, U.S. Department of Labor, serving as a Latin American specialist. Father McIntire is a graduate of Harvard University, with an A.B. in government and an A.M. in international affairs. He joined the Maryknoll order in 1961, and during his theological preparation traveled to eight Latin American countries to study the Latin American Confederation of Christian Trade Unions (CLASC).

WILLIAM A. DOUGLAS

During the academic year 1969–1970, Mr. Douglas has been a senior fellow at the Center for International Studies, New York University, on leave of absence from the American Institute for Free Labor Development (AIFLD). He has been with the AIFLD since 1964, serving part of that time in Lima as director for Peru, where he managed the AIFLD education program through the Centro de Estudios Laborales del Peru (CELP) and the social projects program involving $13 million in housing projects. Mr. Douglas received his B.A. in political science from the University of Washington, his M.A. in international relations from Johns Hopkins University School for Advanced International Studies, and his Ph.D. in politics from Princeton University. He has been an instructor in the Department of International Studies at the University of South Carolina and an instructor in Political Science at Sung Kyun Kwan University, Seoul National University, Yonsei University, Korea University, and Chung An University in Seoul, Korea.

Robert G. Myers

Professor Myers has been a faculty member in the Comparative Education Center of the University of Chicago since 1967. His teaching and research in the economics of education has a Latin American emphasis. In his research he has explored (and continues to explore) Peruvian training abroad in a "brain drain" context and the manner in which graduates of Peruvian universities subsequently utilize their training. Mr. Myers was a resident in Peru from 1962 to 1964 as a teacher in the binational school, Colegio Roosevelt, and again for six months in 1969–1970 as a visiting professor in the Catholic University. He received his B.A. from Oberlin College, his M.A. from Stanford University, and his Ph.D. from the University of Chicago and was a member of the Peru Study Group.

Dan C. McCurry

The youngest member of the Peru Study Group, at 23 Mr. McCurry has just received his M.S. at the University of Chicago Divinity School. He lived in a small community in southern Appalachia until a scholarship took him to the University of North Carolina at Chapel Hill. In 1967 a Richardson Foundation Field Research Grant sent him to the mountains of Colombia for a study of the results of Protestant-Catholic conflict during the 1948–1958 period of *la violencia*. His findings were published as *El Conflicto Colombiano* in 1968. While receiving degrees in Latin American history and International Studies from the University of North Carolina, Mr. McCurry was associated with the International Studies Center of Washington, D.C. as coordinator for traveling seminars of Latin American student, business, and political leaders, which were sponsored by the Department of State. He has served as consultant to various ecclesiastical conferences on the military-industrial complex, U.S. imperialism and Latin America, and has had articles published in distinguished church periodicals such as the *Christian Century* and *Una Sancta*.

Project Participants and Sponsoring Organizations

PROJECT PARTICIPANTS

The project participants are enumerated below because neither this book nor the project would be possible without them, and because the significance of this book derives from the broad and representative nature of this group and from its high quality and high policy level. They fall into the following major categories: (1) members of the permanent study group that met in Chicago twelve times during 1969 and 1970; (2) special guests who attended meetings of the study group and final conference; (3) sponsoring organizations and key officers thereof who participated in special sessions appropriate to their interests; (4) Peruvian government officials; (5) U.S. government officials; and (6) other individuals whose advice and contributions were obtained on various phases of the subject. So many helpful people were involved that the editor must ask forgiveness for any errors of omission or spelling.

PERMANENT STUDY GROUP MEMBERS 1969–1970

Robert A. Abboud
Senior Vice President
The First National Bank
  of Chicago

Emery Biro
Regional Director for
  Middle West
U.S. Job Corps

George I. Blanksten
Chairman, Department of
  Political Science
Northwestern University

Bruce Blomstrom
Assistant to the President
Libby, McNeill & Libby

David Chaplin
Associate Professor of Sociology
  and Ibero-American Studies
University of Wisconsin

Mr. & Mrs. Edgar Griswold Crane
Staff Consultants
Illinois Senate Public Welfare
  Committee

W. Bowman Cutter
Special Assistant to the President
Northwest Industries

Ronald O. Decker
Consultant
The Fantus Company

James H. DeVries
Attorney
McBride, Baker, Wienke
& Schlosser

Paul Doughty
Director of Latin American
Studies
Indiana University

Verne H. Evans
Attorney
Mayer, Friedlich, Speiss, Tierney,
Brown & Platt

Marshall Frankel
Vice President
J. D. Marshall International
Company

Charles T. Goodsell
Professor of Government
Southern Illinois University

S. Lorenzo Harrison
Associate Professor of Latin
American History
Northeastern Illinois University

Euan W. Hill
Vice President in charge of
South America
Continental Bank

Joseph A. Hopkins
Vice President
Business International Corp.

John C. Hussey
Director of Latin American
Operations
The Quaker Oats Company

Martin J. Koldyke
Vice President
Dean Witter & Company, Inc.

Kenneth A. Manaster
Attorney
Leibman, Williams, Bennett,
Baird and Minow

William P. Mangin
Professor of Anthropology
Syracuse University

Daniel McCurry
Presbytery of Chicago

Robert G. Myers
Assistant Professor of Education
University of Chicago

Kenneth O. Page
Director of Public Relations
Sears Roebuck and Company

David J. Rosso
Attorney
Isham, Lincoln & Beale

Antonio R. Sarabia
Attorney
Lord, Bissell & Brook

Daniel A. Sharp
Mrs. Jacqueline B. Sharp

Norton Shapiro
Vice President
National Superior Fur Processing

John Strasma
Land Tenure Center
University of Wisconsin

Edward Sunshine, S.J.

Robert Wood Tullis
Attorney
Isham, Lincoln & Beale

David Harris Ward (inactive)
Attorney
Sidley & Austin

Robert E. Weigand
Coordinator of the Marketing Area
College of Business Administration
University of Illinois
at Chicago Circle

MEETINGS OF THE STUDY GROUP

*First Meeting: September 30, 1969—First Planning Meeting,
Special Guests:*

Ralf Brent
Assistant to the President of the
   Council for Latin America

Dr. William G. Cole
Executive Director of Chicago
   Council on Foreign Relations

James Connolly
IBM World Trade

Dr. William R. Polk
Director of Adlai Stevenson
   Institute

Alex Seith
President of Chicago Council
   on Foreign Relations

Second Meeting: November 3, 1969—special guest:

J. Wesley Jones
Former U.S. Ambassador to Peru

Third Meeting: November 18, 1969—special guest:

Fernando Berckemeyer
Peruvian Ambassador to the U.S.

Fourth Meeting: December 11, 1969—Second Planning Meeting

Fifth Meeting: February 11, 1970—special guests:

To discuss Powelson's chapter:
   Frank Fisher
   Former Deputy AID Director for Colombia

   Prof. J. Powelson
   Author of chapter on International Lending Agencies

Evening session:
   Charles A. Meyer
   Assistant Secretary of State for Inter-American Affairs

   Arnold Harberger
   Chairman, Department of Economics of the University of Chicago

Sixth Meeting: March 5, 1970—special guest:

> Fernando Belaúnde Terry
> Former Peruvian President

Seventh Meeting: March 20, 1970 (all-day meeting on the role of the private sector)—special guests:

Miles Cortez
Director of Corporate Programs
IBM World Trade Corporation

James F. Dean
President
ESSO International

John C. Duncan
Executive Vice President
W. R. Grace & Company

John F. Gallagher
Vice President,
 International Operations
Sears Roebuck and Company

James R. Greene
Senior Vice President for
 Latin America
Manufacturers Hanover Trust

John Guilfoyle
President of ITT—Latin America

Tracy Hastings
Area Director, S. C. Johnson
 and Son, Inc.
Region IV, South America

Richard A. Hoefs, Partner
Arthur Andersen and Company

Richard Pettit
Vice President and Treasurer
Marcona Mining Company

Alfred Roberts
Executive Vice President,
 International Operations
S. C. Johnson & Son, Inc.

Harvey L. Schwartz
Vice President for Public Affairs
IBEC (International Basic
 Economy Corporation)

Raymond C. Weigel
Director, Western Hemisphere
International Division
Sunbeam Corporation

Joseph W. Welsh
Vice Chairman
Continental Bank International

Dwight Williams
Vice President—Latin America
International Harvester

The Johnson Foundation Staff:

Leslie Paffrath
President

George Goss
Senior Program Associate

Sister Rosita Uhen
Senior Program Associate
 for Urban Affairs

Rita Goodman
Program Associate

Jayne Bogard
Program Assistant

Eighth Meeting: April 14, 1970 (the 200-mile fishing issue)—special guests:

Ambassador Donald McKernan
Assistant Secretary of State
   for Fisheries
Department of State,
   Washington, D.C.

August Felando
General Manager
American Tuna Boat Association

David Loring
Author of the paper on the
   200-mile issue

Richard Hoefs
Arthur Andersen & Company

Georgie Anne Geyer
Chicago Daily News
Foreign Correspondent

Ninth Meeting: April 21, 1970 (agrarian reform)

Thomas Carroll
Inter-American Development
   Bank Specialist in Peruvian
   Agrarian Reform

Fred Mann
Head of the University of Iowa
   Agrarian Mission to Peru

Russell Marks
Grace & Company, Peru

Tenth Meeting: May 11, 1970 (papers on the military and on the Alliance for Progress)—special guests:

Luigi R. Einaudi (author of the
   paper on the military)
Head of Latin American Research
RAND Corp., Santa Monica,
   Calif.

David Bronheim
Former deputy coordinator
   of the Alliance for Progress
   and Head of the Center for
   Inter-American Relations

David Collier
Ph.D. candidate, University of
   Chicago, recently returned from
   sixteen months field work in
   Peruvian squatter settlements

FINAL CONFERENCE AT WINGSPREAD: MAY 24–26, 1970

The final conference participants included the study group members previously listed, the authors of this book, official delegations from both the Peruvian and U.S. governments enumerated below, and representative citizens of both countries, also enumerated below.

Peruvians

Carlos Alzamora
Under Secretary for Economic
  Affairs
Ministerio de Relaciones
  Exteriores

Jorge Bravo Bressani
Instituto de Estudios Peruanos

Julio Cotler
Instituto de Estudios Peruanos

Samuel Drassinower Katz
Presidente Directorio
Moraveco

General E. P. Marco Fernández
  Baca
Presidente Ejecutivo
Petroperu

Helan Jaworski C.
Presidente Ejecutivo
Centro de Estudios y Promoción
  del Desarrollo

Admiral Luis Edgardo Llosa
Member of the Advisory Committee to the Foreign Ministry

Marcelo Llosa G.
Lawyer

Gonzalo Martin-Mandly
Padres de Santa Cruz

Ing. Agustín Merea
Director Superior
Ministry of Agriculture

Ramón Remolina
Consultant
Banco de Credito

Ricardo Saettone
Principal Manager
Price Waterhouse Peat &
  Company

Daniel Schydlowsky
Assistant Professor of Economics
Harvard University Center
  for International Affairs

José Valle
President
Freno S.A.

Otoniel Velasco
Director Técnico
Instituto Nacional de
  Planificación

John Watmough
Director Gerente
Pesquera América, S.A.

Richard Webb
Chairman
Economics Department
Universidad Católica

Carlos Zuzunaga-Florez
Corporation Lawyer
Presidente
Acción para el Desarrollo

Patricio Ricketts
El Correo

Alejandro Tabini

*International Organization
  Representatives*

Shiv S. Kapur
Senior Loan Officer for Peru
I.B.R.D. (World Bank)

Fernando A. Vera
Deputy Director
Western Hemisphere Dept.
International Monetary Fund

North Americans

Colin J. Bradford, Jr.
Economist
Overseas Development Council

Thomas Carroll
Chief, Agricultural Economics
  Group
Inter-American Development
  Bank

John Clark
Assistant to the Chairman
  of the Board
Deltec International Ltd.

Humberto Cortina
Regional Representative for Peru
Council for Latin America

William A. Douglas
Senior Fellow
Center for International Studies
New York University

Richard W. Dye
(Representative-to-be, Lima,
  Peru)
Ford Foundation

David Farrell, C.S.C.
Congregación de Santa Cruz
Peru

Alan Flanigan
Chief, Peruvian Political Affairs
U.S. Department of State

Fred Gibbs
Director of Latin American
  Operations
ITT Latin America

Robert C. Helander
Vice President
IBEC Management Services, Inc.
Lima, Peru

Amb. Douglas Henderson
U.S. Representative CIAP
Former chargé d'affaires Lima
Department of State

Richard A. Hoefs
Partner
Arthur Andersen & Co.

Shane Hunt
Associate Professor of Economics
  and International Affairs
Woodrow Wilson School of Public
  and International Affairs

J. Wesley Jones
Former U.S. Ambassador to Peru

Joseph Michenfelder
Former Maryknoll priest in Peru
New York Director
Public Affairs Analysts, Inc.

Richard Pettit
Vice President and Treasurer
Marcona Mining Company

John Plank
Senior Fellow
The Brookings Institution

Leigh Ratiner
Chairman, Defense Advisory
  Group on Law of Sea
Department of Defense

Wilvan G. Van Campen
Foreign Affairs Officer
Department of State

John G. Waggener
Colonel, U.S. Army
Office of Assistant Chief of Staff
 for Force Development

Raymond C. Weigel
Director—Western Hemisphere
Sunbeam Corporation

John Duncan
Executive Vice President
W. R. Grace & Co.

John Gallagher
Vice President in charge of
 International Operations
Sears Roebuck & Co.

SPONSORING ORGANIZATIONS

ADELA
Adlai Stevenson Institute

PRINCIPAL CONTACTS

Ernst Keller, President
Dr. William R. Polk, President
Sumner G. Rahr, Assistant
 Director
Peter Diamandopoulos, Director
 of Studies
Kathryn Wirtz, Project Assistant

Arthur Andersen
The Cerro Corp., N.Y.

Richard Hoefs, Partner
Robert P. Koenig, President &
 Chief Exec. Officer

Chicago Council on Foreign
 Relations
The First National Bank
 of Chicago

Alex Seith, President

Robert A. Abboud, Senior Vice
 President
Head of International Section

Grace & Co.

John Duncan, Executive Vice
 President

IBEC

Harvey L. Schwartz, Vice
 President Public Affairs
Robert C. Helander, Vice
 President, Lima

IBM

Robert A. Bennett, Vice President
Miles Cortez, Manager Corporate
 Programs

ITT

J. W. Guilfoyle, President,
 ITT Latin America
Peter T. Jones, Vice President
 & Staff Director ITTLA
Richard R. Dillenbeck, Vice
 President, Secretary and
 General Counsel ITTLA
Charles N. Goldman, Attorney

Johnson Foundation	Leslie Paffrath, President
	George Goss, Senior Program Associate
Manufacturers Hanover Trust Co.	James R. Greene, Senior Vice President for Latin America
Sears Roebuck & Co.	John F. Gallagher, Vice President in charge of International Operations
	Kenneth O. Page, Director Public Relations
Sunbeam Corporation	Raymond C. Weigel, Director of Western Hemisphere International Division

PERUVIAN GOVERNMENT CONSULTANTS TO THE PROJECT

Ambassador Carlos Alzamora
Ministerio de Relaciones
  Exteriores

Dr. Luis Alvarado
Peruvian Ambassador to the
  OAS & UN

General Luis Barandiarán
  Pagador
Head, Office for Economic
  Integration (ONIT)

General Jorge Barandiarán
  Pagador
Ministro de Agricultura

Amb. Fernando Berckemeyer
Peruvian Ambassador to the U.S.

General Guillermo Marco
  del Pont
Minister of Planning

Ing. Eduardo Dibós
Mayor of Lima

Oscar Espinoza
Instituto Nacional de
  Planificación

Gral. Brig. E. P. Marco
  Fernández Baca
Presidente Ejecutivo de Petroperu

Amb. Carlos García Bedoya
Sub-Secretary of Foreign
  Relations—Planning

Admiral Luis Edgardo Llosa
Advisory Committee to Foreign
  Ministry

General Edgardo Mercado Jarrín
Minister of Foreign Relations

Ing. Agustín Merea
Director Superior
Ministry of Agriculture

Ministry of Foreign Relations:
  Ambassador Juan José Calle
  Hubert Wieland
  Felipe Valdivieso
  Ricardo Leguía
  Raúl Pinto Alvarez
  Harry Belevan McBride

Armando Prugue
Banco Industrial de Perú

Director Ejecutivo Suplente,
Banco Interamericano de
Desarrollo

Dr. Alberto Ruiz Eldredge
Ex Decano del Colegio
de Abogados

Germán Tito Gutiérrez
Minister of Mines and Energy

Dr. Otoniel Velasco Fernández
Director Técnico
Instituto Nacional de
Planificación

U.S. GOVERNMENT

Curtis Cutter
Foreign Service Officer

Marion Czarnecki
Foreign Affairs Committee
U.S. Congress

Dante B. Fascell
House of Representatives

Wilmot Hastings
Special Assistant
Office of the Under Secretary
Department of State

Douglas Henderson
Ambassador
U.S. Representative CIAP

Pat Holt
Office of Senate Foreign Relations
Committee

John Wesley Jones
Ambassador
Department of Defense

William Lang
Department of Defense

Sol Linowitz
Ambassador

George T. Lister
State Department

Donald McKernan
Assistant Secretary of State
for Fisheries

Charles A. Meyer
Assistant Secretary of State for
Inter-American Affairs

Bradford F. Morse
Congressman

William Stedman
Country Director Peru and
Ecuador
U.S. Department of State

Ben S. Stephansky
Former U.S. Ambassador
to Bolivia

Viron P. Vaky
White House Staff

OTHER PARTICIPANTS

In addition to all of the preceding, the following people representing various elements in our diverse constituency made their own special contributions to the success of this project.

Peru

Jorge Alvarez Calderón
Parroquia San Cristóbal
(Oficina Nacional de
Investigación Social)

Enrique Ayulo Pardo
Banco de Crédito

Luis Banchero
President
National Society of Fisheries

Alberto Benavides
President
The Cerro Corporation

Oscar Berckemeyer
Celanese

Art F. Beynon
Lima, Peru

Harry Bright Ferreyros
Lima, Peru

Dr. José Carlos Mariátegui
Director de Asuntos Económicos
Ministerio de Relaciones
  Exteriores

Emilio Castañón Pasquel
Consejo Nacional de Investigación

Manuel Checa
IBM
Lima, Peru

Leopoldo Chiappo
Vice Rector
Cayetano Heredia University

Enrique Chirinos Soto

Dr. Máximo Cisneros Sánchez

Federico Costa y Laurent
Managing Director
Cemento Pacasmayo S.A.

Tulio De Andrea
Dean
Escuela de Administración de
  Negocios para Graduados

Carlos Delgado
Advisor
Instituto Nacional de
  Planificación

Enrique East
Vice Presidente y Consejero Legal
Marcona Mining Co.

Alberto Escobar
Vice Rector
Universidad Nacional Mayor
  de San Marcos

Ing. Rómulo Ferrero
Director
Banco de Crédito

James Freeborn
Vice President
W. R. Grace & Co.

Dr. Enrique García Sayán
Secretary General
Permanent Commission of the
  South Pacific

Oscar Granados Aliaga
IBEC

Jorge Grieve
Asociación Peruana Automotriz

Darryl L. Hunt
Catholic Information Office

Ernst Keller
President
ADELA

Henry La Motte
Gildemeister & Co.

Abraham F. Lowenthal
Assistant Representative
Ford Foundation

Dr. Carlos Mariotti
Director and General Manager
Empresas Eléctricas Asociadas

Carlos B. Martijena
Assistant Manager
ADELATEC Technical and
  Management Services Co. S.A.

José Matos Mar
Director
Institute of Peruvian Studies

José Miró Quesada
Head of Public Relations
The Cerro Corporation

Eduardo Neira
Lima, Peru

Eduardo Orrego V.
Arquitecto

Gardner Patrick
Banco Continental

Dr. Pedro Reiser
Manager
Reiser y Curioni S.A.

Patricio Ricketts
El Correo

Fernando Romero
Rector
Universidad del Pacífico

J. Frazer Ross
Presidente del Directorio y
    Gerente General
Cía. Peruana de Teléfonos S.A.

John Ryan III
Pesquería Santa Margarita S.A.

Nancy and Javier Sacio
Lima, Peru

Dr. Frank B. Savage
Director
Instituto Interamericano de
    Educación

John Gardner
President, Sears, Roebuck del
    Perú, S.A.

Steve and Pilar Stein
Lima, Peru

Víctor Villanueva
Lima, Peru

Enrique Zileri Gibson
Director
Caretas

U.S.A.

CALIFORNIA

Henry Colen
Vice President
Homestake Mining Company,
    Exploration

Henry Dietz
Stanford University

Dr. John J. Johnson
Director
Center for Latin American Studies

FLORIDA

James F. Dean
President
Esso International

ILLINOIS

Mrs. Ruth Pollak
Council on Foreign Relations

William McDonough
Vice President
First National Bank of Chicago

INDIANA

Dr. David B. Burks
Department of History
Indiana University

Prof. Paul Doughty
Department of Anthropology
Indiana University

MASSACHUSETTS

Dr. Albert O. Hirschman
Professor of Political Economy
Harvard University

Peter T. Jones
Vice President, ITTLA

Prof. George Cabot Lodge
Graduate School of Business
 Administration
Harvard University

MINNESOTA

Whitney MacMillan
Group Vice President
Cargill Inc.

NEW YORK

Frank Archibald
President
Southern Peru Copper

Carlos A. Astiz
Associate Professor of Political
 Science
State University of New York

Robert A. Bennett
Vice President
IBM

Ralf Brent
Council for Latin America

David Bronheim
Dreyfus Fund

Emilio G. Collado
Executive Vice President
 and Director
Standard Oil Company of
 New Jersey

J. M. Connolly
IBM World Trade Corporation

Miles Cortez
Manager of Corporate Programs
IBM World Trade Corporation

William MacEachron
Council on Foreign Relations

William T. Dentzer, Jr.
Supt. of Banks. (Former USAID
 Director, Peru)
New York State Banking Dept.

Richard R. Dillenbeck
Senior Counsel for Latin America
ITT

Henry Geyelin
Executive Secretary
Council for Latin America

Charles N. Goldman
Attorney for Latin America
International Telephone and
 Telegraph Corporation

John N. Irwin, II

Robert E. Kingsley
Public Relations Department
Standard Oil Company

Russell E. Marks
Vice President
Latin American Group
W. R. Grace and Co.

John Stephan Nagel
Deputy Head
Office for Latin America and
 the Caribbean
Ford Foundation

Jay R. Reist
President
Celanese International Co.

Joseph W. Welsh
Vice Chairman
Continental Bank International

Dr. William Whyte
Cornell University

Washington, D.C.

James P. Grant
President, Overseas Development
 Council

Frank Mankiewicz
First Peace Corps Director, Peru

George D. Woods
Director
First Boston Corporation

TEXAS

Dr. Thomas McGann
Department of History
University of Texas at Austin

Antonio Tarnawiecki
World Bank

Adlai Stevenson Institute Fellows and Staff

Eqbal Ahmad
Barbara Fields
Kathryn Wirtz Gude
Sydney Hyman
Juan Maiguashca
Ted Marmor

Molly Older
Richard Rubenstein
Reinaldo Scarpetta

Index

Abanto Morales, Luis: 215

Acción Popular: and 1962 election, 292; influence of, in executive branch, 293; controls labor ministry, 327. SEE ALSO Belaúnde Terry, Fernando

Act of Bogotá: 161

Act of Talara: signed, 249; as temporary settlement, 252. SEE ALSO International Petroleum Company dispute

ADV. SEE Peruvian Sales Management Association

Adventists: need for communication with, 405; antipathy toward, 410; and earthquake relief, 438. SEE ALSO Protestantism; religion, organized

Adventist School and Hospital: 207

AFL. SEE American Federation of Labor

AFL-CIO. SEE American Federation of Labor–Congress of Industrial Organizations

Agency for International Development (AID): aids road-building procurements, 42; supports civic-action activities, 55; authorizes no new loans, 128; authorizes loans, 129, 247–248; and slowdown of loans, 137, 149; activities of, 146; disbursements from, 150; concerned with Bolivian land reform, 159–160; finances land registration, 160; report of, on Guatemalan Counterrevolution, 160–161; favors land reform, 167; funds agricultural credit program, 182; and Indians, 206, 207, 209, 229; pressure from, against Peru, 250; cutbacks in, 264; incorporates risk management analysis, 278; and expropriation, 279; and labor, 302, 318, 320, 434–435; assists independent unions, 326–327; involves changing U.S. policy, 346; and educational development, 346, 347, 430–432; and TCCU, 346, 360; and educational loans, 348, 349, 350; funds Catholic activities, 403; refusal of, to fund missionary programs, 404; and birth control, 411; direct assistance by, 424; technical assistance of, to agriculture, 425–426; agricultural loans of, 426–429; and assistance to public administration, 429, 430; assists private enterprise development, 432–433; and housing institutions, 433; assists community development, 433–434; assists police, 435; and earthquake relief, 436, 437; mentioned, 10, 125, 144

agrarian reform: included in discussions, xxi; role of international lending agencies in, 5; as government program, 5, 421; Catholic support of, 31; administration of, 194–195; and marketing, 196; need for, 425

Agrarian Reform Law: 309

Agrarian Tribunals: 189–190

Agrarian University: loans to, 354, 355; resists 1969 reform law, 363; development of, 425, 426, 427

Agricultural Development Bank: state-owned, 174; favors large landowners, 174–175; and agricultural credit, 182, 427; and production credit, 196–197

CCLA. See Committee on Cooperation in Latin America

CDU. See German Christian Democrats

CECLA. See Special Commission for Latin American Coordination

CELP. See Centro de Estudios Laborales del Perú

Center for Higher Military Studies (CAEM): trains Peruvian officers, 18; civilians lecture at, 30; and social philosophy of government, 387

Central American Common Market: 143

Central Bank: corruption in, 35; offers economic training, 359

Central Intelligence Agency (CIA): as harmful to U.S. interests, 75; overthrows Arbenz government, 160, 161; and peasant syndicates, 229; academic ties feared, 368

Central Reserve Bank of Peru: shake-up in, 135

Centro de Estudios Laborales del Perú (CELP): founded, 304; activities of, 304–305; prospects for, 311; government supervision of, 313; raises workers' social awareness, 323–324; Labor Ministry participation in, 327; and future of Peruvian economy, 328; and collective bargaining, 329; and political reform, 332

Cerro de Pasco Corporation: expropriated, 173, 183, 187; participates in agrarian reform commission, 177; intransigence of, 183; and Indians, 207, 232; involved in disputes, 242–243; seeks European collaboration, 260; ranch lands of, expropriated, 261; backs AIFLD, 303; and miners' strike, 307

Cetepé: militant stance of, 307

CGTP. See Confederación General de Trabajadores del Perú

Chaco War of 1932–1935: 20

Chemical Bank: provides loan to Peru, 182

Chile: issues first two-hundred-mile declaration, 66–67

Chimbote steel mill: 130

Chinese: in Peru, 212

Chipaya Indians: traits of, 225–226. See also Indians

cholos: and social class, 214–216; and Indian nativism, 227; mentioned, 224, 225, 226

Christian Democrats: associated with military regime, 31; and agrarian reform bill, 179; of little interest to Indians, 227; influence of, in executive branch, 293; and contacts with MOSICP, 294; union ties with, 324

Christian Trade Union Movement of Peru. See Movimiento Sindical Cristiano del Perú

"Church and Society": 400

Church World Service: seeks to preserve tax privileges, 392; and earthquake relief, 437

CIA. See Central Intelligence Agency

CIAP. See Inter-American Committee for the Alliance for Progress

CIO. See Congress of Industrial Organizations

CISC. See International Federation of Christian Trade Unions

CISM: training program of, 358; modern techniques of, 430

CIT. See Confederación Interamericana de Trabajadores

citizens' constituency: definition of, xviii–xix

Civil Aviation Law: asserts sovereignty over air space, 92

civilian bureaucracy: relation of, to military, 36

CLASC. See Latin American Confederation of Christian Trade Unionists

CLUSA. See Cooperation League

Cold War: effect of, on U.S.-Peruvian relations, 9–10; and military pre-